WAR at SEA
1939–1945

WAR at SEA

1939–1945

John Hamilton

Blandford Press
Poole . New York . Sydney

First published in the UK 1986 by Blandford Press
Link House, West Street, Poole, Dorset BH15 Ill

Copyright © 1986 John Hamilton

Distributed in the United States by
Sterling Publishing Co Inc,
2 Park Avenue, New York, NY 10016

Distributed in Australia by
Capricorn Link (Australia) Pty Ltd
PO Box 665, Lane Cove, NSW 2066

British Library Cataloguing in Publication Data

Hamilton, John
  War at sea.
  1. World War, 1939-1945—Naval operations
  —Pictorial works
  I. Title
  940.54'5'0222   D770

  ISBN 0-7137-1660-6
  ISBN 0-7137-1739-4 de-luxe

War at Sea was conceived, edited, and designed by Thames Head Limited,
Avening, Tetbury, Gloucestershire, Great Britain.

Editorial and Marketing director   Design and Production director
Martin Marix Evans   David Playne

Art editor   Editor
Tony De Saulles   Alison Goldingham

Designers
Nick Allen   Heather Church   Nick Hand
Barry Chadwick   Tracey Arnold

Typeset in ITC Garamond on Scantext by Thames Head Limited and
processed by Topic Typesetting Limited, London UK

Printed by   Reproduction by
New Interlitho, Milan, Italy   Redsend Limited, Birmingham

The painting on page 40 is reproduced with the permission of
Wing Commander G.W. Leatherbarrow and on page 242 of Mr H. Rolfes.

General guide to map symbols

Allied forces		Light cruiser	
Japanese and Axis forces		Destroyer	
Aircraft carrier		Submarine/U-boat	
Battleship		Aircraft/airbase	
Heavy cruiser		Merchant ship	

*To those who were spared the horror and
who never knew, this book is dedicated*

Introduction

by Admiral of the Fleet the Lord Lewin and Admiral Arleigh Burke

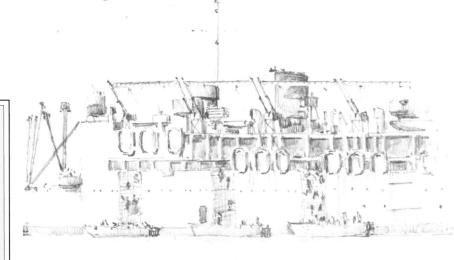

Forty years and more have passed since the events described and depicted in this book occurred and it is all too easy to forget the enormous scale of the war at sea. Across all the oceans, many thousands of ships moved to convey the men and material with which the campaigns were fought. Warships, aircraft and submarines were continually struggling for control of the seas, for although it is on land that final victory is secured, without naval control it is at sea that wars can be lost.

In this beautifully presented and comprehensive volume John Hamilton relates the history of the sea war, drawing on a wide variety of sources from many countries. His long, painstaking and detailed research has enabled him to set before the reader an account that will fascinate the participant whose memories are inevitably subjective, and which will provide for others an accurate and rounded version of great events.

The paintings bring the whole story to life. It is almost shocking to the senses to read the words then turn to see them translated into a visual image. I have known the artist's work for many years and have great admiration for his dedication to accurate representation. Sailors now grown old will catch their breath as scenes forever vivid in their memories appear before their eyes, and they will be able to say to their children and grandchildren: 'That is exactly how it was.' Particularly can John Hamilton bring to life the many moods of that common enemy of all seamen, the sea itself.

Read this saga of the greatest war at sea, study the truthful representation of the dreadful ordeals that ships and men endured. May we be wise enough to ensure that this chapter of history is not repeated.

Admiral of the Fleet the Lord Lewin KG, GCB, LVO, DSC

It is a great privilege and pleasure for this old sailor to write a foreword to John Hamilton's unique book — the visual recording of the battles at sea during World War II.

There is no way that words alone can convey the excitement, the awe and the unyielding resolution that the men in those battles felt. But the vivid, precise paintings of John Hamilton do express the intensity and the emotion of being at sea in the 1940s. The men who fought those battles are now old, but these paintings will stir memories of those actions, and of shipmates who shared the hazards of mighty endeavours.

It is remarkable that the artist and the author of this book, a Britisher and a soldier, has achieved such a great contribution to the understanding of the Second World War at sea. Obviously, many years were involved in conducting the research and making the story come alive.

His paintings will not only remind old sailors of days gone by, but may point out to those who never knew, the sacrifices that their fathers and grandfathers made over forty years ago. As John Hamilton has said to me 'It is possible that the young people of today, who sometimes seem to be beset by bewilderment and uncertainty, may gain a respect and a feeling of pride in viewing history through the eyes of an understanding painter, even though he was a soldier.'

There is a need in the United States, as well as in Japan and Britain, for a collection of accurate paintings to preserve a visual record of what actually happened. The lessons of the past are learned through the heroic actions of people. God help any nation which neglects to study its past.

Admiral Arleigh Burke, USN ret.

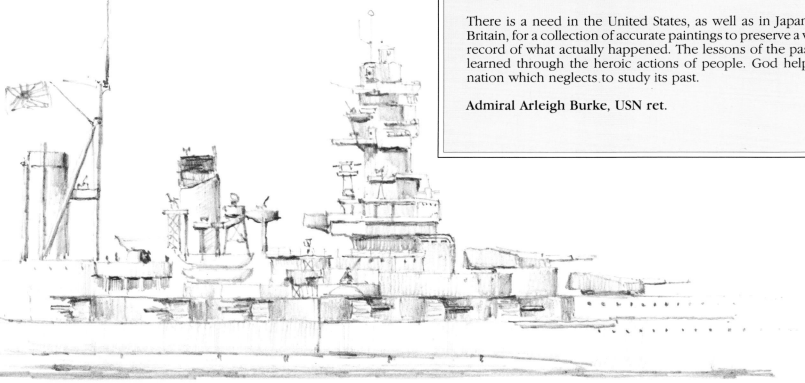

Preface

It may well be asked why anyone should spend over seven years of their life researching and painting a history of naval operations in the Second World War and so bring to life again the terrible days of 1939 – 45. To many it would seem wiser to bury the horror and misery of those days, and let a sea mist gradually roll in and cover the last resting place of so many brave men and brave ships. But I believe deeply that it should be recorded. The naval operations in the Pacific, which burst upon the world on 7 December 1941, were the greatest conflict at sea that the world has ever known. However, they form only a part of the global war at sea which began in September 1939 and continued relentlessly until the summer of 1945.

Official histories have been written by many participants and a mass of material has been published covering every conceivable aspect of the global conflict. War artists have painted thousands of sketches and pictures, so many in fact that the majority are stored away in museum archives. So after over forty years have gone by why expose the whole thing all over again? The answer lies in the fact that no one has made use of the privilege of hindsight to attempt to paint a balanced history with all the factual detail available to the historian. I have tried to do this without bias, as an attempt to illustrate historical fact.

During my researches a whole new concept of war at sea became available to historians to create what must be a fourth dimension. So great was its effect that it must take a prominent part in this story. Throughout the war cryptanalysis — the breaking of secret codes — played a vital part in naval operations and its revelations form an integral part of the strategy of the war at sea.

This is first and foremost a book of paintings; thus for the first time it will be possible to have a visual account of the course of the war, with each painting linked by an explanatory text or chart to bring the events to life. This is not a full history of the war by any means — it is confined to the sea and to the naval and United States Marine Corps actions in the air and on the ground.

In his writing the historian can describe all the facts which took place over many hours and days. The painter has no such facility. He must weigh up the significant actions and activities on both sides and try to bring to life those which had a bearing on the outcome of the war. When action is joined or an assault is made on a lonely Pacific atoll there must be a particular moment which will capture the essence of the action.

This is the artist's dilemma. Should he concentrate on the naval bombardment at 05.00 or the actual assault at 08.00? When was the crucial moment? In the same way the relentless battle to protect a convoy, spread over miles of ocean and only making seven knots, must be framed in such a way as to typify the courage of those who carried lethal cargoes and could not take avoiding action, the escorts who sought to protect them and the

incredibly brave men who attacked them from beneath the surface. At some point the scene must be frozen.

The decision is made and the moment stands still. The historian now takes over and pinpoints the position of the ships and the bearing of the guns with historical accuracy. He must convey truthfully the state of the sea and amount of daylight. The aircraft must have the correct markings and be at the correct height. But the painter must also, while retaining accuracy, at the same time try to produce some sort of a work of art. This is the dilemma, and I can only say that the inaccuracies and imperfections of the finished work are my failings despite all the help that I have been given in Washington, Tokyo, Stuttgart, London and Canberra.

Over forty years have gone by and the majority of those living who took part on land, at sea or in the air, in their own country or overseas, have either retired from active work or shortly will contemplate doing so. Meanwhile two generations have taken their place. These new generations come from different nationalities and from all walks of life. But they share one thing in common. Their fathers or grandfathers were involved in combat. Their mothers and grandmothers also knew the strain of waiting and the terrible suffering of war. Is it not right, and I would go further, is it not the duty of those who never knew to seek to know what happened and to remember those older generations, and from whatever viewpoint they look upon the past, to honour their memory? For some of us, their memory can never be erased, and to me it seems unthinkable that the events of those days should not be remembered with all the benefits of hindsight and historical research.

It is important to place that part of the conflict at sea in the Pacific within the global conflict taking place on every other ocean. For that reason I have had to switch from one theatre to another and have based the narrative in sections in chronological order of dates. I fully realise that there will be criticism and disappointment that many important actions and incidents have been left out, and that in some cases historians may well point to discrepancies of fact both in the written commentary and in the paintings. I can only say that in selecting subjects to paint I have tried to give an overall picture of what took place covering an area of sea far greater than the whole land mass of the world. For these mistakes I must accept entire responsibility.

While my reference library is extensive, I am a painter and not a historian. I have tried to acknowledge the debt I owe to the authors of the period but it may be I have omitted some. To these I apologise. The help I have received has been generous and unstinted. To the Historical Branch of the United States Navy under the leadership of Rear-Admiral John D.H. Kane jun. USN ret. I am deeply indebted. Dr Dean Allard who heads the Operational Archives Branch has been my guide and friend, and with him I include Mike Walker and the rest of the staff. The photographic

section under Mr Charles Haberlein and Mrs Agnes Hoover have given me of their time and expertise, as has Mr Henry Vadnais of the Curator Branch. In a very special sense, Rear-Admiral Thompson has given me the benefit of his advice and help from the very start of the project and I am most grateful both to him and to his family.

I thank the Historical Branch of the United States Marine Corps under Brigadier General E.H. Simmons USMC ret. and particularly Mr Ben Frank. On the other side of the Pacific, in Tokyo, I have had the generous help of the Historical Section of the Japanese Self Defence Force and I would like particularly to thank Professor Nomuru and his staff, and especially Commander Masafumi Kikuta. My thanks go to Professor Dr J. Rohwer of Stuttgart and to Mr MacKenzie of Canberra. Thanks are also due to Lady Donaldson, Mr Peter Bowring, to Dr Jonathan Steinburg and to Commander John Jacob. For the continuing interest of Admiral of the Fleet the Lord Lewin of Greenwich and Admiral Watkins USN Chief of Naval Operations, to that great American sailor, Admiral Arleigh Burke, the Naval Attachés at the Embassy of the United States in London and at the Japanese Legation in Washington, I extend my grateful thanks.

To the HMS *Belfast* Trust under Rear-Admiral Morgan Giles RN ret. and to the Imperial War Museum must go a special word of thanks, for they have presented my collection to the general public on board HMS *Belfast* as a permanent collection, through the generosity of a number of shipping companies. At the time of writing a permanent home for the Pacific Collection has yet to be found. However, two great and generous Foundations in Texas enabled me to complete the paintings. Without them it could never have been done.

Although there is an abbreviated Bibliography at the end of the book, a special word of thanks must go to three people. To the late Captain S.W. Roskill RN ret. for his masterly volumes of *War at Sea,* to the late Rear-Admiral Samuel Eliot Morison for the fifteen volumes of the *History of the United States Naval Operations in World War II,* and to the late Ronald Lewin whose books on the story of Ultra and Magic have opened a new dimension to our knowledge.

Finally to Martin Marix Evans and David Playne of Thames Head on the publishing side, I can only say that their enthusiasm matches their patience, and to my wife Betty, that she still believes all things are possible! My deep and sincere thanks to them all.

John Hamilton
The Studio Tresco
Isles of Scilly Cornwall Great Britain

Contents and list of paintings

5

6

Chronology of the War at Sea

One of the problems inherent in a work of this nature is the vastness of the oceans and the fact that events were taking place simultaneously all over the world. In order to cover this huge canvas, I have divided the book into six sections and in case this may tend to confuse the reader, I have compiled a chronology which brings the conflict at sea together by dates. This is based on the work of J.N. Westwood and Rohmer and Hummelchen to whom I acknowledge my thanks. It may be helpful to refer to this section from time to time.

1939

September 1 Old German battleship *Schleswig-Holstein* begins Second World War by opening fire on the entrance to the free port of Danzig.

September 3 Britain and France declare war. U-30 sinks liner SS *Athenia*.

September 17 U-29 sinks aircraft carrier HMS *Courageous* off Ireland.

October 14 U-47 sinks battleship HMS *Royal Oak* in Scapa Flow.

November 23 German *Scharnhörst* sinks armed merchant cruiser HMS *Rawalpindi*. A magnetic mine, dropped by the *Luftwaffe* on English mudflats, recovered and examined, enabling counter measures to be devised.

December 13 Battle of the River Plate, followed by destruction of the German *Admiral Graf Spee*.

1940

February 16 Destroyer HMS *Cossack* disregards Norwegian neutrality to enter fiord, boards German naval supply ship *Altmark*, and rescues British merchant seamen captured earlier by the *Admiral Graf Spee*.

April 8 Destroyer HMS *Glowworm* rams German cruiser *Admiral Hipper* after being reduced to sinking conditions by the latter.

April 9 HMS *Renown* encounters German *Scharnhörst* and *Gneisenau* and scores hits. German Navy lands troops in Norway, losing cruiser *Blücher* to Norwegian coastal defences.

April 10 First Battle of Narvik; two German and two British destroyers sunk. German cruiser *Karlsruhe* irreparably damaged by submarine HMS *Truant* off Norway. Land-based Fleet Air Arm bombers sink German cruiser *Königsberg* at Bergen.

April 13 Second Battle of Narvik; eight German destroyers sunk.

May 10 German invasion of Holland and Belgium.

May 26 Troop evacuation from Dunkirk begins and continues until June 4. During this period only nine destroyers out of forty-one and nine personnel ships out of forty-five remain serviceable. In all 366,162 troops were evacuated and landed in England but lost nearly all their equipment.

June A peak month for U-boats, which sink over half a million tons of Allied shipping.

June 8 Allies end land operations in Norway. Aircraft carrier HMS *Glorious* and two destroyers sunk by German battlecruisers *Scharnhörst* and *Gneisenau*.

June 11 Italy declares war against France and Britain.

June 17 SS *Lancastria* with 5,800 troops on board is sunk by bombing at St Nazaire — 3,000 troops were drowned.

June 22 France signs armistice. The evacuation of Allied troops from France is now almost complete. A further 191,870 (48,000 French) were landed in Britain.

July 3 French warships in British ports seized by Royal Navy. British bombard French squadron at Oran; French retaliate by bombing Gibraltar two days later.

July 7 Aircraft from carrier HMS *Hermes* damage French battleship *Richelieu* at Dakar.

July 9 Encounter off Calabria of British battleships and Italian squadron; one Italian battleship damaged.

July 19 Australian cruiser *Sydney* sinks Italian cruiser *Bartolomeo Colleoni*.

September 5 USA agrees to transfer to Britain fifty old destroyers in exchange for bases in western Atlantic.

September 23 Beginning of unsuccessful British and Free French attempt to 'liberate' Dakar from Vichy government.

October 10 German pocket battleship *Admiral Scheer* begins cruise against British shipping which will last until April.

HMCS Snowberry — *Flower class corvette.*

October 18-20 Seven U-boats sink seventeen out of thirty-four freighters in Atlantic convoy SC 7 while six U-boats sink fourteen out of forty-nine ships in convoy HX 79.

November 5 *Admiral Scheer* sinks armed merchant cruiser HMS *Jervis Bay*.

November 11 Fleet Air Arm attacks Taranto, sinking three Italian battleships at their moorings.

1941

January 10 German dive-bombers badly damage aircraft carrier HMS *Illustrious* in Mediterranean.

January 11 German dive-bombers sink cruiser HMS *Southampton* in Mediterranean.

February 25 Submarine HMS *Upright* sinks Italian cruiser *Armando Diaz*.

March 28 British and Italian fleets meet off Cape Matapan; Italian heavy cruisers *Pola*, *Zara* and *Fiume* and two destroyers sunk by British battleships after Italian withdrawal, which is slowed down by air attacks from carrier HMS *Formidable*. U-boats attack convoy SL 68 off the West African coast.

March 31 Italian submarine sinks cruiser HMS *Bonaventure*.

April 24 Royal Navy begins troop evacuation from Greece, losing three destroyers and several transports.

President Roosevelt commits US naval forces to protect Atlantic shipping west of 30 degrees.

May 9 U-110 boarded by HMS *Bulldog* capturing secret codes.

May 20 German invasion of Crete begins. Cruiser HMS *York*, damaged earlier by Italian motor torpedo boats, is abandoned when Crete is evacuated.

May 22 Cruisers HMS *Gloucester* and HMS *Fiji* sunk by German aircraft off Crete.

May 24 German battleship *Bismarck* and cruiser *Prinz Eugen* sink HMS *Hood* and damage HMS *Prince of Wales* off Iceland. *Bismarck* damaged.

May 27 *Bismarck* destroyed.

June 3-23 Nine German naval supply ships intercepted in Atlantic and Indian Oceans.

June 22 Germany invades Russia.

August 21 First convoy, of seven freighters, leaves for north Russia.

September 4 US destroyer *Greer* attacks U-boats.

October 31 US destroyer *Reuben James*, escorting a convoy, sunk by a U-boat.

November 8 First big success of Force K from Malta: seven Axis supply ships and one Italian destroyer sunk near Tripoli.

November 13 U-81 sinks aircraft carrier HMS *Ark Royal*.

November 19 Engagement off Western Australia between cruiser HMAS *Sydney* and German armed merchant cruiser *Kormoran*, both ships sunk.

November 23 U-331 sinks battleship HMS *Barham* in eastern Mediterranean.

December 7 Japanese carrier aircraft attack Pearl Harbor and put US Pacific Fleet battleships out of action, destroying *Arizona* and *Oklahoma*, but ignoring oil storage tanks and repair facilities.

December 8-10 Japanese landings in Malaya and air attacks in Philippines

December 10 Japanese naval aircraft sink HMS *Prince of Wales* and HMS *Repulse* off Malaya. Japanese land in Philippines. Japanese capture Guam.

December 13 Anglo-Dutch destroyer force sinks Italian cruisers *Alberto di Guissano and Alberico da Barbiano* off North Africa.

December 14 U-557 sinks cruiser HMS *Galatea* near Alexandria.

December 17 First Battle of Sirte; British light cruisers pursue two Italian battleships off Benghazi. Beginning of six-day battle between Atlantic Convoy HG 76 and U-boats; U-boats defeated but escort carrier HMS *Audacity* sunk.

December 19 Italian two-man torpedoes severely damage battleships HMS *Queen Elizabeth* and HMS *Valiant* at Alexandria; damage successfully concealed but subsequent damage to HMS *Malaya* leaves Britain without any serviceable battleships in the Mediterranean. Force K caught in minefield, losing cruiser HMS *Neptune* and sustaining damage to other ships.

1942

January 23-4 Four US destroyers sink four Japanese transports off Borneo. U-boats begin operations off the east coast of the US with disastrous American losses.

February 12 'Channel dash' by German battlecruisers *Scharnhörst* and *Gneisenau* and cruiser *Prinz Eugen*.

February 15 Singapore, Britain's eastern naval base, surrenders to Japanese Army.

February 19 Japanese carrier aircraft devastate Darwin.

February 25 German battlecruiser *Gneisenau*, under repair after 'Channel dash', bombed by RAF; never repaired.

February 27 Battle of the Java Sea; Dutch cruisers *De Ruyter* and *Java* and two British destroyers sunk by Japanese cruisers.

February 28 Cruisers USS *Houston* and HMAS *Perth* sink in night action off Sunda Strait.

March Half a million tons of Allied shipping sunk in this month, mostly by U-boats sent to American waters.

March 1 Cruiser HMS *Exeter* and two destroyers sunk by Japanese cruisers near Java.

March 11 U-565 sinks cruiser HMS *Naiad* in Mediterranean.

March 22 Second Battle of Sirte; British light cruisers and destroyers using smokescreens and torpedoes drive off Italian battleship and cruisers attacking Malta convoy, but German aircraft destroy almost all cargoes.

March 27 British naval and commando raid on St Nazaire puts out of action only dry dock on Atlantic suitable for German battleship *Tirpitz*.

April 1 Italian cruiser *Delle Bande Nere* sunk by submarine, HMS *Urge*.

April 5 Japanese carrier aircraft raid Colombo, and also sink cruisers HMS *Dorsetshire* and HMS *Cornwall*.

April 9 Japanese carrier aircraft raid Trincomalee and sink aircraft carrier HMS *Hermes* and other ships. Japanese forces operate against shipping in Bay of Bengal, twenty-three merchant ships of 112,312 tons are sunk.

April 18 US carrier aircraft bomb Tokyo.

April 20 Aircraft carrier USS *Wasp* makes first of two deliveries of new RAF fighters to Malta, where German air bombardment has intensified.

May 2 Cruiser HMS *Edinburgh* sunk by German destroyers in Barents Sea.

May 4-8 Battle of the Coral Sea; carriers USS *Lexington* and smaller IJN *Shoho* sunk. IJN carrier *Shokaku* badly damaged but Japanese landing at Port Moresby frustrated.

May 5 Madagascar invaded by British forces; three Vichy French submarines sunk while opposing landings.

May 15 Cruiser HMS *Trinidad*, after torpedoing herself with errant torpedo, is sunk by German aircraft in Barents Sea.

May 29 Japanese midget submarine badly damages battleship HMS *Ramillies* off Madagascar.

May 31 Japanese midget submarines fail at Sydney.

June This is a peak month for U-boats, over 800,000 tons of Allied shipping being sunk.

June 3 Japanese forces occupy the Aleutian Islands.

June 4-6 Battle of Midway; timely intelligence and good fortune enable US ships to destroy Japanese carriers *Akagi*, *Kaga*, *Soryu* and *Hiryu*, the cruiser *Mikuma* and 322 planes for the loss of carrier USS *Yorktown*, a destroyer and 150 planes, thereby changing the course of the war in America's favour.

June 11 Two convoys sent to Malta but only two freighters arrive; in these operations Italian cruiser *Trento* and British cruiser *Hermione* are sunk by submarines.

June 27 Convoy PQ 17 leaves for North Russia but only thirteen of its thirty-three merchant vessels arrive; convoys to Russia suspended until September.

July Air attacks on beleaguered Malta decline in this month, and first British submarines return to their base there.

August 7 US marines land on Guadalcanal, the first step in recovering territory occupied by the Japanese.

August 8 Battle of Savo Island; Japanese cruisers achieve surprise in night attack and sink cruisers USS *Quincy*, *Vincennes*, *Astoria* and HMAS *Canberra*.

August 9 US submarine S-44 sinks Japanese cruiser *Kako* off Rabaul.

August 11 Aircraft carrier HMS *Eagle* sunk by U-73.

August 12-13 Convoy battle to relieve Malta — five ships out of fourteen arrive.

August 13 Cruiser HMS *Manchester* sunk by Italian motor torpedo boats.

August 19 British raid on Dieppe which results in heavy casualties and confused withdrawal

August 24-5 Battle of Eastern Solomons; aircraft from USS *Saratoga* sink Japanese carrier *Ryujo* but USS *Enterprise* damaged; Japanese abandon operation to reinforce their Guadalcanal troops.

September 15 Japanese submarine sinks USS *Wasp* and damages battleship USS *North Carolina*, leaving USA with one operational carrier and one operational new battleship in South Pacific.

October 11 Battle of Cape Esperance; US cruisers in a confused night action sink a Japanese cruiser and destroyer. One American destroyer sunk.

October 26 Battle of Santa Cruz Islands; Japanese carrier aircraft sink USS *Hornet*, and damage USS *Enterprise* but Japanese lose 100 aircraft against US loss of seventy-four.

November 8 Allied troops conveyed safely to Morocco and Algeria. Opposition by French naval forces.

November 12-15 Naval battles of Guadalcanal. Night action on 12-13 results in sinking of IJN *Hiei* and two Japanese destroyers while American cruisers *Atlanta* and *Juneau* and four destroyers are sunk with other cruisers and destroyers badly damaged. On the night of 14-15 Japanese forces return to bombard Guadalcanal and clash with American battleships. IJN *Kirishima* and two American destroyers are sunk and USS *South Dakota* is damaged. These confused night actions result in the withdrawal of heavy Japanese warships from the area and add to the difficulties of supporting Japanese ground forces, leading to their final withdrawal.

November 15 Escort carrier HMS *Avenger* sunk by U-155 in Atlantic.

November 30 Battle of Tassafaronga; unsuccessful US night operation in which cruiser USS *Northampton* sunk and three other cruisers badly damaged by Japanese destroyers' torpedoes.

December 4 Italian cruiser *Attendolo* sunk by air attack at Naples.

December 30 German heavy ships repelled by destroyer escort of Russian convoy JW 51B. Admiral Raeder is replaced as Commander-in-Chief of German Navy by Admiral Dönitz.

1943

January 3 Italian cruiser *Ulpio Traiano* sunk by British 'human torpedo' while being completed at Palermo.

January 30 USS *Chicago* sunk by Japanese aircraft off Rennell Island, Solomons.

March Worst ever Allied losses in battles in the Atlantic involving convoys SC 122 and HX 229.

March 2 Battle of the Bismarck Sea, in which US land-based aircraft sink eight transports and four destroyers of a Japanese convoy attempting to reinforce New Guinea troops; future reinforcements are sent by submarine or barge.

April 10 Italian cruiser *Trieste* sunk by air attack.

April 28 Beginning of eight-day convoy battle, marking turning point of Battle of the Atlantic; fifty-one U-boats confront convoy ONS 5 but seven escorts with air assistance sink six submarines and drive off others for the loss of twelve freighters.

May In this month forty-one U-boats are destroyed.

July For the first time, Allied merchant ship construction exceeds losses.

July 6 Battle of Kula Gulf, a night cruiser action in which USS *Helena* is torpedoed by Japanese destroyers.

July 9 Troops conveyed safely to Sicily and Allied ships give gunfire support to landings.

July 13 Battle of Kolombangara, a night cruiser battle in which a Japanese light cruiser and US destroyer are sunk.

Oiling at dusk — the Third Fleet off Okinawa.

August 6 Battle of Vella Gulf, a night destroyer action in which US ships sink three Japanese destroyers.

August 17 Aleutian Islands evacuation by Japanese forces.

August 17 Evacuation of Sicily by Axis forces.

August 31 Allied forces land in Italy.

September British Eastern Fleet transfers its base from Kenya to Ceylon.

September 8 Italian armistice signed.

September 9 Salerno landings begin; cruisers HMS *Uganda* and USS *Savannah* badly damaged by glider bombs. Italian fleet surrenders to Allies but battleship *Roma*, *en route* to Malta, is sunk by German glider bomb.

September 22 British midget submarines damage German battleship *Tirpitz* in Norwegian fiord.

October 6 Battle of Vella Lavella, a night action in which both USA and Japan lose a destroyer, but the Japanese succeed in evacuating their troops from the island.

October 23 Cruiser HMS *Charybdis* and destroyer HMS *Limbourne* sunk by German torpedo boats off French coast.

November 2 Battle of Empress Augusta Bay, another confused night battle in the Solomons. Japanese naval forces prevented from attacking United States support for landings on Bougainville.

November 20 Assault on Tarawa by US Marines after heavy naval bombardment. Fierce fighting before the atoll is captured on 27 November.

November 25 Battle of Cape St George, a night destroyer action in the Solomons in which two Japanese destroyers are sunk by US torpedoes and gunfire.

December 26 German battlecruiser *Scharnhörst* sunk in Battle of North Cape.

December 28 Cruisers HMS *Glasgow* and HMS *Enterprise* sink three German destroyers in Bay of Biscay.

1944

January 22 Allied forces land at Anzio in Italy.

January 29 Cruiser HMS *Spartan* sunk by German aircraft off Anzio.

February 1 US forces assault Kwajalein Island after heavy naval bombardment.

February 17 US carriers, battleships and submarines attack Truk, sinking two Japanese cruisers and four destroyers. Over 137,000 tons of Japanese shipping are destroyed. Truk ceases to be a major Japanese base.

February 18 Cruiser HMS *Penelope* sunk by U-410 in Mediterranean.

April In this month U-boat campaign in Atlantic is suspended, pending delivery of improved types of submarine.

April 3 British carrier aircraft damage German battleship *Tirpitz*.

June 6 D-Day. The major Allied landing in France on four beaches in Cherbourg Peninsular. Air attacks by over 5,000 bombers supported by 5,400 fighters with 2,316 transport aircraft. Heavy naval bombardment. During the day seven battleships, two monitors, twenty-three cruisers, 103 destroyers and 1,073 smaller naval vessels are employed. Over 130,000 troops are landed.

June 14 American troops assault Saipan in the Marianas, after a naval bombardment and heavy air strikes on surrounding Japanese bases.

June 18-22 Battle of the Philippine Sea. Japanese air attack on US forces fails with the loss of over 400 aircraft. US losses are: thirty-one aircraft. Japanese carriers *Taiho* and *Shokaku* sunk by US submarines. US carrier aircraft attack Japanese forces at dusk, sinking carrier *Hiyo* and damaging one carrier and two cruisers. US losses are: seventeen aircraft, but during night recovery eighty-two aircraft are lost.

August In this month U-boats are transferred from threatened French ports to Norway.

August 15 Invasion of southern France.

August 15 Peleliu Atoll assaulted by US forces.

September U-boats begin campaign in British coastal waters.

October 10-15 US carrier planes attack Okinawa, Luzon and Formosa in preparation for assault on the Philippines.

October 20 American 6th Army lands on Philippines at Leyte supported by massive air cover and sea bombardment.

October 23-5 Battle of Leyte Gulf. Two cruisers sunk by US submarines on 23rd. Battleship *Musashi* sunk by carrier aircraft, and battleships *Yamashiro* and *Fusu* sunk in

Leyte Gulf — American escort carriers under attack off Samar on 25 October 1944.

night gun action. Japanese forces attack US light carrier force off Samar (two escort carriers and three destroyers sunk and three escort carriers damaged), but Japanese cruisers *Chikuma* and *Chokai* are sunk by aircraft. TF 58 (Halsey) moved north to intercept Japanese carriers of which four are sunk including *Zuikaku*. The Leyte Gulf battles form the largest naval engagement of the war and the last occasion when the Japanese Combined Fleet is in action.

November 12 British bombers sink German battleship *Tirpitz* in Norwegian fiord.

November 21 US submarine *Sealion* sinks Japanese battleship *Kongo*.

November 28 US submarine *Archerfish* sinks new Japanese aircraft carrier *Shinano*.

December 17 US Navy loses three destroyers and 186 planes in typhoon.

1945

January 4 US escort carrier *Ommaney Bay* sunk by kamikaze plane off Philippines.

January 29 Aircraft from British Pacific Fleet attack oilfields in Sumatra causing serious disruption.

February 19 Iwo Jima landings begin; kamikaze planes sink escort carrier USS *Bismarck Sea* and badly damage USS *Saratoga* in these operations.

March 18-19 US carrier planes bomb airfields in southern Japan.

March 30 US aircraft sink German cruiser *Köln* at Wilhelmshaven.

April 1 Okinawa landings begin after massive bombardment. Kamikaze attacks on US naval forces cause considerable damage and dislocation. These attacks continued throughout the following three months.

April 6-7 'Last sortie' of Japanese Navy; battleship *Yamato* and cruiser *Yahagi* with two destroyers sunk by carrier aircraft *en route* to Okinawa.

April 9 German *Admiral Scheer, Emden*, and *Admiral Hipper* irreparably damaged by RAF bombing at Kiel.

April 16 German pocket battleship *Lutzow* damaged by RAF and never repaired.

May 4 U-boats ordered to cease hostilities.

May 7 Admiral Dönitz, former U-boat commander and C-in-C German Fleet and Hitler's successor, authorizes Germany's surrender.

May 16 British destroyers sink Japanese cruiser *Haguro* near Penang.

June 8 British submarine *Trenchant* sinks Japanese cruiser *Ashigara* off Sumatra.

June 21 Americans complete capture of Okinawa.

July 17 US carriers and battleships, with British Pacific Fleet, begin raids on Yokosuka, Kure, and Japanese airfields.

July 30 US cruiser *Indianapolis* sunk by Japanese submarine. British midget submarines irreparably damage Japanese cruiser *Takao* at Singapore.

August 6 Atomic bomb destroys Hiroshima.

August 9 Second atomic bomb destroys Nagasaki.

August 15 Final air attacks on Japan and cease-fire ordered. Japan surrenders.

September 2 Japanese surrender signed on board battleship USS *Missouri* in Tokyo Bay.

1

The Western Oceans

September 1939 to December 1941

U-309 on Atlantic patrol

John Hamilton

The Battle of the Atlantic opens

Battles might be fought and won, enterprise might succeed or miscarry, territories might be gained or quitted, but dominating all our power to carry on the war, or even keep ourselves alive, lay in the mastery of the ocean routes and the free approach and entry to our ports. The only thing that really frightened me during the war was the U-boat peril.

Winston Churchill

On 19 August 1939 the first of thirty-nine U-boats slipped their moorings and proceeded to sea to their secret operational area. Within a week the German pocket battleships *Admiral Graf Spee* and *Deutschland* were rounding the north of Scotland to proceed south through The Faeroes-Iceland Channel, the former heading for the mid-Atlantic, and the latter for the North Atlantic.

On 3 September Germany and Great Britain were at war, and on the same day the liner *Athenia* was sunk by U-30. She was to be the first of 5,150 Allied merchant ships with the staggering figure of 21,570,720 tons to be destroyed at sea in the global war which raged for the next six years.

From the British point of view, every phase of the war against Germany was dominated by the need to ensure the safe arrival and departure of ships from all over the world. Every drop of oil had to come by sea. It was only by the destruction of shipping that the British Isles could be vanquished. This story tells of the bitter struggle that followed Hitler's decision to try to force Britain to surrender. It was only twenty-one years since the Great War of 1914-18 had ended and the lessons learned were to dominate the strategy of the opening phases of this war at sea. The only major change was that during the intervening years, the aeroplane, which had come upon the scene in the closing years of the First World War, was now to become the most potent weapon in this second great war. It was a lesson that both Germany and Britain had to a great degree neglected.

In the first few months of the war U-boats were positioned around the approaches to Britain and it was to be some time before they ranged far and wide across the Atlantic. Hitler relied upon his commerce raiders to disrupt the flow of shipping in the oceans of the world. In order to maintain secrecy, the German High Command decided to wait until war was declared before turning fast merchant ships into armed merchant cruisers, but the arming of these ships was now a priority.

The effectiveness of surface raiders was not measured only by the number of ships they destroyed. To locate a large warship in the centre of the ocean was difficult enough, but to destroy it meant the deployment to the last known sighting of overwhelming strength. In this way the presence, or even the suspected presence, of one such surface raider could seriously dislocate and dissipate the defender's naval strength and throw into confusion the sailings of ships in its path. Such was the situation in 1939. Germany therefore decided to make use of heavy capital ships in the North and South Atlantic while the conversion of armed merchant cruisers was being undertaken. To protect the shipping which approached or departed from Britain, it was essential to introduce a convoy system and this was put into operation at once. To do this required escorts and Britain was woefully short of such ships. U-boats had to be destroyed or kept submerged and thus their mobility reduced, and escorts to accompany all convoys even for short distances were just not there in sufficient number. In this way, a small nucleus of U-boats positioned in the distant approaches to the British Isles was able to inflict losses which mounted as month followed month.

Contingency plans to protect the inshore convoy routes and harbours included the laying of mine barrages in shallow coastal waters around Britain, in river estuaries and in the approaches to naval and mercantile ports. In addition the Straits of Dover were to be closed to Germany and thus the shortest U-boat route to the Atlantic was blocked by a mine barrage across the narrow strait. The daily flow of traffic between the Scottish ports and London was protected by a continuous minefield to deter surface warships and U-boats. However, the mine is very much a two-edged weapon. Offensive mining by aircraft, submarines and surface ships can cause enormous damage until they are located and swept up.

In this story we shall see the development of air power and the struggle for supremacy. Maritime strategy demands the control of the area of sea during the passage of a convoy, not only on the surface or under the keels of ships, but also in the air. To deny the passage of ships by local control of the skies is just as lethal as the menace that may lurk below. The Battle of the Atlantic was fought in order to maintain and to extend this control over an ever-widening area of ocean.

The fleet destroyer was to be the backbone of North Atlantic convoy escort and above all it was claimed that the new submarine sonar detection gear — Asdic — was to have great value and to be the main weapon of detection and destruction of the U-boat.

This was not to say that there was complacency — far from it — but in the event RAF Coastal Command lacked the number and quality of reconnaissance aircraft needed, and Asdic, while effective against submerged U-boats, was almost totally ineffective when boats attacked on the surface at night. Added to that, the lack of sufficient trained operators delayed the mass introduction of this instrument into escort vessels in the early months of the war.

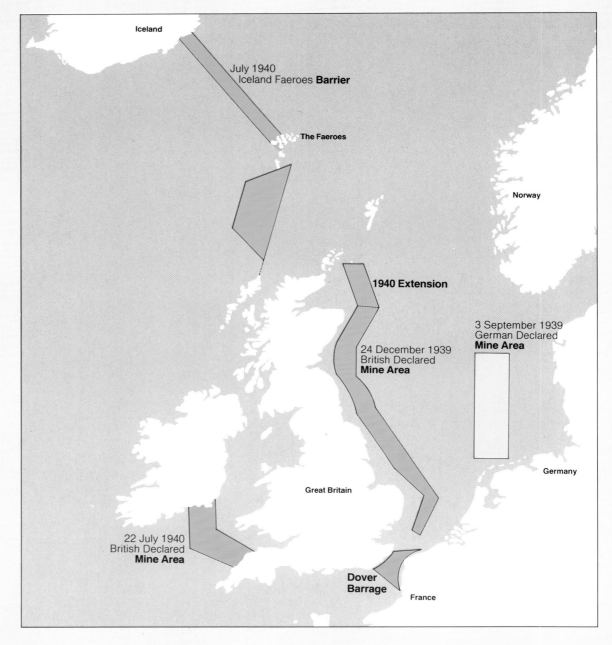

British and German declared mine areas 1939-40.

However, it must be said that in the years leading up to 1939, the inter-service rivalries and their differences of emphasis prevented the co-operative planning which, thankfully, was to take its place as the war progressed. On the German side, controversy and jealousy between the German Navy and the *Luftwaffe* continued throughout the war. The Navy was never allowed to develop its own air power and this led to the *Luftwaffe* being only partially successful in its maritime role. Had Germany concentrated on the employment of maritime attack aircraft in co-operative harmony with naval forces at sea, then truly the chances of Britain's survival would have been minimal.

Let us now look at the situation at sea at the outbreak of war in September 1939. The Admiralty decided to attack and destroy U-boats by sending forces of destroyers and carriers into the Atlantic as hunting groups. It was a mistake for, on 14 September, HMS *Ark Royal* narrowly escaped a spread of torpedoes and her attacker U-39 was sunk. Within days the carrier *Courageous* was sunk with the loss of 518 lives. Britain had lost one of her few carriers and this form of independent U-boat hunting was not repeated until 1943.

By the end of September the British Expeditionary Force had been carried across to France without loss, but there then followed a disaster at the Home Fleet's anchorage at Scapa Flow in the Orkneys. U-47 (Lieutenant Prien) with great skill and courage had penetrated the defences on the surface and in the pitch darkness of 14 October sank the battleship *Royal Oak* with a spread of torpedoes, causing great loss of life. This daring raid by Prien was the first of many notable successes by this very skilled U-boat commander — before his boat was finally destroyed in an Atlantic battle.

In the meantime, the two specially built German commerce raiders were at sea. The *Admiral Graf Spee* and the *Deutschland* were purpose built. Their armament consisted of 11 inch guns, larger than those of a cruiser, and they had a speed superior to a battleship. Equipped with light spotting aircraft and supported by supply ships stationed at strategic positions, they were ideal for the job. Their method of attack was to close a ship, to forbid the use of wireless on pain of instant shelling and to invite the crew to abandon their ship before sinking it by gunfire. The *Deutschland* had little success and was undetected for two months, returning to Germany in November 1939 to be renamed the *Lutzow*. However the *Admiral Graf Spee* was a different matter, operating in the South Atlantic, with one sortie into the Indian Ocean.

While both ships were known to be at large since survivors had been rescued and told their story, their actual position was not known. It was the SS *Doric Star's* distress call on 2 December in the South Atlantic which gave the first indication of the presence of the raider. In order to bring the raider to battle, it was necessary to concentrate a balanced force heavy and fast enough to catch and sink her. No less than eight hunting groups including four battleships, fifteen cruisers and three carriers, a total of twenty-two major warships, were deployed over the vast areas of the South Atlantic and Indian Oceans. This was not all. Homeward bound Atlantic convoys were given

battleship escorts and other major moves were made which depleted the forces available to the Home Fleet.

The northern patrol between The Faeroes and Iceland in the Denmark Strait, whose duty it was to stop and search all German and neutral merchant ships proceeding round the north of Scotland, was largely carried out by armed merchant cruisers. HMS *Rawalpindi* was sunk by gunfire on 23 November in a totally unequal struggle, when the battlecruisers *Scharnhörst* and *Gneisenau* sortied out to draw attention away from the *Deutschland*. Thankfully they never entered the North Atlantic, but returned home in heavy weather. In the South Atlantic, the hunting groups had stopped and sunk five German merchant ships, but refuelling was a permanent problem as the ships were continu

ally steaming at high speed, whereas the *Admiral Graf Spee* could make use of her supply ships which were in fact not caught until much later.

It was the view of Commodore Harwood, commanding Force G, that sooner or later the raider would make for the rich pickings to be found in the sea lanes off Rio de Janeiro and the River Plate on the east coast of South America. He therefore ordered his force — HMS *Exeter* (8 inch cruiser) and HMS *Achilles* and HMS *Ajax* (flag — 6 inch cruisers) to concentrate 150 miles off the entrance to the River Plate on 13 December. The heavy cruiser *Cumberland* remained in the Falklands. Meanwhile the *Admiral Graf Spee's* ninth victim was sunk on 7 December, and the raider steamed west towards the River Plate and the waiting cruisers.

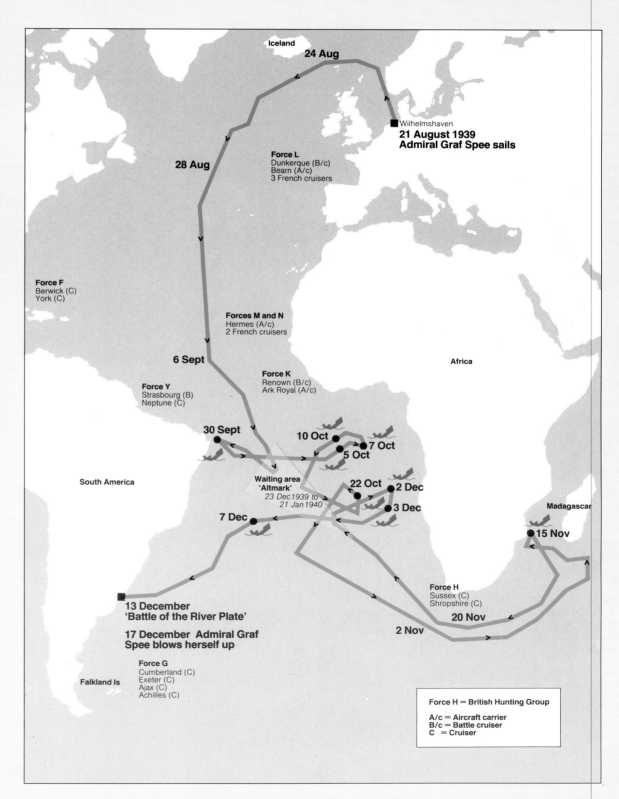

The Voyage of the Admiral Graf Spee *August to December 1939.*

Sightings were made at 06.08 on 13 December and action was joined. Harwood's tactics were to divide his force, with the heavier *Exeter* moving to the west and *Ajax* and *Achilles* to the east to divide the raider's fire. German gunnery was accurate and since it seemed that *Exeter* was the more dangerous with her 8 inch guns, Captain Langsdorff of the *Admiral Graf Spee* gave orders to concentrate on her. Soon she was crippled and turned away out of the fight. Meanwhile *Ajax* and *Achilles* had been firing continuously and had been engaged by the raider's secondary (5.9 inch) armament. The range was closing rapidly and the British ships were obtaining hits. *Admiral Graf Spee* now turned her attention to the two cruisers and each was hit, *Ajax* losing both her rear turrets. The fact that *Admiral Graf Spee* was making smoke added to the problems which were becoming one-sided. The fire power of the British cruisers was scarcely more than that of the German's secondary armament and the range had closed to 8,000 yards. Commodore Harwood then turned to the west to open the range and preserve his ships from further punishment, taking up a shadowing position. Fire was exchanged from time to time as the *Admiral Graf Spee* continued on her course towards the port of Montevideo, which she entered. Harwood's task was to ensure that she did not get away after she had effected repairs. His force of two cruisers, one with half her armament out of action, was no match for the *Admiral Graf Spee* should she renew the fight. The heavy cruiser *Cumberland* had been ordered up from the Falkland Islands but could not reach the scene until 16 December. All other reinforcements were several thousand miles away, but an overwhelming concentration of ships was ordered to the scene.

Diplomatic representations to the Uruguayan Government were directed at delaying the departure of the *Admiral Graf Spee*. Meanwhile signal traffic made out that a superior force was converging or had arrived at the River Plate. However, Captain Langsdorff had expended a considerable amount of ammunition and was faced with a major gun action in shallow water as he tried to force his way out. It was fairly certain that he would now be left with empty magazines, and his supply ships many hundreds of miles away. Thus Captain Langsdorff reported to Berlin that a large group of ships was awaiting him and that he proposed to fight his way out, but pointed out his dilemma and asked for a decision on whether he should scuttle if his attempt to break out resulted in certain destruction of his ship without causing appreciable damage to the British Forces. Hitler's reply was that in such a case it was better to scuttle. At 18.15 on 17 December the *Admiral Graf Spee* sailed and at 19.56 she blew herself up. *Cumberland* and the two damaged light cruisers sailed into Montevideo.

The need to deny sea communications to an enemy was just as important as obtaining control over them for oneself. Germany had ordered all her merchant ships to seek neutral ports and of the 206 ships bottled up in the Atlantic ports alone, only a few returned to the

The British light cruisers Ajax *and* Achilles *turn to open the range during the Battle of the River Plate on 13 December 1939.*

Fatherland. This seizure of ships outside Germany was to have a serious effect on her merchant tonnage in time to come. The early months of the war were dominated by mine-laying on both sides. Thousands of mines were laid at the entrance to ports and as protective barrages. This nightly action by German surface ships, submarines and aircraft caused dislocation in the movement of shipping, for during the first four months of the war seventy-nine Allied merchant ships of over a quarter of a million tons had been sunk by mines. Comparing this with the total tonnage sunk we see that the mine accounted for just over one-third of all Allied losses at this time — a potent weapon. It took some weeks for flotillas of converted trawlers to augment the Royal Navy's mine-sweeping fleet, but from then on these little ships proceeded to sea day after day on their dangerous mission of sweeping up mines which had been recently dropped from the air or laid by other means. Mine-sweepers were attacked regularly off the east coast of Britain and full air cover could not be provided. As the months passed, new and more deadly mines were laid — the magnetically fired variety being the latest weapon of destruction for it lay on the sea bed and was detonated automatically by the passing of a ship. They could not be swept like conventional mines and it was fortunate that one such device dropped from the air landed on mud flats in the Thames Estuary, where it was defused and its secret laid bare.

The mine was one of the most effective weapons of the Second World War at sea. It was laid by aircraft, surface ships and by submarines, and the sea lanes required continual sweeping. Mine-sweepers working in all weathers were frequently subjected to air attacks. The painting shows an attack by Junkers 87 aircraft in the Thames estuary in October 1940.

The convoy system had been instituted at the outset of the war. However, a large number of ships were returning to Britain unescorted and it was these, and the very slow vessels, which were easy to attack. By the end of the year only four ships in convoy out of 5,756 which sailed were sunk by U-boats, whereas 110 independents had been lost. These easy pickings were to continue until all ships could be gathered under the protection of escorts. The map illustrates the very small area within which ships had the benefit of close convoy on the Atlantic route. Outside these perimeters they were on their own.

At sea the successes of the small number of operational U-boats only confirmed the need to provide all but the fastest ships with extended convoy protection. U-boats had learned that there was easier prey to be had outside the convoys, for a full escort only accompanied the convoy for some 100 miles west of Ireland, and from then on ships made their own way across the Atlantic or down to the Mediterranean. It was essential to extend this area, and there-

fore the first priority was a massive building programme to increase the number of escort vessels available to give greater protection to convoys into the Atlantic.

These were but the opening skirmishes of battle. The full horror of war on land, in the air and at sea was to follow as 1939 slipped into 1940.

The year opened on a relatively quiet note. The time had not yet arrived when Admiral Dönitz was to order his boats to widen their range far out into the Atlantic, and convoys sailed virtually unescorted except for close escort for the extended 200 miles into and away from British ports. Inshore convoys suffered from magnetic mines but the problem was beginning to be controlled. Nevertheless German aircraft were making repeated attacks on coastal shipping.

While there appeared to be stalemate on land and the armies watched and waited, activity at sea was increasing, and the assistance of RAF fighter patrols went some way to controlling the losses from air attack.

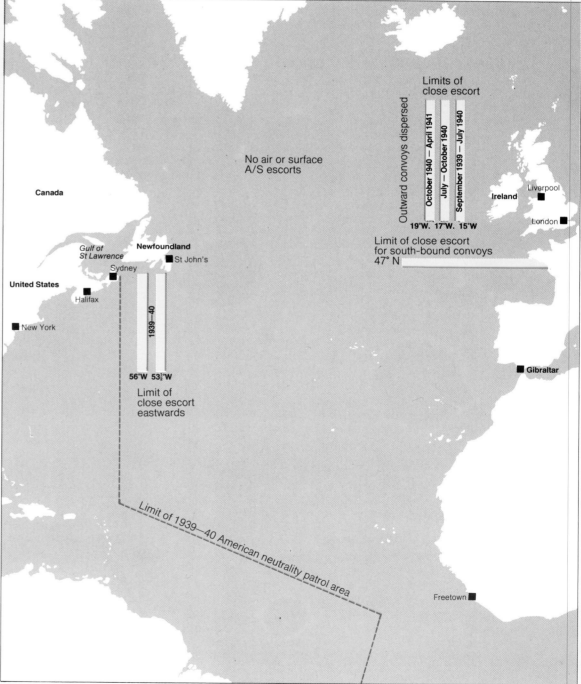

The limit of close escort for the Atlantic route, September 1939 to April 1941

The Norwegian campaign

HMS Renown *in a gale in the North Sea on 8 April 1940.*

An incident in February 1940 caught the imagination of the world. The supply ship *Altmark* was believed to have on board a large number of British seamen from the ships sunk by the *Admiral Graf Spee*. Sea and air patrols sighted her in a Norwegian fiord. HMS *Cossack* (Captain Vian) boarded her against the wishes of the neutral Norwegians and released 299 British prisoners, returning to Rosyth with an escort of the Home Fleet. The story continues in Norway for Swedish iron ore was vital to the German war effort. When the Baltic ports were closed by ice in winter, it was from Narvik that the ore was shipped. From then on it was possible for ships to return to Germany inside Norwegian territorial waters for most of the way. After considerable Allied discussion it was decided to mine the inshore waters, but this mining coincided with the news of heavy German ship movements in the North Sea, indicating a possible imminent invasion of Norway by German troops. Part of the Home Fleet sailed under Admiral Whitworth in *Renown* and on 8 April a fierce gale raged in the North Sea. HMS *Glowworm*, one of the destroyer-escorting screen, fell behind to search for a man overboard and lost contact. Two days later she encountered the German heavy cruiser *Admiral Hipper* and was over-whelmed, sinking in heavy seas, but not before she had fought an unequal action and rammed and damaged the cruiser. During this time, with the Home Fleet at sea, conflicting reports gradually gave way to a certainty that an invasion of Norway was under way.

The German High Command risked almost the whole of its naval strength in supporting a surprise attack on Norway. It was indeed a gamble but it came off, although at heavy cost. The British Admiralty was concerned to head off a large sortie into the Atlantic and the Home Fleet was well to the north. The likelihood of this threat was reinforced by a sighting in atrocious weather of the German battlecruisers *Scharnhörst* and *Gneisenau* far to the north of the invasion forces. This is exactly what the German High Command wanted. The battlecruiser HMS *Renown* on her own obtained three hits on the *Gneisenau*, after which the battlecruisers disappeared into the mist. Meanwhile the seaborne invasion of Norway had been effected without interference from the Allies, who were without doubt caught off balance and German troops were landed by warships at five ports simultaneously and captured their objectives. However, the light cruiser *Königsberg* was damaged by Norwegian shore batteries and sunk by Royal Naval air-craft next day; the heavy cruiser *Blücher* was crippled and sunk in Oslo Fiord by Norwegian defences.

The question now posed was how to come to the aid of Norway and the maritime control of the coast of Norway became vital. German air supremacy over the area soon made itself apparent and it was largely left to submarines to intercept the returning German naval forces. The submarine *Truant* torpedoed the cruiser *Karlsruhe* which was sunk, while on 12 April the pocket battleship *Lutzow* (ex *Deutschland*) was seriously damaged by torpedoes from HM submarine *Spearfish* and put out of action for twelve months.

Far to the north, German troops had landed in Narvik from ten large destroyers, and the British destroyers *Hardy, Hotspur, Havock, Hunter* and *Hostile* proceeded up Ofotfiord arriving off Narvik as dawn broke early on 10 April. Complete tactical surprise had been achieved after an approach in darkness in a strange channel beset with navigational hazards and the added problem of snow showers.

At 04.30 *Hardy, Hunter* and *Havock* entered the harbour and with torpedoes and gunfire sank the two German destroyers *Wilhelm Heidkamp* and *Anton Schmidt* and damaged three more. In addition some merchant ships were also sunk and as the destroyers withdrew a pall of smoke hung over the port. On with-

drawing, the British destroyers were pursued by three more destroyers which had anchored in nearby Herjangsfiord and their escape was barred by two more destroyers (*Georg Thiele* and *Bernard Von Arnim*) which entered Ofotfiord. A fierce action ensued. *Hardy* was soon disabled and was beached at 06.30 with heavy casualties.

As they dashed down the fiord *Hunter* was hit and came to an immediate halt. At the same moment a shell hit the bridge of *Hotspur* which was close behind, putting her out of control.She crashed into the sinking *Hunter* which turned over and sank. Her captain survived the hit on the bridge of *Hotspur* and standing on X turret he extricated his badly

damaged destroyer. *Hostile* and *Havock* had flashed by untouched. They now returned at speed and shepherded the damaged *Hotspur* out of the action.

The German forces had not escaped damage and they withdrew, allowing the British force to reach the open sea, but not before *Havock* had sunk the ammunition ship *Rauenfels* which exploded. The Commander-in-Chief decided that all of the remaining German destroyers inside Narvik fiord should be destroyed, so the battleship *Warspite* and nine destroyers proceeded up the fiord. The unequal fight was over by 17.00 and despite the fact that every one of the German destroyers fought to the end, they were overwhelmed

by *Warspite*'s 15 inch guns. In addition her Swordfish aircraft also scouted ahead and bombed and sank a U-boat.

German forces had occupied the key strategic areas of Norway necessary for final conquest, and the Allies had not yet landed a single soldier to challenge this. As we have seen, and will continue to see over and over again, control of the skies was a crucial part of this domination

British destroyers enter Narvik Harbour in the early morning of 10 April 1940. The German destroyers Wilhelm Heidkamp *and* Anton Schmidt *were sunk and three more damaged. As the destroyers withdrew a great pall of smoke hung over the port.*

of the sea areas into which any expeditionary force was to penetrate and in the main Germany had that control. They had risked almost the whole of their fleet and had sustained losses, but these losses were acceptable when balanced against the results.

The Commander-in-Chief of the Home Fleet, Admiral Sir Charles Forbes, now faced an impossible task. The German forces on shore were critically short of stores and ammunition for the first few days, but from then on their position improved, so that the chances of defeating them diminished.

A British expeditionary force was embarked in the Clyde on 11 April, but in such haste that the

ships were not tactically loaded. Thus on arrival there was much confusion in locating each unit's equipment. They were bound for Narvik and also for Namsos from where an assault on Trondheim was to be mounted. Further troops were landed near Trondheim on the 18 April, but from then on the troops were bombed throughout the daylight hours.

There was no fighter cover, as the distance from England was too great and the few planes which landed on a frozen lake were promptly destroyed by bombing. What protection they had came from the anti-aircraft cruisers *Carlisle* and *Curacao* since no anti-aircraft guns had been landed. These valuable ships were able to do little more than protect themselves.

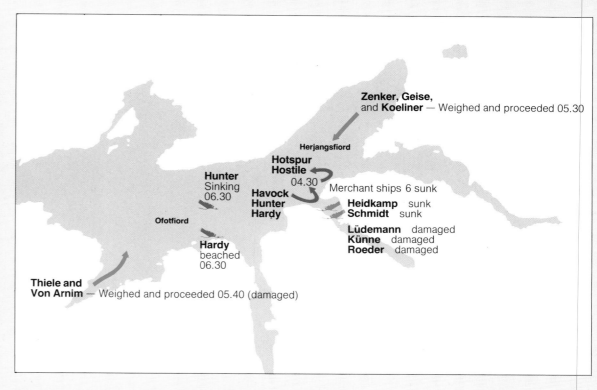

The first Battle of Narvik took place on 10 April 1940.

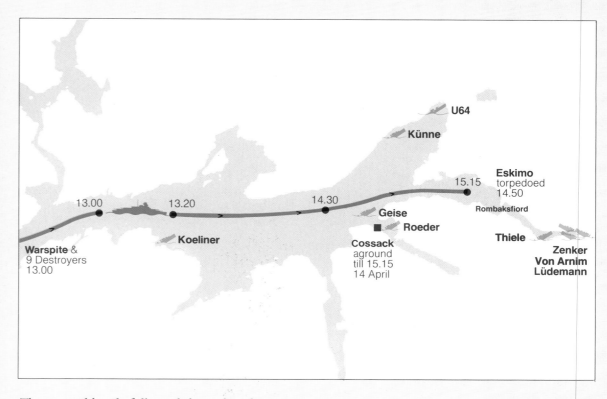

The second battle followed three days later.

During the withdrawal from Narvik Harbour the British destroyer Hardy *was disabled and beached. A fierce action with the German destroyers* Bernard Von Arnim *and* Georg Theile *followed in which the leading British destroyer HMS* Hunter *was torpedoed and stopped dead in the water.* Hotspur, *with her bridge wrecked, crashed into the stationary* Hunter *and as she pulled away,* Hunter *rolled over and sank.*

The orders for an attack on Trondheim were cancelled and luck and seamanship resulted in the re-embarking of the forces which had been landed only days before. In this latitude the nights were becoming shorter and cruisers and destroyers together with two French transports, their decks crammed with troops, made their escape. The King of Norway and his Government were embarked at Tromso and proceeded to England.

Moving further north, nearly 30,000 British troops were ashore in the Narvik area. After delays due to lack of equipment, inadequate air cover and the thick snow, Narvik was finally taken on 28 May, only to be evacuated within days. The RAF were operating under impossible conditions from a makeshift airfield and German bombers appeared in force.

Aircraft from *Ark Royal* and *Glorious* had flown continuous sorties because it was still light at midnight in this latitude but could not control the skies, while the ships themselves were extremely vulnerable. However, under the cicumstances, the evacuation was achieved without serious loss.

The brave Acasta *sinks after torpedoing the battlecruiser* Scharnhörst.

One of the problems facing Admiral Dönitz was the malfunctioning of a high percentage of torpedoes fired by his U-boats which had been sent to attack the evacuation. This led to a number of lost opportunities, but the German High Command was determined to draw heavy Allied warships away from the inshore waters of northern Norway. To this end they sailed the *Scharnhörst, Gneisenau* and *Admiral Hipper,* together with four destroyers. They found and sank a tanker and an empty troopship and then Admiral Marschall detached *Admiral Hipper* and the destroyers to fuel in Trondheim. He was now convinced that an evacuation was in progress and set off at high speed with the two battlecruisers to search for other quarry in the North Sea. On 8 June they sighted the carrier *Glorious* with her two attendant destroyers *Ardent* and *Acasta.* The previous day *Glorious* had completed the difficult task of taking on the remaining RAF Hurricanes and Gladiators, a remarkable feat since none of the pilots had ever landed on a carrier. Although her decks were crammed with aircraft she none the less had not flown off any reconnaissance or patrol aircraft, or even a torpedo strike squadron. She was thus defenceless when the two battlecruisers opened fire at 16.00. Her escorting destroyers made smoke to protect her and then turned at high speed towards the two giants.

Glorious rolled over and sank at 17.40. *Ardent* fired all her torpedoes before being overwhelmed by the fire of the battlecruisers, leaving *Acasta* turning and twisting as she closed her adversaries. Repeatedly hit and gradually losing way, she fired her last torpedo which hit the *Scharnhörst* abreast her aft turret, and caused sufficient damage to put the *Scharnhörst* out of action for six months. This fact did not come to light until after the war despite a report by the single survivor, and the gallant destroyer finally went down close to the *Scharnhörst.*

The loss of one of Britain's few carriers was bad enough, but the loss of the ships' companies together with naval and RAF pilots was grievous. Orders had been given to destroy the RAF fighters but their pilots elected to try to save them by attempting a deck landing, but it was to no avail. From the three ships, forty-six men survived and no rescue efforts were made by the German force. The final torpedo from *Acasta* probably saved the remainder of the Norwegian evacuation fleet, for the two battlecruisers returned to port. *En route* they were attacked by *Ark Royal*'s dive-bombers which did no damage, and the whole unfortunate escapade for the defence of Norway was over.

Defeat of the Allied forces in Europe

While the campaign in Norway was being undertaken, it became plain to the Admiralty that the German advance in the Low Countries begun on 10 May was going to result in the loss of the Belgian and Dutch ports. To deny them to the advancing German Army was a priority and from 11 May onwards destroyers were sent into the harbours to evacuate all shipping and to ensure that the port installations, and particularly the oil, did not fall into German hands. Demolition parties were put ashore and non-essential troops and wounded were brought back to Harwich. The destroyer flotillas worked feverishly to carry out their assorted tasks and at the same time to hold back the advancing German tanks. Throughout this time German aircraft kept up incessant bombing raids. Twenty-three destroyers were involved in demolition, evacuation and the landing of beach parties, three of which were sunk by bombing and four badly damaged. But the Navy had done a remarkable job, only leaving when German troops were actually in occupation in the coastal towns.

It was now plain that an immense task faced the Admiralty. Allied troops were being forced back towards the coast at Dunkirk. The defence of Calais in fact gave the British Expeditionary Force (BEF), assisted by French and Belgian units, the crucial few hours needed to consolidate and hold the perimeter round Dunkirk, but German aircraft bombed the retreating Allied force constantly and few RAF fighters were to be seen. The facts are that nearly every available RAF fighter aircraft was used in an attempt to destroy the bombing force. Between 26 May and 4 June the RAF flew 4,822 hours in the defence of the evacuation, losing 106 aircraft.

The start of the main evacuation of the BEF from France began on 26 May. Hundreds of ships and small craft were mustered in home ports along the south coast and made their way singly or in convoy across the Channel, their destination made clearly visible by the pall of smoke rising into the air. Cross-Channel ferries, destroyers, drifters, mine-sweepers and a host of smaller ships converged on the beaches and the port of Dunkirk.

Over 17,000 men were taken off on the first day, but the sight of lines of troops stretching back along the beaches into the distance under continuous air bombardment made it certain that even the smallest ships, yachts, ships' boats and any other shallow draught vessels were going to be needed to pick up the waiting soldiers who waded out in the shallow water from the open sand dunes.

The inner harbour was a shambles, but troops were still being taken off in large numbers by ships berthed alongside the outer harbour mole. Fierce fighting took place continuously by the units defending the perimeter and holding back the advancing German forces. It was a race against time. The vulnerable and very valuable personnel ships with their large capacity and high speed were being attacked relentlessly and were withdrawn during the hours of daylight. On the night of 28 May the outer harbour was again used by twenty destroyers and thirty-six mine-sweepers and drifters, while numerous Dutch barges, motor boats, tugs, lifeboats and ships' boats hauled men out of the water off the beaches and, dangerously overloaded, made their way back to England. Nearly 18,000 men were rescued that night. German efforts to impede the evacuation included the laying of magnetic mines, attacks by E-boats and a U-boat in addition to the continuous bombing. One destroyer was sunk, five were damaged, three personnel ships were sunk and one damaged.

Troops massed on the Mole at Dunkirk Harbour being taken off by destroyers and fast transports. The port itself together with its oil storage tanks was demolished by bombing and a pall of smoke hung over the area.

To this must be added an assortment of other valuable ships and many smaller craft manned by volunteer civilian crews. However, 29 May saw over 47,000 troops landed back in England. Next day saw a peak number of 53,000 men evacuated. Naval beach parties took control of embarkation points and waiting men were transferred from the water's edge to the miscellaneous craft which lay close inshore. By now a veritable host of small boats were waiting their turn to approach the shore and on 31 May the previous day's numbers were exceeded when 68,000 men were brought home. The outer

harbour was a desperately dangerous place but more than half of the evacuation took place from there.

The events were rising to a final crescendo. As dawn broke on 1 June the destroyers and steamers slipped out of the harbour crowded with troops, and as daylight flooded over the scene a swell breaking on to the beaches made evacuation hazardous as ships standing off were being sunk by bombing and artillery fire from the shore. None the less the evacuation proceeded and 64,000 men reached England.

It is not hard to imagine the exhaustion of the ships' companies and the skippers of the small craft who had been working night and day to effect this miraculous evacuation, nor the plight of the waiting soldiers. It seemed as if evacuation would have to stop during daylight hours as losses simply could not be sustained. But during the next three nights, the destroyers led a host of smaller ships back to the beaches and the harbour. Only nine of the forty-one destroyers originally earmarked for the operation remained serviceable and nine of the forty-five personnel ships. The last ship to leave Dunkirk

was the destroyer *Shikari* at 03.40 on 4 June and Operation Dynamo was over. Between 20 May and 4 June, 366,162 men had been evacuated, but nearly all their equipment had been

While French and British troops held the advancing German forces, the British Expeditionary Force, together with allies, were evacuated from open beaches despite heavy bombing. Every available small craft was pressed into service and with almost miraculous fine weather 366,162 troops were successfully rescued.

left behind. Apart from the almost miraculous fine weather it was a truly combined operation, and the courage of the rescuers and the pilots above them was matched by the patience of the soldiers waiting to be taken off and the bravery of those who defended the perimeter to the last.

Despite this a large number of troops and RAF personnel who had not been involved in the main withdrawal still remained in France and a second evacuation was necessary. Again flotillas of destroyers and personnel carriers, including transatlantic liners, assembled on the south coast and made the dash across the Channel to French ports to the west, and in the Bay of Biscay: The tale of the evacuation of Dunkirk has been told in some detail and the scenes witnessed there were repeated from ports as far south as Bordeaux. Despite *Luftwaffe* bombing, casualties were surprisingly light, except for the sinking of the liner *Lancastria* with 5,800 troops embarked. Of these some 3,000 perished. This was the greatest single loss.

When the French Armistice was signed on 22 June, evacuation almost ceased. The totals lifted from other French ports are impressive. In all, 191,870 fighting men reached England, of whom 48,000 were French troops, and adding this figure to the Dunkirk evacuation the total is in the region of 560,000 troops - a remarkable achievement.

There now occurred an incident which was horrific and tragic. The terms of the French surrender included the condition that the French fleet should be immobilized in French ports. It was the view of the British Cabinet that Hitler would in fact take over the French fleet despite promises to the contrary. Had the large French fleet become a part of the *Kriegsmarine* the results would have become catastrophic for the Allies. Apart from a relatively small portion of the French fleet which had sailed either to British ports or beyond the reach of German forces, the remainder was still at risk mainly at Oran and Dakar.

The British Cabinet therefore informed the French commanders at naval ports that the fleet must either sail to British or neutral ports or be disabled in such a way that it could not be used. In Alexandria, in the Mediterranean, French ships agreed to be immobilized, but elsewhere the pressure on those on the spot was intolerably severe, and involved disobeying the orders given to them as a result of the surrender terms. There was no alternative but for the Royal Navy to use force. A fierce action off Oran ensued on 3 July in which the loss of life among the French seamen was tragically heavy. While the operation was not wholly effective the impact was immediate. Our ally had suffered a terrible blow which was to colour relations for the rest of the war and for long afterwards.

While the evacuation of Allied troops was at its height, Italy declared war on Great Britain and France on 11 June. By the end of the month the British Commonwealth stood alone.

Hitler now laid plans to invade the south coast of England. As a prerequisite he had to destroy the Royal Air Force and gain control of the English Channel and the North Sea. Only then could the invasion take place. To counter the

invasion fleet there was no alternative but to withdraw escorts from the convoy routes and position them ready to deny Germany the passage across the Channel. This resulted in a rising toll of destruction at sea during the months of May and June 1940. Sinkings increased from 107,000 tons in March to 585,000 in June, when every available ship was needed to evacuate the troops from France. Had the U-boat operational strength been greater then the situation would have been even worse.

The situation was critical and its solution almost impossibly difficult, since it was not feasible to release the anti-invasion forces until the outcome of the air war over Britain was known, and a continuous watch had to be kept on Channel ports to report on the build up of the German invasion forces.

With the whole of the west coast of France in German hands, U-boats could operate from these French ports without the long voyage round the north of Scotland, Lorient receiving its first boats in July.

The immediate response was to route convoys round the north of Ireland, and the south-west approaches to our ports were virtually closed. This meant that all shipping destined for London and the south now passed around the north of Scotland and so extended the area of close escort by many miles.

The tactical situation gradually became clearer. The RAF, despite mounting losses, had held the *Luftwaffe*, whose daylight raids on fighter airfields in August and early September had failed to crush the defenders. German tactics now changed from daylight to nightly raids on London and other cities. It became reasonable to conclude that a full-scale invasion of Britain was no longer imminent.

However, even if the invasion was postponed, starvation was not impossible and the destruction of merchant shipping was rising to appalling heights. Not only had the army to be re-equipped after losing almost all its equipment in France, but sufficient food and raw materials had to be brought into British ports to enable Britain to continue the war. It was the Atlantic trade routes which were vital.

With the entry of Italy into the war alongside Germany, the Mediterranean was now virtually closed to merchant shipping, which meant that all convoys to the Middle East had to steam an extra 20,000 miles for the return journey round South Africa and up to the Suez Canal.

Each of these vital convoys carrying troops and stores for General Wavell's campaign in the Middle East had to be escorted by ships not only to deal with U-boats, but also to repel armed raiders which were known to be at large in the South Atlantic and in the Indian Ocean.Thus, cruisers and armed merchant cruisers had to accompany each convoy on its passage round South Africa.

The German armed raiders

By the end of 1940, Germany had six armed merchant cruisers operating. These were formidable ships usually armed with six or eight 5.9 inch guns, torpedo tubes, and one or two aircraft and mines. They were not particularly fast but were capable of very long endurance. To enable them to remain at sea for many months, a succession of supply ships, both tankers and dry cargo vessels, were sailed to a secret rendezvous to remain in the vastness of the oceans or in some cases in neutral ports from which they sailed to replenish both U-boats and raiders. To augment these supply ships, the raiders also used captured ships, notably tankers, which housed captured crews until they could be landed on some remote and desolate shore.

The method of attack was based on surprise. Posing as harmless merchantmen they closed in on their unsuspecting victims, and on declaring their true identity ordered complete radio silence. If this was kept, the ship was stopped, the crew taken off, and the ship sunk. If, however, the master disregarded the instructions and with considerable bravery sent out a distress signal, the raiders opened fire with devastating results. There were instances of great courage on the part of radio operators, which resulted in the tracking down of raiders by Allied cruisers — which had to be released in large numbers to hunt for these raiders. Accurate descriptions of these armed raiders were difficult for they could be disguised with dummy funnels, deckhouses, derrick posts and deck cargoes.

Repainting was often carried out at sea also so as to make the ship unrecognizable. As we have seen in the case of the *Admiral Graf Spee* the problem was not only the damage that they did, but even the continual threat of their very presence, and the fact that their whereabouts were unknown. Nothing less heavily armed than a cruiser could tackle them and so a large number of these valuable ships were tied down both as escorts and in hunting groups, steaming many thousands of miles in what was often nothing more than a wild-goose chase.

The table on page 36, taken from the official history of *The War at Sea* by Captain S.W. Roskill, gives the facts of these important and dangerous ships, which began operations in 1940. In order to achieve continuity, it is well to continue the story of the armed raiders beyond the period of this section.

The pocket battleship *Admiral Scheer* had entered the Atlantic through the Denmark Strait at the end of October 1940. On 5 November she found her first victim and then fell·on a homeward bound convoy only escorted by the armed merchant cruiser *Jervis Bay*. The convoy scattered at once, making smoke, but the *Jervis Bay* bravely faced the pocket battleship. Before she was sunk she gave the convoy valuable time to scatter and only five ships were sunk in what could have been a massacre. The Home Fleet immediately sailed from Scapa Flow but the *Admiral Scheer* had vanished into the vastness of the South Atlantic, where she was refuelled from the tanker and supply ship *Nordmark*. This remarkable vessel had disguised herself first as the *Dixie* and then the *Prairie*, both United States ships, but in fact not tankers at all. She had painted USA on her bows, and

had once been stopped by the Royal Navy and had then been allowed to proceed. Having refuelled the *Admiral Scheer*, which proceeded to the Capetown-Freetown area, she assisted the armed raiders *Thor* and *Pinguin* also in the South Atlantic. When replenished they proceeded farther south, the *Pinguin* to attack the Allied whaling fleets in the South Atlantic. But to continue with the *Admiral Scheer*. Having captured a loaded Norwegian tanker and sent her back to Brest, she proceeded to assume the guise and signals of a British warship. No distress signals had been sent out by two ships sunk in this area, but nevertheless she considered it prudent to cruise in other waters.

Proceeding south of the Cape of Good Hope she entered the Indian Ocean where she sank four ships to the north of Madagascar. However, a distress signal had been picked up and six Allied cruisers and the small aircraft carrier *Hermes* on convoy escort in the area were formed into a hunting group. *Glasgow*'s aircraft sighted her, but then lost contact, and she slipped away. Refuelling again from the *Nordmark*, *Admiral Scheer* moved north to prepare for her return to Germany. Finding suitable thick weather she slipped through the Denmark Strait and returned to Kiel on 1 April. To facilitate her return the battlecruisers *Scharnhörst* and *Gneisenau* had previously been sailed into the Atlantic to divert attention away from her. Their presence was discovered and the whole convoy system was disrupted, a battleship having to be included as escort with each convoy in mid-Atlantic. There is no doubt about the extreme efficiency of the German back-up supply ships, or of the tactical ability of the captains of the major warships engaged in commerce raiding. The distress signals and brief sightings of these ships kept the Home Fleet and cruiser squadrons together with Force H stationed at Gibraltar constantly at sea to protect convoys and search for the raiders. The *Admiral Scheer* had sailed nearly 50,000 miles and sunk nearly 100,000 tons of shipping, together with the armed merchant cruiser *Jervis Bay*. Germany could be well satisfied with the disruption caused, and the British Admiralty had failed to close the Iceland-Faeroes gap through which all those ships sailed.

The heavy cruiser *Admiral Hipper* had made an unsuccessful sortie in December 1940 and was in Brest from where she departed on 1 February 1941 and made a sweep into the Atlantic. Here she encountered an unescorted convoy and sank seven ships amounting to 32,806 tons. Her presence was reported and because of a shortage of fuel she made a fast passage back to Brest, finally returning to Kiel via the Denmark Strait. The need to block that passage was now of paramount importance.

The battlecruisers *Scharnhörst* and *Gneisenau* were also at large, having been sighted by the cruiser *Naiad*, but they disappeared in bad weather and narrowly avoided the trap set by the Home Fleet which had sailed to intercept. Refuelling off southern Greenland and proceeding south they sighted a large convoy on 22 February. As they closed they saw the tripod masts of the battleship *Ramillies* and withdrew to the west where they fell on a convoy 300 miles west of Newfoundland which was dispersing to Canadian and American ports. Five ships of 25,734 tons were sunk. As Admiral

Lütjens, who was in command of the German Squadron, knew he had been seen, he proceeded to the west coast of Africa, where he was again unable to attack a large convoy owing to the presence of the battleship *Malaya* as part of the escort, but steaming back across the Atlantic he approached the Canadian east coast where he found and sank no less than sixteen ships of 82,000 tons. The Home Fleet was stretched to the limit. Not only was it essential to protect North Atlantic convoys by allocating a battleship to each, but Admiral Tovey had to retain sufficient strength in the Iceland-Faeroes area to bring these two big ships to battle.

However, Admiral Lütjens made for Brest instead, where he arrived on 22 March. Despite intense air patrols and thousands of miles of steaming by a large proportion of the Home Fleet and all of Force H based on Gibraltar, these two ships sank or captured twenty-two ships of 115,622 tons and completely dislocated the sailings of convoys vital for the survival of Great Britain.

At the same time they diverted attention from the return passage of the *Admiral Scheer* and the *Admiral Hipper* which, as we have seen, made a successful passage home.

Atlantis was at sea for a successful and harassing career which started on the last day of March 1940 and did not end finally until 22 November 1941 when she was sunk by the cruiser *Devonshire* which had been ordered to intercept as a result of decrypted German U-boat signals and radio communication between the German High Command and the merchant cruiser. However *Atlantis* had sunk or captured twenty-two ships with a total tonnage of 145,697. It was a remarkable achievement and there were numerous occasions when she managed to avoid capture, sometimes by an extremely narrow margin.

With Japanese assistance the raider *Orion* had undergone a refit in the Pacific in January 1941, was narrowly missed by the cruiser *Cornwall* and proceeded westward to enter the South Atlantic. While her presence at large had dislocated shipping and tied up warships in a fruitless hunt, she had achieved little in her 510 days at sea, though that in itself was a very considerable achievement. She had disposed of 57,744 tons of shipping and returned safely to Bordeaux, never again to be used in that role.

The raider Kormoran *sinking an Allied merchant ship in the Indian Ocean.*

35

The *Thor* had been in action against two British armed merchant cruisers and had survived, and on 4 April 1941 she engaged and sank the armed merchant cruiser *Voltaire*, a smaller and more lightly armed ship which fought to the end and 197 of whose crew were rescued by the *Thor*. Her total sinkings were eleven merchant ships of 83,301 tons as well as the armed merchant cruiser and she passed undetected up the English Channel arriving safely at Hamburg on 30 April.

Let us turn now to the *Pinguin* which had proceeded to the Antarctic after refuelling in company with the *Admiral Scheer*. She came upon a Norwegian whaling fleet, capturing three factory ships of 12,000 tons each and sinking eleven of the attendant whale catchers. This was no mean feat for a single ship which put prize crews on board and sailed the ships back to French ports. Reappearing in the Indian Ocean she sank three ships, but the last victim, the *British Emperor*, sent off a distress signal which was picked up by the cruiser *Cornwall* some 500 miles away. The chase was on.

Cornwall's two aircraft sighted a suspicious ship which sent out a distress call when the cruiser arrived and for some moments it was unclear whether it was in fact the *Pinguin*. She was ordered to heave to and the *Cornwall* closed to inspect her. The *Pinguin* opened rapid fire, hitting the *Cornwall* repeatedly, but at 17.26 the *Pinguin* blew up. Twenty-two British and Indian prisoners and sixty of her

The German supply ship Nordmark *disguised as the neutral American tanker* Prairie *(which was in fact non-existent), at a secret rendezvous point in March 1941 with the cruiser* Admiral Scheer.

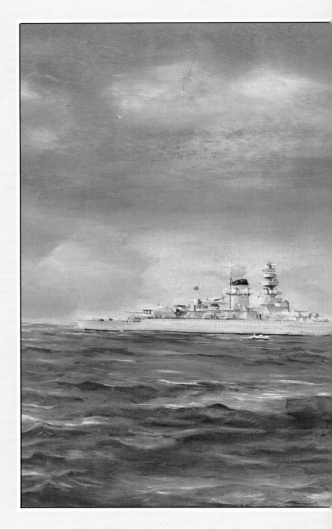

crew survived and were picked up. She had been at sea for ten months and had sunk or captured twenty-eight ships of 136,551 tons. The fact that the *British Emperor* had the courage to send out the distress call with an accurate position before she was sunk by gunfire ended the cruise of a very dangerous ship. But the question of identification had proved difficult. The British warship had doubts and approached too close. It was to be some time before the procedure was perfected, whereby the Admiralty in London was able to identify each suspicious ship, but not before a disaster occurred for the Allies in Australian waters.

Also at large and operating were three more raiders — the *Komet*, which had proceeded by way of the Northern Passage, *Kormoran* and *Ramb I*. The last-named, an Italian, was sunk by HMS *Leander* without having achieved a successful sortie. The *Komet* returned to Germany at the end of November 1941. The *Kormoran* had sunk or captured eleven ships of 68,000 tons and evaded capture for eleven months. On 19 November 1941 she was cruising off the coast of Australia when she was intercepted by the cruiser HMAS *Sydney*. The Australian cruiser closed to within 2,000 yards on a parallel course

Operations by German armed merchant cruisers

Name and duration of sortie	Armament	Shipping sunk or captured Number	Tonnage	Operating area	Remarks
Atlantis 31 3 1940 to 22 11 1941	6 4.9 inch 4 T.tubes 2 Aircraft 93 Mines	22	145,697	Atlantic, Pacific and Indian Oceans	Sunk by HMS *Devonshire* 22 11 1941
Orion 6 4 1940 to 23 8 1941	6 5.9 inch 6 T.tubes 2 Aircraft 228 Mines	9½ [3½ shared]	57,744	Atlantic, Pacific and Indian Oceans	Returned to home base
Widder 6 5 1940 to 31 10 1940	6 5.9 inch 4 T.tubes 1 Aircraft 60 Mines	10	58,643	Central Atlantic	Returned to home base
Thor 6 6 1940 to 30 4 1941	6 5.9 inch 4 T.tubes 1 Aircraft 90 Mines	11	85,000	South and Central Atlantic	Engaged HMS *Alcantara* and *Caernarvon Castle*. Sank HMS *Voltaire*. Returned to home base
Pinguin 22 6 1940 to 8 5 1941	6 5.9 inch 4 T.tubes 2 Aircraft 300 Mines	17 plus 11 whalers	136,551	Atlantic, Indian and Antarctic Oceans	Sunk by HMS *Cornwall* 8 5 1941
Komet 9 7 1940 to 30 11 1941	6 5.9 inch 4 T.tubes 1 Aircraft 25 Mines	6½ [3½ shared]	42,959	Pacific	Sailed by north-east passage and Bering Sea. Returned to home base
Kormoran 3 12 1940 to 19 11 1941	6 5.9 inch 6 T.tubes 2 Aircraft 320 Mines	11	68,274	Central and South Atlantic Indian and Pacific Oceans	Sank and sunk by HMAS *Sydney* 19 11 1941

and demanded to know her identity. *Kormoran* opened fire and the few seconds initiative she obtained were decisive. The cruiser was hit heavily around the bridge and forward turrets as well as by a torpedo. *Kormoran* was hit repeatedly and was also on fire. As the action continued in the dusk both ships were disabled and drifted apart. The raider was abandoned and scuttled, 312 of her crew reaching Australia. During the night an explosion was seen on the horizon; HMAS *Sydney* sank with no survivors.

An epic of the sea. The American Liberty ship SS Stephen Hopkins *was stopped by the German raider* Steir *in the South Atlantic. She had left the South African ports some days before and was on her way back to the United States. The raider was accompanied by the tanker* Tannenfels, *and despite instructions not to use her radio she opened fire with her single 4 inch gun. The* Steir *replied by destroying her bridge and radio and then proceeded to sink the ship. The entire gun crew were killed at their posts but the damage they inflicted on* Steir *caused her to catch fire, explode, and sink. Fifteen survivors from* Stephen Hopkins *endured thirty days in an open boat before reaching the coast of Brazil.*

The Mediterranean

The Mediterranean was the vital link between Britain and the Far East, and in September 1939 it was feared that Italy would join forces with Germany at some stage. These fears were realized on 11 June 1940.

The French fleet ceased to exist with the surrender of France, and the British Commonwealth was faced with the grim task of not only ensuring that Germany did not annex these valuable ships and turn them against her, but also of taking over the defence of this vast area. Tactical dispositions were as follows: Britain had stationed altogether five battleships, two aircraft carriers, twelve cruisers, forty-two destroyers and ten submarines. Ranged against them was the Italian fleet of six battleships commissioned or nearing completion, nineteen cruisers, fifty-four destroyers and 107 submarines with seven destroyers and eight submarines in the Red Sea. In addition to this, Italy possessed no less than sixty-seven small but fast escort and local defence destroyers.

Another very important consideration was the positioning of both the opposing fleets and the available bases. The maritime strategy of both Great Britain and Italy was to dominate the Mediterranean. On paper the Italian fleet, with a number of large, fast and heavily armed vessels, and its large submarine force and overwhelming air superiority, clearly was in a position to do this. Her air bases were conveniently placed in the central Mediterranean and only the tiny island of Malta gave the Allies a toehold in that area. In peacetime Malta had been neglected and now, with all the forces ranged against her by the subjugation of Europe, it was too late for Britain to build up the necessary air strength to protect the skies above the island. Italy only had to dominate the central Mediterranean area, while Britain had to face the need for maritime control over an area covering the North Atlantic, together with the South Atlantic and the route to Suez, India and Australasia, or to starve.

It can be well understood how the British Government had grave doubts as to whether the country could spare the ships and aircraft to hold the whole of the Mediterranean, and still maintain strategic control elsewhere.

The first brush between the opposing forces occurred on 9 July when both sides were escorting convoys. The old capital ships *Royal Sovereign* and *Malaya* were too slow to maintain contact with the Italian escorts and a torpedo attack by aircraft from the old carrier *Eagle* failed. None the less when the Italian battleship *Cesare* was hit by long range gunfire, the whole Italian force turned away under cover of smoke. This aggressive action, which was to be repeated time and again in the future, redressed the tactical imbalance and helped to establish ascendancy over the Italian fleet. It was to become a feature of the naval campaign in the Mediterranean. This incident was followed almost at once by another in which the Australian cruiser *Sydney* and three destroyers met two Italian cruisers and sank the *Bartolomeo Colleoni* after a running fight.

Reinforcements for the Royal Navy in this area had to be found and at the end of August the battleship *Valiant* with the new aircraft carrier *Illustrious* and with two anti-aircraft cruisers reached the Commander-in-Chief, Admiral Cunningham. These were followed in November 1940 by the battleship *Barham*, two cruisers and three destroyers from Britain.

There were two matters of strategic importance. Italy's large fleet of submarines, some eighty of which were operational at this period, were thought to pose a very serious threat. However, in comparison with the effective and deadly use by Germany of her much smaller number of boats, the Italian submarines accomplished relatively little. The same must be said for British boats, which were too large to work safely in the shallow waters used by the Italian convoy routes and were in need of refits, having been transferred from the China Station. By the end of the year over half the British force had been lost, and twenty Italian submarines had also been destroyed.

Admiral Cunningham had been on the offensive since July, bombarding Benghazi, Rhodes and Tripoli. However, there was still urgent need for greater offensive action, and it was decided to mount a night attack by torpedo aircraft on the large naval base at Taranto in south-east Italy. Malta possessed one or two long range reconnaissance aircraft and photographs of Taranto Harbour showed the position of the Italian fleet at anchor on 10 November. On the following day the aircraft carrier *Illustrious*, protected by the Mediterranean fleet, flew off twenty-one Swordfish torpedo-bombers from a position 150 miles from the Italian naval base.

These remarkable biplanes with a maximum speed of 138 miles per hour and with open cockpits were the British Fleet Air Arm's first line operational aircraft. The first strike of twelve aircraft flew off at 20.40 followed by a second strike forty minutes later. The base was illuminated by flares as the aircraft bore in. Three torpedoes struck the new battleship *Littorio* and the battleships *Duilo* and *Cavour* each received one hit. *Cavour* sank at her moorings and *Duilo* was beached. All but two of the aircraft returned to *Illustrious* after this remarkable operation. The damage done did not go unnoticed on the other side of the world and was studied in great detail by the Japanese for their attack on Pearl Harbor a year later.

The attack on Taranto had an effect which went beyond the crippling of three battleships, which in itself helped to redress the balance of power. It showed that Britain's hold on the Mediterranean could be maintained by the aggressive handling of her naval forces; no one was more capable than Admiral Cunningham in this respect. The night's work was rounded off by a sortie into the nearby Straits of Otranto with light forces sinking three out of four ships in an Italian convoy bound for Albania. Thus was British maritime power reasserted in the central Mediterranean at a critical moment.

The question remained whether it was possible to pass convoys through the Mediterranean. Troops and supplies were badly needed by General Wavell in his North African campaign to destroy the Italian threat to the Suez Canal, and Malta had to be reinforced. At the end of

The Fleet Air Arm attack on Taranto — 11 November 1940. Lit by flares, British Fairey Swordfish aircraft attack with torpedoes, sinking the new battleship Littorio *and the older* Cavour, *and beaching* Duilo. *All but two of the aircraft returned to HMS* Illustrious *after this remarkable operation. The damage done to the Italian fleet did not go unnoticed on the other side of the world and was studied in great detail by the Japanese for their attack on Pearl Harbor a year later.*

November 1940 a fast and heavily escorted convoy was taken through from west to east, and during its passage the Italian Commander-in-Chief, Admiral Campioni, despatched a strong force to intercept. Leaving only a close escort, the British covering forces closed the Italian fleet and action was joined at long range off Cape Spartivento in Sicily. The two Italian battleships, seven cruisers and sixteen destroyers were driven off and despite heavy attacks from the air the convoy and its escort arrived safely.

The Vichy Government in France seemed determined that French naval forces would not fall into British hands, while it was unthinkable to allow them to take sides against the Allies. Thus an abortive and distressing encounter took place off West Africa at Dakar in September 1940 where damage was done to both sides. In the event the naval forces under control of the Vichy Government did not interfere with Allied convoy routes.

As 1940 came to an end the position in the Mediterranean was as follows. While some successful convoys had been pushed through from Gibraltar, the large quantities of stores required by General Wavell in his land campaign necessitated the supply route taking the long passage round the Cape and up the Suez Canal. It placed an almost intolerable strain on the available shipping. None the less General Wavell had forced the Italian Army out of Egypt by 9 December, and Cyrenaica had been cleared by 7 February 1941 — a very significant victory. Italian reinforcements were still getting through and Malta was threatened. But the island was vital, not only as a naval base but because its strategic position in the centre of the Mediterranean made it an essential staging post and springboard for offensive operations against the Axis powers. However, each time it was supplied, nearly the whole of the large Mediterranean fleet and Force H were required. The main British fleet was stationed at the eastern end at Alexandria, not only assisting in support of the land warfare but ready to strike at the Italian fleet should it dispute the control of that area. Force H — a powerful squadron — was based at Gibraltar available to operate in the western Mediterranean and also to move into the Atlantic should it be needed.

The action between two Italian cruisers and the Australian light cruiser Sydney *with three destroyers resulted in the sinking of the Italian* Bartolomeo Colleoni *after a running fight.*

Back to the Atlantic

The battle in the Atlantic had never ceased and Britain was confronted by increased U-boat activity from the new German bases on the west coast of France facing the Atlantic. Just as dangerous was the vulnerable sea route down the east coast of Britain. All arriving convoys had been diverted round the north of Ireland to west coast ports such as Liverpool and Greenock, while those heading for the east coast, and notably the port of London, were passed round the north of Scotland. The whole of the east coast was vulnerable, despite mine barrages laid to protect the shipping. While the entrance to the English Channel was blocked, an inshore convoy route was maintained for the use of smaller slower vessels which were subjected to incessant attack by dive-bombers based a few miles away on the French coast. The RAF maintained fighter cover but with the small number of planes available it was inevitable that some dive-bombers would get through. An additional hazard was in the form of E-boats — fast and heavily armed motor torpedo boats which attacked the convoys, mostly at night, from Norfolk to Dorset. Fierce action took place between British coastal forces and the E-boats. Finally it was the RAF cover which enabled the south coast routes to be sustained in daylight, though the loss of seventy-five aircraft in the summer and autumn of 1940 was a high price to pay for the delivery of coal to the West Country.

If this was not enough in the German attempt to halt shipping, the danger of mines increased with the continuous mining of the swept channels by E-boats and aircraft operating at night. Many variations of these deadly weapons were laid, some lying on the sea bed with a delay fuse of up to fourteen days and then activated by the presence of a steel hull or by the noise of propellers passing over them. Minesweeping went on continuously — though at the height of the dive-bombing attacks it was carried out at night. Meanwhile losses by mines increased: 201 ships of half a million tons were lost in 1940.

While the battle to keep open coastal convoy routes was going on, the war at sea in the Atlantic increased in intensity. It was still only possible to give close escort to convoys arriving and departing up to a distance of 200 miles west of Ireland, increased by some 150 miles by the end of the year. From then on they were on their own, accompanied in some cases only by an armed merchant cruiser or one or two sloops, the only escort vessels with the endurance to enable them to accompany a convoy throughout its journey. Ships in convoy sail at the speed of the slowest vessel and transatlantic convoys were divided into slow and fast convoys. The average time taken for a slow convoy from Nova Scotia to a UK port was fifteen days, while fast convoys from Halifax clipped two days off that time. From Freetown in West Africa the time was nineteen days. The winter weather played havoc with the schedules, and escorts waiting at ocean rendezvous were in danger of running out of fuel.

The last six months of 1940 were a time of extreme peril for the British Commonwealth. The U-boats were now 450 miles nearer their operational areas, having moved from Germany to Lorient and Brest. Coastal Command aircraft were needed for reconnaissance of hostile shores to give warning of invasion plans and

thus only a few were available to assist in convoy protection. Above all there was a lack of escort vessels. Two gestures of vital importance to Britain were provided by the United States at this time. First was the declaration by President Roosevelt that America would provide all aid short of war and secondly the gift of fifty obsolete destroyers laid up since 1918 in return for base facilities in the West Indies, Bermuda and Newfoundland. They were unmodernized, had only received minimal maintenance and were difficult to handle, being extremely wet and uncomfortable. But these 'four stackers' as they were called had one important advantage. After modification they had sufficient endurance to accompany a convoy throughout its voyage and so were pressed into service before the end of the year.

There was some concern that Germany would occupy Iceland and The Faeroes which were both Danish. Their strategic position meant that it would be catastrophic if U-boats could establish a base in these areas. The British Government therefore proceeded to occupy a base in Reykjavik and Hvalford in Iceland and Thorshavn in The Faeroes in June 1940 and these were built up into naval and air bases of immense value. Escorts could now refuel or join a convoy from Iceland.

Germany had only sixteen U-boats in action in operational areas at any one time during this period but the boats were handled by such aces as Prien, Kretschmer, Schepke, Frauenheim and others and they were deadly. There was no lack of targets and in June the sinkings rose to fifty-eight ships of 284,113 tons. The Italian Navy joined their allies by sending twenty-six boats into the Atlantic but their performance was extremely poor. This period of the U-boat war was called the Happy Time by their commanders, and Hitler proclaimed a total blockade of the British Isles and neutral ships were to be sunk on sight.

The U-boats were joined by long range Focke-Wulf 'Condor' (FW 200) four-engined long range reconnaissance aircraft which reported the position of convoys to the U-boats and attacked unescorted vessels, or were vectored to the scene by U-boat sightings. In August U-boats sank fifty-six ships of 267,618 tons and the Condors a further fifteen of 53,283 tons. In September the sinkings rose to seventy-four ships (351,660 tons). October was still worse — sixty-nine ships of 361,159 tons. These were caused by U-boat and aircraft but the actual total sinkings of Allied ships from all causes read as follows:

June 1940	140 ships of 585,496 tons
July	105 ships of 386,912 tons
August	92 ships of 397,229 tons
September	100 ships of 448,621 tons
October	103 ships of 442,985 tons
November	97 ships of 385,715 tons
December	82 ships of 349,568 tons

However, these stark statistics give little account of the horror of war in the Atlantic from

whichever viewpoint it is approached. The U-boat commander was subjected to depth charging beneath the cold Atlantic and the escort commander faced an almost impossible task. As an illustration, the story of slow convoy SC 7 is now recalled in some detail.

In October 1940 convoy SC 7 sailed from Canadian ports. It consisted of thirty-five slow and elderly ships and the convoy speed was no more than 7 knots. The ships carried a vital cargo at a time of the gravest peril, after Dunkirk and during the Battle of Britain, which could have been the prelude to invasion. The formation in which the convoy sailed was a broad front rectangle. It was made up of five columns of four ships and three columns of five ships, the longer columns being in the centre. Each column was half a mile apart. Thus the convoy covered a sea area of some four square miles. In this formation — as opposed to a few long columns — it was easier for the escorts to protect and for the commodore in command of the convoy to control in one of the leading ships. Convoys manoeuvred using flag signals by day and coloured lights at night.

The ocean escort for SC 7 was the little sloop *Scarborough*, lightly armed and employed pre-war in policing tropical foreign waters. She had escorted an outward bound convoy which had been set upon between Iceland and Scotland. Six ships had been sunk in six hours and no trace of the U-boats had been found. This one little sloop was the sole defence of the thirty-five ships until a local escort could meet them in the Western Approaches. However, on 16 October as dusk was falling two more escorts met the convoy, unusually far out in the Atlantic. They were the *Fowey* (a sister ship of the *Scarborough*) and the *Bluebell*, one of the new Flower Class corvettes. None of these ships had ever worked together, and there was no accepted and laid down action drill at that period of the war. The ships took station, *Scarborough* and *Fowey* on port and starboard and *Bluebell* astern. Thus the distance between them was some six miles and a full moon was shining down on them in a smooth silver sea.

Away on the port side from where the black hulls stood out in the moonlight, U-48 (Bleichrodt) reported the position and speed of the convoy. As a result six U-boats were positioned in the path of the convoy east and north of Rockall. But U-48 couldn't wait and two ships were torpedoed. The convoy commodore in the freighter *Assyrian* ordered an emergency turn to starboard, and the two sloops sped off to attack the U-boat.

The *Bluebell* stopped to pick up the crews of the sunken ships and the convoy had no escort. U-48, though forced to remain submerged, was still in the vicinity. HMS *Scarborough* searched but failed to find her and was then so far behind the convoy that with a maximum speed of fourteen knots could not rejoin and was out of the fight. The convoy now had *Fowey* on the starboard and *Bluebell* on the port side. Two further escorts were to arrive, the sloop *Leith* and the corvette *Heartsease*. U-48 had lost the convoy but it was sighted during the day by U-38. In the early hours of 18 October U-38 fired a salvo and only succeeded in hitting the freighter *Carsbreck* which was loaded with timber that kept her afloat. Leaving one escort, the

The destruction of Convoy SC 7 off the coast of Scotland. In October 1940 thirty-five slow and elderly ships, escorted by three lightly armed escorts, were attacked by six German U-boats. Twenty out of the original thirty-five ships were sunk. The painting shows the Commodore ship Assyrian *with her bows in the air. The* Empire Brigade *and* Soesterberg *are sinking around her.*

remainder went off to attack the U-boat and U-38 fired again, but missed. During the day, the convoy saw wreckage and the escorts picked up survivors of a previous convoy.

Ahead of the convoy was the wolf pack strung out to wait for the dusk. Among the German commanders were Schepke in U-100 and Kretschmer in U-99. As dusk fell the convoy was sighted as a cloud of smoke and a forest of masts came over the horizon.

Unaware of what lay ahead, the convoy settled down for the night, turning 40 degrees to starboard to confuse the U-boats. But nothing could stop the disaster.

At 20.15 the first ship was sunk. Soon after 23.00 a series of explosions was heard and two

submarines boldly entered the convoy line. U-99 (Kretschmer) sank six ships and the escorts vainly scoured the sea on the flanks and picked up survivors. A sloop came upon the Commodore ship *Assyrian*, her bows in the air, with the *Empire Brigade* and the *Soesterberg* sinking round her.

The sea was filled with wreckage and survivors in the water. The *Leith* picked up the crews from the sunken ships and set off to rejoin the convoy. At this stage the weather closed in with pelting rain and visibility was reduced to a few hundred yards. Twenty ships out of the original

thirty-five had been sunk, and the weary and dispirited escorts returned to base. Following on the heels of SC 7 was convoy HX 79 which, despite a strong escort, lost twelve ships before the U-boats, having expended all of their torpedoes, returned to their bases on the west coast of France.

It is thus understandable that some authoritative minds in the United States doubted whether Britain could survive. This defeatist and isolationist lobby was stoutly attacked by those who were more far-sighted and realized that Britain's defeat would be unacceptable

to the United States. Nowhere was the position being studied with greater interest than in Japan where plans were being advanced for an extension of her control in the Pacific.

However, at the end of the year there was perhaps reason for some slight optimism. Escort vessels damaged or used for anti-invasion duties were returning to duty in the Atlantic. The fifty American destroyers were in service and it was now possible to provide two escort vessels per convoy throughout the journey, as the new Flower Class corvettes were beginning to come forward.

It was an optimism which tended to be short-lived. Eight U-boats had been sunk between July and December, but these losses were soon eclipsed by the new boats which were coming into service.

To lift some of the strain from the Atlantic, the U-boat bases in Brest and Lorient were heavily bombed by the RAF. How ineffective this was only became clear at the end of the war. Up to the invasion of Europe in 1944 only one U-boat was destroyed by all the thousands of tons of bombs dropped on the U-boat pens protected by massive concrete structures.

1941 - the assault of the wolf packs

A year of extreme peril, 1941 was to end with the extension of the war to the Pacific with the Japanese attack on Pearl Harbor in Hawaii and American's entry fully into the war. During those twelve long months Britain and the Commonwealth, together with her small but devoted band of Allies, stood alone, fighting to fend off starvation at home and to retain a foothold in the Middle East to protect the vital Suez Canal. At sea, it was the Battle of the Atlantic which raged throughout the year, while in the Mediterranean the disastrous defeat of Allied land forces in Greece and Crete was followed by very heavy losses in the fleet. But our story continues in the Atlantic.

Alone among the Axis strategists, Admiral Dönitz realized that the only way to defeat the Allies was to starve Britain into surrender. The massed air raids on London and the fighter bases had failed to destroy the RAF and invasion was thus impossible. Hitler disregarded his demands for all-out U-boat construction and for the building of long range aircraft to fly far out into the Atlantic and attack shipping. On the British side, escort vessels were given priority, but the one really important element for the defence of convoys and for an offensive to destroy the U-boat was for aircraft to accompany all convoys and this was not given the priority it required. Eventually, when the value of long range and close support aircraft was finally recognized, it was found that aircraft were a more effective deterrent to U-boats, preventing them from attacking shipping, than were the surface vessels. But that is hindsight. Coastal Command continued to take second place to Bomber Command. It was not until June 1941 that HMS *Audacity*, the first converted merchant ship, came into service with a flight deck capable of operating aircraft within a convoy.

Towards the end of 1940 Admiral Dönitz had introduced the wolf pack system of employing several U-boats to attack a convoy at night on the surface. It was not a new concept, having been used with great success in 1917. The system required that a convoy should be located — by long range aircraft or by U-boat — and shadowed. The pack then converged upon the convoy and proceeded to attack on the surface during the night, withdrawing by day and resuming the attack next night. This required considerable wireless activity. The convoy escorts had been fitted with Asdic (sonar) sets which could detect submerged U-boats but were useless when the U-boat had surfaced. Only radar could pinpoint a surfaced U-boat and radar was not available to many escort vessels at the start of 1941. Shadowing the convoy was all important and a change of course by day could put the wolf pack off the scent and in some cases result in days of fruitless searching. But when the attack did go in the speed of the sloops and corvettes was inferior to that of a surfaced U-boat. Starshell was used by escorts to illuminate the scene, and later a system known as Snowflakes, where merchant ships sent up rockets which turned night into day and disclosed the presence of U-boats in the vicinity of the convoy. But a submarine approaching on the surface was a very small target to detect.

With a convoy spread out in five lines covering an area of six miles by two miles and with only one or two escorts on the flanks or ahead or astern, it was easy for a U-boat to slip in among the lines of ships unnoticed.

However, there were drawbacks. German U-boat pack tactics necessitated the extensive use of wireless telegraphy, and by setting up Direction Finding Stations (HF/DF) it was possible to give a fairly accurate position of the source of transmissions. By July 1941 these interceptions became almost instantaneous, and were shortly followed by centimetric radar. When these facilities were available to escorts at sea the results were spectacular.

The wolf pack gathers. A meeting of U-boats to discuss tactics in October 1940 included the most successful of Germany's commanders: U-99 (Kretschmer), U-100 (Schepke), U-101 (Frauenheim) and U-123 (Moehle).

Meanwhile the slaughter of the convoys went on. The painting on page 46 shows the last action by U-99. In company with U-100 (Schepke) and others, U-99 shadowed a convoy until she was able to slip between two escorting destroyers and position herself inside the convoy. Selecting the tanker *Fern*, Kretschmer fired a torpedo at close range and the sheet of flame from the high octane petrol illuminated the U-boat which was forced to dive. Surfacing later he worked his way round the end of the convoy on the surface, and crept back into the line of ships, selecting another tanker — the *Bedouin*. At this moment he was hemmed in by ships on either side of him, and he weaved his way through the lines until he was able to torpedo another tanker, which erupted. Again he was revealed in the glare and heat of the blaze. He sheered away and entered another line. The escorts were firing starshell but he kept close to the ships in convoy and was not spotted. Finding a third tanker he fired again and the tanker stopped, with black smoke pouring from beneath its decks and angry red flames consuming the upper works of the doomed ship. Travelling along under the clouds of smoke he sighted two large freighters and fired a torpedo at each. The smaller ship sank immediately but the larger settled only slightly in the water. As the convoy sailed slowly by he fired again and the ship sank beneath the sea already strewn with wreckage and struggling seamen. Finally with his last torpedo he selected another tanker, which broke in half and sank.

Meanwhile, Commander Macintyre, commanding the escort in the destroyer *Walker* was fighting back. Hampered by having to pick up survivors, he none the less made Asdic contact with a U-boat, and going into attack with depth charges he forced U-99 to the surface and in a gun action sank her. Kretschmer and his crew abandoned ship and were taken on board. *Vanoc*, the only other destroyer, located U-100 (Schepke) by radar and rammed her. Schepke was badly wounded and died; only five of his crew survived. To the loss of those two 'aces' was added that of Commander Prien in U-47, whose boat was sunk with all hands.

While there is no doubt that the morale of the U-boat arm of the *Kriegsmarine* was high and

Table one   U-boat and Italian submarine losses (including the Mediterranean*)

	U-Boats	Italian submarines
September 1939 to December 1940	32	20
January 1941	0	3
February	0	0
March	5	2
April	2	0
May	1	0
June	4	2

Table two   German U-boat strength

	Operations	Training and trials	Total	Boats recently commissioned
January 1941	22	67	89	22
April	32	81	113	30
July	65	93	158	47
October	80	118	198	53
January 1942	91	158	249	69

Table three   British, Allied and neutral merchant ships lost in action   Figures show tonnage with number of ships in brackets

	January to December 1940	January 1941	February	March	April	May	June
North Atlantic	1,805,494(349)	214,382(42)	317,378(69)	364,689(63)	260,451(45)	324,550(58)	318,740(68)
UK approaches	1,793,748(650)	36,975(15)	51,381(26)	152,862(73)	99,031(40)	100,655(59)	86,381(34)
South Atlantic	55,269(8)	58,585(17)	0	0	21,807(3)	11,339(2)	10,134(2)
Mediterranean	64,183(13)	0	8,343(2)	11,868(2)	292,518(105)	70,835(19)	9,145(3)
Indian Ocean	173,416(24)	10,298(2)	26,291(5)	0	14,094(2)	3,663(1)	7,625(2)
Pacific	99,531(15)	0	0	287(1)	0	0	0
Total	3,991,641(1059)	320,240(76)	403,393(102)	529,706(139)	687,901(195)	511,042(139)	432,025(109)

Cause of destruction

	January to December 1940	January 1941	February	March	April	May	June
Submarine	2,186,158(471)	126,782(21)	196,783(39)	243,020(41)	249,375(43)	325,492(58)	310,143(61)
Aircraft	580,074(192)	78,597(20)	89,305(27)	113,314(41)	323,454(116)	146,302(65)	61,414(25)
Mine	509,889(201)	17,107(10)	16,507(10)	23,585(19)	24,888(6)	23,194(9)	15,326(10)
Warship raider	96,986(17)	18,738(3)	79,086(17)	89,838(17)	0	0	0
Merchant raider	366,644(54)	78,484(20)	7,031(1)	28,707(4)	43,640(6)	15,002(3)	17,759(4)
E-boat	47,985(23)	0	2,979(3)	20,361(9)	4,299(3)	0	0
Unknown/other	203,905(101)	532(2)	11,702(5)	10,881(8)	42,245(21)	1,052(4)	27,383(9)
Total	3,991,641(1059)	320,240(76)	403,393(102)	529,706(139)	687,901(195)	511,042(139)	432,025(109)

their successes had been spectacular, the losses of U-boats, and particularly of their remarkably efficient and highly trained crews, was a serious defeat for Admiral Dönitz. During March 1941 one-fifth of the U-boats operating in the Atlantic had been sunk, and from the Allies' side the facts were becoming plain. Powerful surface escorts trained in conjunction with aircraft were to be the means of stemming the tide of ever-increasing losses.

The tables on page 45 give the stark reality of the position during the first six months of 1941.

The totals of ships sunk show clearly that the effect of sinkings by aircraft was highly significant. In January, U-boats sank twenty-one ships and aircraft twenty ships. In February the U-boat total rose to thirty-nine and another twenty-seven were sunk by aircraft (some in port at Liverpool and in the Thames), and in March, each sank forty-one with a total tonnage of 847,781. But this was not all, for in the same quarter warship raiders accounted for thirty-seven ships (187,662 tons) and merchant raiders twenty-five (101,322 tons). From all causes, 1,253,339 tons of Allied shipping were sunk in the oceans of the world in the first quarter of the year 1941.

Although an enormous expansion of escort vessels was taking place, the need to train the crews and to exercise the ships together meant that the actual number available for operations was only increasing gradually. Too often it became necessary to send out newly commissioned escorts who had never worked together, and this resulted in a less effective convoy escort. Yet training was beginning to show and in the long months to come was to provide the means finally to defeat the U-boat onslaught.

From the German side it was essential to increase the pressure on shipping round the beleaguered shores of Great Britain. This could only be achieved by the combined and co-ordinated action of all arms of the *Kriegsmarine* and the *Luftwaffe*. The German High Command did not provide sufficient long range reconnaissance bombers to make a really decisive contribution. In addition, while U-boat production was stepped up, it did not receive the necessary complete priority. However, the German U-boat strength did grow considerably in 1941, as shown in table 2 on page 45.

German tactics resulted in U-boats penetrating the escort screen at night and attacking on the surface from inside the convoy. While deadly in its effect, this was highly dangerous and demanded nerve and seamanship on the part of the U-boat commanders. The painting shows one of the most daring and successful of Germany's commanders, Captain Otto Kretschmer(U-99) in March 1941. His boat is visible against the burning tanker Fern *taking violent avoiding action. Next day U-99 was so severely damaged that he was forced to the surface and taken prisoner with his crew. The month of March also saw the death of Captain Prien in U-47 (who had sunk the battleship* Royal Oak *in Scapa Flow in 1939) and also another remarkably successful commander, Captain Schepke in U-100.*

The Bismarck action

The strategy of the German *Kriegsmarine* was not conceived to deal with a Jutland type confrontation with the Royal Navy. Their capital ships were intended to destroy Britain's merchant fleet which was supplying the war effort, and in so doing to be strong enough to defeat the dispersed squadrons sent out to hunt them. They were fast enough to draw away into the anonymity of the oceans when they met overwhelming force, and their guns were of sufficient calibre to defend themselves from all but the heaviest adversary. However, these ambitious plans were upset for a number of reasons. On 6 April, the *Gneisenau* was hit and severely damaged while docked in Brest, while the *Scharnhörst* was still undergoing a major refit after her damage off Norway. The *Admiral Hipper* was under repair in Kiel and the battleship *Tirpitz* was not yet completed. Thus plans for a mass attack on shipping to supplement the U-boat campaign were dislocated at a critical moment. Sufficient battleship or battlecruiser strength in the North and South Atlantic never actually materialized.

Nevertheless it was decided to sail the giant *Bismarck* with the heavy cruiser *Prinz Eugen* from Germany. News of the departure of the two ships reached London on 21 May and they were seen in Bergen the same day. It was now likely they would break out into the Atlantic via the Denmark Strait in the gap between the Greenland icefields and the mine barrage laid to the north-west of Iceland. There the heavy cruisers *Norfolk* and *Suffolk* were patrolling.

Admiral Tovey, the Commander-in-Chief, at once sailed the battleship *Prince of Wales* and the old and unmodernized battlecruiser *Hood* (Admiral Holland) with six destroyers from Scapa to Iceland. The *Prince of Wales* had just been completed and had not finished her working up trials, but the position was so grave she was none the less despatched. The remainder of the Home Fleet remained at Scapa at short notice to await definite information of the progress and route of the German squadron. On the evening of 22 May, in very bad weather, a Fleet Air Arm aircraft from the Orkneys penetrated the Bergen fiords and reported that the squadron had left. The Home Fleet sailed to the north-west of Scotland to cover the patrolling cruisers between Iceland and The Faeroes and to be in a position to intercept when it was known which route the German force would take. The overriding consideration in Admiral Tovey's mind was the question of fuel supply should a long chase ensue. The weather was such that air patrols were of little use, but at 19.22 on 23 May the cruiser *Suffolk* sighted the *Bismarck* and *Prinz Eugen* at a distance of about seven miles. Slipping into the mist to avoid these powerful adversaries, she shadowed the German squadron by radar in company with her sister ship *Norfolk*. The news reached the battle squadron under Admiral Holland cruising to the south of Iceland some 600 miles away, who immediately set course to intercept. Surprise was essential and the admiral ordered radio silence, relying on the information supplied by the shadowing cruisers. At these latitudes in May, twilight lasts for most of the night, and shortly after midnight the shadowing cruisers lost contact and Admiral Holland altered course towards the south. At 02.47 *Suffolk* regained contact and Admiral Holland, who had detached his

destroyers to search to the north, was in an unfavourable tactical position. He had to turn north to close his enemy and so prevented the use of a full broadside in the opening stages of the battle. Thus the main advantage of heavier fire power from the British ships was lost.

The opposing forces sighted each other and fire was opened at 25,000 yards at 05.32. The *Bismarck*'s guns all bore on the two British ships which were in close order and the weight of broadside favoured the German squadron.

The opening salvoes from both ships were extremely accurate and as the British squadron altered course to bring a full broadside to bear, the *Hood* was hit and a fire started amidships. She was hit again and blew up with a huge explosion between the after funnel and the main mast. The *Prinz Eugen*'s gunnery officer said afterwards that 'the whole forward section

of *Hood* reared up from the water like a spire of a cathedral towering between the upper works of the *Prince of Wales* as she altered course to avoid the wreck.' There were only three survivors from her company of ninety-five officers and 1,324 men.

Now the full weight of broadsides from both German ships concentrated on the *Prince of Wales*. The range was closing and at 18,000 yards enabled their secondary armament to be used, and 15 inch shells began to hit the ship. Mechanical breakdown in two main turrets in the *Prince of Wales* made it imperative to break off the action and to turn away under cover of smoke. But the *Bismarck* had herself been hit by two 14 inch shells causing a leak of fuel oil and sea water contamination. Admiral Lütjens, commanding the German squadron, decided that all hope of the Atlantic programme must be cancelled and he must make for a French port as

soon as possible. The *Prince of Wales* and the shadowing cruisers tried to keep in touch with the German squadron (which was using every means to shake them off) to enable Admiral Tovey with *King George V, Repulse,* the aircraft carrier *Victorious,* four cruisers and nine destroyers to close the German squadron.

At this moment the British ships were 330 miles away to the south-east and the Admiralty in London now ordered a massive array of warships to close the area. Force H, consisting of the battlecruiser *Renown,* the carrier *Ark Royal* and the cruiser *Sheffield,* was ordered north from Gibraltar. The battleship *Rodney* and four destroyers which were escorting a convoy over 500 miles to the south-east were ordered north, the battleship *Ramillies,* then in mid-Atlantic also escorting a convoy, was detached and even the battleship *Revenge* in Halifax, Nova Scotia, was sailed to join the encircling forces.

It was imperative to slow the *Bismarck* down to enable the opposing force to converge. At 14.40 on 24 May the aircraft carrier *Victorious* was detached with an escort of four cruisers to launch an air strike. *Victorious,* like the *Prince of Wales,* was new and not fully worked up. She was about to leave for Malta with a cargo of Hurricanes and had only an inexperienced squadron of nine Swordfish and six Fulmars for her strike. In very bad weather the Swordfish took off for their target. It was just after midnight in the dusk of a foul night that the Swordfish attacked. One hit was made amidships causing no very serious damage in itself, but the need to manoeuvre at high speed increased the damage caused by the earlier action, and contaminated more fuel oil. It was thus doubly important to return to harbour, and after the strike this remarkably well led squadron found *Victorious* and managed to land on her safely.

The German battleship Bismarck *and the heavy cruiser* Prinz Eugen *were ordered to break out into the Atlantic and attack Allied shipping. Sighted and shadowed by British cruisers they were engaged by the battleship HMS* Prince of Wales *and the battlecruiser HMS* Hood *in the Denmark Strait between Iceland and Greenland at 06.00 on 24 May 1941. Within minutes* Hood *blew up and* Prince of Wales *was damaged.*

Instead of returning to Germany round the North of Scotland (while all major units of the Home Fleet were to the south of him) Admiral Lütjens continued to make for a French port and decided to detach *Prinz Eugen* to continue on into the Atlantic. A diversionary move suddenly confronted the shadowing cruisers when the huge bulk of the *Bismarck* loomed out of the fog at 8,000 yards, and fire was opened before the cruisers were able to reach the

Following the sinking of Hood *and despite an air strike from HMS* Victorious, Bismarck *and* Prinz Eugen *parted and vanished into the Atlantic. However,* Bismarck *had sustained damage in the earlier actions and Admiral Lütjens decided to make for the French coast at Brest. British naval forces were converging from as far as Gibraltar and Halifax, Nova Scotia, but it was not until 10.30 on 26 May that she was sighted by a Catalina aircraft of the Coastal Command.*

safety of the mist. No damage was done but *Prinz Eugen* had slipped away. Within hours the *Bismarck* had shaken off her pursuers and all contact was lost. She now turned towards St Nazaire on the French coast. At that moment the Commander-in-Chief in *King George V* was barely 100 miles away and the change of course meant they missed by a very small but sufficient margin. Admiral Lütjens had set a direct course for Brest on the French Atlantic coast and knew that for the moment he had shaken off his pursuers. Admiral Tovey considered that he might be making for a rendezvous with a supply tanker south of Greenland to refuel before breaking out into the Atlantic. He therefore disregarded the sector between the north and the south-east, which was consequently left for the time unwatched. It was through the south-east corner of that sector that *Bismarck* was now steaming.

At the Admiralty in London, wireless transmissions were being monitored and it seemed probable that Brest was the destination. Due to an error in the Admiralty's signalling of bearings, Admiral Tovey was given the impression that *Bismarck* was breaking back to the north and reversed course for some hours, until at 18.05 on 25 May he resumed his original course. This left him still further behind in the chase. Meanwhile Force H was steaming north from Gibraltar at high speed to cut *Bismarck* off from Brest. In addition the battleships *Ramillies* and *Rodney* and two cruisers were in an area to the south of the German battleship, but apart from the knowledge that a western

French port was the probable destination, the vast stretches of the ocean gave no clue to *Bismarck*'s whereabouts.

Searches were being carried out by all available long-range Coastal Command aircraft and it was at 10.30 next day — 26 May — that a Catalina (with a US Navy ensign as co-pilot and technical adviser) sighted the *Bismarck*. She came under heavy fire but escaped and her position was given as 690 miles north-west of Brest. Within minutes a Swordfish from *Ark Royal* was on the scene and regular accurate shadowing began. It was now a race against time, for unless *Bismarck* was slowed down she would reach the coast of France on the morning of the following day. However, the outcome was to be influenced still further by shortage of fuel. All British ships had been steaming at high speed and might have to break off the chase to refuel. Already the destroyers screening Admiral Tovey's battle squadron had had to return to port, and added anxiety was caused by the near certainty that all U-boats would have been called to the assistance of *Bismarck*. The only way to prevent her escape was a torpedo attack

Throughout the night destroyers kept station round the damaged battleship, being unable to close for a torpedo attack due to defensive gunfire and very heavy seas. The painting shows HMS Zulu *receiving a near miss during the gale.*

The only way to bring Bismarck *to action was to force her to reduce speed. HMS* Ark Royal *coming up from Gibraltar was ordered to fly off an air strike despite bad weather and deteriorating visibility. The aircraft were met by heavy defensive fire and nearly every torpedo was avoided. Then a torpedo from the last aircraft hit* Bismarck*'s stern, jamming the rudder. This finally sealed her fate.*

from *Ark Royal*'s aircraft. Force H had been steaming at high speed into a rising gale and was now only seventy miles from the last reported position of the German ship. *Sheffield* was detached to shadow her and *Ark Royal*'s aircraft were in contact with her. An immediate strike by fourteen Swordfish was flown off at 14.50 in bad weather, but the pilots were unaware of *Sheffield*'s movements and mistook her for the *Bismarck* in the uncertain light and gale-torn sea. At 15.50 the aircraft broke cloud, found their target and dropped their torpedoes. Only then was the mistake realised, and *Sheffield*, some twenty miles from *Bismarck*, avoided all torpedoes by taking drastic avoiding action. In fact, some of the torpedoes had detonated prematurely, having been armed with magnetic pistols which exploded in the heavy swell. *Bismarck* was still steaming defiantly at high speed towards the safety of Brest. A second strike was flown off at 19.10 this time with contact pistols in the torpedoes which were set for a shallower depth.

At 20.47 the attack went in. Low cloud, rain squalls, high wind and a heavy sea were added to the defensive gunfire from *Bismarck*. The slow aircraft came in from all quarters over a prolonged period in an unco-ordinated attack. Two hits were obtained. One struck amidships at the heavily armoured side of the great battleship, and did no real damage, and then the last torpedo to be dropped hit the stern of the ship, damaging *Bismarck*'s propellers, and jamming the rudders. It was this hit which sealed her fate.

Closing in from the south were five destroyers which were guided to the scene by *Sheffield*. *Bismarck*'s speed had been reduced and she was steering an erratic course as the destroyers surrounded her in the darkness. All attacked with torpedoes during the night in tempestuous seas and all were driven off by the battle-

ship's guns. As dawn broke and daylight uncovered the scene the battleships *King George V* and *Rodney* were within range and opened fire. It is unnecessary to record the last moments of the short life of this gallant ship. She fought to the end and sank with her colours flying. She was a very powerful adversary indeed and had she succeeded in her role as commerce raider the results would have indeed been serious. To corner her in one sector of the Atlantic had cost the lives of 4,000 sailors, British and German, and involved eight battleships or battlecruisers, two aircraft carriers, eleven cruisers, twenty-one destroyers and eight submarines. Over 300 air sorties had been flown, sixty torpedoes had been expended, and lack of fuel in the final stages nearly resulted in the chase being abandoned.

The *Prinz Eugen* had developed engine defects and after refuelling it was decided that she should return to Brest, which she reached on 1 June. Although it was unknown at the time, the German High Command reversed their decision to use heavily armed warships to disrupt the convoys and this was the last attempt at what could have been a very dangerous aspect of the Battle of the Atlantic.

The Fourth Arm — Naval Intelligence

Naval Intelligence, which could be called 'the fourth arm' of the Services, had a vitally important effect on the war at sea. For some years prior to the war, Germany had been studying British ciphers and the *Beobachtungsdienst* or the Observation Service (*xB-Dienst*) under Captain Bonatz had made considerable progress in penetrating the British naval codes. However, only some 10 per cent of messages could be decrypted in time for operational use. It is of paramount importance to understand that while it might be possible to decrypt an entire message, unless this was achieved in time to pass it to the appropriate operational command to be acted upon, its value was little more than academic. It was this fact and the battle by both sides to obtain decrypted messages early enough to be of operational use which was so very important.

The immensely complicated convoy system necessitated considerable radio traffic and this was studied in detail by the highly efficient *xB-Dienst*. Although only 10 per cent of messages were effective for operational purposes, nevertheless inspired guesswork and the study of signal traffic analysis was extremely valuable and in the early days of the war Germany had the edge over the British Service.

In April 1940, during the Norwegian operations, the *xB-Dienst* was able to decrypt about 30-50 per cent of the signals in the naval cipher. Although only a small part of this was in time for operational use it was enough to provide useful estimates of the location and movement of the Home Fleet. But Germany never mastered the British ciphers used by the Commander-in-Chief or Flag Officers. Even when British codes and ciphers were changed, the *xB-Dienst* were again able to piece together an increasing amount of the radio traffic as the months went on, particularly in 'naval cipher Number Three' which dealt with convoy routing. The difficulty facing the *Kriegsmarine* was that still only some 10 per cent were received in sufficient time to be acted upon.

Germany used an enciphering method which was called 'Enigma' and for the first six months of the war was virtually secure, despite the fact that a machine had been in British hands since shortly after the outbreak of hostilities. When the *Admiral Graf Spee* was being chased all over the South Atlantic and the *Scharnhörst* and *Gneisenau* were operating in the North Atlantic, the Royal Navy was blind.

The U-boats operating in the Atlantic sent and received a large number of transmissions, and by the use of Direction Finding Stations positioned at two or more places on land it was possible to obtain an accurate fix of the position of the transmitting U-boat. To this must be added the radio traffic intelligence which gave an indication of operations which were imminent. Bletchley Park in Buckinghamshire was the headquarters of the Special Intelligence department of British Naval Intelligence and the part played by the staff of that department was to have a marked effect on the war at sea in general and a decisively vital role in the Battle of the Atlantic. That branch of the Service was classified as 'Ultra' — and ultra-secret it was, for any hint that ciphers were being penetrated would have resulted in a complete change of German coding methods. The whole system

would then be put back months if not years. However, like the German *xB-Dienst*, fragments of deciphered material formed patterns of a mosaic which began to make sense.

But remember that in all these endeavours on both sides of the war at sea, intelligence is only useful if it is delivered in time to those who are in a position to act upon it.

The popular belief that Ultra made a vital contribution in the chase for the *Bismarck* is not borne out by the facts, for the intercepts were just not decoded in time to bring the German battleship to action.

However, the first real breakthrough which resulted in a successful fleet action occurred at the Battle of Matapan on 28 March 1941. The Italian naval cipher had been penetrated and it was known that Hitler had pressed the Italian High Command to intercept the convoys of British troops moving from Egypt to go to the aid of Greece. Thus when the Italian fleet put to sea, and even before they left harbour, British Intelligence at Bletchley had signalled their probable intentions to Admiral Cunningham in Alexandria. It was now possible for him to intercept. This was not due to complete decrypting in time for operational action. Rather the quick and inspired guesswork of a series of connecting signals pointed towards a possible Italian operation, and it was Admiral Cunningham who decided to act upon this information. With great secrecy the Mediterranean fleet put to sea, and although the Italian battleships did escape, a shattering blow was dealt to the cruisers *Zara*, *Fiume* and *Pola*, as will be seen.

The result was to be far reaching. The Italian fleet took no further part in intercepting the withdrawal of British forces from Greece and Crete, and it was left to the *Luftwaffe* to cause the catastrophic damage to RN ships and their cargo of British soldiers. Had the Italian fleet been at sea during this critical time, the result could have been even more devastating to the Royal Navy. After the evacuation when so many Allied warships had been sunk or badly damaged, Ultra information of a very detailed nature was fed to Admiral Cunningham daily, but to have this information without the forces with which to strike at targets was galling. Malta was under constant attack and U-boats harried the remaining Allied forces and the few merchant ships that were afloat. However, the information available included the timing of convoys, naming actual ships and cargoes, and their course and speed. This meant that the minimum use of the slender forces available could achieve remarkable results. Arriving at a given time and a given place could result in a submarine finding a convoy in sight, and pilots flying a given course sometimes found their targets dead ahead. All this was achieved by the staff at Bletchley.

Statistics speak for themselves. From January to July 1942 Axis forces in the Mediterranean lost 100 ships of 191,000 tons and from August to December the figures rose to 174 ships of 320,000 tons. It is little wonder that General Rommel's advance was held up and the effect on the desert war was profound.

However, in considering the overall contribution of Ultra to the war at sea we must return to

the Atlantic. All German ships carried the Enigma machines and the Admiralty made every effort to capture from them any documents or machines which would help to increase the decoding facilities. On 23 February 1941 during the raid on the Lofoten Islands a spare pair of rotors for an Enigma machine were found aboard an abandoned vessel, and two trawlers were located in the Iceland area which had been transmitting regular weather reports. By a carefully planned operation both ships were boarded and invaluable documents were obtained. However, the really crucial event occurred on 8 May. U-110 (Commander Lemp), had attacked a convoy and was itself attacked. The U-boat was forced to the surface and abandoned after her commander had set demolition charges. These failed to explode and it was possible to board the vessel. The destroyer *Bulldog* sent a boat across and this is the moment when history holds its breath. The U-boat commander had failed to destroy his marked charts, code books, cipher documents and above all his Enigma machine. The small boat lurched across the Atlantic swell and a human chain carried the priceless documents down the slippery deck to the waiting boat. During the three hours necessary to extract every bit of information not one mishap occurred and the whole consignment was safely aboard *Bulldog*.

Here indeed was a real breakthrough. The haul included the daily settings for the Enigma machine covering the three months of the U-boat's cruise. It contained material carried on all German ships except the armed raiders. Taken together with other information derived from the two trawlers and other sources, British Intelligence was able to read an increased amount of the German Hydra codes, the big ship Neptune codes and the two ciphers used in the Mediterranean. Just as remarkable were the marked charts giving details of replenishment ships and so it was possible to pinpoint the position of the large number of tankers and supply ships stationed in the vast areas of the North and South Atlantic.

Seven tankers had been assigned to the *Bismarck* and *Prinz Eugen*, and four of these were sunk in the North Atlantic during the month of June, together with three weather reporting ships and two U-boat supply ships. These supply ships played a vital role in operations off the coast of West Africa and their destruction was a severe blow to Admiral Dönitz. We are used to considering naval victories in terms of fleet or air actions, but this one episode must in itself rank as a major victory.

By the use of Ultra with its newly acquired haul of information, the whole concept of the U-boat war changed, and the Admiralty could act more on indisputable evidence rather than inspired guesswork. Admiral Dönitz was suspicious that his secret ciphers had been penetrated, and evidence seemed to point to this fact. A thorough investigation was made, but no proof was found and the ciphers remained unchanged until February 1942 when the Atlantic U-boats on operations were put on a new cipher named Triton. This proved to be a deadly dangerous moment for the Allies in the Atlantic, but codes were still being read from other German naval commands. These flowed into Bletchley and from the spring of 1943 were decrypted speedily to give a wealth of information. Signals from the Baltic enabled British Intelligence to follow the history of each U-boat from the moment it was commissioned, right through its working up period until it left for its operational cruise. It was thus possible to gauge the extent of the building programme and the actual number of U-boats which would be added to the operational fleet. By including the intercepted messages ordering escorts and mine-sweepers to accompany a U-boat to or from harbour, it was possible to provide the Submarine Tracking Room at the Admiralty with vital information. Although there was silence from that quarter as soon as the U-boat left for patrol, the direction finding system picked up signals from boats in mid-Atlantic and their position could be pinpointed.

The Submarine Tracking Room was given almost immediate information on the position of each U-boat every time a signal was sent, and, because of the type of short signal used, of the moment when a U-boat had established contact with a convoy. A threatened convoy could now be warned to take immediate evasive action by altering course. Space precludes any description of the methods used by Bletchley to decrypt signals more quickly, but as time went on 'Hut 8' was able to decipher all intercepted messages of the day within an hour of receiving them after discovering the daily settings. Even when, as in 1941, the time needed to decrypt was between two and four days on average, the Direction Finding System still enabled the Submarine Tracking Room to re-route a convoy threatened by German U-boat patrol lines. From July to December 1941 the Allied convoy routing worked so well that despite heavy losses no convoys were actually intercepted as planned. It has been estimated that in the second half of 1941 possibly some 1.6 million tons of shipping losses were avoided by re-routing. The work done by the Submarine Tracking Room with its minute staff led by Rodger Winn and Patrick Beesley made an outstanding contribution to the outcome of the battle.

An example taken from October 1941 may convey some sense of this. There were three eastbound convoys and four westbound convoys in the North Atlantic at this time. In addition two southbound convoys were entering the Bay of Biscay. Admiral Dönitz had twelve U-boats converging on the southbound convoy and only four in the Atlantic. To these four he had allocated a meeting point and a patrol line. Within two days Bletchley had decrypted these positions, but found two ways of interpreting the superimposed grid letters. Convoy SC 48 was 200 miles out from Canada on its journey to Britain and it was allowed to proceed as planned so that it would sail close to Cape Farewell off the southern tip of Greenland. On 9 October there were indications that the four U-boats were heading for a patrol line in that area, so it was re-routed further south. The westbound convoys ON 23 and 24 were also in the vicinity and were ordered to alter course to the south.

The exact position of the first four U-boats was determined on 10 October by Direction Finding and also the fact that nine more boats had been ordered into the Atlantic from the Bay of Biscay area. Each was given an 'attack square'. The position looked extremely ominous for the

convoys which were nearing that area of the Atlantic, particularly as they had all been re-routed to pass close to each other. It seemed to the Submarine Tracking Room that the course of SC 48 was known to U-boat Headquarters and that a concentration of boats would bar its way. Messages were being decrypted fast, and within two hours and thirty-five minutes of the Admiralty receiving a message three convoys had been given new courses to avoid the U-boat patrol line which was now becoming evident. There was no time to lose. Five convoys had to pass through the narrow gap between the already positioned U-boats, and those that were coming up from the south-east. At a critical moment Bletchley were unable to decrypt messages on 12 and 13 October due to changed settings on the German cipher machine, but the Submarine Tracking Room estimated a strong patrol line correctly from the information it already had. All seemed well, and by re-routing it was going to be possible to pass the convoys

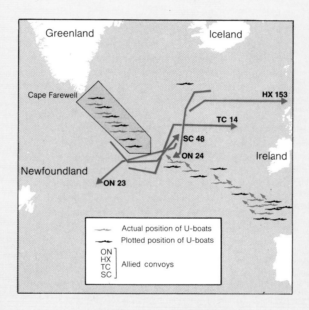

Using a combination of Direction Finding and de-coded messages from Bletchley Park, the British Admiralty was able to re-route the convoys at sea. In some cases convoys only just succeeded in avoiding being sighted as the wolf packs took up positions in a line south of Greenland. This was the situation in the North Atlantic on October 12-13 1941.

through the shrinking gap and so evade the threatened attacks. However U-553 encountered a convoy which had to go further south to avoid too close a contact with the other converging convoys. Two ships were torpedoed and hourly signals were sent by U-553 as she shadowed the convoy. The messages were picked up and while they could not be decrypted immediately, the make up of the messages and their prefix identified them as being shadowing signals. The exact position of the U-boat was now known and it was possible to send immediate assistance to the threatened convoy. Convoy ON 24 was not immediately threatened and was ordered to disperse while its escort of five destroyers proceeded at once to the assistance of the threatened convoy. It happened that this was an American escort — and America was not yet at war with Germany. A large combined American, British, Canadian and Free French escort was now formed. During some confusion another six ships were

torpedoed in a hectic night action, but the result could have been much worse. Had the British Admiralty had the ships and long range aircraft to make full use of the invaluable information presented to them at that time the results would have been spectacular.

During the first six months of 1942 U-boats sank a vast amount of shipping, but it was off the eastern seaboard of the United States and the reasons for this will be discussed later. Activity in the Atlantic slackened and the re-routing of convoys was not so necessary. This merciful break for Britain came at a time when German ciphers were changed and U-boat signals were separated from the general naval cipher Hydra into a new cipher circuit, Triton, as has been noted. The Allies were now virtually blind in the field of cryptanalysis. Had the U-boats remained concentrated in the Atlantic at the time when Bletchley were grappling with the problems of breaking into the new ciphers, the losses would have been far greater in that area than they were. If the battles of the early months of 1943 are any comparison, then the eventual outcome would have been even more in doubt than it was.

Another breakthrough occurred in October 1942 when a boarding party captured codes and cipher material from U-599 before it sank in the Mediterranean. This made it possible to crack the new Triton cipher. Here was another victory at sea because Bletchley and the Submarine Tracking Room were together able to re-route convoys away from the German U-boat patrol lines. The difference was that now there were more than forty boats in the North Atlantic and three or four long patrol lines had to be avoided. The German commanders were assisted by the work of their *xB-Dienst* which was able to decrypt more and more routing and re-routing signals from the British Admiralty due to their having gained access into British Naval Code 3 dealing with convoys.

The German Naval Intelligence introduced a new weather code book on 10 March 1942 which was crucial as a key for other codes, so once again Bletchley were operating in the dark, and the Submarine Tracking Room was unable to re-route convoys with anything like the confidence of earlier days. In the first twenty days of March 1942 four west-east convoys (SC 121 and 122 and HX 228 and 229) lost up to 20 per cent of their ships and if such losses continued it would have been intolerable. The Battle of the Atlantic was swinging in Germany's favour once more. So much depended on how fast Bletchley could solve the new cryptological problem. With a considerable amount of good fortune the problem was solved in ten days. This was probably the greatest single achievement at Bletchley. The situation was now rescued and the catastrophe for the Allies averted. At a time when the first escort carriers and trained support groups were entering service, and long range aircraft were at last being used where they were most required — in the gap south of Greenland, convoys could now be fought through with sufficient escorts. The story of that battle must come later, but the work of the Special Intelligence Department at Bletchley Park and that of the Submarine Tracking Room was of paramount importance in enabling Britain to survive and to go on to win the Battle of the Atlantic.

The critical months in the Atlantic

Before turning to the worsening situation in the Mediterranean we must remain for a while in the North Atlantic, for it was here that Britain's struggle to sustain the war effort and to ward off starvation was fought.

The British Western Approaches Command had gradually increased the area within which it was possible to give a close escort to convoys. By April 1941 the refuelling bases in Iceland had enabled ships in convoy to have some escort for nearly half the journey across the Atlantic. More important still, the emergency building programme was beginning to produce escort vessels in large numbers; it was now possible to release more destroyers and mine-sweepers fitted with Asdic detection equipment.

Air cover, which was to prove decisive in the battle, began to be increased. Coastal Command stationed a few long range aircraft at Reykjavik in Iceland to meet the convoys on the dangerous lightly escorted areas in mid-Atlantic. The problems facing those pilots were indeed great. Ferocious gales and bad visibility added to the hazards of very long endurance flights. Pilots had to seek out a minute spot in

Air cover was of vital importance in the defence of a convoy against U-boats. U-boats had to make a wide detour on the surface, keeping out of sight, to get into a position to attack at night. By forcing them to submerge their speed was reduced and they could not maintain contact. In the Battle of the Atlantic it was the presence of an escort carrier which did so much to redress the balance in favour of the Allies.

the ocean to locate a convoy. The position given was not always accurate and the aircraft might have flown — often by dead reckoning — for many hours. It was remarkable that so many did make contact and the value of such aircraft is hard to over-emphasize. By circling a convoy during daylight hours it was possible to sight any U-boat on the surface trying to make a wide detour so as to get into position for a night attack, and to force it to dive. From a speed of 17 knots it was reduced to 4 or 5 and used up its battery strength, and thus was unable to attack as night fell. While there were few U-boat sinkings, a convoy commodore could alter course after being informed of a U-boat sighting and thus had a chance of avoiding a dangerous confrontation at night. There were other factors which, fully implemented, would redress the balance of power. The V and W Class destroyers of First World War vintage had until now borne a large measure of the escort work. They had not been modernized and their open bridges gave little protection to the lookouts. Green seas swept their decks and sea water found its way to nearly every part of the ship. It was from the open bridge of these ships that an escort commander had to navigate his own ship, control the convoy and fight the U-boats. Help was to come in the form of sloops of the Black Swan class, although by the end of 1942 there were still only four in commission. Modern ships with a speed of 19 knots and an armament of six 4 inch high-angle guns, their anti-aircraft capabilities made them invaluable to counter air attacks. Deep sea trawlers joined the escorts. They were of little use in offensive action but they relieved the work of other escorts by rescuing survivors. The Flower Class corvettes

were also coming forward in large numbers. Slow but good sea boats despite their vicious roll, they had the great advantage of being able to cross the Atlantic without refuelling. They could not catch a U-boat on the surface, but once they pinpointed a submerged U-boat their handling qualities made them excellent fighting ships. However, lack of sufficient escorts still allowed U-boats access to the heart of a convoy.

From the middle of 1941, escorts could be re-fuelled from the base in Iceland. Thus an east-bound convoy, heavily laden with war materials and food, could be met much further out in the Atlantic and taken on further east to meet an escort coming out from Britain, while the original escort picked up a westbound convoy and returned to Canada. But the most potent defence was to be a fully trained escort group, working together with the confidence that each ship would react according to plan in an emergency. These groups were now under training. Led by an experienced commander, they consisted of one or two destroyers or sloops of the Bittern or Black Swan Class and some six Flower Class corvettes. They were the new adversaries with whom Admiral Dönitz's U-boats had to contend. Gone was the 'happy time' when virtually unescorted ships could be picked off at will. Now it was necessary for the U-boats to take on the escorts before they could get at the merchant ships. But the number of U-boats was increasing also. Admiral Dönitz knew full well that untrained crews stood little chance of survival and the new boats coming forward in great numbers were held back for rigorous training. So the number available actually in operational areas was still relatively small,

Depth charges from HMS Woodpecker *are fired as a result of an Asdic (sonar) contact.*

and a lull in operations ensued. Few U-boats were sunk but at the same time few successful attacks on convoys occurred, and there were far fewer unescorted ships.

On the other side of the Atlantic the signing of the Lease-Lend Bill in March had altered the balance in favour of the Allies. British warships were repaired in American yards and, in July, the relief of the British garrison in Iceland by United States troops and the announcement that in future US Naval forces would escort shipping of any nationality to and from Iceland, brought America further into the conflict.

None the less one disastrous convoy at the end of August 1941 made it plain that the battle could still be one-sided. Admiral Dönitz had had little success in finding convoys, which had been routed further and further north. He therefore positioned sixteen U-boats in a line from Iceland to Greenland and on 9 September a convoy was sighted and the first ship sunk.

The Royal Canadian Navy had expanded greatly since the outbreak of war and the demands put on it were equally great. Thus it was a very small Canadian escort of one destroyer and three corvettes which was shepherding sixty-five ships in twelve columns. The weather was so bad that the convoy hove to and in four days only averaged 3 knots. The corvettes had never worked together before and when the U-boats finally fell on the convoy the escort was

virtually powerless to prevent a massacre. Searching for U-boats left two of the corvettes many miles behind and the escort commander in the destroyer *Skeena* raced from one sinking to another. The dull roar of a torpedo finding its mark was followed by illumination which showed a U-boat inside the convoy. Machine gun fire sent the destroyer hurrying to the spot, only to hear another explosion elsewhere in the strung out lines of ships. It was a nightmare, and the exhausted crews who had been at action stations for over twenty-four hours had no respite. Two newly commissioned corvettes on a training cruise were ordered to join the escort. Approaching from ahead they surprised a U-boat 700 yards away. A pattern of depth charges forced the U-boat to the surface and the first round of a corvette's 4 inch gun smashed into the conning tower. This was a memorable success for the partly trained corvette crew, but still ships were being sunk, and the sea was littered for miles with men clinging to wreckage in the heavy swell.

On the afternoon of 11 September an escort group from Iceland of five destroyers, a trawler, and a further three corvettes reached the convoy. Additionally, aircraft from Iceland circled the convoy, and, acting on a contact report, U-207 was sunk. The survivors of the convoy plodded on towards their destination, the escort being augmented for a few hours by three United States destroyers. This was an early instance of American participation before she

was officially at war. However, out of sixty-five ships, fifteen had been sunk with the loss of many lives.

During the same month U-boats struck at the Freetown and Gibraltar convoys. These convoys were doubly vulnerable being within easy range of Focke-Wolf Kondor aircraft from bases in France as they entered the Bay of Biscay. Sloops and corvettes made up the escorts for these long distance convoys with the addition of Gibraltar-based destroyers for a part of the voyage. Convoy SL 87, consisting of eleven ships, was found far out in the Atlantic and only four reached port.

However, for the first time an outward-bound convoy (OG 74), heading for Gibraltar, was to be accompanied by the first auxiliary aircraft carrier, HMS *Audacity*. She was a merchant ship stripped down and then provided with a wooden flight deck, and carried Martlet fighters. The rest of the escort consisted of a sloop and five Flower Class corvettes. There were twenty-seven merchantmen and they sailed on 13 September 1941. Although the Martlet aircraft forced all the U-boats to submerge, two ships were sunk on the night of 20 September. Next day a Focke-Wolf Kondor bombed and sank a ship which was picking up survivors, but was itself shot down by the air escort.

Before reaching their destination five ships out of the twenty-seven had gone. Some days later four U-boats attacked and sank nine vessels out of a convoy of twenty-seven ships in three successive nights — this convoy had no air escort. These sinkings highlighted a serious weakness in this convoy route which, because of the long distance, had to have lightly armed slow escorts of the necessary endurance. It also showed the value of air cover. *Audacity*, which had a short life, was the first of many such vessels which were to have a profound effect on the Battle of the Atlantic. But these successive attacks on the West Africa — Gibraltar — UK route required immediate attention. In the North Atlantic, the lessons of the disaster of convoy SC 42 forced the Admiralty to re-think their methods of escorting these vital convoys. What was needed was air cover and a series of offensive escort groups, and this had been foreseen. But the pace of the battle and the need to keep every available escort at sea had left little room for the highly professional training needed to bring these escort groups to the pitch of efficiency that was required.

It is worth remembering that it was only fifteen months since Dunkirk and the invasion scare which followed had kept many destroyers in home waters. However, training had gone on and success was beginning to be shown in the North Atlantic. It was essential that the same consideration should be given to the West African convoys.

Convoy HG 76 was forming up at Gibraltar, consisting of thirty-two ships, and it was expected that the convoy would be heavily attacked. The escort consisted of HMS *Stork*, a modern sloop with six 4 inch guns in twin dual purpose mountings and a speed of 19 knots. With her were seven Flower Class corvettes and an old sloop. The difference between this escort and other similar ones was that the crews had been trained to a very high degree of efficiency and they were led by Commander F.J. Walker who was to become the most successful group commander in the whole of the Battle of the Atlantic. Commander Walker had trained his ship's company to peak performance and the rest of his team were similarly indoctrinated and were capable of carrying out his wishes unbidden. They were a formidable force. Three destroyers, two sloops and three Flower Class corvettes augmented the escort for the first dangerous days when it was breaking through the line of U-boats. They would also have the services of Gibraltar-based Swordfish aircraft for the critical hours ahead. With them went the auxiliary aircraft carrier *Audacity*. It was certainly a very heavy escort. They sailed on 14 December in nine columns. A U-boat was sighted by a protecting Martlet from *Audacity* and Commander Walker's well drilled team sank it, although the aircraft was lost. Next day another U-boat was sighted as the wolf pack closed. Again the escort went into action and U-434 was forced to the surface and the crew abandoned ship and were picked up. The following night one of the escorts and a convoy ship were torpedoed and sank, but the U-boat was also sunk, after being rammed by *Stork*, following a chase where each

An escorting corvette closes to pick up survivors from a torpedoed liberty ship while a frigate patrols the area.

57

vessel went into tighter and tighter turning circles. When daylight came a swooping Kondor was shot down by *Audacity*'s aircraft who also forced a U-boat ahead of the convoy to submerge. Three U-boats had now been sunk but Admiral Dönitz ordered two more to the scene, one of which was U-567 whose commander was at the time the most successful in the German fleet.

By 21 December the wolf pack was seen to be closing despite the efforts of *Audacity*'s three remaining aircraft. As night fell the convoy altered course while four escorts pushed on and staged a mock battle to draw the U-boats away. Unfortunately one of the ships in the convoy sent up snowflake rockets, illuminating the convoy, which resulted in one ship being torpedoed. Against the lights of the convoy *Audacity*, which had moved out on her own, was torpedoed by U-751 and sank.

Meanwhile Asdic or visual contacts were made by three of the escorts who went into the attack and U-567 was sunk. The night ended with a collision between the escorts *Stork* and *Deptford*. The dawn of 22 December found the escort exhausted after four days of continuous fighting. *Audacity* had been lost as had *Stanley* and two escorts damaged by collision. Against this only two of the convoy ships had been sunk and four U-boats had been destroyed. A long range Liberator, one of the first allotted to

Coastal Command, had flown 800 miles to find the convoy and now circled the area, finding U-boats still in the vicinity. The aircraft forced these to submerge by using depth charges, and the attack was called off.

The results of the new strategy were clear. From the German side it had been an encounter with unacceptable losses, despite a series of determined and brave attacks against a large and well trained escort. The valuable Kondor aircraft had been kept away by air cover and no longer had the U-boats been able to enter the convoy lines. On the Allied side the presence of an auxiliary carrier was of immense help and the loss of *Audacity*, in part by ill luck, did not diminish the value of its inclusion in the escort. Only two merchant ships had been sunk in a running battle with an experienced Wolf Pack of nine submarines. Even though the escort strength was far in excess of those available for the North Atlantic, the message was clear.

Trained groups with combined sea and air escort had proved their worth. In time, as training and new ships became available, it would be possible to counter the mass attacks of U-boat wolf packs and the Battle of the Atlantic eventually could be won by the Allies.

Meanwhile America was becoming further involved in the war effort. Huge quantities of food and every conceivable piece of equipment

were being shipped across the Atlantic under lease-lend agreements. British ships were being repaired in American yards, American troops had occupied Iceland, and American escort groups were assisting in the convoy of shipping destined for that area.

Further heavy units of the United States fleet were at sea to counter any threat by German surface raiders in the Atlantic, and American destroyers were permitted to escort convoys of any nationality as far east as the mid-ocean meeting point. Here they would put into Iceland to refuel and pick up a westbound convoy, handing it over to Canadian and Royal Navy escorts for the last part of its journey.

It was obvious that the US would eventually be involved in a clash since U-boats were operating between Iceland and Greenland. The first incident occurred on 4 September 1941 when the American destroyer *Greer* on passage to Iceland was attacked and replied with depth charges. On 17 October the *Kearny* was damaged by a torpedo and finally the destroyer *Reuben James* was sunk on 31 October

A Liberator of 120 Squadron RAF based in Iceland has flown hundreds of miles into the Atlantic by dead reckoning to find a convoy. The presence of these aircraft over the convoy for only a few hours forced U-boats in the vicinity to submerge.

From September 1941 the US naval forces participated in the Battle of the Atlantic. On 31 October they sustained their first loss; USS Reuben James *was sunk escorting a British convoy.*

while escorting convoy HX 156, and became the first American warship to be lost in the Atlantic struggle.

Looking back over the history of those days, the events just recounted were of paramount importance. For two long years Britain, with the assistance of the small but growing Royal Canadian Navy, had taken the full force of the Battle of the Atlantic. Desperately few escort vessels, many of them totally unsuited to the task they undertook, in gales and mountainous seas, had only just enabled Britain to survive.

Now American ships were beginning to take their part in the grim task of ensuring this survival. Germany had thrown every possible U-boat and some long range aircraft into the fight. Despite the enormous successes they had achieved with their small number of U-boats, handled with daring and great bravery, they had failed to force Great Britain out of the war. And now Admiral Dönitz, at a moment when it was essential to keep up the momentum of attack, was ordered to send a force of U-boats to the Mediterranean to protect the sea routes of German troops proceeding to North Africa. It must have been a bitter blow to him for it produced a much needed lull in the fighting in the Atlantic.

A lone survivor of unknown nationality, covered in oil; the painting tells its own story of the horror of war at sea.

The Mediterranean and Matapan

At the beginning of 1941 there was some confidence that the Italian Navy could be held, and if brought to battle could be defeated.

On land, General Wavell's advance into the desert had forced the Italian Army into full retreat and the Royal Navy was called upon to supply the 8th Army from an advanced base at Benghazi. Suddenly there was a major setback. German reinforcements poured into North Africa and the highly efficient Flieger Korps X of the *Luftwaffe* was posted to Sicily. This unit specialized in attacking shipping and with their air superiority, Benghazi had to be closed, and the advance on land slowed to a halt.

A small fast convoy was pushed through to Malta from the west, escorted by Force H and met by Admiral Cunningham's fleet from Alexandria. His ships were shadowed and on 9 January the *Luftwaffe* struck. Concentrating on the aircraft carrier *Illustrious*, the JU 87 aircraft dived through the protective gunfire of the fleet. Six hits and several near misses damaged the ship very severely, but her armoured deck saved her and she limped into Malta after dark with many casualties. Here she was bombed repeatedly as emergency repairs were effected, but she escaped some days later and reached the United States for a complete refit, leaving the Mediterranean fleet with only one carrier, the old unarmoured *Eagle*.

To cap it all, German troops invaded Greece in April. The War Cabinet decided to send 58,000 troops from General Wavell's command to assist the Greek Army, escorted by the Navy. The port of Piraeus was bombed by the *Luftwaffe* and an ammunition ship blew up, sinking ten other ships, closing the port and destroying much of the equipment for the expeditionary force. From now on reinforcements had to use small, poorly equipped bases.

For Admiral Cunningham this was a shattering blow. His lines of communication were overextended and he had virtually no air cover. While German troops were massing in Greece, General Rommel was advancing from the west. Insufficient aircraft were available to obstruct the passage of supplies from the Italian mainland, though destroyers recently stationed in Malta destroyed a convoy of five ships of 14,000 tons in a night action on 16 April, with the loss of one destroyer. British submarines were active, causing some disruption, but the German advance bypassed Tobruk which was invested and had to be supplied from the sea. Without air cover, severe losses were inevitable.

This was not all, for Malta desperately required fighter aircraft and further supplies. In a series of hazardous operations *Ark Royal* sailed from Gibraltar to supply Hurricanes to the island. But, despite this support, by mid-April General Wavell's forces had been driven back to the Egyptian border. Admiral Cunningham ordered the bombardment of the port of Tripoli, the

Following the air strike on Taranto, the Luftwaffe *singled out the British aircraft carrier* Illustrious *for attack. JU 87 aircraft dived through the protective gunfire of the fleet and although the ship was saved by her armoured deck, six hits and several near misses did serious damage to the ship.*

61

destination of the bulk of Rommel's supplies. While this difficult operation was taking place, a fast supply convoy was slipped into Malta, and a fleet of empty merchant ships sailed for Alexandria. Virtually the whole of the available naval strength was needed for this major operation, and during the night of 21 April the port of Tripoli was badly damaged by gunfire from battleships, cruisers and destroyers, illuminated by aircraft from *Formidable*. It was successful and the fleet returned to Alexandria, but Admiral Cunningham was fortunate to have effected complete surprise.

Although British troops had reached Greece, they had to be supplied and it seemed highly probable that the Italian Navy would dispute the passage of supply ships. Air reconnaissance proved that just such an operation was, in fact, building up.

As a result of the fast and accurate decrypts of the German and Italian radio signals, Admiral Cunningham was in a position to act. He knew that the Italian fleet was at sea and dispatched four cruisers — *Orion, Ajax, Gloucester* and *Perth* — and nine destroyers to a position fifty miles to the west of Crete. On the evening of the 27 March with a continuous flow of information from Bletchley Park, Admiral Cunningham sailed the Mediterranean fleet consisting of the battleships *Warspite, Barham* and *Valiant*, together with the carrier *Formidable* and nine destroyers.

Meanwhile the British cruiser force had intercepted three Italian cruisers and found itself hemmed in on the disengaged side by the Italian Admiral Pachino's battle fleet consisting of the battleship *Vittorio Veneto* and accompanying cruisers and destroyers. Admiral Cunningham ordered the cruisers to withdraw towards him and this was done without damage. Meanwhile aircraft from *Formidable* were ordered to attack the Italian battleship in an attempt at least to slow her down. Two air strikes resulted in one hit, the aircraft flying through intense anti-aircraft fire emanating from the Italian force.

The Italian fleet had by then reversed course to the west and one torpedo hit was insufficient to slow up *Vittorio Veneto*. Air reconnaissance now reported the Italian fleet consisting of the *Vittorio Veneto* screened by four destroyers in the centre with three cruisers on either side, and an outer ring of three or four destroyers. It was into this concentration of defensive fire that a third strike of ten slow Swordfish and Albacores attacked at dusk. The only hit was on the cruiser *Pola* which came to a stop. The Italian Commander-in-Chief detached the cruisers *Zara* and *Fiume* with two destroyers to stand by the damaged *Pola*.

Admiral Cunningham realised that only a night action could bring the Italian fleet to battle before they reached the air cover waiting for them in southern Italy and Sicily at dawn.

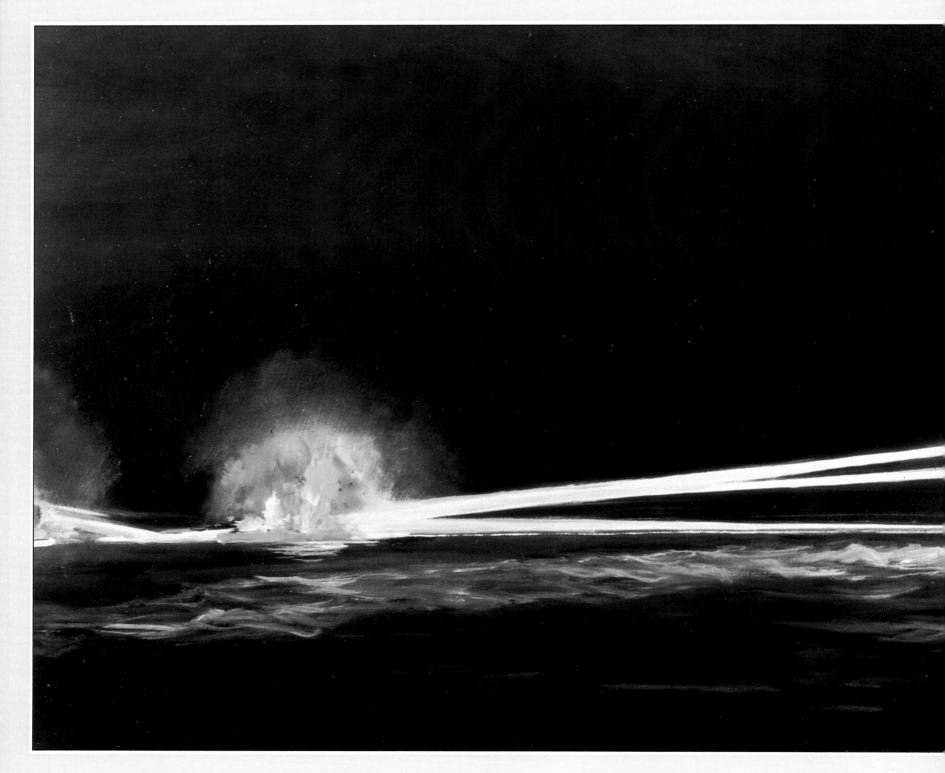

Reports on the reduced speed of the *Vittorio Veneto* as a result of the torpedo hit had been exaggerated and, unbeknown to Admiral Cunningham, she had by now worked up to 19 knots, making for the safety of air cover.

Destroyers were sent ahead to attack, passing close to an unknown ship which was seen to be stopped. The Commander-in-Chief decided to investigate. Ordering the *Formidable* to move away out of line, the battle fleet approached, in radar contact. Taken completely unawares with their guns fore and aft, the two cruisers *Fiume* and *Zara* were subjected to devastating fire at 3,000 yards and both ships sank. The stopped cruiser *Pola* was found by the destroyers *Nubian* and *Jervis* and was sunk after many of her crew had been taken off. Finally the two accompanying Italian destroyers were sunk by the destroyers *Stuart* and *Havock*. The *Vittorio Veneto* was never found and the British forces returned to Alexandria. However, this night action had resulted in the sinking of three of

Italy's fast heavy cruisers and two fleet destroyers, with the loss to the British fleet of one aircraft. This Battle of Cape Matapan showed that aggressive action gave Britain an ascendancy over the Italian Navy, even though the *Luftwaffe* was dominant in the air. Of even greater consequence was the fact that the Italian Navy did not put to sea to contest the forthcoming operations in the eastern Mediterranean. Had they done so the result would have been even more catastrophic than it turned out to be.

To sum up the position. On land it seemed that the German Afrika Korps was about to imperil the whole Allied position in North Africa. Benghazi was lost and Tobruk surrounded, having to be supplied by a small inshore squadron. Some relief had been afforded by surface and submarine action to disrupt Axis supplies, but far more serious was the position in Greece where the recently arrived British troops were in danger of being driven into the sea. Finally Malta had to be held at all costs.

Some aircraft and stores had got through, but the continuous bombing made it impossible to operate with any safety in such a situation.

These events in the Mediterranean came only ten months after the Allied defeat in Europe and the evacuation from Dunkirk. The Battle of the Atlantic was at its height and raiders were at large in the North and South Atlantic. Within three months the *Bismarck* action was further to deplete the overstretched Allied naval forces, and the Royal Navy was now called upon to become stretched almost to breaking point.

The naval actions which ended in the Battle of Matapan on 28 March 1941 ensured that the Italian fleet did not dispute the withdrawal of British forces from Greece and Crete. Here the battleships Warspite *and* Valiant *open fire at point-blank range on the Italian cruiser* Fiume.

Evacuating the Army

It was against this background that the decision was taken to evacuate Allied forces from Greece. It was to be a perilous undertaking scarcely reminiscent of the other evacuation ten months previously from the coast of France. Instead of a short sea crossing and air cover from bases close at hand, the Allies were now faced with a 400 mile sea journey and arrival in a dubiously neutral country like Egypt. Instead of

the prospect of home and England with its grimly determined people where the Army could be re-equipped and damaged ships repaired, the fleet had to run the gauntlet of the *Luftwaffe*'s undisputed control of the skies, and return to a base which was itself threatened.

Evacuation would have to take place from smaller ports or from the beaches at night. It

was a chaotic situation. Due to the presence of the *Luftwaffe*, the area had to be cleared by 03.00 and evacuation vessels could not arrive until well after dark. But the Navy had to go to the assistance of the Army at whatever cost; every available ship in the eastern Mediterranean was needed except for the battle fleet which was stripped of its escorting destroyers. Even the inshore squadron supply-

The Royal Navy suffered very severe casualties in men and ships when they evacuated the Army first from Greece and then from Crete. Day after day they were subjected to intense air attack when out of range of Allied air cover. The painting shows HMS Orion *and the destroyer* Kimberley *as seen from the crowded deck of HMS* Hotspur.

the operations were not seriously damaged and were able to set out once again at short notice to make another attempt to reinforce Malta with aircraft and stores and to pass a fast convoy with tanks and other equipment under escort right through to Alexandria. Force H sailed from Gibraltar on 18 May and forty-seven fighters were flown off and arrived safely in Malta. The pitifully small number available to defend the island had shot down seventy-seven Axis planes over the island but the cost had been heavy. Thirty-two had been lost in combat and as many destroyed on the ground, but the Royal Air Force succeeded in holding on by a thread and preventing the total collapse of the defences.

With Greece and its principal islands in Axis hands it was almost certain that Crete and Cyprus and the land areas approaching the Dardanelles would be occupied also, thus imperilling the Suez Canal and all Allied forces in North Africa. The Navy's tasks were to deny the sea routes necessary for a seaborne invasion of Crete; to keep the garrison supplied with what meagre equipment was available, and in the last resort to evacuate the British forces. When they were forced out of Greece they left behind their equipment and guns and these had to be made up from stocks held in Egypt. But with the *Luftwaffe* controlling the air, the port of Suda Bay in Crete could not be used as an advanced naval base, and all operations had to be based on Alexandria, 420 miles to the south. For a week before the German assault Axis bombers struck at the island and this was followed early on 20 May by parachute and glider landings and then by transport aircraft. The fleet put to sea but kept out of sight of the islands. Next day it was heavily bombed and the destroyer *Juno* was sunk. Air reconnaissance sighted a sea invasion force composed of light craft making for Crete and escorted by Italian torpedo boats. These were intercepted by three cruisers and four destroyers and the convoy was dispersed with much loss of life, and the first seaborne invasion was broken up.

Another convoy was sighted next day and forced to return with heavy losses, but the *Luftwaffe* had attacked the British naval forces continuously throughout the day. Anti-aircraft ammunition was running low and the light cruiser *Naiad* was badly damaged, as was the anti-aircraft cruiser *Carlisle* and the battleship *Warspite*, where the damage was serious. The destroyer *Greyhound* was sunk. The cruisers *Gloucester* and *Fiji* were sent to pick up survivors, but *Gloucester* was hit and set on fire. *Fiji*, now completely out of anti-aircraft ammunition, was forced to leave the survivors and she too was hit and sunk. For ships with no fighter cover the best protection against air attack was a concentration of force able to put up a protective barrage. By detaching these two cruisers they became vulnerable and paid the price. As dawn broke on 23 May the destroyers *Kelly* and *Kashmir* came under heavy attack and were

ing Tobruk had to be withdrawn. The evacuation forces consisted of six cruisers, nineteen destroyers, three corvettes, some small landing craft with three transports and eight merchant navy transports — this was all that was available.

The evacuation started on the night of 24 April and went on for the next five nights without a break; 50,732 troops, about 80 per cent of those who had landed under a month before, were taken off, including a large number of wounded, and landed in Crete or Egypt. The cost was not light. Four merchant ships were sunk and destroyers *Diamond* and *Wryneck* were bombed and sunk when picking up survivors. Only one officer, forty-one ratings and eight soldiers survived from the destroyers. However, the other naval forces engaged in sunk, the survivors being picked up by the destroyer *Kipling* which escaped after being heavily bombed. The fleet, now running short of oil and almost out of ammunition, returned to Alexandria. Then on 26 May the carrier *Formidable* with a heavy escort struck at the airfields at Scarpanto to attempt to break up air attacks on the fleet. During the withdrawal she was hit by dive-bombers and as a result was forced to leave the Mediterranean for repair in the United States.

There was to be no respite. The position of the land forces on Crete had deteriorated. The hastily organized defence of the island with insufficient equipment was no match for the German onslaught. Once more the Navy was called upon to evacuate the Army against the full weight of the *Luftwaffe*. Every ship of the eastern Mediterranean fleet had been in continuous action for weeks and their ship's companies were stretched to the limit of endurance. They were now called upon to rescue some 32,000 troops from one unsuitable port or over open beaches at night, without any air cover and with unrelenting bombing by the highly effective *Luftwaffe* and the Italian Air Force. On 28 May — exactly a year after Dunkirk — the cruisers *Orion*, *Ajax* and *Dido* and ten destroyers sailed from Alexandria for the port of Heraklion 400 miles away on the north coast of the island. On entering after dark the destroyers ferried troops out to the waiting cruisers and by 03.20 they sailed with the entire garrison of 4,000 men. Meanwhile four destroyers took

men off the beaches to the south of the island and returned almost unmolested. It was a different story for the cruiser force. The destroyer *Imperial* had been near missed on the outward journey but seemed to be undamaged. However as soon as she started on the homeward journey her steering gear jammed. The *Hotspur* was sent back to take off her troops, and to sink the ship. Admiral Rawlings realised that on her own, crowded with 900 troops, *Hotspur* would have no chance of survival and he slowed down to wait until she had rejoined. But day was now breaking and the Axis aircraft kept up a continuous attack on the overcrowded ships. All fighter support possible had been sent, but the Blenheims were the only aircraft with the necessary endurance, and due to the lateness of the withdrawal they had to return to Alexandria. Thus the ships had no air cover.

The destroyer *Hereward* was damaged, left behind and lost, and the survivors taken prisoner. The squadron kept up a barrage and manoeuvred violently as the bombers dived from all quarters. *Dido* had 'B' turret completely demolished, while in *Orion* 'A' turret was hit and fires started. A bomb had exploded below the mess decks killing 260 men, wounding 280. The carnage was indescribable. Water had contaminated the fuel and blazing fires were fought and put out with great gallantry. The depleted and shattered squadron entered Alexandria at 20.00. *Orion* had only two rounds of 6 inch ammunition left and ten tons of fuel — but the Navy had kept its pledge.

Next day Admiral Cunningham despatched the cruisers *Perth* and *Phoebe* with two anti-aircraft cruisers *Calcutta* and *Coventry* as protection for the squadron's three destroyers and the landing assault ship *Glengyle*. The rearguard of Australian, New Zealand and British soldiers with a Royal Marine battalion were fighting desperately to hold a perimeter around the Sphakia beaches to the south of the island. The whole force — naval personnel and soldiers alike, were beyond exhaustion, but by 03.30 that night, 6,000 men had been taken off the beach, and the squadron sailed for Alexandria. Fighter aircraft had been sent out to rendezvous at dawn with orders to stay above the ships until their fuel was exhausted and then to ditch and be picked up. They broke up the attacks and although *Perth* received a direct hit in her boiler room the squadron returned safely to Alexandria. By now 11,000 troops had been lifted off the beaches but it was estimated that 10,000 remained. Four destroyers set out next day; two returned due to engine trouble and a near miss. They took off 1,500 troops and returned, damaged by further near misses.

Axis forces in North Africa relied wholly on supplies from the Italian mainland, while for Britain, after the losses at Crete, the submarine was the only arm of the services available to dispute their passage. They were eminently successful despite the shoal waters, but they suffered cruel losses. Among them was Upholder, *seen here in a night surface attack on Italian transports.*

There remained in Alexandria just enough small ships for one more evacuation. Vice-Admiral King, flying his flag in the cruiser *Phoebe*, the fast minelayer *Abdiel* and the destroyers *Kimberley, Hotspur* and *Jackal* sailed at 06.00 on Saturday 31 May for the final evacuation. Four thousand troops were taken off and the remainder were forced to surrender. Among them were the Australian, New Zealand and Royal Marine rearguard whose gallantry had made the evacuation possible.

The anti-aircraft cruisers *Calcutta* and *Coventry* were ordered to rendezvous with Admiral King for the return journey. *Calcutta* was bombed and sank, and after rescuing survivors *Coventry* returned to Alexandria alone. The evacuation was over, but at great cost. The Royal Navy had lost three cruisers and had six destroyers sunk, while one aircraft carrier, four battleships, six cruisers and seven destroyers had been damaged, putting many of them out of action in the months to come. This left the Mediterranean fleet with only two battleships, two cruisers, one minelayer and nine destroyers and no carrier fit for service.

The effects of this catastrophe on Admiral Cunningham were profound. He could not sweep into the Mediterranean to pass convoys to Malta and seek out the Italian fleet — neither could he supply the Army by sea without incurring an immediate response from the *Luftwaffe*, who had control of the skies from their advanced bases which surrounded him. He was bottled into the eastern end of the Mediterranean. Yet somehow he had to stop reinforcements and supplies reaching General Rommel's forces in the desert. There now followed a period in which the submarine forces which had performed so well from their base in Malta were reinforced from Gibraltar and home waters. These boats operated from Alexandria as well and achieved spectacular successes. The nightly flow of traffic across the short sea route began to become seriously disorganized. The *Clyde, Severn* and the Dutch *023* and *024* operating from Gibraltar were particularly successful. From Malta itself, despite bombing which often meant submerging the submarines while in harbour, patrols covered the Narrows inflicting heavy losses. *Upholder, Upright, Unbeaten, Ursula, Unique* and *Urge* attacked any convoy they could sight. In conjunction with the submarine campaign, the effective air strength on Malta had been increased. Ferry operations using *Ark Royal* and *Furious* brought forty-five Hurricane fighters while Blenheim and radar-equipped Wellington bombers flew direct from Gibraltar. It was now possible to reconnoitre the Italian ports which resulted in daylight attacks on convoys at low level by the bombers and night torpedo attacks by naval Swordfish and Albacores, which achieved surprise and remarkable accuracy with their torpedoes. The Blenheims particularly had predictably heavy losses but the combined attacks from the air and under the sea dislocated the Axis plans. The German General Staff reported that between July and September eighty-one Axis ships of 312,000 tons had been attacked and forty-four sunk together with sixty-four smaller ships.

In September 1941 Malta was again supplied. Once more Force H augmented by the Home Fleet fought their way through to the island,

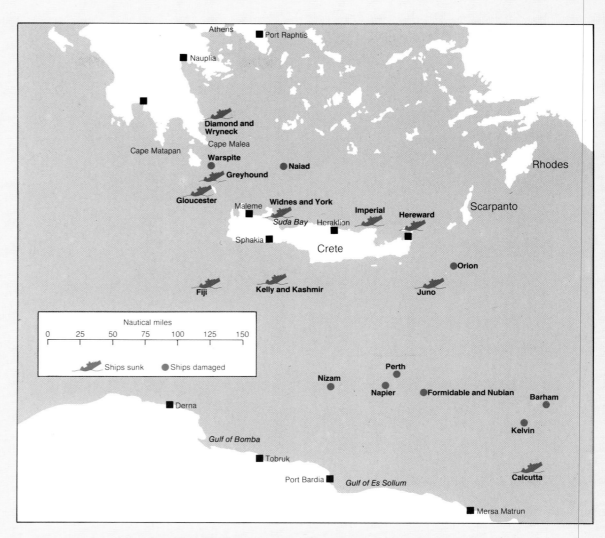

Ships lost during the campaign to evacuate the Army from Greece in 1941.

Nelson receiving one torpedo hit but only one of the fifteen merchant ships being lost. The escort consisted of three battleships, five cruisers and eighteen destroyers, together with *Ark Royal* whose fighters broke up numerous air attacks. The Italian Navy did not interfere.

During the last three months of 1941 it was decided once again to station surface ships at Malta. Thus Force K came into being. The cruisers *Penelope* and *Aurora* and two destroyers arrived on 21 October and on 9 November gained contact with an Italian convoy of seven merchant ships escorted by six destroyers and a support force of two cruisers. In a brief night action all the merchant ships (39,000 tons) were sunk together with one destroyer. A second destroyer was sunk by the submarine *Upholder*, and a week later two tankers carrying much needed oil to General Rommel were sunk.

Two further sorties from Gibraltar by Force H increased the effective air strength on Malta, but, returning to Gibraltar, *Ark Royal* was torpedoed on 14 November by U-81 and despite all efforts to save her this splendid ship sank within twenty-five miles of the Rock. This left no modern aircraft carrier in the Mediterranean.

Meanwhile Force K was again active with the addition of the cruisers *Ajax* and *Neptune* and two more destroyers. They further disrupted the flow of men and materials to General Rommel, who complained that hardly any regular transports had reached their destinations. The Italian Navy suffered a severe defeat when

two light cruisers were sunk in an engagement with four destroyers which were on passage to Alexandria through the Narrows, due in no small part to the timely arrival of Ultra intelligence. But these successes were more than offset by the activities of German U-boats. The battleship *Barham* was torpedoed and blew up with very heavy losses. This was followed by the cruiser *Galatea* and finally disaster struck Force K. While searching for a convoy on the Tripoli route on 18 December they ran into a minefield. *Neptune* was sunk, *Aurora* badly and *Penelope* lightly damaged and *Kandahar* sunk. Now the whole future of the North African campaign and the denial of supplies to General Rommel depended once again on the submarines and the aircraft from Malta.

With hindsight it is clear that the German advance in the Western Desert came close to a complete halt through the Allied attacks on shipping. By December 1941, 30 per cent of Italy's merchant fleet in the Mediterranean had been destroyed, but this success must be balanced against the inevitably severe losses sustained by British and Allied submarines.

As a final blow to the Allies at the end of 1941 came the crippling of the battleships *Queen Elizabeth* and *Valiant*. Three Italian 'human torpedoes' were launched from a submarine outside Alexandria harbour and penetrated the boom defences. With great courage the Italian frogmen attached limpet mines to the hulls and when these exploded both vessels settled on the mud. For a time the battle fleet in the eastern Mediterranean had all but ceased to exist.

The dawn fly-off from the Japanese carrier strike force north of Pearl Harbor, 7 December 1941.

2

The Pacific
December 1941 to June 1942

America's entry into the war

We now turn to the other side of the earth and consider the opening stages of what was to be the greatest conflict at sea that the world has ever known. It covered a vast area and was beset with problems of logistics hitherto unknown. It was fought with no quarter asked for or given, and it started with a suddenness and in a manner which shocked the world.

This book deals only with the actual events and readers must look elsewhere for the complex reasons which led to the catastrophe which followed. Japan had decided upon a course of action which was to expand her territories and so to dominate the Pacific. She had been engaged in total war with China for over three years and so her pilots had had combat experience, were an efficient and elite corps, and her aircraft had been tested in action. Similarly, her navy was thoroughly competent and the morale of the armed forces, indeed of the whole nation, amounted almost to euphoria. The country was gripped by a fever of war which bred a hatred of America and Britain containing all the ruthlessness which was to be experienced during the long war years ahead. This patriotic fervour demanding complete obedience was the hallmark of the militarist regime which ruled Japan.

There was a vocal non-interventionist lobby in America, but the country was bracing itself to go to the aid of Britain in her lone fight against the Axis powers. To the casual observer the events in and across the Atlantic gave little indication that Great Britain would win the battle for survival unaided despite the massive support given by American industry under the lease-lend arrangements. If Britain should succumb to the U-boat onslaught, although the United States Government was determined that she should not, then would America be prepared to fight a two-ocean war? Some of Japan's leaders believed that a lightning strike on the territories she wished to annex would result in America agreeing to some form of status quo. Thus the timing of the action was all important. The two vital ingredients were secrecy and speed.

Japanese strategy was based on her overriding need for oil. Without sufficient stocks, and Japan had none of her own, all her expansionist plans would come to nothing, and even the war with China could not be sustained. When in 1941 America, who had provided nearly eighty

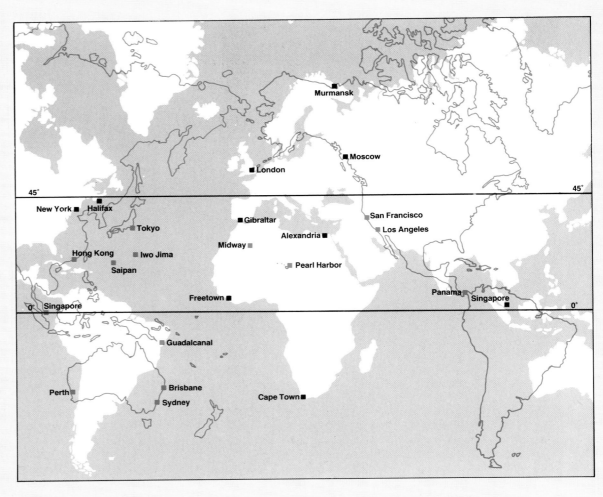

Superimposed maps of the Pacific and Western Oceans show the relative distances.

per cent of her requirements, cut off all oil supplies, war was inevitable. The only other available sources were in the areas of the Dutch East Indies, Sumatra, Java and in Borneo. Japan was now poised for war. For years her ship-building programme had been on an unprecedented level and the aircraft carrier was now to become the striking force, and so she had concentrated on building large and powerful vessels able to act independently or in conjunction with their awesome battle fleet. The United States had also embarked upon an enormous ship-building programme with carriers as a priority. But America and Britain had agreed that should war come to the Pacific, their first priority was to defeat Germany and Italy, even at the expense of denuding the Pacific of a

proportion of America's naval strength. This concept of 'Beat Hitler first' was a courageous and farsighted decision on the part of President Roosevelt, but inevitably was to have very serious consequences in the Pacific.

In April 1941 the United States Government decided to transfer to the Atlantic three battleships, one carrier, four cruisers and two squadrons of destroyers. As a result of this Allied and Japanese strength in the Pacific in December 1941 is shown below.

Japan thus had a marked superiority in carriers, and her fleet was a well trained, integrated force. In comparison, the United States was inferior in numbers in every class of warship,

Allied naval strength in the Pacific in December 1941

	US Pacific fleet	US Asiatic fleet based on Manila	British Commonwealth	Royal Netherlands Navy	Total
Battleships and Battlecruisers (mostly from World War I)	9	0	2	0	11
Carriers	3	0	0	0	3
Heavy cruisers	12	1	1	0	14
Light cruisers	9	2	7	3	21
Destroyers	67	13	13	7	100
Submarines	28	28	0	13	69

Japanese strength in December 1941

Battleships (mostly modernized)	10
Carriers	10 (6 fleet, 4 light)
Seaplane tenders	6
Heavy cruisers	18
Light cruisers	20
Destroyers	113
Submarines	64

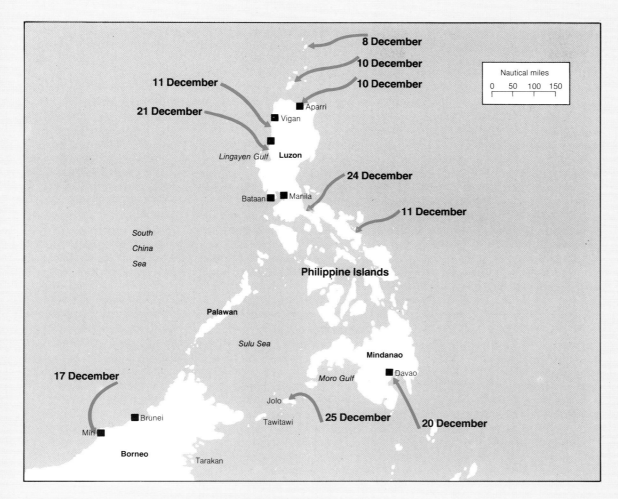

Japanese invasion of the Philippine Islands in December 1941.

none of which had had any battle experience, and the majority of the American fleet was concentrated at the main naval base at Pearl Harbor in Hawaii.

The Japanese plan of conquest in South East Asia was as follows, and was finally ratified on 5 November 1941.

1 Landings by amphibious forces at a number of different sites in the Philippines, followed by the destruction of American air power and of the naval base at Cavite. Simultaneous landings to be made on Guam, the British Malay Peninsula, Hong Kong and British North Borneo.

2 A carrier air strike to be mounted on the United States fleet at Pearl Harbor.

3 Rapid exploitation of initial success by seizing Manila (the capital) and Mindanao (the largest southern island of the Philippines), Wake Island, the Bismarcks, and also Bangkok and Singapore.

4 The occupation of the Dutch East Indies (with its oil) and the continuation of the war with China.

This invasion plan puts two points into their correct perspective. Firstly, the question of oil. Oil in plenty was to be had in the Dutch East Indies and in Borneo. To transport this oil safely back to Japan required the occupation of the Philippines which lie on the flank of the direct route to the Homeland. Secondly, in order to achieve this it was essential to immobilize the United States battle fleet at Pearl Harbor so that the landings could take place without the threat of major US intervention. For the same reason Singapore had to be captured.

Thus the destruction of America's battleships and carriers was, essentially, a protective measure. A fleet action to destroy the remaining Allied forces could wait until the Japanese combined fleet had finished covering the invasion forces which stretched far to the south.

The Americans were unaware of these actual detailed preparations, but it was obvious that Japan was about to invade territories in South East Asia. For some years American cryptographers had been working on, and had penetrated successfully, the Japanese diplomatic cipher — named Purple. They were able to read the secret messages flashed between Berlin and Tokyo and between the embassies abroad. Ample warning should therefore have been available but secrecy dictated that this ultra secret information be restricted to a 'need to know' basis. The mistake lay in excessive secrecy and it is no part of our story to delve into this question. However, the sense of urgency which was so lacking in Naval Intelligence at the time and the price paid for the omission resulted in a remarkable change in the system. The weapon of intelligence, 'the fourth arm', was to become so finely tuned that it would become one of the major instruments in the defeat of Japan.

However, it is necessary to make a distinction between the Japanese diplomatic cipher and the Japanese naval code JN 25. At this time, despite all efforts to crack it, JN 25 still remained secure. It was possible to amass a vast amount of information from Purple, to collate it, and to produce an undeniable pointer to events in the future, but the actual naval radio traffic signals were, at this stage, denied to the American service chiefs.

So Japanese envoys were still engaged in endless negotiations with Washington. To maintain secrecy they were still talking at the very moment their aircraft struck at Pearl Harbor.

Possibly the best way to understand the events which shattered the peace of the Pacific is to tabulate the Japanese invasion from day to day from the last two weeks in November 1941 to the end of December.

10-18 November Japanese strike force to attack Pearl Harbor departs from Japan. It consists of six aircraft carriers (423 planes) with an escort of one light cruiser and nine destroyers. The support force comprises two battleships, two heavy cruisers, three submarines and seven supply ships. Twenty-seven submarines are to proceed independently to form a ring round Pearl Harbor.

4 December Japanese invasion fleet for Malaya leaves Hainan in southern China with eighteen transports, escorted by twenty-one destroyers and one heavy cruiser, with a support group of three cruisers and three destroyers. A distant escort to cover operations in Malaya and the Philippines is provided by two battleships, two cruisers and four destroyers cruising in the South China Sea. Next day the convoy is joined by nine transports, a cruiser and a minelayer and mine-sweepers. British reconnaissance aircraft reports units at sea, but is promptly shot down. Eleven submarines lay mines round Singapore and eastern Malaya.

6 December The North Philippine (Luzon) invasion force leaves Palau Atoll consisting of fourteen transports escorted by four cruisers, twelve destroyers and three sea plane carriers. A southern force destined for the central Philippines departs from Palau on 16 December consisting of twenty-one transports, escorted by four cruisers, twelve destroyers, one seaplane and two light carriers.

7 December A massive air attack is mounted on Pearl Harbor.

7-8 December Japanese forces land on the east coast of Malaya.

8 December Japanese air attack on Clark Field, the main air base in the Philippines, effectively destroys United States air power in that theatre.

10 December Japanese air attack destroys United States naval base at Cavite near Manila.

10-11 December Japanese forces land at points in northern Luzon (Philippines) and at Legaspi in the central Philippines.

10 December HMS *Prince of Wales* and *Repulse* sunk by Japanese aircraft off Malaya. Japanese forces from Kwajalein (Marshall Islands) attempt a landing on Wake Island and are repulsed by the Marine garrison with the loss of two destroyers. Wake is again attacked a few days later but holds out until 23 December, and the American relief operation mounted from Pearl Harbor is recalled.

13 December The invasion convoy leaves Camranh Bay in Indo-China for North Borneo consisting of ten transports, escorted by one light cruiser and four destroyers.

16 December Japanese invasion forces land in North Borneo, and in Sarawak on 23rd.

17-18 December Leaving Formosa, seventeen transports with a heavy escort set sail for the south Philippines.

20 December The Japanese forces capture Davao (southern tip of the Philippines) and establish air bases.

21 December Further Japanese landings on Luzon at Lingayen Gulf.

25 December Hong Kong surrenders to the troops attacking from the Chinese mainland.

The Japanese conquest of South East Asia was a devastating blow to the Allies. The plan was executed with brilliant efficiency, at a speed hitherto unknown in the history of sea warfare and conquest.

It is now possible to put into perspective the massive air raid on Pearl Harbor. Its object was to cripple all heavy units of the United States fleet in the Pacific. As we have already seen, the Japanese conquest of South East Asia depended upon minimum interference. The strength of their naval forces was such that in addition to convoy duty they could take on scattered Allied units or squadrons, but it was essential to avoid a major fleet action at this stage. It was also essential to avoid a counter-attack supported by battleships and carriers until the Japanese had consolidated their position. Only then could they concentrate sufficient naval force for a final showdown.

The strike at Pearl Harbor was planned as follows. By sailing far to the north towards the Aleutian Islands in winter weather in fog and heavy seas, it was assumed that complete surprise could be effected. Fuelling at sea was a problem, but this was an acceptable risk. As a precaution against the problem of refuelling at sea in bad weather, a rendezvous was planned in the isolated and virtually uninhabited Kurile Islands. Here extra drums of fuel were also to be taken on board.

Specific training in great secrecy had been carried out on a small island off Japan and particular attention was given to dropping torpedoes in shoal waters. This was perfected. The attack by torpedo planes was to strike the initial and lethal blow, but high level and dive-bombers were to follow; these destroyed planes and installations on the ground and caused heavy casualties.

There were 423 planes on board the six carriers, and of these thirty-three were used for combat air patrol to protect the fleet, forty were held in reserve and 350 comprised the attack force.

About 104 'Kates' were designated for high level bombing, another forty for the torpedo attack and 135 'Vals' were allocated for dive-bombing. Eighty-one Zero fighters were to be used as escort and for the strafing of installations and personnel.

It was a well thought out and diligently rehearsed air strike. The only impediment to success was if security was blown and the United States fleet was alerted, so as to be deployed and waiting for the attackers.

The Pearl Harbor strike force of six carriers with its escort sortied from the naval base at Kure on the Inland Sea in echelons between 10 and 18 November 1941 under the command of Vice-Admiral Nagumo. Of the twenty-seven submarines which were to be stationed round Pearl Harbor to torpedo any ships that escaped the air attack, five carried midget submarines with two man crews whose job it was to penetrate the harbour and act independently.

It was a formidable force, the largest air strike in naval history to date. But history was to ensure that before the end of this cataclysmic war every single one of these warships, except one destroyer, was to be sunk by gunfire, mines, torpedoes or bombing.

Strict radio silence was maintained but the rest of the fleet at Kure increased the volume of radio traffic so that American surveillance would not notice the departure of the fleet.

By 22 November the striking force had rendezvoused in the Kurile Islands, and the extra fuel was taken on board.

On leaving the Kuriles the fleet encountered thick fog and heavy seas. The six carriers steamed in two parallel columns with a battleship at the rear and two heavy cruisers ahead. Destroyers were stationed on either flank, and a screen of four were some six miles ahead of the fleet in order to detect shipping. Orders were given to sink any American, British or Dutch ships on sight, and a boarding party was to take over any neutral ships which appeared on the scene. With the exception of one Japanese ship the ocean seemed to be empty.

In order to conserve fuel and to enable the oilers to keep up, the average speed was restricted. At the same time a careful radio watch was kept on transmissions from Pearl Harbor, but the secret had not leaked out and everything was normal. This good luck was partly attributable to the weather, as there were high seas and bad visibility — both of which made station keeping difficult.

On 1 December the Japanese Cabinet ratified General Tojo's decision to commence the hostilities on 7 December 1941. The striking force darkened ship and set Condition Two, the second degree of readiness for action. Meanwhile the weather moderated sufficiently for successful refuelling to take place, and the latest and most accurate data on ships present at Pearl Harbor was received — seven battleships, seven cruisers, but no carriers.

At 21.00 on 6 December 1941 the strike force reached a point 490 miles north of the target. There was a moment of great emotion when all hands were summoned to the flight deck and the actual 'Z' flag which had been displayed from Admiral Togo's flagship *Mikasa* before the Battle of Tsushima in 1905 was hoisted to the masthead of the flagship *Akagi*. Course was altered due south and the speed increased to 26 knots.

The heavy cruisers pushed on ahead and launched two float-type 'Zero' aircraft to reconnoitre Pearl Harbor. With the exception of the carriers, the United States fleet lay below them. By a remarkable piece of good fortune, at that time America's three carriers were at sea. This gratuitous advantage was to have a decisive effect on the war in the Pacific.

The attack on Pearl Harbor

In the darkness before dawn it was heavily over-cast at 6,000 feet and with a moderate sea running the flight decks pitched badly. Turning into wind the carriers commenced launching the first strike. Forty 'Kates' armed with torpedoes, forty-nine more equipped for high level bombing, fifty-one 'Val' dive-bombers and forty-three 'Zero' fighters orbited the force as dawn broke.

It was 07.50 on 7 December 1941. The Japanese air armada was approaching Pearl Harbor. Visibility was perfect and below them lay the United States Pacific Fleet.

For some weeks some precautionary measures had been taken and a modified form of readi-

ness was in force throughout the fleet, though totally inadequate to deal with any surprise attack. It was a Sunday morning and at 07.55 the first wave of torpedo-carrying 'Kates' swung in low and attacked the seven battleships moored along 'Battleship Row'.

A single plane attacked the light cruiser *Helena* and three more planes circled to the north side of Ford Island and attacked cruisers in the position normally occupied by the carriers. Within five minutes of the first torpedo attack, the battleships were combed fore and aft by the 'Kate' high level bombers. After delivering their attack the Japanese aircraft then flew low over the area strafing viciously to kill men running to positions for General Quarters.

The attack was devastating. Within half an hour, battleship *Arizona* was a burning wreck, *Oklahoma* had capsized, *West Virginia* had sunk, *California* was going down and *Nevada* and *Tennessee* were damaged, the latter being in danger of catching fire from *Arizona*. The *Maryland* was virtually unscathed, while *Pennsylvania* in dry dock received some hits but was not seriously damaged. The battleships of the Pacific fleet had been crippled.

The forward magazines of *Arizona* had exploded due to a direct bomb hit beside the second turret and in addition she had taken a torpedo forward. The repair ship *Vestal* moored outboard took two bomb hits but was able to beach herself sometime after 08.45.

USS Neosho — *a fleet oiler — stands out from her berth ahead of the* Maryland *narrowly missing the sunken* Oklahoma. *She was later to be sunk at the Battle of the Coral Sea. Oilers were just as much an indispensable part of the war at sea as any major warship as they enabled the task forces to remain at sea for long periods.*

Meanwhile flames shot hundreds of feet in the air as more bombs rained down on the battleship. *Arizona* was ablaze and endangering *West Virginia* moored ahead of her, and the *Arizona* blew up and sank so fast that she did not capsize and took with her 1,100 of her ship's company, wounding a further forty-four.

Moored astern of *Arizona* was the old battleship *Nevada*. She suffered only one torpedo hit, due mainly to the quick action of the ship's company in opening fire and destroying at least two Japanese aircraft. Despite one serious hit from the bomber force, *Nevada* immediately stood out and headed for the harbour entrance and the open sea. At 09.00 during the second big wave of the attack she attracted the attention of the dive-bombers and was hit repeatedly and set on fire. To avoid sinking in the fairway she was beached and her crew set about fighting the many fires.

Just ahead of *Arizona* was the battleship *West Virginia* outboard of *Tennessee*. *West Virginia* took six or seven torpedoes on her port side and sank rapidly on to the mud. Quick action in sounding General Quarters undoubtedly saved many lives. However, the flames from the exploding *Arizona* and the repeated bomb hits started serious fires which were not brought under control until the afternoon.

Inboard, the twenty-one year old battleship *Tennessee* was only lightly hit by the air strike, being protected by the *West Virginia*. The fires which took hold later came from the *Arizona* moored seventy-five feet astern, and were not brought under control until the next night.

The remaining pair of battleships moored to the next berth forward were *Maryland* and *Oklahoma*. The latter was outboard and was struck by three torpedoes very early in the attack. General Quarters was sounded but there was no time to counter-flood. As the ship began to roll over, her crew abandoned ship over her starboard side amid dive-bombing and strafing.

She came to rest when her masts caught in the mud, leaving only her keel showing. Over 400 members of her crew were killed or missing and a further thirty-four wounded — a third of the ship's company. *Maryland* was the luckiest of them all and received only one heavy bomb hit which detonated and she was back in service within three months.

At the southernmost berth was *California* and she was hit by two torpedoes within five minutes of the attack. Listing badly she was then hit by a bomb which set off the anti-aircraft magazine and caused serious fires. Before she was able to get under way, burning oil on the surface of the water threatened to engulf her and 'abandon ship' was ordered. The threat receded and the ship's company returned to fight the fires. But she slowly settled on to the mud with her decks awash.

Aircraft directed to the north of Ford Island did little damage and came under accurate fire. The light cruiser *Raleigh* was hit but her crew promptly counter-flooded and assisted in destroying several planes, while the destroyer *Monaghan* was already under way. She sighted a midget submarine and sank it before standing out of the harbour.

Battleship Row in flames. In the foreground the battleship Arizona *has blown up. Ahead of her* West Virginia *is resting on the bottom while inboard* Tennessee *is on fire. Next ahead* Oklahoma *has capsized and only her keel is showing while inboard* Maryland *is virtually untouched. In the middle distance* California *is sinking,* while in the far distance Nevada *is under attack. Despite an earlier torpedo hit in the bow which caused flooding, the battleship stood out into the channel. As she passes* Pennsylvania, *the flagship of the Pacific Fleet in dry dock, the destroyer* Shaw *in the near floating dock blows up. The time is 09.06 and the date is 7 December 1941.*

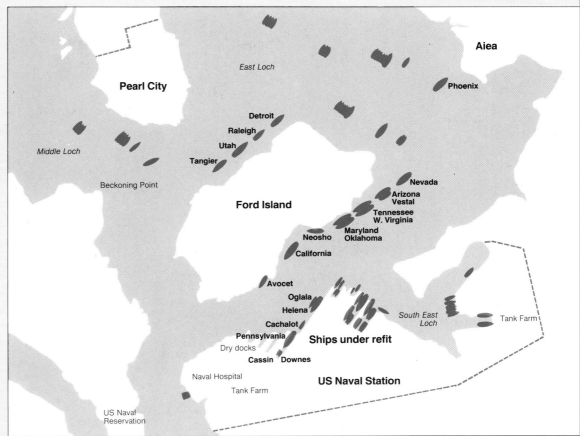

Pearl Harbor at 07.55 on Sunday 7 December 1941.

Also getting under way was the oiler *Neosho* which had just discharged her cargo of aviation spirit and was berthed ahead of *Maryland* and the sunken *Oklahoma*. She manoeuvred into the stream narrowly missing *Oklahoma*'s keel and proceeded to sea only receiving near misses from the Japanese aircraft.

Let us now turn our attention to the Navy Yard on the opposite side of the main channel. The minelayer *Oglala,* moored outboard of the light cruiser *Helena*, was sunk and *Helena* suffered damage. *Pennsylvania*, flagship of the Pacific Fleet, was in the dry dock with destroyers *Cassin* and *Downes* occupying the space at the head of the dock. By 09.00 the second attack by fifty-four high level 'Kates', seventy-eight dive-bombing 'Vals' and thirty-five 'Zeros', which had been launched from the carriers an hour after the first, began to arrive. By this time a heavier anti-aircraft defence had been organized, but as *Nevada* was moving slowly down the channel opposite the Navy Yard she was attacked again, as were the ships in the dry dock. *Downes* and *Cassin* were badly damaged although they were subsequently salvaged and rebuilt. *Pennsylvania* was not seriously damaged, but opposite in the floating dock the destroyer *Shaw* was hit, the forward magazine blowing up with an enormous explosion which ripped the bow from the ship.

The docks and piers of the Navy Yard were filled with ships undergoing refit, but little damage was inflicted on them. Only one or two tanks at the oil tank farm to the south of the Navy Yard

Japanese aircraft attacking the burning hangars on Ford Island. The aircraft shown was in fact piloted by Commander Fuchida who led the air strike.

were set on fire though dense smoke added to the scene of destruction.

As well as the ships, there were two large airfields, at Wheeler's Field on Ford Island and Hickham's Field behind the oil tank farm south of the Navy Yard. Also the seaplane base at Kaneohe Bay contained three squadrons of Catalina PBY reconnaissance aircraft.

While the torpedo carrying and high level bombing 'Kates' were attacking the fleet, the dive bombing 'Vals' of the first wave, 'Kates' of the second wave and the 'Zeros' concentrated on the aircraft and installations at the airfields and seaplane base. Every one of the Catalinas which was anchored at the base was destroyed or damaged, and the destruction of the closely packed aircraft at the airfields was hardly less disastrous. Hangars burst into flames to add to the holocaust of burning aircraft. The Marine Corps airfield at Ewa to the west was attacked by 'Zeros' and all but two of the forty-seven aircraft were destroyed or suffered major damage. The Army lost fifty-six aircraft amid much structural damage to installations. The air strike had been successful. The Japanese crippled the battle fleet at a critical moment, although they had missed the carriers which were an even more important target. However, they would have done more lasting damage if they had also destroyed the repair shops and the oil installations — and this would have been possible.

By just 10.00 the strike was over. Never in modern history had a war begun with so overwhelming a victory by one side, and never did the initial victor pay so dearly for that victory. However, the weeks and months ahead were to witness an even greater victory over a vast area of sea until the Japanese advance was checked in the Coral Sea, and halted at Midway.

77

Japanese supremacy and Allied disasters

We have seen how essential it was to Japan that she cripple the United States Pacific Battle Fleet. That air strike destroyed any hope of the United States remaining neutral or allowing the Japanese Government to continue with their plan to occupy South East Asia. The American people responded with shock and fury, and demanded immediate retaliation.

What structural damage actually had been done? The stricken battleships were without exception elderly, with a speed of around 21 knots, and lacking sufficient anti-aircraft armament. On the other hand the carriers which survived the raid could maintain a speed of at least 23 knots. Although the battleships had enormous fire power, in modern carrier warfare they could not keep up with the rest of the fleet.

The building programme had called for no less than seventeen battleships ordered between 1937 and 1940, but the first of these was not yet ready for action.

The destruction of aircraft was serious but the Navy Yard with its repair shops was untouched, and was able to function normally, although the major dry dock was a shambles. The oil stocks had not been destroyed, but above all, by providential good fortune the three carriers in the Pacific were at sea and escaped the fate of the battleships. However, the Japanese had partly succeeded in their stated objective. They could now invest Borneo and Sumatra and obtain oil and complete the conquest of South East Asia with overwhelming strength without having to maintain a battle fleet to combat the United States fleet.

The Japanese invasion force was now nearing Malaya and the Philippines and it was essential that no hitch should occur. The United States base in Manila Bay could interfere seriously with these operations. While USS *Houston* was the only heavy cruiser at the naval base at Cavite, the base did contain facilities for ship repair and maintenance, particularly for submarines, and carried a large stock of torpedoes. In addition there was a large balanced force of fighter, bomber and reconnaissance aircraft.

On 8 and 9 December, two days after the Pearl Harbor raid, Japanese carrier borne aircraft struck in strength and in three major air raids destroyed the United States Army Air Force Far East. On 10 December they struck at Cavite, the naval base. Flying above the range of the 3 inch anti-aircraft guns, and with no fighter interception, they reduced the Navy Yard to rubble, totally destroying installations and repair yards. Just in time USS *Houston* in company with the light cruiser *Boise*, a seaplane tender and oilers had been ordered south, arriving off Borneo on 14 December.

The campaign on land which followed is outside the scope of this narrative. Japanese forces landed in the north, central and southern Philippines. Little help could be given by the Navy, and American submarines failed to inflict any significant damage on the Japanese invasion fleets anchored off the beaches. General MacArthur's troops fell back to Bataan, and when forced to evacuate, a last stand was made on Corregidor Island. This held out until May 1942, but it did not upset the Japanese plans for South East Asia.

It was essential for Japan to hold the Philippines, not particularly for its minerals, but for its position sitting astride the route to and from Sumatra, Java and the South-west Pacific. A glance at a map is all that is needed to show the strategic significance of the area.

To round off a week of disaster, Guam was captured on 10 December. Wake Island was attacked on 10 December but the Marine garrison repulsed the landing. They held the island against increasing odds until forced to surrender on 23 December.

We now turn our attention to the south. Malaya and Thailand had been invaded from Indo-China and Japanese reinforcements were pouring in all along the east coast. The British

Government had reinforced Singapore with a troop convoy, but more important still, by the presence of the new battleship *Prince of Wales* and the battlecruiser *Repulse*. What Britain had not been able to do was to build up air support with modern aircraft. Now reinforcements were just not available. In fact there were 332 combat aircraft in Malaya and the Dutch had another 200 in the Netherlands East India against about 560 Japanese planes. The difference lay entirely in their obsolescence in comparison with the modern Japanese Air force which was highly trained and highly effective.

Thus the fleet, British, Dutch and American, was without adequate air cover. None the less, with news of Japanese landings in the north, the two heavy units of the British Fleet, escorted by four

The speed of the Japanese conquest of South East Asia was breathtaking. Unopposed landings were made in Malaya and the Philippines within hours of the air attack on Pearl Harbor.

destroyers, left Singapore on 8 December to intercept a reported Japanese convoy. No air cover was provided as the squadron proceeded north. At 14.00 on 9 December 1941the

Having immobilized the United States Pacific Battle Fleet, Japanese aircraft immediately destroyed the main airbase in the Philippines at Clark Field, Manila. Then with no American opposition at all from the air they destroyed the large naval base nearby at Cavite.

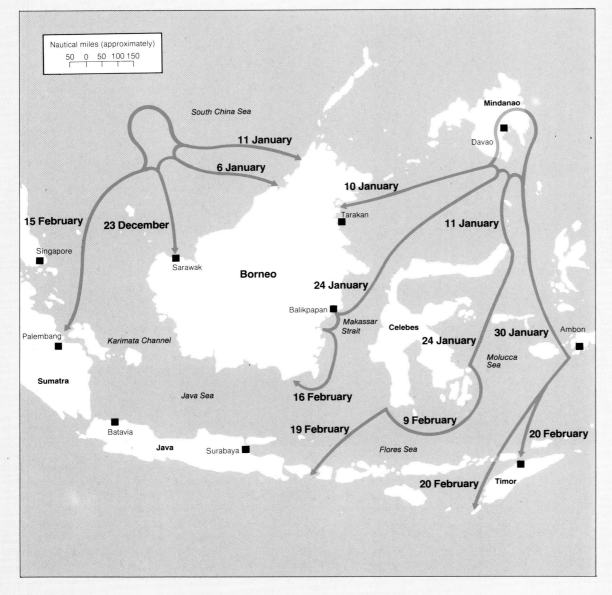

Amphibious movements of the Japanese Octopus, January to February 1942.

Japanese submarine I-65 sighted and reported the position of the squadron. As dusk fell Admiral Phillips in *Prince of Wales* prepared to turn to the west for a dawn attack on the beaches where the Japanese troops would have been unloading. But, during the night, he realised that he had been seen from the air and made the difficult decision to break off and return to Singapore.

Meanwhile another submarine, I-58, had fired a spread of torpedoes at the force, all of which missed, but the position of the British ships was again reported. Signals that Japanese forces were landing at Kuantan to the south had also been received in the flagship.

This was serious as it would cut off the ground troops to the north, and Admiral Phillips turned west to investigate. On arrival nothing was discovered and the squadron resumed course to the south.

The aircrews of the Japanese 22nd flotilla were readied and flown off from Saigon at 07.30 on 10 December and were picked up on *Repulse*'s radar at 11.00. They attacked at high altitude and despite the anti-aircraft barrage were extremely accurate. *Repulse* was hit amidships but without impairing her efficiency.

The torpedo aircraft came half an hour later . They appeared out of low cloud, some diving towards the port side of the *Prince of Wales* and others making for *Repulse* which avoided the spread by turning to starboard.

Prince of Wales was too late and two torpedoes struck aft, jamming the rudder and port propeller shafts exactly as in the case of the *Bismarck.* In addition power for half her secondary armament was lost.

A second and perfectly co-ordinated attack by torpedo aircraft now closed the squadron

which was in a desperate position with no air cover of any sort. Nine aircraft approached at low level, six making for *Prince of Wales* and three for *Repulse.*

At the last moment three aircraft heading for *Prince of Wales* veered away and made for *Repulse* so that she was attacked simultaneously from both sides. Unable to combat the attack she was hit by four torpedoes and her fate was sealed. She rolled over and sank.

The remaining three aircraft bore in on *Prince of Wales* which was unable to manoeuvre and all three torpedoes hit the starboard side. A destroyer closed to take off the ship's company, but the battleship began to roll over and then disappeared beneath the surface.

The effect of this action was stunning. Never before had capital ships at sea been destroyed with such ease by aircraft alone.

The British battleship Prince of Wales *and the battlecruiser* Repulse *with a destroyer escort sailed from Singapore on 8 December 1941 to intercept a landing in eastern Malaya. All available aircraft were heavily committed and no air cover was made available. Sighted and attacked by Japanese aircraft, first* Prince of Wales *was disabled, and then both ships were sunk by torpedoes.*

The Allies now set up a joint American, British, Dutch and Australian command (ABDA) to cover the whole area to the south and east, and to include the north coast of Australia. Land, air and sea forces were under unified command.

The British and Australian naval forces consisted of one heavy and one light cruiser and three destroyers — while the Netherlands naval forces were composed of three light cruisers and seven destroyers, together with thirteen submarines.

Japanese troops advanced south through the jungles of Malaya and captured the main British naval base in the Far East at Singapore after just seventy days of war.

The ABDA forces stood between Japan and the oil and rubber of the Indies, the most essential source of strategic materials, and vital to the whole Japanese war effort. It was to this area that the invasion forces now turned, entering the Celebes Sea and landing on the east coast of Borneo. An American destroyer squadron attacked the invasion transports at Balikpapan on 23/24 January 1942, sinking four in a night action, but this did not stop the invaders. Like some vast octopus the Japanese strategy relied on strangling many small points rather than concentrating on a vital organ, and so avoided meeting the full strength of the ABDA naval forces. At all times they were within range of the security of their land or carrier based aircraft. There was little that the overworked Allied naval forces could do to stop them. Without air cover they were vulnerable and though the few surviving PBY Catalina aircraft flew to the limit of the endurance of both men and machines, the Japanese forces were virtually untouched in the huge areas of the South Pacific Ocean. Between 23 December and the middle of February, the Japanese had swung south from the Philippines and attacked Borneo and Sumatra. On 15 February Singapore fell. This much acclaimed fortress was over-run, not by a frontal attack from the sea, on which for decades British strategic defensive planning had depended, but from the north, through 'impenetrable' jungle. History has already made its judgment. Throughout these critical weeks the land forces in Malaya fought a rearguard action, but with a feeling that the cause was already lost, and they had as yet not learned the lessons of jungle warfare. Elsewhere the story was the same: outposts of Allied forces, insufficient to hold the flood of invasion and without adequate air cover, fought on until they were overwhelmed.

With the Allied threat from Malaya removed, the Japanese invading forces made for Palembang in Sumatra and by the end of February half the oil reserves in the East Indies were in their hands. It cannot be stressed too strongly that it was upon oil and key strategic minerals, but above all upon oil, that the whole of Japan's war effort depended. Tankers were loading at the oil ports and taking their precious cargoes back to Japan without interference. The major objective had been achieved.

Java was the next target, but before invading, it was considered essential to sever the island's communications with Australia, and especially the Allied base at Darwin. Two Japanese battleships and three heavy cruisers escorted four carriers into the Timor Sea. There was nothing capable of stopping them for one moment. The air attack on Darwin took place at 09.30 on 19 February under a clear sky. The port was crowded with shipping and the attackers made for the docks and the airfield. The latter was demolished and the bombers now set about the shipping. Eleven ships were sunk with their valuable cargoes. The 250 casualties were increased by the strafing of survivors in small boats, and the town was severely damaged.

Japanese troops make unopposed landings at will in the Philippines in December 1941.

In order to protect their eastern flank, a Japanese strike force of four carriers, two battleships and three heavy cruisers approached Darwin in north-western Australia. There was nothing to stop them. After destroying the nearby air base they attacked the port, setting fire to the oil depot and sinking eleven ships. Much damage was done to the port and the town was abandoned temporarily.

The way to Java was now open. Allied forces tangled with the Japanese invasion fleet in a night action off Bali but with only minor damage inflicted. It takes little imagination to realise that the Allied ships continually at sea were grossly overworked and in need of upkeep and repair, and their crews nearing exhaustion. The efficiency of the ABDA forces was being whittled away through breakdowns and losses and damage from bombing near misses; but a final showdown had to come.

The available Japanese forces in the area consisted of four battleships, four carriers, six heavy and four light cruisers together with thirty-eight destroyers in two main commands. Ranged against them were the remaining forces of the three Allied nations, which formed a concentrated force of two heavy cruisers, four light cruisers, and eleven destroyers.

The invasion of Java began and the Dutch Rear-Admiral Doorman commanding the Allied squadron sortied from Surabaya to intercept. They had no air cover and were short of fuel and ammunition. In this action the Allied forces consisted of two heavy (*Houston* and *Exeter*) and three light (*De Ruyter, Java* and *Perth*) cruisers with nine destroyers. They were spotted and at 16.16 on 27 February 1942 were engaged at the extreme range of 28,000 yards by the Japanese heavy cruisers *Nachi* and *Haguro* which were accompanied by two light cruisers and thirteen destroyers under Rear-Admiral Takagi. The opposing forces then closed rapidly and the Japanese fired forty-three torpedoes, but all were avoided.

Later at 17.08 the British heavy cruiser *Exeter* was hit by gunfire and pulled out of line. She was followed by *Houston, Perth* and *Java* and it was some minutes before Admiral Doorman in the lead in *De Ruyter* could sort out the confusion. *Perth* made a wide sweep towards the oncoming Japanese force laying a smoke screen to protect *Exeter*, while the British destroyers *Encounter, Jupiter* and *Electra* were ordered to counter-attack through the smoke. At point blank range *Electra* took the full force of the Japanese attack and she was sunk in a matter of minutes at 17.10. As the Allied squadron withdrew to the south-east, American destroyers counter-attacked to cover the withdrawal, but by then the range had opened and their torpedoes were avoided. The crippled *Exeter* was escorted by the Dutch destroyer *Witte de With*, but her sister ship the *Kortenaer* had already been sunk. In the greatest possible danger, the Allied squadron turned south as darkness fell.

But the four Allied cruisers were not left alone. Japanese float planes shadowed them, dropping flares to mark their course. The American destroyers needed fuel and more torpedoes, so left the squadron and proceeded to Surabaya. *Jupiter* hit a mine and was lost. At 23.00 the two heavy cruisers *Nachi* and *Haguro* were sighted and fire was opened. At 8,000 yards the Japanese launched torpedoes and in the spread *De Ruyter* was hit and burst into flames. *Perth* following behind at high speed scraped by the stationary leader and then *Java* was hit by a torpedo and sank in a sheet of flame. The brave Doorman was lost with his ship and the first part of this disaster was over. In one afternoon and night, half the Allied squadron was lost in what is now known as the Battle of the Java Sea.

The Battle of the Java Sea. The action at 17.25 on 27 February 1942. The British destroyers Encounter, Jupiter *and* Electra *counter-attack through the smoke to defend the damaged* Exeter. *All were sunk in the days that followed.*

The only hope for the survivors of this battle was to make for the Indian Ocean and Ceylon via the Sunda Strait, or to Australia via the Bali Strait. Unknown to the Allies, the route had already been closed. Rear-Admiral Kurita had chosen Banten Bay on the north coast of Sumatra to land troops from the invasion fleet. Covering them were four heavy cruisers, a carrier and at least twelve destroyers. The exhausted crews of USS *Houston* and HMAS *Perth* having returned to Surabaya now turned to the west to make for Ceylon, desperately low on ammunition.

At high speed they approached the Sunda Strait and at 23.00 on 28 February sighted the convoy for which the Allies had been searching for

so long, anchored in Banten Bay. As they flashed past, all guns plastered the Japanese troopships, destroying four, but within minutes they were embroiled in a fight to the finish. Huge water spouts hid the cruisers as they turned and twisted to avoid the torpedoes which approached from all directions. The Japanese searchlights held them in a pitiless glare as they returned fire with everything they had.

Perth exhausted her six inch ammunition and fired starshells into the destroyers as they closed in. She was finally torpedoed and sank at 00.25 on 1 March. *Houston* was without number 3 turret and the heavy 8 inch shells were manhandled to the forward guns. Twisting and turning she fought to the end, but her

turn came at 00.33. With her decks strewn with dead and wounded, she came to a standstill and Japanese destroyers closed in, tearing the ship apart. Finally in a blaze of light she rolled over and sank at 00.46.

Next morning the damaged *Exeter* escorted by the destroyers *Encounter* and *Pope* tried to slip away to the west. Sighted and closed by four heavy cruisers, they were all overwhelmed despite the efforts by the destroyers to shield the wounded cruiser. All three ships were lost by midday.

The Japanese Western Attack Group had now crushed all naval opposition and proceeded at leisure to consolidate and to move inland to take Batavia. Java surrendered on 8 March.

The tale of defeat and disaster in the Far East is not yet complete. Thailand fell to Japan on the first day of the war and was the springboard for the invasion of Burma. Rangoon fell on 8 March and by 1 May China was cut off from outside aid. The strategic Andaman Islands in the Indian Ocean would become very useful as a forward base to the Allies in reconquering Burma, Malaya and Sumatra.

In order to occupy these islands and to clear the Indian Ocean, and also to damage the bases in Ceylon, the Japanese planned a sortie into the Indian Ocean.

The not inconsiderable British fleet based on Ceylon consisted of five old but serviceable battleships, two large and one small aircraft carriers, eight cruisers and five submarines. Vice-Admiral Nagumo sailed into the Indian Ocean with five large carriers, three battleships, two heavy and one light cruiser, nine destroyers and escorted supply vessels.

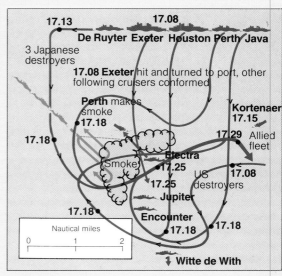

The Java Sea Battle, 27 February 1942.

Night action at the Battle of the Java Sea when the Allied squadron was shadowed and attacked by a Japanese naval force. The Dutch light cruiser De Ruyter *(flagship of Rear-Admiral Doorman) was torpedoed and burst into flames. HMAS* Perth *following close behind just managed to avoid a collision. Minutes later the light cruiser* Java *was also torpedoed and exploded.*

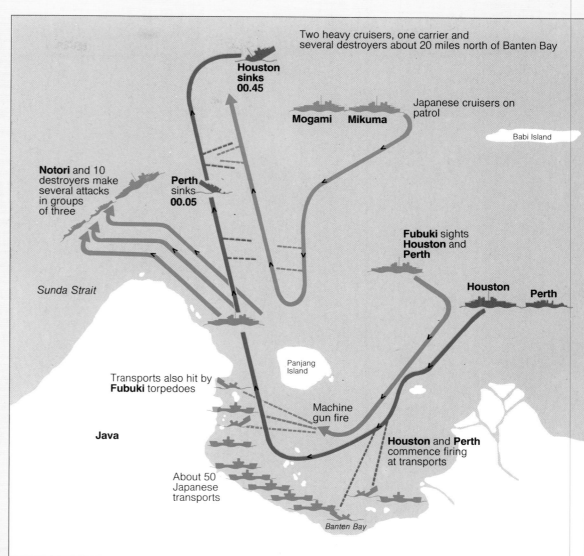

Two heavy cruisers, one carrier and
several destroyers about 20 miles north of Banten Bay

**Houston
sinks
00.45**

Mogami   **Mikuma**   Japanese cruisers on
patrol

Babi Island

Notori and 10
destroyers make
several attacks
in groups
of three

**Perth
sinks
00.05**

Fubuki sights
Houston and
Perth

Sunda Strait

Houston   **Perth**

Transports also hit by
Fubuki torpedoes

Panjang
Island

Machine
gun fire

Java

Houston and **Perth**
commence firing
at transports

About 50
Japanese
transports

Banten Bay

Battle of the Sunda Strait, 28 February to 1 March 1942.

*The only Allied cruisers in the South Pacific to survive the Battle of the Java Sea were the
American.* Houston *and the Australian* Perth. *Barring their escape was a heavy escort to a
Japanese convoy. Both ships fought courageously before being overwhelmed and sunk.*

Word of this intended attack reached the British Commander, Admiral Somerville, who decided against a headlong conflict with a force superior in strength, battle practice, morale and technique. He withdrew from Japanese air range by day and closed at night, hoping for a quick gunfire attack and withdrawal. The results could be said to have been predictable had this conflict come about, and he later decided wisely to keep away from Ceylon. The air attack on Colombo was made on 5 April and much damage was done to workshops and shore installations. Of the thirty-three RAF and RN planes that intercepted, sixteen were lost, but they shot down seven of the attackers. At the time there were twenty-one merchant ships in Colombo Harbour together with five warships and eight auxiliaries. One destroyer and a depot ship were sunk. The British heavy cruisers *Dorsetshire* and *Cornwall* were at sea and steaming towards Colombo when they were set upon by Japanese carrier borne dive-bombers. In a brilliantly accurate attack both ships were sunk. The old aircraft carrier *Hermes* escorted by a destroyer were sighted on 9 April and they also went to the bottom, *Hermes* receiving at least forty bombs. Trincomalee was attacked next and some damage was done to the port.

Still the tale of Allied disaster was not complete. A Japanese squadron, acting independently, attacked shipping in the Bay of Bengal and within one week twenty-eight ships (135,000 tons) were sunk by the combined force which suffered no losses.

This sortie did considerable damage and at the same time forced the British Eastern Fleet to remain in the western half of the Indian Ocean or in East African bases. It could therefore be

A Japanese carrier strike force entered the Indian Ocean and attacked Colombo in April 1942. The old carrier HMS Hermes *was sunk together with the cruisers* Dorsetshire *and* Cornwall *in a series of decisively accurate dive-bombing attacks.*

The Japanese carrier strike force returning after their successful sortie into the Indian Ocean. They had destroyed all Allied opposition in the South-west Pacific, and now awaited the first big carrier battle.

quite safely disregarded by the Japanese High Command in its later operations to the east. The victorious Japanese fleet then withdrew from the Indian Ocean.

To sum up, Admiral Nagumo had good reason to feel proud. He had sunk five battleships, one aircraft carrier, seven cruisers and seven destroyers; severely damaged several more capital ships and disposed of hundreds of thousands of tons of fleet auxiliaries and merchant ships. Hundreds of Allied aircraft and important shore installations had been destroyed. Yet not one major ship of his striking force had been sunk or even badly damaged by Allied action.

In addition the invasion of South East Asia had gone through as planned and the Imperial Japanese Navy had seen to it that there had been little interference from the sea or air. Japanese tankers and ore-carrying merchant ships could now return to Japan with their holds filled with the precious oil and raw materials so desperately needed to continue the war.

The victorious fleet returned to Singapore, and the three large carriers then proceeded to Japan for refit, thus missing the build up of forces which was to result in the Battle of the Coral Sea.

With the exception only of a part of New Guinea, Japan had conquered the whole of the South-west Pacific north of Australia. This area contained enough oil, rubber, tin and other strategic raw materials to satisfy the needs of the Japanese war machine.

With complete control of the air space over the sea lanes it was now possible for loaded tankers and supply ships to return to Japan almost unescorted. Throughout their long journey north they were under the protection of the Imperial Japanese Navy.

The first strike back

The disaster at Pearl Harbor and the following defeats throughout the Pacific, while rocking America to its foundations, also welded the people into a determination to fight back, to use to the full all the massive industrial output that the nation possessed.

Upon the shoulders of Admiral Ernest J. King, Commander-in-Chief of the United States Navy, fell the task of directing operations in a two-ocean war. To ease the burden, the President and Secretary of the Navy made the immediate decision to appoint Admiral Chester Nimitz to the post of Commander-in-Chief Pacific. This officer was to mastermind the events which were to follow and to lead the United States naval forces to final victory in the Pacific. Few men have had to take on the awesome responsibilities allocated to Admiral Nimitz from the dark days of 1941 to final victory in 1945; and the world may be thankful for his brilliant leadership and his inspired selection of commanders at sea.

In the gloomy atmosphere at the beginning of 1942 it was essential that the American people be given tangible evidence that the Navy was ready to strike back. It is true that raids on Wake Island on 23 February 1942 and on Marcus Island on 4 March, together with the air strikes by *Yorktown* and *Lexington* in New Guinea had been widely reported. However, something more substantial was urgently required. As early as January 1942 Admiral King and his staff were discussing how the Navy might pull off a really spectacular raid on Japan. As the months wore on and one disaster followed another this need to strike back became all the more important for morale at home and in the Pacific. The problems were great. Shore-based aircraft from the Japanese mainland were capable of operating 300 miles off shore and it was known that a ring of picket boats patrolled 500 miles off Tokyo Bay. How could aircraft be launched from outside these defences to bomb Tokyo? Conventional carrier borne aircraft lacked the range, but the Army Air Force Mitchell medium bombers — the B-25s — had the range to do the job. Could they be launched from a carrier? It was theoretically possible but it had never been tried before. Certainly they could not be recovered and would have to over-fly their targets and land in mainland China.

Sixteen B-25s could just be accommodated on the deck of the brand new carrier *Hornet* and after training in secret they were hoisted aboard the carrier on 1 April 1942 and sailed next day from San Francisco. To make room for the bombers, *Hornet*'s own aircraft were struck down, and to provide air cover the carrier *Enterprise* met the task force on the 13 April north of Midway Island. They refuelled 1,000 miles from Tokyo and continued westward. In order to reach the Chinese airfields which were 1,100 miles away, the launch had to take place within 500 miles of the Japanese coast, and it was decided to attack at night. Lieutenant-Colonel Doolittle who commanded the raid was to precede the rest of the squadron and drop incendiary bombs on Tokyo to illuminate the target. The date was fixed for 18 April. When more than 800 miles from the Japanese coast, air reconnaissance found picket boats and the aircraft were spotted. Surprise was lost, but an instant and bold decision was made to launch at once and raid Tokyo by day. It was not

even certain if the B-25s now had the range to reach China, but at 07.25 Colonel Doolittle led his aircraft off *Hornet*'s deck 668 miles from the target. Each aircraft carried four 500 pound bombs. The wind and sea were so strong that green water was breaking over the carrier's ramps, but all the aircraft rose safely into the air. Colonel Doolittle circled the carrier once and

they set off. By a coincidence Tokyo was having an air raid practice that day and the bombers arrived over the target as the all clear was sounded! Military targets were selected in the capital and surrounding cities and at 12.35 the attack went in. The actual damage done was negligible by subsequent bombing standards but the effect on the Japanese High Command

was immediate. Four Army fighter plane groups which were urgently needed elsewhere were pinned down in Japan in order to maintain the defence of the Homeland.

More important still, future plans for a final showdown were pushed ahead, and so were over-extended. This led to the Battle of Midway.

Seventy-seven out of the eighty pilots and crewmen, including Colonel Doolittle, survived the raid although four died subsequently as Japanese prisoners. One plane landed at Vladivostok and the others landed in China. The lift to American morale was tremendous and very badly needed. This historic flight, so small in comparison with what had gone before and

The United States retaliated with a daring raid on Tokyo on 18 April 1942. Sixteen B-25 bombers, which had never flown from a carrier before, were hoisted aboard Hornet. They could never be recovered. The raid was launched 668 miles from the target and after bombing, flew on to the Chinese mainland. Little damage was done but the effect on Japanese morale was profound.

what was to come in the future, left a deep impression on Japanese planning. It showed that the very heart of the victorious Japanese nation was, in fact, vulnerable. It was the first strike back.

However, the fact remained that the situation in the Pacific was very grave. Indeed, it was very grave everywhere, and the agreement between Roosevelt and Churchill to 'beat Hitler first' meant that the United States was committed to a strategic defensive role in the Pacific for some time to come.

Nevertheless we must not lose sight of the intense preparations going on in the United States as the vast industrial potential of the country was turned over to war production and planning. Factories and shipyards were working night and day to produce the war materials needed to sustain the Allied forces all over the world.

In no sphere was this more dramatic than in shipbuilding and aircraft production. A huge naval construction programme was under way. To offset losses in the Atlantic and to build up tonnage to prosecute the war, standardized merchant ships were being produced on a scale that had been unheard of before. Using assembly line techniques the famous Liberty and other standard type ships were being produced in American and Canadian yards in enormous numbers.

The Kaiser Corporation took 197 days to produce their first Liberty ship, but by August 1942 this time had been reduced to sixteen. However, in November 1942 the record time in which a ship was built from the laying of the keel to the final completion was probably that of the *Robert E. Peary.*The complete vessel containing more than 250,000 different items was completed in four days and fifteen hours. In twenty-four hours the hull had taken shape and the 1,450 tons of steel — all prefabricated sections — and the 135 ton engine were in place. By the end of the second day the upper deck was finished. On the third day, deckhouses, masts and deck equipment were installed. Final welding, wiring and painting was completed on the fourth day, and the ship was ready for launching. She went into service three days later.

To work this shipbuilding miracle, construction time was cut from months to weeks by rigid uniformity of design, specification and procurement. Sixty-one per cent of the ship was prefabricated, with more than 152,000 feet of welding performed on the assembly line. Similar procedures were applied in other spheres of manufacture from aircraft to trucks.

The vast industrial potential of the United States was nowhere more apparent than in shipbuilding where, together with Canadian yards, prefabricated ships were built in very large numbers. The maritime and aviation construction programmes were to attain proportions that would eventually overwhelm Japan.

The Battle of the Coral Sea

The Japanese strategy was to occupy New Guinea, dominate the Coral Sea area as a preliminary to future expansion and so to cut off Australia from her main sources of supply. Port Moresby was the key to Papua and its capture would bring northern Australia within range of Japanese bombers. A glance at a map shows that the occupation of Tulagi in the Solomon Islands and the construction of airfields and a naval base in the area would close off the eastern flank. This was regarded as a major threat in Washington, and Port Moresby was not just a place to be denied to Japan; it was essential to hold it at all costs for General MacArthur's plans to re-conquer lost territory.

The Combat Intelligence Unit in the Navy Yard at Pearl Harbor was engaged in a round-the-clock effort to break the Japanese naval code JN 25. By early April the Japanese plan to press southwards against Port Moresby was clearly identified. Admiral Nimitz had been warned of the build up in that area and it was obvious that within weeks or even days a clash was inevitable. To assault Port Moresby would require a large covering force with continuous air cover and the call signs of a number of carriers and other heavy units had been identified in the area of the Coral Sea towards the end of April.

On the American side the carriers *Enterprise* and *Hornet* had just returned to Pearl Harbor after the raid on Tokyo and could not cover the 3,500 miles to the Coral Sea in time. This left Admiral Fletcher's Task Force 17 comprising the carrier *Yorktown* which was reinforced on l May 1942 by *Lexington* with five cruisers and nine destroyers — together with Rear-Admiral Crace's squadron of two Australian cruisers, the USS *Chicago* and two destroyers coming up from Australia.

The exact whereabouts of the Japanese Admiral Inouye's forces were not known, but while the Allied squadrons were refuelling, Tulagi in the

Solomons was occupied on 3 May. Admiral Fletcher attacked the next day with an air strike without hindering the occupation. At this moment and as yet unseen, a Japanese invasion force for Port Moresby was leaving Rabaul. It was covered by the two large carriers *Zuikaku* and *Shokaku* and six destroyers with two heavy cruisers, *Myoko* and *Haguro*. The invasion force itself was escorted by four heavy cruisers and two light cruisers and by the light carrier *Shoho*. The date 6 May was one which marked the low point of the war for America, for General Wainwright had just ordered the defenders of Bataan to lay down their arms. However, the depression was short lived, for the build up for the first great carrier battle was nearly complete. The oiler *Neosho* (which had boldly escaped from Pearl Harbor on 7 December) and the destroyer *Sims* were sighted by the Japanese and mistaken for a carrier and a cruiser. They were set upon and after an unequal fight both ships were sunk.

At the same time as Admiral Fletcher's Task Force 17 was proceeding west to intercept, the invasion force was sighted by reconnaissance aircraft from the task force and was seen to be heading for the Jomard Passage preparatory to the run in to Port Moresby. At 06.25 on 7 May Admiral Fletcher detached Admiral Crace's Support Group to continue on a westerly course at high speed to intercept, while he turned north with the carriers. This was a risky move. Crace had no air cover and by detaching this squadron he greatly weakened his small force. They were heavily bombed, but skilful ship handling and aggressive retaliation by the squadron's guns drove off the attackers. None the less it was providential for the Allies that the whole squadron was not destroyed.

Yorktown's air reconnaissance to the north reported 'two Japanese carriers and four heavy cruisers' on 7 May and both American carriers launched a powerful strike. The information

The first major naval action in history where the opposing ships never met. Aircraft from both sides attempted to sink the opposing ships. Here SBD Dauntless aircraft from USS Yorktown *attack IJN* Shokaku *obtaining two bomb hits. She was saved by the efficiency of her damage control parties.*

was incorrect due to a mistake in encoding. Admiral Fletcher was now in deep trouble with his strike force heading at right angles to the approach of Admiral Takagi's fleet carriers. The Japanese realized that a carrier battle was imminent and Admiral Inouye ordered the Port Moresby invasion force to reverse course and keep out of the area until the battle was over.

By a stroke of good fortune the abortive air strike sighted the invasion force support group and it included the light carrier *Shoho*. American aircraft dived to attack, and *Shoho* was set on fire and sank. For the first time in the war a Japanese carrier had been sunk.

Admiral Fletcher decided to wait until the following day before searching for Admiral Takagi's big carriers. Meanwhile a twenty-seven plane strike from *Shokaku* and *Zuikaku* narrowly missed their targets and were set on by Fletcher's fighters, from which only seven Japanese returned.

In carrier actions bands of low cloud and rain and generally foul weather frequently played a decisive part in the actions which followed. This was the case in the Coral Sea action. Admiral Fletcher had been under a protective cloud cover until dawn broke to reveal clear skies and high visibility on the morning of 8 May, while Admiral Takagi was still under an umbrella of cloud. Each side had about 120 operational aircraft and Admiral Fletcher sent out a 360 degree search. At 08.38 the Japanese force was found and reported, and Admiral Fletcher at once despatched air strikes. At 09.30 they found the big carriers each screened by two heavy cruisers and two or three destroyers. The Dauntless dive-bombers orbited at 17,000 feet to await the slower low flying Devastator torpedo aircraft, while *Shokaku* turned into wind to launch additional combat air patrol Zero fighters. At 10.57 the attack on *Shokaku* went in. The Devastators attacked at sea level but their torpedoes were launched at too great a distance and all were avoided.

These were followed by the dive-bomber attack and three hits were made on *Shokaku*. Dog fights between the escorting Wildcats and the Japanese Zeros enabled the bombers to complete their runs, and one of the attacking pilots released his bomb 300 feet from *Shokaku*'s flight deck. The explosion killed the pilot but started fires and made the carrier inoperable. *Shokaku* was in a bad way from two other hits, but the efficiency of the damage control parties saved the ship. One hundred and forty-eight of the ship's company were killed or wounded and, screened by her escort, she made for Rabaul. Meanwhile, *Zuikaku* had eluded the American strike by entering a rain squall and was untouched. The American strike was over.

At the same time as Admiral Fletcher's aircraft were setting off, Admiral Takagi's strike force was heading for *Yorktown* and *Lexington*, visible for many miles in the brilliant sunshine. The attack was better co-ordinated and the combat air patrols were not strong enough over the carriers. The 'Kate' torpedo-bombers attacked *Lexington* from both sides, and despite violent

manoeuvring two serious hits were made on her port side. This was followed by a dive-bomber attack which scored two hits with light bombs, neither of which caused much damage. It was all over in nineteen minutes. *Lexington* had a 7 degree list, three boiler rooms flooded and plane elevators inoperable, but despite this within an hour she was able to launch and recover aircraft. However, three separate fires were burning inside the ship.

Meanwhile *Yorktown* was not left unscathed. She avoided all torpedoes but took a 550 pound bomb in the centre of the flight deck which did considerable damage. Fires which raged down to the fourth deck were tackled and soon put out, and although scarred *Yorktown* was still fully operational.

At this moment the first carrier battle seemed to have gone to the American task force. One Japanese light carrier had been sunk and one carrier damaged, against two US carriers damaged. Fourteen American aircraft failed to return while the Japanese lost twenty-nine. But the fires in *Lexington* were never extinguished, although she was able to operate aircraft. Her aviation petrol system had been very badly shaken, and inflammable vapour penetrated the ship. At 12.47 a devastating internal explosion rocked the ship. Even then she was still just able to operate her aircraft, but the fires spread further until an even greater explosion at 14.45 engulfed the carrier. She was abandoned and sank at 20.00.

The actual battle of the Coral Sea was a tactical victory for the Japanese, but strategically the victory went to the Allies. The invasion threat to Port Moresby had been thwarted. The Japanese never did reach Port Moresby due to intense bombing by land-based Australian aircraft. Admiral Inouye dared not subject his invasion fleet to another sortie without air cover and he had lost the light carrier *Shoho*. *Shokaku* had returned to Japan to make good the damage, and a far larger and fundamental conflict was being planned to the north.

The American Yorktown *and* Lexington *were visible under clear skies and* Lexington *was attacked simultaneously from all quarters by Japanese torpedo carrying 'Kates' sustaining two hits, together with two further hits by dive-bombing 'Vals'. Although the carrier seemed to have survived and was soon recovering aircraft, a huge internal explosion, followed by an even heavier blast, caused the ship to be abandoned.*

The Battle of Midway

The overall objective of the Japanese was to maintain an impenetrable perimeter around their newly acquired terrritories. They had gained control of an area of sea so vast, in such a short time and at so little cost, that it was almost breathtaking. In that time they had destroyed virtually all naval, air and military opposition which they had come up against. The exception was in New Guinea, where as a result of the Coral Sea battle, the invasion force for Port Moresby had been turned back and without air supremacy would not be able to take this last Allied stronghold in the area. To the north, America still held Midway Island, a vitally important forward naval and air base for both sides. To complete and protect their conquests and to obtain a forward base for further conquest, Midway had to be assaulted by the Japanese. In so doing a fleet action was inevitable in which the United States carrier force could be destroyed.

Admiral Nimitz was aware that a full scale offensive in the Central Pacific was imminent. The events of the past five months had included not only feverish activity in the field of intelligence and cryptanalysis but also solid results. It is only now, some forty years after the events, that the work of the dedicated men involved is becoming recognized and their contribution to final Allied victory appreciated. One major mistake made by the Japanese was in not changing the JN 25C cipher until too late and allowing it to become broken.

Both Midway and the Aleutians were still in American hands, and for Japan the immediate objective was to occupy both places. The reaction to such an assault would inevitably result in bringing the United States carriers to battle.

Signal intelligence (Sigint) was accumulating conclusive evidence that the Aleutians were to be occupied. Admiral Nimitz never believed that it was to be the major threat, but none the less it was American territory, and a force of five cruisers and ten destroyers was allocated to this area under Admiral Theobald. On 28 May Admiral Nimitz informed Admiral Theobald that the Japanese objective was probably Kiska and Attu. Decoded Japanese signals pointed to this, but Theobald considered that Dutch Harbour was the more likely spot and concentrated his force in that area. Thus he was in the wrong place at the wrong time and in the mists shrouding these islands Japanese forces landed on 6 and 7 June on Kiska and Attu. This was of no great importance. What was vital was the fact that signal intelligence had identified it as a feint recognizing that a bigger offensive was to come. Had Admiral Nimitz sent his carriers north, all would have been lost. The Japanese deception plan had failed. They had sent a force of two carriers, four battleships and screening cruisers and destroyers; sufficient to maul American forces had they been drawn northward in strength.

Admiral Nimitz knew that an occupation force was heading north-east from Saipan and Truk. Small sections of routine decoded signals made this abundantly clear and indicated that a major offensive was even now under way. On 16 May the Japanese First Air fleet was signalling: 'As we plan to make attacks from a generally north-westerly direction from J-2 to N-day inclusive, please send weather three hours prior

to take off . . . on the day of attack we will endeavour to . . . at a point fifty-one miles north-west of AF and move pilots off quickly.'

Where was AF? Was it Midway or Pearl Harbor? To find out, the simplest of deceptions was made. Midway was linked by undersea cable to Pearl Harbor, and through this secure channel Midway was ordered to send a signal in clear that the fresh water plant had broken down. Hawaii replied also in clear that a water barge was on its way. All intercept stations waited for any reaction. It came on 21 May, when a signal via Wake Island reported AF to be short of water! Midway was the target — but when? To an admiral commanding the precious few carriers that the United States possessed, it was essential to pinpoint the date. Seldom in history was that one fact of more crucial importance. By a remarkable effort of round-the-clock concentrated activity, signal intelligence discovered that the date was 3 June for the Aleutians and 4 June for Midway. Captain Rochefort, a man whose contribution to victory in the Pacific was immense, informed Admiral Nimitz that his team had finally cracked the code. The breakthrough came only days before the Japanese cipher JN 25C was altered. The fact that Admiral Nimitz was able to place his forces in a brilliant set of dispositions was due to the accurate early warning intelligence he was given, and to the fact that Nimitz himself had the confident courage to trust this signal intelligence.

It was known that the Japanese Carrier Divisions 1 and 2 (comprising *Akagi, Kaga, Soryu* and *Hiryu*) were approaching from the north-west of Midway, and that the occupation forces were coming up from the south-west. In addition to the four Japanese carriers were two battleships, two heavy cruisers and twelve destroyers all under the command of Admiral Nagumo. The occupation force of 5,000 men in transports was covered by two battleships, eight cruisers and nine destroyers under Vice-Admiral Kondo, and the main body under Admiral Yamamoto comprised three battleships including the mighty *Yamato* with a strong screen of destroyers; it was to form a covering force but its presence was unknown to Admiral Nimitz until after the battle. Finally, air reconnaissance was to cover Pearl Harbor, but signal intelligence thwarted this move by ensuring that the large Japanese flying boats were denied a refuelling point at French Frigate Shoals, a cluster of islets 500 miles from Pearl Harbor where Japanese submarine tankers awaited the arrival of the aircraft. American forces arrived there first.

The Japanese plan was to attack Midway Island from the air and destroy the defences. When all air opposition had been overcome the covering battleships and cruisers would bombard Midway while the troops assaulted and captured the island coming in from the south-west. Meanwhile the carriers would be ready for the expected appearance of the American carrier force and in a swift and well co-ordinated attack by the pilots and their superior aircraft the United States carrier fleet would be crippled and pursued by the main body, while the Aleutians covering force was brought south to assist as required. Such was the plan — somewhat complicated and vulnerable, but none the less the overwhelming strength of the Japanese meant it should have succeeded.

Signal intelligence had pieced together most of the dispositions, except for the unknown main body under Admiral Yamamoto. So the date was known, and the critical position of the Japanese carrier strike force at dawn on 4 June was estimated — as it turned out — with uncanny accuracy.

To meet the Japanese threat, Admiral Nimitz was eagerly awaiting the arrival at Pearl Harbor of the damaged *Yorktown*, coming up from the Coral Sea. She arrived on 27 May, and with the remarkable speed and ingenuity which is the hallmark of American industrial capacity, the damage inflicted upon her three weeks before was patched up in three days and she was ready to sail on 31 May.

Of the other carriers in the Pacific, *Lexington* had been sunk and *Saratoga*, after repairs following an earlier torpedo hit, was training at San Diego on the west coast of America. That left *Enterprise* and *Hornet* which had returned at speed from the Doolittle raid on Japan, arriving at Pearl Harbor on 26 May. They were now augmented by the patched-up *Yorktown* to make a total of just three carriers.

At this critical moment Admiral Halsey, the Task Force commander, became ill and had to be admitted to hospital so the tactical command was given to Rear-Admiral Fletcher. Rear-Admiral Spruance who had commanded Halsey's cruisers was given command of Task Force 16 comprising *Hornet* and *Enterprise*. *Hornet* had had no battle experience and *Yorktown*'s pilots were augmented by the survivors from *Lexington* after the Coral Sea battle. So the total strength of the American fleet positioned to deny Midway to the Japanese and to thwart their intentions was as follows:

Task Force 17 — Rear-Admiral Fletcher with *Yorktown*, two heavy cruisers and six destroyers.
Task Force 16 — Rear-Admiral Spruance with *Enterprise* and *Hornet* with five heavy and one anti-aircraft cruiser and nine destroyers.

The American air strength was seventy fighters, 111 SBD Dauntless dive-bombers and forty-two Devastator torpedo-bombers.
Twelve submarines were positioned in a ring to the west of Midway (and seven covered Pearl Harbour).
The available battleships at Pearl Harbor were not included as they could not keep up with the carriers and would have needed extra air cover.

On Midway itself was a mixed collection of aircraft comprising thirty PBY Catalina reconnaissance aircraft, twenty-eight fighters, sixteen light and eighteen dive-bombers, and six torpedo-bombers. In addition the Army Air Force had twenty-one bombers, but none of these was trained to attack moving targets.

Generally, the types of aircraft which faced the coming battle were much inferior in performance to those of the Japanese, with the exception of the PBYs.

The Japanese carrier strike force for Midway was comprised of eighty-four fighters, ninety bombers and ninety-three torpedo-bombers, all of which were highly efficient aircraft flown by battle-hardened and competent pilots.

While the total numbers of aircraft show a superiority on the American side, they were dispersed between the fleet and Midway Island. Furthermore the Japanese Zero fighter was the best carrier-borne fighter in the world at that time and the American Buffalos, Vindicators and Devastators were thoroughly obsolete. The Catalinas were invaluable for reconnaissance and rescue but the Army Air Force detachment had had no training for war at sea.

The orders Admiral Nimitz gave to his commanders were 'to inflict maximum damage on the enemy by employing strong attrition tactics.' He ordered Fletcher and Spruance to take up initial positions to the north-east of Midway, positions dictated by the early warning system provided by signal intelligence.

They were well beyond the search range of Admiral Nagumo's carrier strike force which was advancing under a fortuitous blanket of cloud and, at times, fog. Admiral Nimitz also added '. . . you will be governed by the principle of calculated risk . . . the avoidance of exposure of your force to attack by superior enemy forces without good prospect of inflicting . . . greater damage on the enemy.'

Finally the Midway garrison was reinforced with additional anti-aircraft guns. From Midway, Admiral Nimitz ordered intense air searches by Catalina aircraft to the north-west, west and south-west to a depth of 700 miles.

It was a Midway based PBY which first sighted the opposing forces — in this case the Japanese occupation force, and they were then attacked from Midway but with little success.

The first sighting of Japanese carriers was made at 05.34 on 4 June 1942, again by a Midway based PBY, with the report that 'many planes' were heading for Midway. The Japanese carriers were 200 miles from Fletcher and Spruance and an air strike was prepared. The 'many planes' heading for Midway were 108 Japanese aircraft determined to destroy all opposition from the island, and the Marine Corps fighter squadrons went up to meet them. The Buffalo fighters were outclassed in every way by the Zeros and only eleven out of twenty-six returned, but together with the anti-aircraft fire they did inflict a number of casualties to the air strike. While damage on the island was severe, the runway was still usable and there had been relatively few casualties on the ground. Ten Midway based torpedo-bombers had set off to attack the Japanese carriers as soon as their whereabouts were known. Unescorted by fighters they attacked, but were set upon by Zeros from the Combat Air Patrol before reaching the target and only three badly damaged planes returned.

Admiral Nagumo had reserved ninety-three planes, armed with bombs and torpedoes, for the moment when his search planes found the American carriers. Three search planes had been catapulted from the escorting cruisers and

no word had been received from them. However, Lieutenant Tomonaga, commanding the Midway air strike, informed Nagumo that 'there is need for a second attack wave'. Admiral Nagumo then made a fatal decision.

As the whereabouts of Admiral Fletcher's carriers were unknown he decided at 07.15 on 4 June that his ninety-three aircraft on instant readiness should be struck below and orders were given to replace the torpedoes with bombs for a second strike on Midway Island. At 07.30 came the first report from the search plane from the cruiser *Tone.* This aircraft had delayed its take off for half an hour, due to a fault. That half an hour was to be crucial to the outcome of the battle. The message read 'what appears to be ten enemy surface ships' and gave position, bearing, course and speed. There was no hint of carriers and the work went on below decks. At 08.20 a further message was received: 'The enemy is accompanied by what appears to be a carrier.' Admiral Nagumo was in trouble. He had to cancel the second strike on Midway and immediately began to rearm his aircraft to attack the newly found carrier. But at the same moment his decks had to be kept clear for the returning Midway strike force.

The Battle of Midway opened when a Midway based PBY Catalina sighted a part of the Japanese fleet on 3 June 1942. The following day the carrier force was located, also by a Catalina, flying from Midway.

To add to these problems, sixteen Marine Corps dive-bombers from Midway attacked the fleet and fifteen Army Flying Fortresses bombed from 20,000 feet, but with no results. This was followed by an attack by eleven Vindicators, but again no hits were registered. The unescorted Marine Corps pilots were set upon by Zeros in every attack and ten out of the twenty-seven aircraft were destroyed.

One other incident occurred which was to have a crucial bearing on the events which followed. One of the eleven submarines stationed round Midway to attack any Japanese forces in the area found herself in the centre of the Japanese fleet. USS *Nautilus* fired torpedoes which either missed or did not detonate, and she was heavily depth charged. A destroyer was left behind to continue the hunt.

The first phase of the battle ended in Japan's favour. With the loss of sixty planes, and with his ships intact, Admiral Nagumo had destroyed well over half the Midway based aircraft, and badly damaged the installations. But he was in deep trouble. His decks were crowded with

The Japanese air strike on Midway was met by the Marine Corps pilots in fighter aircraft which were both outnumbered and outclassed by the protecting Zeros. The bombers got through and few of the defending fighters were undamaged.

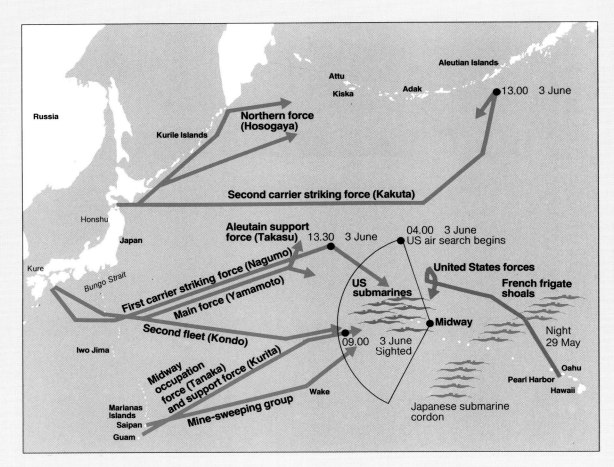

The Japanese forces sailed between 25 and 28 May 1942 (Midway dates).

In an attempt to destroy the air base, together with the defences and installations on Midway, 108 Japanese aircraft attacked at 06.00 on 4 June. Considerable damage was done, but a second strike was called for to complete the mission.

returned aircraft from Midway and these had to be struck down. He had already reversed the decision to remove torpedoes, and mechanics were working feverishly to rearm his ninety-three aircraft for an air strike. He knew there was at least one American carrier near him, that he had been seen and that he would be attacked and his planes were not yet ready to make a counter-attack.

To return to the American Carrier Striking Force. Admiral Spruance originally planned to launch his strike at 09.00 when he would be only 100 miles from the Japanese carriers, but as reports came in of the strike on Midway he decided to launch at 07.00, hoping to catch Admiral Nagumo in the act of recovering his air-craft which had returned from Midway. It was a difficult decision, as his obsolete torpedo planes only had a combat radius of 175 miles.

The second major decision he made was to strike with everything he had, leaving only enough Wildcats for a continuous combat air patrol over his carriers, and a handful of SBD Dauntless for anti-submarine patrols. The launch took longer than intended but by 08.00 twenty Wildcat fighters, sixty-seven Dauntless dive-bombers and twenty-seven Devastator torpedo-bombers were in the air.

Admiral Fletcher in *Yorktown* delayed his launch thinking there might be other carriers at present unknown, but at 08.38 he gave orders to launch half of his dive-bombers (seventeen) and all of his torpedo-bombers (twelve) together with six fighters.

The fourth of June was a cool and cloudless day with maximum visibility, but between the two forces was a weather front with its protecting cloud base. While the American strike was on its way, Admiral Nagumo's carriers with their attendant battleships, cruisers and destroyers steamed towards Midway, lessening the dist-ance for the recovery of their aircraft and making a feverish attempt to prepare for a strike. At 09.05 Admiral Nagumo changed

course, and as a result the thirty-five Dauntless dive-bombers from *Hornet* with escorting Wildcats missed their target and ran out of fuel, some landing at Midway and some ditching. As a consequence they missed the battle entirely. On neither side did the aircraft carry radar, and so they were forced to rely entirely on the last known sighting position of the enemy. One third of Admiral Spruance's strike force was now ineffective.

Japanese air reconnaissance by float planes from the cruiser force failed to find the American carriers. One aircraft mistakenly failed to see and report the carriers when over a part of the American fleet. This resulted in Admiral Nagumo making a fatal decision.

Commander Waldron led *Hornet*'s torpedo-bombers and as they neared their target they entered the weather front. Escorting Wildcats flying above the clouds were watching for Zero fighters and at this critical moment radio contact between the torpedo-bombers and their escort failed. Sighting the Japanese carrier force at eight miles, the torpedo-bombers approached their targets in a shallow dive, but they were spotted by the keen-eyed Zero combat air patrol orbiting above the Japanese fleet, and suddenly they were beset on all sides by Zeros and literally torn to pieces. One by one they splashed into the sea until every single aircraft was destroyed. One torpedo was fired before the last lone aircraft crashed close to a Japanese carrier.

The *Enterprise* torpedo-bombers led by Commander Lindsey fared no better. They too lost their escorts and ten out of the fourteen aircraft were destroyed. Finally at 10.00 *Yorktown*'s Devastators led by Commander Massey and escorted by six Wildcats were set upon. The fighters overpowered the slow, low flying Devastators, which were shot down into the sea by the victorious Zeros. Only two of the ten aircraft returned to the carrier. Thus out of forty-one torpedo planes which comprised the mass torpedo attack only six returned and there were no hits. The attack went in piecemeal and the escorting fighters were detached or overpowered. Disaster faced the American forces because the entire mass torpedo attack had failed utterly.

Providentially for the American forces this was not the end of the story. The SBD Dauntless dive-bombers were approaching their targets. Commander McCluskey leading the *Enterprise* strike arrived at his target area and found nothing, as Admiral Nagumo had altered course. He searched beyond the safe limit of fuel endurance and when on the point of returning to his carrier he saw the Japanese destroyer *Arashi* 19,000 feet below. She had been left behind to attack the submarine *Nautilus*, and failing to sink the submarine was proceeding at speed to rejoin the fleet. McClusky at once realized that the destroyer could be on course to join the Japanese fleet, and made the decision to take his course from her. Within a few minutes he found himself over the fleet with his thirty-seven dive-bombers. Almost simultaneously the seventeen dive-bombers from *Yorktown* reached the target. They had been launched an hour after the others, but had calculated a direct route and the whole force was orbiting the Japanese fleet which was under broken cloud.

The majority of the large and victorious combat air patrol of Japanese Zero fighters had been drawn down to sea level and had smashed the torpedo attack, but in so doing had left their carriers without adequate protection. All eyes were on the unequal slaughter on the horizon, while Admiral Nagumo was completing his preparations for a massive strike on the American forces. Turning into wind, his carriers' decks packed with aircraft flown by the elite of Japan's pilots, he gave the order to launch.

At that very moment the Dauntless dive-bombers struck without warning. Selecting the three carriers which were immediately visible they dived. Within minutes the *Akagi, Kaga* and *Soryu* were ablaze.

Tightly packed aircraft were incinerated on the smashed flight decks and an indescribable and ghastly holocaust followed. It was all over. The torpedo attack, disastrous as it was, had not been in vain because it had removed the fighter protection over the Japanese fleet and diverted attention at a crucial moment. All three Japanese carriers later sank.

Admiral Nagumo transferred his flag from the blazing *Akagi* to the light cruiser *Nagara* and orders were given for his one remaining carrier, *Hiryu* to attack the American carrier force. At the same time Admiral Kondo's powerful forces supporting the Midway occupation force were ordered to the scene and the carriers *Ryujo* and *Junyo*, far to the north covering the Aleutians, were ordered south. Admiral Yamamoto was moving up from the west at high speed and it was hoped that a fleet action could destroy the American task force that night.

At about 12.15 aircraft from the remaining Japanese carrier *Hiryu* were approaching the American task forces, heading directly for *Yorktown*. The combat air patrol destroyed or turned back nine of the eighteen 'Val' dive-bombers and six Zeros, but the rest got through. The escorting cruisers and destroyers accounted for three more, but the remaining eight Japanese dive-bomber pilots bore bravely on. *Yorktown* was hit by three bombs, and seriously damaged. Admiral Fletcher transferred his flag to the cruiser *Astoria*, and the fight to save *Yorktown* went on. By 14.00 the carrier was making 18 knots and recovering and refuelling aircraft. At 14.40 a second attack from *Hiryu* came in. *Yorktown* only had time to launch a further eight Wildcats (all of which were very low on fuel). Ten Japanese torpedo planes and six escorting Zeros attacked at sea level. Commanded by Lieutenant Tomanaga who had led the Midway raid they were the only aircraft available from the whole of the Japanese fleet. An enormous curtain of fire greeted them from an augmented cruiser screen as they again made for *Yorktown*. They came in from four different angles at masthead height, and one by one they fell. Four aircraft were left and at 500 yards they dropped their torpedoes. Immediately after dropping his torpedo, Lieutenant Tomanaga's plane was destroyed by a direct hit. Two torpedoes had crashed into *Yorktown* and she was in a desperate state. The last air attack was over and she was still afloat but unmanageable. Screened by a flotilla of destroyers, every effort was made to counter her list, but she was abandoned before nightfall.

It was known that there was one Japanese carrier left intact and that a strong force was probably closing in on Fletcher and Spruance. Previously *Yorktown* had flown a search mission and found the *Hiryu* with a powerful escort at 14.45. This last remaining carrier was attacked by twenty-four SBD Dauntless dive-bombers for whom an escort of fighters could not be spared. Four direct hits put her out of action and she sank the next morning.

Admiral Yamamoto pressed on at full speed to bring about a night action which would destroy the American carrier force. During the night he realized that if he was unsuccessful, the probable result would be an air strike against him at dawn and he had no air protection. So at 02.55 on 5 June he ordered a general retirement.

Admiral Spruance had decided not to seek further action. He was unaware of the presence of Admiral Yamamoto's battleships but suspected that heavy forces would endeavour to close him for a gun action. He therefore turned eastward for several hours but then reversed course to be within range of Midway should an attack on that island materialize at dawn.

Yorktown was still afloat and next day, 6 June 1942, she was re-boarded. The fires were

smouldering but it was possible to tow her back to Pearl Harbor. Alongside was the destroyer USS *Hammann*. The carrier had already been spotted by a float plane from a Japanese cruiser and Admiral Nagumo sent submarine I-168 to sink her. This boat manoeuvred with great skill through the destroyer screen undetected and fired four torpedoes of which three hit, one smashing into the destroyer *Hammann* amidships and setting off a number of depth charges. The destroyer broke in two with great loss of

life, but the carrier remained afloat throughout the day. However, during the night she took on a heavy list and rolled over and sank at dawn on 7 June.

There had been one final episode in the battle. Admiral Kurita's column of four cruisers and two destroyers were closing Midway for a night bombardment early on 5 June. They were spotted by the US submarine *Tambor* and their position radioed to Admiral Spruance, who

The painting shows torpedo-bombers from USS Hornet *being destroyed at sea level by an overwhelming force of Japanese combat air patrol Zero fighters. At this stage of the battle the United States forces faced a disastrous defeat.*

turned to the south-west to be in a position to intercept them at dawn. However, Admiral Yamamoto had already decided to withdraw the force. While doing so the heavy cruisers

After searching in vain for the Japanese fleet and on the point of returning to their carriers, the United States dive-bomber pilots saw the whole Japanese carrier strike force below. The combat air patrol which should have been above the carriers to protect them were at sea level destroying the American torpedo-bombers. The SBD Dauntless dive-bombers attacked from 15,000 feet just at the moment when the carriers had turned into the wind to fly off deckloads of Japan's most experienced pilots. The fleet carriers Akagi, Kaga and Soryu were enveloped in flames and all were destroyed. It was a major turning point in the whole of the Pacific war.

The abandoned and blackened Yorktown *with destroyer* Hammann *alongside could be seen through the periscope of the Japanese submarine I-168 which cleverly penetrated the destroyer screen* *round the carrier. Three torpedoes hit. As a result* Hammann *sank in four minutes and* Yorktown *sank early the next morning. The Japanese I-168 escaped.*

Meanwhile aircraft from the remaining Japanese carrier Hiryu were flown off to attack the American carrier force. Yorktown was singled out for attack and was badly damaged. A final attack by the last sixteen aircraft from the whole of the Japanese strike force flew in from all quarters disregarding the intense American defensive gunfire. All but four 'Kates' were destroyed, but two torpedoes hit. As a result of the ensuing fires, Yorktown was abandoned — and Hiryu was later sunk by aircraft from USS Enterprise.

Mogami and Mikuma collided and both were damaged. They were left behind with two destroyers. A dawn search on 5 June from Midway found them, and twelve USMC aircraft, all that were on the island, set off to attack them.

Fierce anti-aircraft fire beat them off with losses but they severely damaged Mikuma. Aircraft from Enterprise and Hornet arrived and in a series of attacks Mikuma was left a blazing wreck. The remaining Mogami had a charmed life. Despite six serious hits she survived and escaped, escorted by her two destroyers. Throughout these intense air attacks, the Japanese gunners stuck to their guns and fought back bravely — but nothing could save Mikuma from destruction.

The crucial Battle of Midway was over. The Japanese plan was a complicated one, but provided all had gone as planned, their overwhelming strength had made the outcome and their success seem a certainty. On the other hand the American forces were pitifully small for the dual task of defending Midway and destroying the huge Japanese fleet, and relied on Midway based air reconnaissance to find the Japanese carriers.

Of major importance was the use of signal intelligence, and despite the disastrous American torpedo attack, the little destroyer Arashi guided the dive-bombers, at the limit of their endurance, on to their target where the skies were clear of defending Zeros and a devastating attack could be launched.

Finally it must be said that the decision of Admiral Spruance to withdraw after the battle, and not to seek further confrontation denied the Japanese the chance of a possibly successful night gun action.

The defeat of the Imperial Japanese Navy at the Battle of Midway was a turning point in the war. While many more desperate actions were yet to take place, the Japanese High Command now seemed to go over to the defensive, while America was able to look forward to an enormous build up of naval strength.

During the night of June 5 1942 the Japanese cruisers Mogami and Mikuma collided and were damaged when withdrawing some ninety miles west of Midway. Both were heavily attacked by aircraft on 6 June and Mikuma was sunk after a brave defence. The destroyer Arashi is standing by the stricken cruiser. Mogami and the two screening destroyers were fortunate to escape.

3

The Western Oceans
January 1942 to September 1943

The fight to save the SS Regent Lion *(Bowring Steamship Company)*

The convoys to Russia

The Arctic convoys to Russia will remain collectively and individually a permanent memorial to the courage and heroism of all those — of whatever nation — who sailed or flew in probably the worst physical conditions in which a human being can survive. Between Greenland and Norway lies one of the most turbulent stretches of water in the world. Across it sweep a relentless and cruel succession of north-easterly gales, bearing rain, sleet, hail and snow. When these mingle with the relatively warmer waters of the Gulf Stream which runs north past Bear Island the effect is to add fog to the horror of the cold. Even so, the sea itself rarely exceeds 4 degrees centigrade, and this temperature, combined with a freezing wind, will kill a human being within a very few minutes.

The drift ice which forms the northern boundary of this tempestuous area advances and recedes with the seasons. Spray freezes where it falls and unless this is chipped away, it can add so much weight that a ship becomes in danger of capsizing.

The concealing darkness, which persists for over 100 days in the winter months, made it harder for German aircraft to locate the ships they were searching to destroy or to guide U-boats to the spot, but the long summer days when the sun never sinks out of sight for the whole twenty-four hours, enabled them to attack 'all round the clock' until the exhausted defenders were down to their last round of ammunition.

This chapter tells of the epic struggle to deliver supplies to Russia for a crucial period of three years and seven months, and the efforts made to thwart that attempt. It depicts a struggle where Germany had a strategic advantage by its occupation of Norway; and shows how officers and men of warships, aircraft and merchant ships displayed a courage and a devotion to duty in the face of odds which no words can adequately convey. It was a battle not just between two enemies locked in mortal combat, where bravery was shared between friend and foe, but one waged also against some of the worst natural conditions in the world.

The first of the Arctic convoys to Russia sailed from Reykjavik on 28 September 1941 to Archangel, at a time when the Soviet Union was on the brink of collapse, with the German Army within striking distance of Moscow. It also followed a period when the Royal Navy had sustained crippling losses in the eastern Mediterranean during the evacuation of the Army from Greece and Crete in May. Additionally, the Battle of the Atlantic was being fought relentlessly, all of which meant that Britain had no reserves whatever.

We should remember that the convoys which sailed to Russia were a truly integrated Allied effort. The enormous output of the industrial war machine in the United States was carried in ships which had to overcome the ordeal of the North Atlantic battles before they attempted the even more hazardous run to Murmansk to aid the Russian war effort. In midsummer 1942 more than half the ships making the Arctic passage flew the American flag.

Heavy seas and bitingly cold winds added to the dangers of the convoys to Russia.

In January 1942 the German battleship *Tirpitz* was moved from the Baltic to southern Norway, and the number of U-boats allocated to northern waters was increased to twenty. By the end of February they were joined by the pocket battleship *Admiral Scheer* and the heavy cruiser *Prinz Eugen* which was torpedoed and damaged by the submarine HMS *Trident*.

This meant that the British Commander-in-Chief had to keep heavy units at sea during the passage of all convoys. In March 1942, the *Tirpitz* made an unsuccessful attack on convoy PQ 12 and despite an attack by Albacore aircraft from HMS *Victorious* she returned to her base unscathed. Subsequently at the end of March the heavy cruiser *Admiral Hipper* was sent to northern Norway to join the German squadron.

The outward-bound convoy PQ 13 hit a savage storm which lasted for four days and the convoy was spread over a distance of some 150 miles. As the weather cleared, dive-bombing attacks began, but only two ships were sunk. German destroyers arrived on the scene and sank one ship before being attacked by the cruiser *Trinidad*. One destroyer was sunk but in the mêlée a torpedo fired by the *Trinidad* ran erratically due to the intense cold and made a complete circle to hit the port side of the ship. Badly damaged, she reached Kola escorted by the destroyer *Fury*.

It was a week before this scattered and mauled convoy could be collected together to reach its destination. German destroyers again attacked the returning convoy QP 15, this time sinking the cruiser *Edinburgh*, which had been disabled earlier by a U-boat. They were driven away from the convoy by the other escorts in a long and spirited defence, and had sustained such casualties that in future they did not proceed to sea other than as escorts for German heavy units.

With the near permanent daylight of the summer of 1942 it was the turn of the *Luftwaffe* and the U-boats to concentrate on the convoy route. PQ 16 had a continuous battle throughout the voyage. Five destroyers and five corvettes with five smaller vessels made up the escort led by the destroyer *Ashanti*. This was augmented by four cruisers when in the vicinity of Bear Island as protection against a possible sortie by German surface units. The first attacks began four days later on 25 May, with high level bombing and an attack by torpedo-carrying aircraft. Little damage was done and German losses included one He 111 shot down by a Hurricane catapulted from the deck of *Empire Laurence*.

The next day was unusually calm and sunny though bitingly cold, and saw a resumption of aerial attacks which claimed six ships. The exhausted crews were now running short of ammunition. Help came in the form of low cloud and mist giving some respite before the following day, when the escort again fought off attacks from the air, without losing any further ships, and they arrived at their destination.

The subsequent convoy — PQ 17 — was the most disastrous of them all. Out of thirty-six ships and one tanker which formed the convoy, only eleven reached port. It was still a period of perpetual daylight and politically it was essential to send a large convoy. Intelligence received at the Admiralty made it abundantly clear that German forces were preparing to attack this convoy in a combined offensive using aircraft and U-boats to the west of Bear Island and heavy units to the east of Bear Island.

Distant escorts to guard against attack by German surface units usually accompanied Arctic convoys. Here HMS Sheffield, Duke of York *and* Jamaica *are on patrol.*

To mount an escort sufficient to accompany the convoy throughout its journey, to destroy a German heavy squadron which included a new and fast battleship and to ward off a mass attack by U-boats and the *Luftwaffe* was beyond the resources of the Allies.

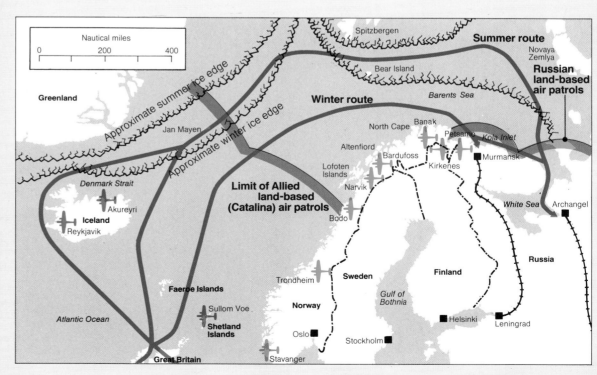

Allied convoys struggled along these routes to keep Russia supplied after the German invasion.

The escort was to consist of a close escort of six destroyers, four corvettes and seven smaller vessels with two ships equipped for anti-aircraft defence together with two submarines. Providentially, two rescue ships were also attached. The convoy sailed on 27 June 1942 and was sighted and shadowed on 1 July. The weather was fine and calm. Meanwhile German heavy units had moved up to Altenfiord and air reconnaissance had shown that their usual berths were empty. It could be surmised that they were at sea making for the convoy. A covering force of cruisers, including two American cruisers, were to be within reach of the convoy as far as Bear Island but not further, since they could not be given adequate protection against U-boats or air attack, and if they were damaged so many miles from home bases it would be difficult to extricate them. The Home Fleet (the battleships *Duke of York,* USS *Washington,* the aircraft carrier *Victorious,* two cruisers and fourteen destroyers) cruised to the north. Finally a strong submarine patrol was positioned round North Cape across the likely route for any German heavy unit which put to sea.

The strong political pressure to resume the Russian convoys was the overall reason for the sailing. Due to lack of escort ships the convoys had been stopped temporarily between May and June because of the desperate need to relieve Malta, but they had to be resumed, and despite the dangers, the convoy sailed. It must be realized that to allow the Home Fleet to accompany the convoy all the way presented acute refuelling problems in addition to a possible fleet action hundreds of miles away from any base, and all the problems of mass air attacks on the fleet. It was a desperate gamble brought about by the political pressure to assist the Russians at a critical time.

Air attacks claimed three ships on 4 July and at the same time there was information that the *Tirpitz* and *Admiral Scheer* had moved up to Altenfiord, and that the German force, possibly augmented by two heavy cruisers and destroyers, could proceed to attack the convoy during the following night in the Barents Sea well to the east. In this case the cruiser and destroyer force would probably be overwhelmed. A decision had to be made, and at 21.00 on 4 July 1942, orders were given for the cruisers and the destroyers of the close escort to withdraw to the westward and for the convoy to scatter. This order to scatter was made in London by Admiral Pound in anticipation that the German fleet would attack. It was made without telling those on the spot whether the intelligence was positive or negative, and the Most Immediate signals gave the commanders the feeling that the German forces were just over the horizon.

In fact the German forces did sail and were sighted and reported by Allied submarines, but when they were informed that the convoy had scattered they returned to port, leaving it to the U-boats and *Luftwaffe* to attack.

SS Rathlin *sailed with Arctic convoys as a rescue ship. In addition to the usual hazards, her ship's company knew that if they did not rescue survivors from the sea within a very few minutes it would be too late. She accompanied sixty convoys during the war and rescued 634 survivors.*

This disastrous Allied decision left the ships with their remaining corvettes and trawlers naked under the overwhelming attacks which followed as they slowly made their way to Archangel, 800 miles distant.

The two rescue ships did valiant work. The *Zaafaran* had been sunk but her crew were saved, and the little *Rathlin* and her consort the *Zamelek* never stopped. Had they too gone down the losses would have been even more horrible as they were crammed with survivors.

Out of thirty-six cargo vessels and one tanker, nine were sunk by U-boats, eight by aircraft and seven by a combination of torpedoes and aircraft. Five ships had turned back earlier due to defects or damage by ice.

In contrast the total cost to the *Luftwaffe* was only six aircraft. They employed 202 aircraft during the action and of the 156,492 tons of supplies loaded, only 57,176 tons arrived, the losses including 430 tanks, 210 aircraft and 3,350 vehicles.

Some 1,300 survivors of sunken ships were landed at Archangel. During the latter part of their ordeal urgent requests for air cover and other help were made to the Russians but in the main fell on deaf ears due in some measure to the lack of long range aircraft in the north.

It was now obvious that it was suicidal to send a further convoy during the period of perpetual daylight, and despite Russian protests the next convoy was delayed. It was vital to supply Malta and some escorts were directed to Operation 'Pedestal' whose story has yet to be told. At the same time an RAF strike force was sent to operate near the Kola Inlet. This move was completed in August, and the next convoy did not sail until the 2 September. Forty ships set out with eighteen destroyers, the cruiser *Scylla,* eight corvettes and trawlers together with two anti-aircraft ships, under the command of Rear-Admiral Burnett. In addition, and for the first time, the escort carrier *Avenger* joined the convoy. The Home Fleet did not sail, but three cruisers gave distant escort. This meant refuelling *en route*. Convoy PQ 18 was located on 12 September but *Avenger*'s air patrols kept the U-boats down, though two ships and one U-boat were lost the next day.

Air attacks began and every effort was made to sink *Avenger*. The main attack came in at 15.30 on 13 September when thirty JU 88s and fifty-five He 111 torpedo-bombers, each carrying two torpedoes, appeared over the horizon. They were flying very low over the sea in a single line about 100 to 150 yards apart and

113

stretching in an arc right round the starboard side of the convoy in perfect formation. It was an awe-inspiring sight. The aircraft lifted as they passed over the outer screen of destroyers, and all the torpedoes were dropped simultaneously at close range. The convoy was threatened by 110 torpedoes racing towards it, the tracks looking like the ever-lengthening teeth of a giant comb. The Commodore executed an emergency turn of 45 degrees to starboard, which would bring the convoy bow on to the approaching torpedoes. Unfortunately, some confusion in two columns meant that they did not effect the manoeuvre and six of the seven ships were sunk. Two more in the centre were also hit and sunk.

The German aircraft were so low that they were unable to rise above the mast height of the merchant ships and weaved in and out of the convoy as they passed through. It was a brilliant attack against the combined fire power of the escort, and only eight aircraft were shot down.

Meanwhile U-boats were trying by every possible means available to them to get at the convoy, but *Avenger*'s aircraft played a vital role at this time. Despite further fierce air attacks the convoy reached port with the total loss of thirteen ships out of the forty which originally started the voyage.

The story of one further convoy, JW 51B, should be told in some detail. It consisted of fourteen ships with an escort of six destroyers and five smaller ships. The cruisers *Sheffield* and *Jamaica* had covered the previous convoy, and now sailed from Kola on 27 December, taking a westerly course, to cover the approaching convoy JW 51B.

The convoy was sighted by a U-boat on 30 December 1942 to the south of Bear Island, and Admiral Kummetz with the German pocket battleship *Lützow* and the heavy cruiser *Admiral Hipper* with six destroyers immediately put to sea. Their orders were to avoid action with equal or superior forces, but to destroy the convoy if at all possible. They were unaware of the presence of the British cruisers.

At 08.30 on 31 December, the destroyer *Obdurate* sighted two German destroyers which opened fire. Captain Sherbrooke in *Onslow* ordered the destroyers *Obedient* and *Orwell* to follow him and closed the German force. This left only the destroyer *Achates* and three smaller escorts with the convoy. They laid smoke around the convoy, which turned away to the south.

Almost at once the British destroyers sighted the German heavy cruiser *Admiral Hipper* which opened fire, and for the next thirty minutes the action continued, with the small destroyers moving in and out of smoke. The visibility was poor with sea and cloud all merging into a uniform grey, and while the sea was relatively calm, the spray which swept over the destroyers as they manoeuvred at more than 20 knots was freezing as it came on board. This made it very difficult to fire the forward guns.

The defence of Arctic convoy JW 51B on 31 December 1942. HMS Onslow *(foreground) following HMS* Orwell, *shielding the convoy from the German heavy cruiser* Admiral Hipper *(distance), the pocket battleship* Lützow *and six destroyers. Five British destroyers defended this convoy until the arrival of the escorting cruisers when the action was broken off.*

While threatening *Admiral Hipper* with torpedoes, Captain Sherbrooke detached *Obedient* and *Obdurate* back to the convoy and continued with *Orwell* to engage the German cruiser. He had no idea whether or not further forces were to the south, and possibly about to attack the convoy.

Admiral Burnett in *Sheffield* had intercepted signals from the escorts and in company with *Jamaica* he turned south-east at full speed. By now the German gunnery had improved and *Onslow* was hit repeatedly and a fire broke out. Captain Sherbrooke was badly wounded and turned over command to *Obedient*.

The damaged *Onslow* now turned to rejoin the convoy and the *Admiral Hipper* disappeared. Meanwhile, *Sheffield* had caught glimpses of the action but could not identify friend from foe. Flashes were seen further to the east but this must have been the unequal action between the *Admiral Hipper* and the minesweeper *Bramble* which had been detached and was overwhelmed and sank with all hands.

The escort commander now received information that a German force was to the south of the convoy. This was *Lützow* and her destroyers closing rapidly. Disaster was avoided by a providential snow storm when the ships were only two miles from the convoy. The German admiral decided to wait for the weather to clear, and *Obedient, Obdurate* and *Orwell* remained with the convoy. At 11.00 the weather cleared and once more the *Lützow* force was sighted, having crossed ahead of the convoy moving north-east. The British destroyers at once engaged while smoke was laid to cover the convoy. *Lützow* opened fire, damaging one merchant ship, but ceased when the smoke became effective.

The *Admiral Hipper* now reappeared from the north and concentrated her fire on the destroyer *Achates*, crippling her and causing many casualties. She then shifted to *Obedient*, putting her wireless out of action. *Obdurate* meanwhile engaged the cruiser which hauled off to avoid being hit by torpedoes.

The situation was critical. Visibility was becoming very poor, made worse by the protective smoke which hung over the scene, and while hiding the convoy, also confused the escort as to the whereabouts of the German force.

On 13 September 1942 Convoy PQ 18 was attacked by eight-five German aircraft with torpedoes and bombs. They came in wing tip to wing tip no more than 50 feet above the sea against the combined fire power of the escorts and the convoy. Six ships were sunk in this action.

At 11.30 the British cruisers arrived on the scene and opened fire at seven miles, quickly obtaining hits. The *Admiral Hipper* turned away making smoke and disappeared at 11.43. Two German destroyers were sighted at a range of only 4,000 yards. One escaped, but the *Frederich Eckholdt* was sunk by the *Sheffield* at point-blank range and with her went nearly all her ship's company.

Throughout this time the damaged *Achates* had continued to make smoke and to protect the convoy. It was not until the action was over, at 13.15, that she called for assistance, but before a rescuing trawler could get to her in the growing darkness of the Arctic winter the gallant little destroyer capsized and sank.

Convoy JW 51B had no further adventures and the ships discharged their precious cargo in Russian ports on 3 January 1943. It was attacked by one pocket battleship, one heavy cruiser and six destroyers, and was defended by five destroyers until the attackers were driven from the area by two six inch cruisers which were then outgunned in this truly memorable action.

The next convoys JW 52 and 53 sent in January and February 1943 were to be the last until November. There were many reasons for this. The number of close escorts and the continual use of the Home Fleet for distant escort duties hampered events taking place elsewhere. The Battle of the Atlantic was approaching a critical stage and in the Mediterranean, as we will see, a

huge escalation of activity was about to begin. There were just not enough ships to cover every aspect of the war at sea, and the Russians sent little assistance to augment the convoys. In view of their desperate need for supplies this is difficult to understand.

However, the German battleship *Tirpitz,* the battlecruiser *Scharnhörst* together with the *Admiral Scheer* were still in northern waters and they could break out into the Atlantic at any time. Some way had to be found to cripple or destroy them. At that time it was not possible for heavily laden bombers to make the return trip, but for some time experiments had gone ahead in the development of midget submarines or X craft. These were 51 feet long, could make

6½ knots on the surface and dive to 300 feet, cruising at 5 knots submerged, with a crew of four. Their weapons were two detachable charges, each containing two tons of explosive to be dropped on the sea bed underneath a warship and detonated on a timed fuse.

It was decided to attack the *Tirpitz* on 22 September 1943. The plan was to tow the X craft behind submarines to within about twenty-five miles of the targets. The escorting submarines would then wait until the attack had taken place and pick up the crews and their X craft for the return journey. On 11 September six submarines with their X craft departed from Scotland. Air reconnaissance pinpointed the German ships and it was decided that three

boats would attack the *Tirpitz*, two would attack the *Scharnhörst* and one would attack the *Admiral Scheer.*

Problems with the tow during the long and tedious passage caused delays, and disaster overtook X9 which had dived and was never seen again, the tow having parted. One other X craft had mechanical troubles and had to be scuttled and her crew picked up. That left four craft which proceeded to the rendezvous.

X10 had to break off her attack due to defects. X5, X6 and X7 were now all directed to the *Tirpitz* in her heavily defended anchorage. X7 led and penetrated the anti-submarine boom, to be followed by X6. Both craft dropped their

charges under the battleship after being spotted and fired upon. The fate of X5 is unknown. In great haste, *Tirpitz* was warped back as far as possible, but four explosions took place and she was damaged. British losses had been heavy and none of the X craft returned home from this dangerous mission. However, the battleship which had caused so many problems to the Royal Navy was immobilized for the following six months.

Atlantic slaughter

Germany and Italy declared war on the United States on 11 December 1941, but as we have seen American warships were operating as convoy escorts in the North Atlantic for some months before this. We now enter a period of appalling losses, with the United States Navy totally unprepared for the massacre which took place on her doorstep. Looking back it seems hardly credible that with all the lessons learned through the bitter fighting in the North Atlantic, and with all the information furnished to our Allies, this catastrophe could have taken place. Admiral Dönitz was ready to switch twelve boats to the east coast of America at once. With his clear vision he saw the opportunity being offered. It was denied to him by Hitler. For him the frustrating fact was that of ninety-one operational boats, twenty-six were in or proceeding to the Mediterranean, six were stationed off Gibraltar, and four in Norwegian waters. Sixty per cent of the remainder were in dockyard hands with a shortage of labour and of the twenty-two boats at sea in the Atlantic half were *en route* to or from their base areas. Thus, unlikely as it may seem, in January 1942 after two and a half years at war, there were not more

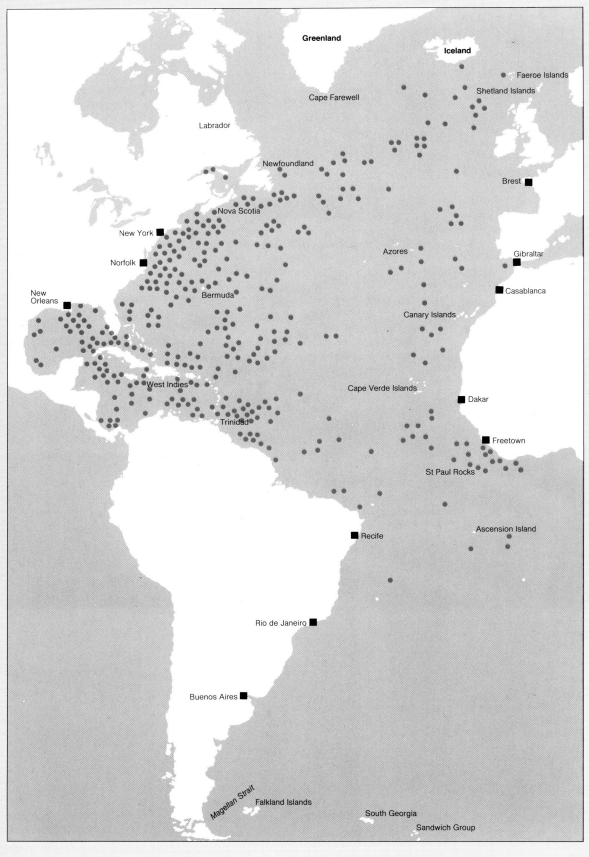

Merchant ships sunk by U-boats in the Atlantic, 7 December 1941 to 31 July 1942.

than ten or twelve boats actively engaged in the battle which could drive Britain to starvation. Admiral Dönitz's plea to concentrate his available force was rejected in favour of the Mediterranean and only five boats sailed to the American east coast. Nevertheless the blow fell with devastating effect.

The eastern seaboard of the United States contained the busiest sea lanes in the world. From the St Lawrence River in the north, down the coast of Nova Scotia and the New England ports, the coastal shipping was continuous. New York and Long Island Sound had no less

than fifty arrivals and departures per day in November 1941. The shipping lane passes south to Cape Hatteras, with important feeders up the Chesapeake and Delaware Bays, to Florida; then from the Florida coast it branches out all over the Caribbean and to the important oil refineries of Texas. Further south lies the continent of South America with the vast oil supplies of Venezuela.

Britain had learned by bitter experience in both World Wars that the convoy system was essential to survival. Up until now America had enjoyed a peacetime economy while her facto-ries and shipyards worked to capacity. That peacetime economy included brilliant illumina-tion of every town along the coast. Miami and its luxurious suburbs put up six miles of neon light glow against which ships were silhouetted. The most striking statistic of losses is shown all too graphically in the map on page 118, but the story must unfold. Such protection as the United States Navy did allocate was pitifully inadequate. The naval air patrols were totally ineffective at the start, and untrained army air-craft were pressed into service, with predictable results. Anti-submarine patrols were conducted by coastguard cutters and converted yachts,

On entering the war America was totally unprepared for the U-boat onslaught off her coasts. There was no convoy system and no effort was made to extinguish lights along the shore. In six months well over one million tons of shipping was lost, much of it almost within sight of land. When at last an interlocking convoy system was introduced these losses almost ceased. A ship sinks outlined against six miles of neon lights from the holiday resort of Miami.

with fourteen armed trawlers on loan from Britain. American destroyers were used in offensive sweeps out to sea with the same lack of results as Britain obtained in 1939. There was no cohesive strategy when the small number of U-boats struck.

Between 12 and 31 January forty-six ships had been sunk in the North Atlantic, forty of which were off the American coast. In February sixty-five ships were sunk in American waters out of a total of seventy-one. March saw eighty-six ships lost in the same area, April sixty-nine, and May 111, to be raised to 121 in June.

Then in July, after the convoy system had been integrated fully, almost total immunity was achieved in areas where previously the sea had been littered with burning and sinking ships.

The U-boats had been able to close to within sight of the shore, surface and pick off the merchant ships one by one, sometimes sinking them by gunfire. Throughout April to June 1942 there were never more than about twelve U-boats on station off the American coast but Admiral Dönitz had despatched two large supply U-boats (milch cows) to the area which greatly extended the period during which U-boats could remain on station. The slaughter went on.

One U-boat commander commented in his log that he could not possibly deal with the ten unescorted ships in sight as he pursued them on the surface in daylight. After the lessons learned on the eastern seaboard had resulted in the formation of a convoy system, Admiral Dönitz switched his forces to the rather more

profitable targets in the Gulf of Mexico for a further period of almost uninterrupted success. Eventually in May an interlocking convoy system began to be introduced. Ships gathered in ports until escorts could be found to take them another stage of their journey and air patrols became more numerous.

The 'happy days' for the U-boats were virtually over except for those in the Caribbean and off the coast of South America.

Admiral Dönitz now shifted some of his U-boat fleet to a position further east.

Seamen clutching any means of buoyancy leap from a burning tanker. The still air is filled with the stench of fuel oil as the flames spread over the sea.

Daylight brings the realization that the survivors are alone in the Atlantic.

The situation of the boats stationed in the Atlantic Ocean in September 1942 was: Twelve boats off the south of Greenland; six off the Azores; six off North-west Africa; five off the Canadian coast; fifteen in the Caribbean; six off Brazil; twenty were on passage and ten new boats were outward bound round the north of Scotland.

U-507 made the great mistake of sinking five Brazilian ships in quick succession. As a result Brazil declared war on Germany. The actual assistance she gave was small, but her huge coastline provided bases for Allied ships and aircraft and was of considerable value. On the Allied side there were some technical advances about to be introduced; in May 1943 the first British Leigh Light, a miniature searchlight, was fitted to bombing aircraft and could illuminate a target as it was homed in on an early form of radar. This resulted in some sinkings, but German U-boats were already equipped with measures to detect the aircraft radar and to dive in time. The major breakthrough was to be in 10 centimetre radar, a British invention (mostly manufactured in the United States). This radar approach system could pinpoint the position of a U-boat with unerring accuracy, and when fitted to aircraft was difficult for U-boats to detect. No surfaced U-boat was safe when air cover was fitted with this device, but by mid 1943 only a few Allied reconnaissance aircraft were so equipped. There were still wide gaps in mid-Atlantic with scant air protection and it was to these gaps that the U-boats moved. On the German side, supply or 'milch cow' U-boats on station at convenient points could increase greatly the operational duration of a patrol. On the Allied side the two vital needs were air cover and better armed, better trained, longer range and faster escorts. German Intelligence still had

the ability to read fragments of Naval Cipher 3, though complete decrypting took too long to be of real use at this time. It was not until May 1943 that a complete change of code stopped this leakage. However British Intelligence services were able to read signals fast enough to enable the Admiralty to re-route convoys away from the concentrations of U-boats. It was a deadly game of cat and mouse.

The passage of American and Canadian troops to Britain posed a problem, for the destruction of a troopship in mid-Atlantic would have been disastrous. Mention must be made of the 'Queens'. Six ships — the *Queen Elizabeth, Queen Mary, Aquitania, Mauretania, Ile de France* and *Nieuw Amsterdam* could all steam at 24 to 28½ knots and sailed independently until met at the Western Approaches. Speed was their main defence, plus the facility to route them away from any known U-boat concentration, though this meant they steamed many hundreds of extra miles on special routes. The Queens could carry up to 15,000 troops per trip and while they caused great anxiety when at sea, and were a calculated risk, they were probably safer than in a slow convoy.

The continuous erosion of shipping in the North Atlantic went on. U-boats attacked with great daring while the escorts fought with the weapons they had. October 1942 was a bad month, which included the passage of convoy SC 107 where fifteen ships were sunk before air escorts could force the attackers to submerge. SL 125 from Sierra Leone was attacked off Madeira and thirteen ships were sunk without damage to a single U-boat.

By early November 1942, Admiral Dönitz disposed his greatly increased Atlantic Ocean U-boats as follows: Forty-two were operating between Greenland and the Azores; sixteen were in the eastern Caribbean and between

Africa and Brazil; seven were off South Africa and six off the central African coast; ten were at that moment attacking SL 125 and twenty-eight were on passage.

By the end of the month no less than twenty-two boats were attacking convoy HX 217, but it had a powerful air escort at the critical moment and only two ships were sunk together with two U-boats. None the less in November 1942 world-wide shipping losses to U-boats reached an all time peak.

Before the end of 1942 came a change of command. Admiral Noble, formerly Commander-in-Chief Western Approaches since February 1941, who had directed the Battle of the Atlantic through a desperately difficult time with courage and great ability, was replaced by Admiral Horton who had directed British home based submarines since 1940. Admiral Horton had been a submariner all his service and brought to the job an unrivalled knowledge of the technical and human problems of submarine warfare. No one knew better the U-boat commander's mind and he was the right man to face Admiral Dönitz in the coming months.

In mid-December Britain had only 300,000 tons of commercial bunker fuel oil and consumption was running at 130,000 tons a month. The Admiralty had another one million tons but it was for exceptional emergency needs only. If it was used, the fleet was immobilized — it was as serious as that. Plans to bring large tanker convoys from the Caribbean area were put in hand, but it was months — critical months — before the position was eased.

Looking back over 1942, Germany's attempt to starve Britain into submission, while not succeeding, did not fall far short. U-boats in all waters had sunk 1,160 ships, more than three per day, and the tonnage was 6,266,215. The other weapons used by Germany had raised this figure to 1,664 ships with the staggering total of 7,790,697 tons. To offset this, over seven million tons of new shipping had been built, thanks mainly to American industry.

The stark fact remains that Allied losses had been accomplished by a considerably smaller fleet of U-boats than Admiral Dönitz had declared was necessary to win the Battle of the Atlantic. Hitler, as ruler of Germany and strategist in chief, had decreed that not all the steel required to build the necessary U-boats would be available, and he had diverted a high proportion of operational U-boats away from the North Atlantic at a crucial moment. The Allies could be thankful that Admiral Dönitz did not have complete freedom.

The Channel dash — February 1942

The German battlecruiser Scharnhörst *(foreground) with* Gneisenau *and the cruiser* Prinz Eugen *break out of Brest in February 1942 and proceed up the English Channel in daylight within sight of the* English coast. They were off Dover before the first attack was mounted, and reached Germany despite all attempts to stop them, though Scharnhörst *was badly damaged by a mine.*

The battlecruisers *Scharnhörst* and *Gneisenau* and the cruiser *Prinz Eugen* were bottled up in Brest. Repeated bombing raids by the RAF against this heavily defended area had caused some damage to the ships and it was essential to move them back to Germany so that they could be available for operations against convoys to Russia. It was vital to the Allies that they did not escape into the Atlantic, for at any moment they could cause havoc to the convoy system. From the German point of view they would be safer in Norway, because the decision had already been made that they would not be used for commerce raiding. The fact that the supply ships had been sunk was a major factor which decided the German High Command to abandon the Atlantic — but this was unknown to the British. It was then decided that the ships should take the Channel route rather than break out round the north of Scotland.

The staff at Bletchley Park had lost the ability to read verbatim the signals passing from the German High Command to U-boats at sea due to the change of ciphers, but from general signal traffic it was evident that a move was to be made, and activity in the Channel pointed to the use of that route. A reconnaissance of the area was maintained but it seems that those who needed to know and had to make the dispositions to ensure that the heavy ships were destroyed, were not informed of even the gist of the information flowing from Ultra. This then became another classic example of priceless information, though highly secret, being frittered away.

For some reason it was assumed that the passage would be made at night but in fact minute planning by the German High Command, covering every mile of this dangerous voyage by day, was undertaken in great secrecy. The German squadron slipped out of Brest at 19.30 on 11 February 1942. The two British submarines *Sealion* and H-34 operating off Brest did not sight the squadron as they had with-

drawn to seaward to surface and recharge their batteries. The squadron headed north and at twelve minutes after midnight had rounded Ushant and set course for the Channel at 27 knots. The night was dark. The RAF Hudson aircraft on patrol had encountered a JU 88 night fighter and after taking avoiding action had lost the use of its radar. It returned to base and it was not until 22.38 that another aircraft was over the area, by which time it was too late and the squadron had gone. The next aircraft covering Ushant had a similar malfunction and the ships passed unnoticed in the dark. The third aircraft covered Le Havre to Boulogne, but as mist was turning to fog it was recalled one hour early. During that hour the German force passed Le Havre unnoticed.

The early recall was not reported. The *Luftwaffe* air cover arrived at 07.20 and at 09.15 ten torpedo boats joined the six destroyers as further escort. The squadron eased down to 11 knots to go through a newly swept channel where mines had been laid the night before. They were now passing Boulogne and more torpedo boats and E-boats joined the escort, making smoke to seaward as by now Admiral Ciliax knew he must have been spotted.

On the British side, unusual activity was noticed and radar stations reported three ships at a range of fifty-six miles. After some delay 825 Naval Air Squadron was alerted and the Swordfish aircraft were armed with torpedoes by 10.45. The weather was rapidly closing in with a rising sea. A strike by Coastal Forces motor torpedo boats (MTBs and MGBs) was ordered immediately and the small force closed the squadron. They then came under fire from the escorts and the attack failed. In the meantime the Swordfish aircraft were circling Manston airfield waiting for a strong fighter escort. By 12.28 only ten aircraft had arrived and the squadron could wait no longer and set off hoping that the six additional squadrons of Spitfires would arrive in time. When only ten miles out from Ramsgate and with twelve miles to go, German fighters attacked. The escorting fighters tried to defend the six Swordfish, but to no avail. The three large German ships were sighted through the smoke screen, but the defensive fire was intense and the torpedo aircraft were overwhelmed. One after another the six Swordfish were shot out of the sky. They had flown towards the German squadron until their planes had literally disintegrated. This gallant attempt was to be repeated four months later by torpedo-bombers at the Battle of Midway.

The story so far is one beset by mechanical fault, confusion and lack of co-ordinated attack, despite many individual acts of gallantry. More confusion was to follow. Twenty-eight Beaufort torpedo aircraft attacked through intense fire from fighters and the German squadron's guns, and scored no torpedo hits, as the weather closed right in. Seventeen were shot down and sixteen German aircraft were destroyed. The German squadron had now passed Ostend. Their good fortune held when they crossed a minefield laid a month previously without damage, but at 14.32 the *Scharnhörst* struck a mine newly dropped by RAF aircraft, and stopped. The rest of the force continued at 27 knots. Fifty minutes later the *Scharnhörst* had rectified the damage and was working up to 25 knots.

From the British side two further attempts were to be made. Six destroyers had been exercising off Harwich and were despatched on an intercepting course, and in the air were 242 aircraft of Bomber Command making for the German squadron. The destroyers were all elderly vessels of World War I vintage whose task was escorting east coast convoys. In order to overtake their adversaries it was necessary to cross the east coast mine barrier. This was accomplished at 28 knots by 14.30. *Walpole* ran a main bearing and had to drop out, but at 15.17 the German squadron was detected on *Campbell*'s radar. No ships were yet visible in the bad light and approaching dusk. The destroyers pressed on, being bombed and strafed in the half light by British and German aircraft alike. Suddenly the squadron was sighted four miles away and the destroyers deployed to attack, while under fire from the combined fire power of both ships and aircraft. The sea was breaking green over the bows and spray flew over the bridges as the little ships plunged into the waves. The destroyers fired their torpedoes amid a hail of shellfire. The *Worcester* was hit continuously and she

stopped. None of the torpedoes found a target as the German ships turned to comb their track.

The battlecruiser *Gneisenau* struck another newly laid mine when north of Vlieland but it did slight damage and she reached port. *Scharnhörst* also struck a mine which was much more serious, though she limped into Wilhelmshaven at 10.00 on 13 February.

The ships had covered some 270 miles of their 550 mile passage before discovery and the 277 bombers which had attacked failed to make even one hit. The sequel to this story is more favourable to the Allies. The *Gneisenau* was placed in dry dock for repair to her mine damage. She was attacked there by the RAF on three successive nights at the end of the month and this time the bombs did severe damage. She was eventually towed to Gdynia where she acted as a harbour defence block ship. The *Prinz Eugen* remained unscathed but was torpedoed *en route* to Norway and put back to Kiel. She took no further active part in operations before the end of the war. The *Scharnhörst* had been badly damaged by mines during the operation and did not reach Norway until February 1943, and in December of that year was sunk at the Battle of North Cape.

We can conclude that despite the air attacks and the surface engagements, it was the mine which was the really lethal weapon in this minutely planned and successful German operation.

Destroyers attack the German squadron without success, due to deteriorating visibility and heavy seas.

The raids on St Nazaire and Dieppe

The raid on St Nazaire on 28 March 1942. Destroyer HMS Campbeltown *has rammed the lock gates and the British commandos are under intense fire as they disembark.*

One hundred and fifty miles south of Brest lies the port of St Nazaire, which contained the only dry dock capable of accepting the German battleship *Tirpitz* for the repair of battle damage if she had entered the Atlantic. Plans were therefore laid for a commando raid to blow up the dock gates and destroy the pumping station. The date was set for 28 March 1942.

The old ex-American destroyer *Campbeltown* was stripped and sufficiently lightened to enable her to proceed up the estuary of the Loire at speed at high water. She was also altered to resemble a German torpedo boat. In her bows were three tons of explosive and she was to hit the lock gates of the dry dock at speed and after a lapse of time blow up and destroy them. At the same time the winding gear which worked the lock gates was to be destroyed.

For this operation, besides the destroyer which also embarked commandos, there were one motor torpedo boat (MTB) and seventeen motor launches (MLs). The force was within two miles of its objective, when, following a series of challenges, the batteries lining the river bank opened fire and floodlit the area with searchlights. As a diversion the RAF were to synchronize with an air raid on the port but there was heavy cloud and therefore the attack did not take place.

Owing to excessive secrecy the RAF crews were completely unaware of the raid. This grave error resulted in the entire defence system of St Nazaire being directed at the small force racing for the lock gates with battle ensigns flying.

The air was filled with coloured tracer and shell splashes as the small force neared their target. Every German gun that could bear was turned on the *Campbeltown* instead of defending the port from a heavy air raid. At 20 knots the destroyer crashed into the centre of the lock, her bows crumpling back for thirty-six feet.

Just astern were the two lines of MLs each going to its allocated task. The commandos were disembarked over the bow of the *Campbeltown* and the hail of fire continued in one long ear-splitting roar in the dazzling light of the searchlights. It seemed impossible that anyone could remain alive.

The demolition teams destroyed the winding gear that opened and closed the gates in a succession of shattering explosions.

On the river Loire the MLs bravely followed the destroyer on the last mile of the run until they came under shattering fire as they attempted to put into their disembarkation points.

Finally the MTB fired her two torpedoes with delayed action charges into the lock gates of the old entrance and prepared to leave.

Other MLs were due to land their troops at the Old Mole with the job of silencing the batteries situated there. The fire was intense and the launches were hit one after another, but a significant number of commandos were landed.

Meanwhile, a fierce battle was taking place in the dockyard. The main objective had been accomplished, the winding gear was smashed and the *Campbeltown* was firmly wedged into the lock gates. The small number of boats still serviceable embarked their survivors and made for the open sea. Out of the 611 men who made up the force and sailed from England, 169 had perished and many more were wounded and taken prisoner.

At 10.00 on 29 March 1942 a tremendous explosion took place. The three tons of high explosive inside the *Campbeltown* had blown up. The object of this daring raid was to destroy the only dry dock that could hold the German battleship *Tirpitz* and the dry dock was now smashed beyond repair.

Further north opposite the south coast of Britain lies the port of Dieppe. In order to gain some experience of an opposed landing in German-held France, the Allies decided to make a reconnaissance in strength. It was to be a frontal assault on the town and a withdrawal.

The plan required complete secrecy, and the objective as shown on the map was to assault the western and eastern outer and inner flanks to capture the coast defence guns. With these in Allied hands the assault on the Dieppe beaches could be effected assisted by 58 'Churchill' tanks. The fleet was to carry over, land and re-embark a total of 4,961 officers and men of the Canadian Army and 1,057 commandos (including a small number of American Rangers), under the command of Major-General Roberts. The command ship was the destroyer *Calpe*.

The assault was postponed once, but was finally scheduled to take place on 19 August. There were two matters of crucial importance. There was to be no pre-assault bombardment by battleship or by heavy bombing, and no airborne troops were to be used. Thus surprise was essential and the attack was to go in at first light. The landing ships arrived ten miles off shore, and by 03.20 had transferred troops into their landing craft. Soon afterwards the eastern assault force ran into an escorted German convoy and a sharp engagement took place, so vital surprise was now lost. Of the twenty-three landing craft in this group only seven reached their allotted beach and landed their troops. On the eastern inner flank it was the same story and as a result the battery was not captured. This seriously affected the assault in the centre, although the western outer batteries were captured successfully.

On the western inner flank the troops landed and proceeded to capture their objectives, but with stiffening German resistance they could not join up with the troops and tanks which should have been coming up from the town. Thus German forces were still in control of the inner defences of the town when the main assault went in. When the destroyers lifted their bombardment the forces coming ashore were overwhelmed by fire from concealed weapons on the cliffs. The tanks landed but none got further than the entrance to the town where they were stopped by road blocks and all were lost. This sealed the fate of the infantry. The reserve battalion was put ashore, and this unit also suffered many casualties. There now came the task of extricating the assault forces from what had to be considered a failure. Despite great gallantry there was shambles on the bullet-swept beaches. The destroyers moved in to give close support from their 4 inch guns — but these were ineffective against the coast defence guns, and only 1,000 troops were rescued. An essential part of the operation was to maintain air cover over the beaches and although this was kept up throughout it was at the cost of 106 aircraft against forty-eight German losses.

The raid was a costly waste of human life. Gallantry alone was not enough — 68 per cent of all Canadian troops were casualties and 23 per cent of the commandos. However, vitally important lessons had been learned and these probably saved thousands of lives when the invasion of France took place two years later.

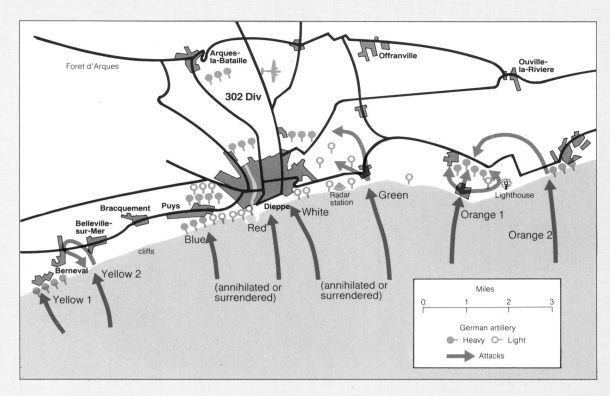

Operation 'Jubilee', 19 August 1942.

The raid on Dieppe in August 1942 took place in daylight and resulted in the Canadian forces suffering dreadful losses. Disabled tanks littered the beaches and casualties mounted in this disastrous operation to test the defences of Occupied Europe. It had been planned as a set piece raid in divisional strength on a fortified town and port, in order to test the German reaction to what would seem to be a full-scale invasion. The lessons learned were many and probably saved many thousands of lives later on but, at the time, it was a costly enterprise.

The Mediterranean

The year 1941 closed with the situation in the Mediterranean being so critical that fears for the continued defence of Malta became acute. In December three human torpedoes carried to the entrance of Alexandria harbour by the Italian submarine *Scire* had penetrated the defences with remarkable courage and then proceeded to drop their charges under the battleships *Valiant* and *Queen Elizabeth*, putting them out of action. Thus at the eastern end for a time there was no battleship in an operational state and the small force of cruisers and destroyers was hard put to support the Army. The only interference to the supply of war materials to the Axis forces was from submarines and such bombers as could be spared from the Desert Air Force. In February three fast merchant ships were sunk from the air before reaching Malta, despite a cruiser escort, and General Rommel's offensive on land forced the Allies to evacuate Benghazi. German U-boats were active and the cruiser *Naiad* was torpedoed by U-565 in March 1942. The little Inshore Squadron operated the only ships available to supply the forward base which was now Tobruk.

A further attempt to send supplies to Malta was undertaken in March 1942 and the hard worked transports with Merchant Navy crews set out, escorted by most of the Mediterranean fleet. The Commander-in-Chief knew that the Italian fleet had sailed to intercept, and what is known as the Second Battle of Sirte took place. Two Italian heavy cruisers and one light cruiser with four destroyers were sighted by Admiral Vian who turned to meet them with his light cruisers making smoke in a rough sea. The Italian cruisers turned away with no damage inflicted on either side, and the British cruisers rejoined the convoy, which had beaten off a heavy air attack. Within minutes a new threat appeared in the form of the Italian battleship *Littorio* and three heavy cruisers approaching from the north-east and working round to head off the convoy. The British cruisers turned to the attack, weaving in and out of the heavy pall of smoke which was drifting in the high wind and obscuring the convoy. A gun action ensued and two British destroyers were disabled by the *Littorio*'s 15 inch guns. The destroyer squadrons now turned to attack. In the rising gale they headed for the Italian battleship and fired torpedoes. None hit, but the Italian squadron turned away to comb the mass spread and broke

The Second Battle of Sirte. British light cruisers attack the Italian fleet under cover of smoke in defence of a convoy to Malta in March 1942.

off the action. The convoy had been saved but next day German aircraft sank two ships, and the remaining two were hit while unloading. Malta had not been sufficiently relieved and great trials and privation were to follow for the civilian and service population of the island. It was obvious that the Navy would not be able to fulfil the triple task of supplying the Army in North Africa and the fortress of Malta and at the same time denying General Rommel access to the supplies he constantly needed from the Italian mainland.

Owing to the continual air raids on Malta, the decision was taken to withdraw the submarine flotilla to Alexandria. They had fought valiantly for two years and had lost no less than half their boats and irreplaceable crews. Owing to the situation in the Atlantic and Arctic it was not possible to send another relief convoy from Britain in May, but the American carrier *Wasp* made two trips to the Mediterranean ferrying Spitfire fighters to the island. A further setback to the operations in the Mediterranean occurred with the loss of four submarines including the famous *Upholder*, while two more submarines were lost to mines. News of an Italian convoy sailing to Benghazi sent the destroyers *Kipling*, *Lively*, *Jackal* and *Jervis* to intercept. They were set upon by German dive-bombers which by extreme accuracy sank first the *Lively*, then *Kipling*, and damaged *Jackal* which later sank. *Jervis* alone was left to take 690 survivors on board and reach the relative safety of Alexandria.

In June a further attempt was made to break the blockade of Malta. Eleven ships with additional escorts from the Indian Ocean set out from Alexandria while six sailed simultaneously from Gibraltar with an escort of Force H, reinforced by units of the Home Fleet. Supplies totalled 43,000 tons and ships were sailing under British, American and Dutch flags. The Gibraltar convoy was attacked from the air during the voyage and four of the six ships were sunk. A heavy attack was made by Italian cruisers after the main covering force had withdrawn on

reaching the Sicilian Narrows. The close escort turned to attack the cruisers and two destroyers were sunk but the Italians were driven off, though mines damaged the remaining supply ships as they entered Malta.

The convoy from Alexandria fared no better. One merchant ship was sunk in air attacks on the first day, and Italian E-boats damaged the cruiser *Newcastle* and the destroyer *Hasty*. The Italian fleet put to sea on 3 December and Malta-based aircraft attacked and disabled the cruiser *Trento* in the evening, while one hit was made on the battleship *Littorio* doing little damage. Due to various causes the eleven merchant ships were reduced to six and with the escorts' anti-aircraft ammunition down to one-third, and under almost continuous daylight air attack, the convoy reversed course and returned to Alexandria. Before reaching the

Damage to Allied naval forces in March and June 1942

Naval forces	From east convoy in March		From east and west convoy in June	
	Sunk	Damaged	Sunk	Damaged
Cruisers	0	3	1	3
A-A cruisers	0	0	0	1
Destroyers	3	2	5	3
Mine-sweepers	0	0	0	2
Submarines	1	0	0	0
Merchant ships which arrived in Malta	3 (all sunk after arrival)	2	0	2

harbour, U-205 sank the cruiser *Hermione* and one destroyer had to be scuttled.

This very serious setback was partly caused by the situation on land in the desert. Aircraft which should have covered the convoy were unavailable due to the loss of forward airfields and the RAF's preoccupation with supporting the Army to relieve the unrelenting pressure of General Rommel's advance. The cost to the Allied naval forces in trying to force through the convoys to Malta in March and June can best be shown by the table on the left extracted from Captain S. Roskill's *The War at Sea* Volume 2.

As a result of the disastrous convoy PQ 17 to Russia, further aid to Russia via Murmansk was suspended during the next few months of the summer. This released warships from the Home Fleet and allowed for one last attempt to relieve

Malta. Meanwhile Tobruk, the British Army's forward base for supplies from the sea, had fallen. This was followed by Sollum with its airfield which now endangered the naval base at Alexandria. As a precautionary measure all non-essential ships were moved south through the Suez Canal to Port Sudan. Supplies to General Rommel's forces were pouring across from the Italian mainland. Admiral Cunningham, who had commanded with such distinction, handed over to Admiral Harwood and proceeded to Washington temporarily to join the Joint Chiefs of Staff.

To Malta itself two more reinforcements of fighter aircraft had been flown off by the carrier *Eagle*. The fast minelayer *Welshman* had made a successful run with a cargo of foodstuffs and the submarine *Unbroken* had returned as advance guard of the famous 10th Flotilla. But none

of this was sufficient to hold Malta without a major re-supply delivery.

The 'Pedestal' convoy upon which Malta's survival depended was to consist of fourteen fast merchant ships including one tanker, the *Ohio*. They left England on 1 August and as they passed the Straits of Gibraltar picked up a massive escort. This included three carriers (and the *Furious* which was to fly off reinforcements to Malta), two battleships, six cruisers, one anti-aircraft cruiser and some twenty-four destroyers. Of these, three cruisers and the anti-aircraft cruiser and twelve destroyers were to go through to Malta under Rear-Admiral Burrough; the whole force being under the command of Vice-Admiral Syfret. Two oilers with their escorts were to be on station in the western Mediterranean and eight submarines were to patrol to the north of the convoy route.

The convoy passed through the Straits of Gibraltar without loss in thick fog on 8 August, and oiling took place as course was set for Malta. Axis submarines were attacked and kept down, but the convoy had been sighted. It was proceeding at 14 knots and air cover from the carriers was driving off reconnaissance planes.

Meanwhile U-73 had sighted the convoy and by skilful handling had managed to close to within 500 yards. The submarine fired four torpedoes all of which hit the carrier *Eagle* which sank in six minutes.

It was a brilliant attack and the convoy had lost 20 per cent of its air cover. U-73 escaped and the convoy proceeded. The carrier *Furious* now flew off the fighters which were to reinforce the garrison in Malta, and all thirty-seven aircraft reached the island. She returned to Gibraltar and embarked a further twenty-three Spitfires which were flown off a week later.

At 20.00 on 11 August a synchronized high and low level assault by German aircraft was broken up and no ships were hit.

First light on 12 August 1942 saw the convoy approaching the main danger area fifty miles north of Bone. Concentrated in this area were a large group of German and Italian submarines. From this point on the heavily defended convoy could expect attention during daylight from every aircraft within range from Sicily and Sardinia. Standing patrols were flown from the carriers on this brilliantly sunny day and all probing aircraft were attacked. A wolf pack of submarines was reported off Bizerta and at 09.00 twenty JU 88s broke through the fighter screen and attacked. They were driven off with the loss of six aircraft.

By midday further Axis bombers were seen on the radar screens, and fighters sent up to intercept this heavily escorted force. It was a cleverly designed attack but no hits were scored.

This raid was followed by thirty-seven JU 88s. They were attacked by the carriers' Martlet and Sea Hurricane aircraft but some got through and the freighter *Deucalion* was hit and badly damaged. She was ordered to try to use the inshore channel through the Tunisian narrows and shoals, while escorted by the destroyer *Bramham*. Finally, as the British pilots were coming in to land, two Italians joined the circuit and in a daring attack on *Victorious* dropped anti-personnel bombs which exploded on the flight deck but caused little damage.

There were now further submarine contacts resulting in the destruction of the Italian *Cobalto* and damage to one escorting destroyer. Throughout the day the Axis forces tried every means they knew to get at the convoy but the escorting destroyers retaliated by plastering each submarine with depth charges.

Later a large build-up of aircraft was taking place twenty miles astern. The original plan was for a massed assault to saturate the fleet's defences. It was to be made by twenty-two torpedo-bombers, fourteen dive-bombers and forty high level bombers all heavily guarded by fighters. In the event, violent avoiding action saved all but the destroyer *Foresight* which was heavily damaged and eventually sank.

The 'Pedestal' convoy to Malta. Brisbane Star *and* Rochester Castle *under attack by German dive-bombers.*

In the midst of the massive defensive fire from the fleet, added to by *Rodney*'s huge 16 inch guns putting up a splash barrage, twelve JU 87 dive-bombers dived from 9,000 feet directly at the carrier *Indomitable*. Regardless of the fighters and the concentrated fire of the carrier's guns, they scored two direct hits and three near misses. *Indomitable* was unable to operate her aircraft for the rest of the action, with heavy loss of life and considerable material destruction.

She was fortunate not to have been lost; meanwhile her fighters had to land on *Victorious*. Up till now the only merchant ship casualty was the *Deucalion* which was still moving slowly towards Malta. At 18.55 Vice-Admiral Syfret turned his covering force to the west, leaving the cruisers *Nigeria, Kenya, Manchester* and the anti-aircraft cruiser *Cairo*, together with eleven destroyers, to escort this vital convoy on the last and most dangerous part of its journey. It had to form into two columns in order to enter the narrow Skerki Channel which lies between Sicily and Tunisia.

All seemed calm, but it was to be a night of disaster. Unknown to the convoy and its close escort, the very narrow deep channel bounded on both sides by sandbars through which the convoy had to pass had been converted into a trap. Five Italian submarines and nineteen motor torpedo boats barred the way.

The submarine *Axum* manoeuvred into a firing position and fired four torpedoes at a cruiser overlapping another cruiser which overlapped a tanker! All four torpedoes hit. It was a brilliant attack. The cruiser *Nigeria*, flagship of Rear-Admiral Burrough, the anti-aircraft cruiser *Cairo* and the tanker *Ohio* were torpedoed, slewing round and causing confusion in the convoy, which took violent avoiding action.

The *Nigeria* assumed a serious list and was obviously out of the battle. As destroyers closed, Admiral Burrough transferred to the destroyer *Ashanti* and the damaged *Nigeria* was despatched back to Gibraltar escorted by two destroyers. The other cruiser settled slowly and after her ship's company had been taken off the *Cairo* was sunk by gunfire. The only tanker in the convoy with vital petrol and oil for Malta was badly hit. She caught fire, but the inrush of water into the 27 feet hole in her side helped to quench the fire which was put out by 20.15.

Vice-Admiral Syfret, on hearing of this attack, detached the cruiser *Charybdis* and the destroyers *Eskimo* and *Somali* in order to reinforce the escort.

As darkness fell a final air attack was made on the convoy, and during the next half hour many ships escaped with near misses. The *Empire Hope* after avoiding no less than eighteen bombs was finally hit and disabled with raging fires. The destroyer *Penn* closed and took off the survivors, but casualties had been very heavy. The *Ohio*, struck again, was now slowly moving in circles. This was rectified and the *Ledbury* was detailed to guide her through the channel. The *Brisbane Star* was hit on the stem but after shoring up the bulkheads this gallant ship set off at 7 knots. She would have no chance of rejoining the convoy and it was decided to steer her close to the Tunisian shore and hope that she was not spotted. It was now the turn of the *Clan Ferguson* to be hit, and with a huge explosion and a sheet of flame she slewed to a halt. Most of her crew escaped, but she was left blazing.

The convoy was now in complete disorder in the darkness but silhouetted against the fire of the *Clan Ferguson*, the destroyers collected the survivors and proceeded as best they could in the direction of Malta. There was one more submarine lying in wait and a torpedo from the *Alagi* hit the cruiser *Kenya* but did not damage her seriously.

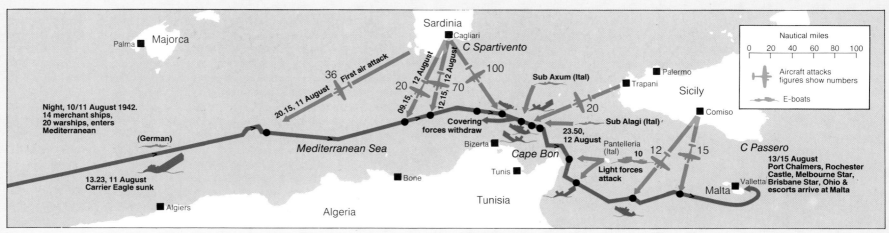

The attacks on the 'Pedestal' convoy in the Mediterranean, 11 to 15 August 1942.

The convoy rounded Cape Bon at 23.50 on 12 August. The leading warship group was followed by the *Glenorchy, Almeria Lykes* (US) and *Wairangi*. A long way behind were the *Melbourne Star, Waimarama, Santa Elisa* (US), *Dorset* and *Rochester Castle*. Astern of these was the *Ohio*, and still further astern the *Port Chalmers*. As we have seen, the *Brisbane Star* was picking her own route close in to the Tunisian coast.

At that moment the Italian MTBs struck — but they attacked the main naval strength ahead of the convoy. A violent action took place with tracer, torpedoes and the heavier armament all being fired at once. No warship was hit and no MTB was sunk. Pulling away from this very hot reception they slid back along the line where they soon found the isolated convoy weakly protected. While avoiding action was being taken, two Italian boats which had been lying stopped ahead of the warships suddenly emerged and moved in bravely and torpedoed the cruiser *Manchester* in the engine room. She came to a stop and the ships following behind in the darkness narrowly avoided collision with the stationary cruiser. The MTBs now turned their attention to the convoy. The *Rochester Castle* was hit, blowing a hole twenty feet long in her number two hold. Although damaged by near misses in an earlier air raid, the ship's company managed to keep her afloat though down by the head. Not so fortunate was the *Glenorchy*. Illuminated by a searchlight, possibly from the shore, she was torpedoed and began to sink and her crew were forced to abandon ship. Meanwhile despite every effort it was obvious that the cruiser *Manchester* would not get back to Gibraltar and her crew took to the boats. Some were picked up by a destroyer next day but many were interned by the French.

The night was not yet over. The convoy, strung out and feeling thoroughly lost and unprotected, was subjected to another MTB attack. First to be hit was the *Wairangi*, and she had to be abandoned. Then came the turn of the *Almeria Lykes*, an American freighter. Her cargo contained ammunition which mercifully did not explode, but the ship did not get under way again and sank during the following day.

At 04.48 the other American ship the *Santa Elisa* was the next to go. The first attack on her was driven off but then an MTB scored a hit at point-blank range. Her cargo included aviation fuel and this ignited in a roaring explosion. At last came the dawn after a night of disaster. The Italian MTBs had caused chaos and had been handled with courage and daring.

Throughout the night the crippled *Ohio* with the destroyer *Ledbury* as escort was making valiant efforts to remain in one piece and to catch up with the convoy.

A force of Italian cruisers had put to sea earlier and it was thought that a gun action was to be fought at first light. Providentially for this convoy no such action occurred. They were intercepted by the British submarine *Unbroken* and two cruisers were torpedoed. Though they reached harbour, neither ship was repaired, and *Unbroken* returned to Malta after a heavy depth charge attack. The remains of the convoy were scattered: the *Santa Elisa* was still afloat with the destroyer *Bramham* standing by.

HMS Ledbury *rescuing survivors in the intense heat following the destruction of the* Waimarama *which was bombed and blew up.*

The *Port Chalmers* was coming up from astern with the destroyer *Penn* while the *Ledbury* was with the *Ohio* some five miles further astern of the main body which comprised the *Melbourne Star*, *Waimarama* and *Rochester Castle*. Meanwhile the *Dorset* had become detached. She was now eighty-four miles from her goal and decided to make a dash for it alone.

The first air attack was on the abandoned *Santa Elisa* and the next covered the *Ohio* with near misses. Next came the turn of the *Waimarama*. She was hit and ignited in a blast which swept the mutilated vessel from bow to stern and spread in a roaring sheet of flame as the ship disintegrated. The *Melbourne Star* was immediately behind and, unable to take avoiding action, sailed through the blistering heat which ignited her ship's boats and blistered her paintwork, but she survived.

The destroyer *Ledbury* sailed four times into the sea of flames while her ship's boats moved around the edge of the carnage. Finally *Ledbury* withdrew, having managed to pick up some forty-four survivors.

In a final effort to deny the vital supplies to Malta, one Axis assault merged into the next, the Stukas coming in from all angles to be met by the combined fire power of the depleted escorts and the Malta based fighters which were now arriving on the scene. One German aircraft crashed on *Ohio*'s deck, but did not blow up. The only other casualty was the *Dorset* which was set on fire.

The survivors were now nearing Malta, and under the protection of the Malta Escort Force. The *Port Chalmers*, *Rochester Castle* and *Melbourne Star* entered the harbour, while the

weary escort hauled round to the west and headed for Gibraltar. The destroyers *Penn* and *Ledbury* were shepherding the *Ohio* while the *Bramham* closed the *Dorset*, taking off the crew and withstanding a very heavy bombing attack. She had been hit almost within sight of Malta. *Bramham* then joined in the struggle to save the *Ohio*. Bombed from every angle and sinking lower and lower the *Ohio* was slowly nosed into Malta with a destroyer lashed to each side. She was finally beached in Grand Harbour, and her precious oil pumped ashore.

Brisbane Star, having survived everything that could be thrown at her, also arrived in the harbour. The *Deucalion* had struggled along the Tunisian coast but in the gathering dusk of 12 August had been bombed and later sank. Out of fourteen ships which had started from England only five remained. But it was enough

The 'Pedestal' convoy to Malta has been told in detail as an example of the problems in the Mediterranean, and although it saved the island, the position of the British 8th Army on land in North Africa was again critical. As an attempt to relieve pressure on the Army, a raid on Tobruk from the sea was planned. It was a failure resulting in the loss of the anti-aircraft cruiser *Coventry*, and the destroyers *Sikh* and *Zulu* together with six coastal craft, and a high proportion of the Royal Marines who made up the attacking force.

However, the long awaited British offensive took place on 24 October at the Battle of Alamein. British forces broke through the German lines and forced them to retreat to the west. Meanwhile the largest and most heavily protected convoy of the war so far sailed from Britain at the end of October bound for Oran and Algiers on the coast of North Africa. The Royal Navy was responsible for its safety. A further large convoy sailed direct from America for a simultaneous landing at Casablanca on the Moroccan coast. This was an all-American force and was escorted by the United States Navy. Together they comprised the 1st Army and the objective was to drive eastwards to meet the advancing 8th Army and so defeat General Rommel's forces. Air cover and support for the landings at Oran and Algiers was to be British and for those at Casablanca, American, while the whole naval operation was under the command of Admiral Cunningham. The code word for this major invasion was 'Torch'.

The scale of the invasion was unprecedented and explains some of the reasons why the Pacific was relegated to second place during the critical months of Guadalcanal. The warships needed for a massive escort and support resulted in cutting Atlantic convoy escorts to a minimum, halting the Russian convoys and also those to the South Atlantic.

It was a logistical test unsurpassed, and the danger of the secret leaking out with an inevitable concentration of U-boat packs was immense. The Signals Intelligence staff in their different locations monitored German traffic and the negative information they gave was of great value. Fortunately for the Allies, the U-boats in the vicinity of Gibraltar had been attracted to a Sierra Leone convoy and the invasion armada arrived without significant loss.

The whole operation depended on avoiding congestion in the Straits of Gibraltar and the 154 combat-loaded ships had to pass the Rock at exactly the right moment and at night. The American convoys comprising 136 ships headed for Casablanca, and proceeded direct to their destination on the Atlantic-facing shore.

As it turned out the landing at Algiers on November 8 was punctual and little opposition was encountered. By 06.40 without a preliminary bombardment the main airfield had been captured; by 09.00 RAF fighters from Gibraltar were using it to patrol over the beaches.

The boom at the entrance to the port was rammed by the destroyers *Broke* and *Malcolm*. Both were badly damaged but managed to disembark their American assault troops. The *Broke* was lost, but Algiers was captured by the end of the day.

In order to prevent the destruction of the port of Oran, a frontal assault was made by two British ex-American coastguard cutters, the *Walney* and *Hartland*, with American troops embarked to capture key positions. By now the port had been alerted and both ships came under heavy fire, very few surviving from the troops embarked and the ships' companies. French destroyers sortied to attack the merchant ships and two were sunk by the light cruiser *Aurora*, the third returning to the harbour where she was scuttled. Although fierce fighting continued ashore for a time, there was little interference from the sea.

The third landing of Operation 'Torch' was the American expedition to Casablanca. It had sailed from America on 24 October consisting of some sixty warships and forty transports and tankers in the first wave. The plan was to land at three points north and south of Casablanca.

The southern force was to capture the port of Safi using two old destroyers with some 400 troops embarked to seize the port facilities, while the covering forces silenced the coastal batteries on either side of the port. With very little difficulty Safi was taken and the Sherman tanks were off-loaded.

The 'Torch' convoy in October 1942. The largest convoy to leave Britain, bound for the invasion of North Africa.

The gallant Ohio *which carried a cargo of oil was essential to the continuing defence of Malta. She had been torpedoed, set on fire and bombed. A crashed German dive-bomber littered her decks and she was slowly sinking as she was brought into Malta with one destroyer lashed alongside. Although her decks were awash the oil was pumped out into the island's empty tanks.*

— Malta was saved — although the loss was extremely heavy. Out of forty-five escorting warships the carrier *Eagle*, the cruisers *Nigeria*, *Manchester* and *Cairo* together with the destroyer *Foresight* were sunk. Moreover, one carrier, two cruisers and three destroyers were all put out of action for some considerable time. Those were the material losses but the loss of life was grievous.

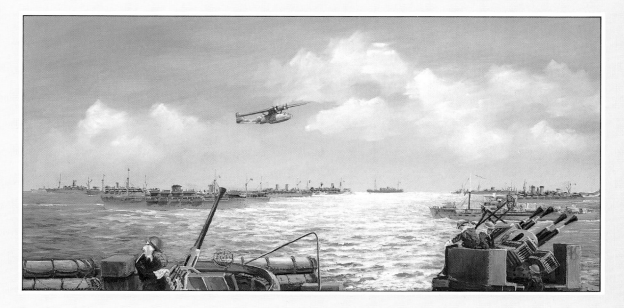

Salerno beachhead 9 September 1943. The British landings took place on the far shores to the left of the painting and American forces to the right of the painting.

The crucial centre force, which was just north of Casablanca, encountered heavy surf and nearly half the landing craft were wrecked, but most of the assault troops managed to get ashore with little resistance before daylight. Then French aircraft, ships and shore batteries attacked the transport area. One French cruiser and seven destroyers sortied out against the overwhelming covering force and all but one destroyer was sunk. Six French submarines attacked but their torpedoes were avoided and they lost half their number. The 16 inch shells of the battleship *Massachusetts* put the French battleship *Jean Bart* out of action and did much damage in the port. By nightfall despite losses in the surf the position was taken.

The northern attack force encountered many problems. As a result the area was not seized finally for three days — at which time all resistance ceased.

It is a sad story. German troops now occupied France and the whole country was enslaved. The Allied assault in Operation 'Torch' was the beginning of a long struggle to eject Hitler's armies and yet French sailors, soldiers and airmen fought the very people who were to liberate France. They obeyed their commander, Admiral Darlan and fought in each of the assault areas with gallantry, only laying down their arms on his orders.

The German reaction, for they had been taken completely by surprise, was to withdraw all U-boats from the North Atlantic and attempt a mass attack on the armada of ships off shore. However, the anti-submarine defences had sufficient warning to be able to deal with them, and for the loss of a few supply ships the U-boats were driven off with losses, but despite the anti-submarine measures, U-boats and Italian submarines did continue to harass the fleet of supply ships and their escorts. A number of valuable ships were sunk, but against this fourteen German and Italian boats were also sunk, a loss too high to be acceptable to Admiral Dönitz, and the pressure eased.

Yet another French tragedy occurred in November, when German troops entered unoccupied France and the French Admiral de Laborde commanding at Toulon refused to sail the French fleet to North Africa. Instead on 27 November it was scuttled to avoid falling into Axis hands. Those splendid ships with their highly trained crews could have been the rallying spearhead for France to fight back at a time when their presence with the Allies would have been invaluable. But it was not to be.

For the Allies the war at sea as well as on land continued to be assisted by the British use of Ultra. Decrypted Italian signals were sent to the commanders in time for operational use and Allied submarines were back in Malta. Together with other naval and air forces they created havoc among Axis convoys vainly trying to supply their beleaguered forces.

As the German Army was squeezed in by the Allied forces advancing from both the east and west, orders for their evacuation were given. A Royal Naval operation was now mounted to ensure that the rescue of Axis forces in a Dunkirk type operation was thwarted. Vigorous patrolling in the air and swift night actions at sea forced the vast majority to capitulate when hostilities in the desert ended on 13 May 1943. The Mediterranean was now open to Allied shipping, although German U-boats continued to operate with the same tenacity, but their numbers were decreasing.

None the less it was essential to keep up the momentum and the next stage of operations was the invasion of Sicily. As a prelude the island of Pantelleria was captured after a heavy air and sea bombardment — which destroyed its airfields and also caused great damage on the ground.

The capture of the island of Sicily was to be a large and complicated operation. Put simply, it was planned to assault the south and southeastern corner of the island and to capture the adjacent airfields. Troops were to come from the Middle East Command and from the United Kingdom and the United States and it was to be a fully co-ordinated Allied invasion. The air strength was to consist of some 4,000 Allied aircraft whose role was to obtain control of the skies and then to support the land forces by bombing. The Royal Navy Task Force commanded by Admiral Ramsay supported the British invasion forces while Admiral Hewitt USN commanded the American Task Force. The complicated logistical problems are outside the scope of this narrative but the naval forces from battleships to troop carrying transport, landing craft and escort vessels, numbered 1,614 British and 945 American ships. They were to transport and to cover the landing of 115,000 British and Commonwealth and 66,000 American troops — all of whom were destined to land on a small stretch of coastline.

The assault began with airborne landings before daylight on 10 July 1943, without an initial bombardment. Before nightfall British troops had entered Syracuse. The seaborne landings had been effected despite a heavy swell and difficult sea conditions on the beaches. Resistance had been slight. On the American beaches the surf was a serious obstacle but by nightfall the troops had reached their initial objectives.

From D-Day onwards the guns of the Allied fleets were on call to support the Army inland. Attacks by Axis submarines were driven off and no less than eleven were sunk in the first week and in the next three weeks a further three German and nine Italian submarines were lost. The Axis air force caused far more dislocation and heavy fighting in the air followed.

On 25 July Mussolini fell from power and was taken into custody, being replaced by Marshal Badoglio. Sicily was now almost completely in Allied hands, but German forces escaped across the narrow Straits of Messina, taking with them much of their equipment and many of their tanks and guns. The Straits themselves were heavily defended and so the Allies found

that it was impossible to prevent this very well executed withdrawal.

It was now essential for the Allies to maintain pressure on the Italian mainland. Landings were to be made across the Straits of Messina early in September while a full-scale assault was to take place further up the coast in the Gulf of Salerno, which afforded the only suitable landing area. There were two drawbacks to this: the narrowness of the beachhead precluded a fast build-up, and the *Luftwaffe* had 700 aircraft in the area. However, it had the advantage of cutting off all German forces in the 'toe' of Italy and was only 180 miles south of Rome.

As a preliminary, the British 8th Army had to be ferried across the Straits of Messina from Sicily into Italy and the same assault craft were needed for the attack on Salerno. The timing and smoothness of the operation were vital. Heavy bombardment of German shore batteries was undertaken by four battleships,. three monitors and a cruiser and destroyer force. The landings were unopposed and the 8th Army with its supplies moved up the coast to join up with the Salerno landings, while the port of Taranto was captured intact both by airborne assault and by troops being landed from five cruisers and a minelayer. The assault on the Salerno beaches took place on 9 September, the Commandos and US Rangers racing inland to capture the heights overlooking the beachhead. This was partially successful but German reinforcements managed to get through and oppose the principal landings.

At a time when the assault forces were positioning themselves for the attack — news came of Italy's surrender. German reaction was swift and the Italian battleship *Roma* was sunk by an FX 1400 guided bomb. The terms of the Italian

surrender decreed that the Italian fleet should proceed to Malta.For three years, the Royal Navy had fought in the Mediterranean without sufficient air cover, and at the same time it had assisted the forces fighting on land. It had sustained grievous losses against a numerically superior adversary and all the participants had suffered the horrors that accompany action at sea. Germany's junior partner now sued for peace. If it had not been for the actions of a dictator seeking power when Britain's fortunes were at the lowest ebb and joining forces in what he believed would be a short war with easy pickings, much misery to the people of Italy and Great Britain would have been avoided.

Back at Salerno, the British had landed at six points on the northern sector and by nightfall had forced their way against stiff opposition to form a bridgehead, but the vital airfield at Montecorvino had not been taken. Their successful assault was greatly assisted by the guns of destroyers which closed the beaches and responded to calls for support from the troops ashore. The American assault on four beaches to the south encountered stronger opposition with the added danger of unswept mines. They had a more difficult time and while a bridgehead was secured the position was still precarious with a gap of five miles between the British and American forces.

Down this gap came a determined thrust of German armour and infantry supported by heavy artillery. It was a moment of crisis. Had the attacking force reached the sea the whole invasion could well have ended in disaster. The Allied navies responded at once. Fresh troops were embarked from North Africa in cruisers and transported at speed to stiffen the beachheads, while cruisers and destroyers closed the shore and at point-blank range fired throughout the day at German concentrations, and in some cases at individual tanks.

The Allied air forces flew over 1,900 sorties in one day and gradually forced the German advance to falter. At one time *Warspite* closed to within a mile of the shore and her guns gave much needed support. On withdrawing she was hit by an FX 1400 bomb and was badly damaged, needing to be towed to Malta.

The appearance of this dangerous new weapon — the wireless-controlled (FX 1400) bomb — caused severe problems. They were released from aircraft at some 18,000 feet and were guided to their targets. In the packed anchorages it was impossible to avoid them and three cruisers were badly disabled. However, the immediate crisis was over and the naval intervention together with the continuous assault from the air played a decisive part, for on 14 September, General Montgomery's 8th Army joined up with the American beachhead, and Salerno was secured.

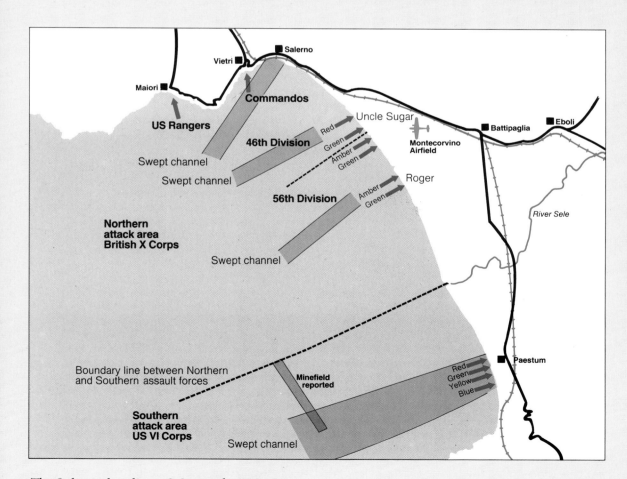

The Salerno landings, 9 September 1943.

The critical convoy battles in the North Atlantic

While the Allies were putting pressure on Germany in the Mediterranean, there was no let up in the battle in the Atlantic. At the end of 1942 food and the raw materials for the war effort were at a critically low level. Above all, oil stocks were below the minimum needed for safety. The new year opened with tempestuous weather and the number of sinkings declined. The problem facing the escort was to keep its convoy together in the wild expanse of ocean, and for the Admiralty to route the convoys away from known concentrations of U-boats. Ships which could not keep up and were forced out of station were an easy prey for attack and could easily disappear without trace.

In Germany there had been a change of command. Admiral Raeder had resigned from his position as Commander-in-Chief and was replaced by Admiral Dönitz. Admiral Raeder had been Commander-in-Chief since 1935, and before that Chief of Naval Staff for seven years. A dedicated naval officer and highly respected leader, he had produced a powerful and effective navy and had served his country well. What he had been unable to do was to stand up to Hitler's erratic and dogmatic opinions. He had tried to obtain the necessary allocation of steel to build a U-boat fleet which would win the Battle of the Atlantic and to acquire the long range aircraft essential to that end — but without success. Admiral Dönitz now stepped in and was given much of the priority he needed for his U-boats, but not the aircraft he so badly required. He obtained some respite for the heavy units which Hitler wished to decommission, but the release of trained seamen and a

crash construction programme meant that, given time, he could fling into the battles an unprecedented number of new boats.

At sea the battle of the convoy routes was to be won by the side that could hold on longest and could endure the relentless pressure of hunting their enemies above and below the Atlantic Ocean. It depended on the stamina of the crews of the Allied merchant navies who were powerless to take avoiding action as they kept station in ships which they knew would explode or burst into flames if torpedoed. It depended on the training and ingenuity of the escorts to remain at sea for long periods, only putting into port for more oil, depth charges and provisions and to effect emergency repairs. They then proceeded to sea again to meet and escort another convoy. It depended on the ability of new and untried U-boat crews to face the hazards of ever-increasing countermeasures and the strong possibility of death below the surface of the ocean. It depended on morale and it was above all a battle between men.

At home in Britain and Germany the crucial battle of Naval Intelligence went on. While the German *xB-Dienst* could read a high proportion of convoy routing signals, the time taken rendered the work mostly operationally ineffective. On the other hand the British at Bletchley Park were again capable of reading U-boat signals, and acting upon them. Taken with the ability to pinpoint the position of a U-boat by Direction Finding while making a transmission, this enabled the Submarine Tracking Room to re-route convoys. This was more difficult as

they had to avoid an increasing number of patrol lines strung out across the Atlantic.

In regard to armaments, 10 centimetre radar which could detect a surfaced U-boat at four miles had been fitted to an increasing number of escorts since its inception in May 1941. Depth charges in patterns of up to twenty could reach 500 feet before exploding and Hedgehog bombs which detonated on impact with a U-boat hull were a new and deadly weapon. Escorts could now be refuelled at sea from specially equipped tankers which meant that they could stay with convoys right across the Atlantic, and rescue ships freed the escorts from stopping to pick up survivors.

Against this, U-boats could remain at sea for longer periods when supply boats were available — U-460 and U-462 replenished no less than twenty-seven boats between 21 February and 5 March 1943, and they could dive to much greater depths and so avoid the depth charges. While the near hurricane force storms in the Atlantic in early January saw a decrease in sinkings, storm damage to ships was serious. Losses from 'marine causes' rose so high as to be second only to those caused by U-boats. The commodore's ship of one convoy capsized and was lost with all hands. But in the calmer waters further south a convoy of tankers coming from the Caribbean was all but destroyed by U-boats. Only two of the nine tankers reached port.

By the end of January 1943, Admiral Dönitz had increased the number of boats in the North Atlantic. A major clash was imminent. Early in February, slow convoy SC 118 of sixty-three ships and ten escorts was found and attacked by no less than twenty U-boats. A furious battle spread over the ocean from 4 to 9 February and thirteen ships were lost for the loss of three U-boats sunk and two damaged.

Then on 10 March the change in German weather codes was introduced which threw the decrypting process at Bletchley Park into confusion. It seemed as though Britain was faced with another complete blackout of the vital information from Ultra. It was now much more difficult to make assumptions upon which re-routing of convoys took place, and there followed some of the biggest and most disastrous convoy battles to face the Allies.

Convoy SC 121 had every form of foul weather on its journey. A gale with towering seas and a driving blizzard of snow scattered the convoy and was followed by fog which made reassembly slow and difficult. Seventeen U-boats had followed the convoy doggedly, showing courage and seamanship of the highest order. Some fell on the stragglers and others got through the disorganized defence. Thirteen ships were sunk without loss to the U-boats. Further south, and missing the gale, another convoy fought off attacks with the loss of only four ships and with two U-boats rammed and sunk by the escorts, one of which was torpedoed. These convoys were followed by HX 229 and SC 122. On 16 March HX 229, composed of forty ships, was attacked and in three days twelve ships were sunk. SC 122, a slow convoy, was 120 miles ahead and gradually the two convoys closed, forming a mass of shipping. Thirty-three U-boats were ordered to the area and in the ensuing three days a total of twenty-one ships of no less than 141,000 tons were lost from both convoys. Air cover was spasmodic and no rescue ships were in the area. This made for agonizing decisions by the escorts when the attack developed, with the bitter choice of staying behind to rescue survivors or keeping up with the convoy. There occurred a single act of cold courage which is recorded in the painting on the next page, but it is by no means unique and only highlights one small part of the Battle of the Atlantic. The SS *Tekoa* had seen five ships torpedoed nearby and no one had stopped. The master (Captain Hocken) stopped his ship and commenced rescuing survivors from the *Irene du Pont*, the blazing tanker *Southern Princess* and the *Nariva*. Lit up by flames, the work of rescue went on while no less than five U-boats passed by on the surface. Six torpedoes were fired and some hit the already sinking ships, but providentially none hit the *Tekoa* although their tracks could be clearly seen. Four hours later she had picked up 146 oil-covered survivors and made her way under escort to rejoin the convoy.

This disaster was followed by bad weather in the Atlantic, but the next convoy SC 123 was escorted by the American escort carrier *Bogue*. The long awaited arrival of these invaluable ships coincided with the start of the use of support groups. These additions to the escorts were highly trained units composed of sloops of the Black Swan class or of faster destroyers released from the Home Fleet or Western Approaches Command. They kept together and worked together and were commanded by men of outstanding ability. By decrypting Ultra signals these groups could be sent to augment convoy escorts as and when required and usually their job was not that of close escort but to hunt U-boats in the vicinity. Working in conjunction with escort carriers they were lethal to the U-boats. At the end of March five groups were operating in the North Atlantic in conjunction with another two escort carriers, one American and the other British.

But March had been a disastrous month. At the end of the month the U-boat strength was distributed as follows:

400 U-boats were in service. An additional 47 were fitting out, and 245 were building.

Of the 400 boats in service about 50 were training boats, 118 were working up, 7 were experimental and 225 (55 per cent) were front line boats.

Of the 225 front line boats 21 were in the Arctic, 22 were in the Mediterranean and 182 were in the Atlantic.

Of the 182 in the Atlantic, 114 were at sea and 68 were in harbour.

Of the 114 at sea 44 were on passage to or from operational areas.

Of the 70 in operational areas 58 were in the North Atlantic, 5 were in the Western Atlantic and 7 were in the South Atlantic.

In the first ten days of March 1943 forty-one ships were lost in all waters, and in the second ten days, fifty-four. More than half a million tons were sunk during those twenty days, two-thirds of them being destroyed in the Atlantic. At the time it was obvious that two or three months of sinkings at this rate would end in an Allied collapse, and at the end of the year the Admiralty recorded that 'the Germans never came so near to disrupting communication between the New World and the Old as in the first twenty days of March 1943.'

However, to look more closely at these statistics reveals that on the critical US/UK route, of the fifty-one ships sunk, twenty-seven were sunk proceeding independently or straggling from the convoy, and only twenty-four were sunk in convoy. During this period, nine U-boats were sunk in this area. This gives a clue to the change of fortune three months later. Provided a convoy could be kept together and the escort be accompanied by one or more support groups and an escort carrier, the protection of the convoy would be far more assured, and the chance of attack or even survival by the U-boat far more problematical. But it can only be considered remarkable that within three months of this disastrous time for the Allies, the tables were turned, the crisis was over and Admiral Dönitz had accepted the fact that he could not win the Battle of the Atlantic. This change of fortune occurred because a number of independent factors coincided to present the Allies with the means to combat the U-boat. Apart from the courage of the seamen and the airmen it was the advent of the support groups, the escort carriers and the long range aircraft which turned the tide — and this was despite the equal courage with which the crews of U-boats continued to press home their attacks — resulting in the destruction of so many of them. Finally there was Ultra.

But firstly the support groups. To spare ships from close escort to form hunting groups was a slow process, and time was taken to withdraw them from operational areas for training. The decision to do so at a time of great anxiety required considerable and far-sighted moral courage on the part of Western Approaches Command. It paid off. Ships' companies and their commanding officers knew exactly what was expected of them in all eventualities and when they went to sea they did so with confidence in themselves and in each other. Ten centimetre radar, Direction Finding equipment, TBS (talk between ships) radio-telephone equipment, deeper exploding depth charges as well as the new Hedgehog (ahead-throwing weapons) gave them an ascendancy over the U-boats whenever they met them.

The escort carriers had taken time to develop. At first they were converted cargo or tanker merchant ships stripped of all upper works and with a wooden platform as a flight deck. Carrying no more than a handful of aircraft, they none the less provided air escort throughout the day, flying patrols around the convoy and over the horizon to pinpoint a U-boat and force it to dive and to stay below the surface. A few were armed with rockets and these gave the U-boat little chance of survival when caught. The U-boats attacked at night and to do so they had to proceed at high speed on the surface by day to be in position to attack. By forcing them to submerge, the speed of the U-boats was less than that of the convoy and they were out of the battle. There were only just enough USN and RN escort carriers to make the vital difference in the critical months of April and May 1943.

We next turn to the Royal Air Force and Coastal Command. Firstly in the Bay of Biscay. The continuous patrols when 10 centimetre radar and Leigh Light equipment was carried resulted in a first success in February 1943. U-boats which had made fast passages on the surface at night to and from their bases now made the passage submerged and when as far away as possible surfaced to charge their batteries. It was a grave error, for they were again set upon by Coastal Command. Admiral Dönitz furnished them with heavier anti-aircraft weapons and told them to fight it out on the surface by day. Aircraft were lost in these encounters, but U-boats were sunk also and many others were forced to return damaged. Far out in the Atlantic very long range Liberators were allocated to Coastal Command just in time. Flying to the limit of their endurance they sought out convoys and in many cases by remarkable feats of navigation they met them in bad weather and at a critical moment in the middle of the Atlantic. U-boats had to submerge before depth charges rained down on them. The question will be asked as to why it took so long to bring these invaluable aircraft into service in the Battle of the Atlantic. The answer lies in differing opinions and pressures both between the Allies and between the needs and rivalries of the Royal Air Force and the Royal Navy. It was a tragic possibility that the Battle of the Atlantic could have been lost literally for want of a handful of aircraft.

Finally but of critical importance was the contribution of Ultra, and the re-routing tactics of the Submarine Tracking Room. Convoys could alter course within hours of the transmission of short signals from U-boats barring their way, and again because of Ultra a convoy which was known to be undetected could have its escort sent to assist a convoy under attack. Ultra was indeed a vital ingredient to the Allied successes in the Atlantic.

We now come to the critical convoys which the U-boats strove to destroy and into which the full weight of Allied resistance was thrown. During the first twenty days of March 1943, sixty-seven ships had been sunk, and in the last eleven only a further ten. At the beginning of April there was only one large concentration of U-boats operating in the North Atlantic, but during this month no less than ninety-eight boats sailed for the battleground. Further south a convoy off Sierra

Leone was cut to pieces at the end of the month. Seven ships of 43,255 tons were destroyed by only one boat — U-515 — which was undamaged. In the Atlantic fifty-six ships of 327,943 tons were lost to U-boats in April (and during the last week seven U-boats were sunk by air and surface escorts). The Italian submarine *Da Vinci* having sunk 58,973 tons of merchant shipping was herself sunk in May. There were five support groups working in the

Atlantic during April, two of them accompanied by an escort carrier. Thirty very long range aircraft were also operational.

The total U-boat losses during April from all areas was fifteen. Twelve of these losses occurred in the Atlantic. The total for the month before had also been fifteen, but half a million tons of shipping had also been destroyed. This time the losses had been halved.

Accepting such losses, Admiral Dönitz had about sixty U-boats waiting on the edge of the Greenland Air Gap and off the coast of northern Spain. Convoy ONS 5 was attacked by a very determined wolf pack in heavy weather, and despite a strong escort.

During the night of 4 May five ships were sunk and in daylight next day a further four, with three U-boats destroyed.

SS Tekoa *(New Zealand Shipping Company) stops to rescue survivors from three sinking ships. No less than five U-boats passed her on the surface as, lit up by the blazing tanker* Southern Princess, *she rescued 146 seamen.*

On the night of 5 May 1943 the U-boats struck again, but the escorts fought back. Not a single ship was sunk but the escort managed to sink a further three U-boats. Thus six U-boats had been sunk in return for twelve merchant

U-boat sinkings in April and May 1943 comparing the total with those in the North Atlantic

	North Atlantic sinkings	Total sinkings
By surface escort vessels	15	16
By surface escort vessels and carriers	2	2
By surface escort vessels and shore-based aircraft	3	4
By shore-based air escorts	10	10
By shore-based aircraft		3
By shore-based air patrols (Biscay and North Scotland)	13	9
By other shore-based air patrols		3
Carrier air escorts	2	2
Submarine patrols	0	2
Other causes - Mine		1
Accident	4	2
Unknown		2
Totals	49	56

ships during the convoy's passage. Of crucial importance to the outcome was the fog which hung over the sea during this battle. The escorts were able to pinpoint by radar the attacking U-boats at some distance, while the U-boats were confronted by escorts which suddenly emerged out of the mist. Despite these losses

SS Bedouin ablaze in the Atlantic with a corvette standing by. At a critical moment in the battle to import enough oil to ensure Britain's survival, Admiral Dönitz ordered his U-boat commanders to give priority to tanker targets in convoys. Unable to take evasive action, these ships were desperately vulnerable. An explosion, followed by a sheet of flame which lit up the sky, told of yet another sinking. Under these circumstances rescue was often impossible.

the U-boats re-formed further south and attacked two convoys. Three ships were sunk but three U-boats had been lost also.

It was a combined operation with an escort carrier, long range aircraft and surface ships all contriving to make an attack on the convoy almost suicidal. Another of the convoys was attacked but two more U-boats were sunk.

The next convoy with air and surface protection of considerable strength got through safely, despite a very fierce battle. The escort included the USS *Bogue* and HMS *Archer* as escort carriers. Some of the latter's Swordfish aircraft carried rockets, and these were used to sink U-752 on 23 May. In fact no less than five U-boats were sunk during the convoy's passage, which was again a combined operation. Convoys were sailing across the Atlantic at ten

day intervals from either end, and from the middle to the end of May only two ships were sunk in transit while an anti-submarine air escort was present.

It can be said with hindsight that the end of May 1943 was the final turning point in the Battle of the Atlantic. It was by no means over and many more actions, sinkings and U-boat losses were to occur in the future, and it was not apparent until early 1944 that the battle was being won. However, the rate of sinkings although acceptable to the Allies, was quite unacceptable to Admiral Dönitz. There was no alternative but for him to withdraw from the battleground.

During May, a total of forty-one U-boats had been lost; thirty-seven were lost within the North Atlantic, one in the South Atlantic, and three in the Mediterranean.

The co-operation between shore and carrier based aircraft, surface escorts and the relentless pressure on the approaches to U-boat bases; all these factors contributed to make attacks on Allied ships in convoy an enterprise too dangerous to be maintained.

The contribution of Ultra was again immense. The effect of almost immediate decrypts can be seen in the increase in U-boat losses by shore-based aircraft acting upon this information. Losses on this scale could not be sustained by Germany's U-boat arm and a period of regrouping was to follow.

Air combat over Guadalcanal.

4

The Pacific

July 1942 to December 1943

Guadalcanal and the Battle of Savo

The Battle of Midway forced Japan to re-think her strategy. It was essential for her to maintain her outer perimeter and the blind spot was far away to the south-east. If a strong base with air-fields capable of operating long range bombers could be established in the British Solomon Islands, then the ever-increasing flow of the American traffic along the direct route to Australia was certain to become seriously threatened. Australia was the obvious secure Allied base from which to mount an attack on newly acquired Japanese territory. The destruction of troopships by air bombing and a fleet action to destroy a convoy would cause a real threat to the reinforcement of New Guinea and the build-up of an Allied campaign.

The American Chiefs of Staff were as aware of this as the Japanese High Command. The Allies also realised that by having to move their slender forces southward they would lessen the protection of Pearl Harbor and Midway. None the less, urgent preparations were begun to deny the Solomons to the Japanese. It was decided to retake the island of Tulagi where a Japanese garrison and a seaplane base had been established, and at the same time Guadalcanal was to be occupied. Here an airfield was under construction and there was a weak garrison. The 1st Marine Division under the command of Major-General Vandegrift USMC had landed in New Zealand and was combat-loaded into fifteen transports.

Their objective was to retake and to hold Guadalcanal and Tulagi against whatever Japanese resistance they encountered.

There were considerable dangers because Japanese reaction would be swift and immediate. They had a well established base at Rabaul which was within easy striking distance and contained seasoned troops, air power and a considerable cruiser squadron.

In April 1942 the Pacific had been divided into two great Allied commands. The South-west Pacific area was under the command of General MacArthur and the Pacific area under Admiral Nimitz, with Vice-Admiral Robert L. Ghormley as Commander South Pacific Force. It was a race against time to attack before the Japanese completed the airfield on Guadalcanal and crippled the American plans.

The invasion force made a mid-ocean rendezvous on 26 July 1942 some 400 miles south of Fiji. By nightfall on 7 August, Rear-Admiral Turner, who commanded the Amphibious Force, had 12,000 Marines ashore at Lunga Point on Guadalcanal without meeting opposition. Resistance was stiffer on the island of Tulagi but this was overcome, and 6,000

Marines dug in. Work started at once on the partially completed airfield which was named Henderson Field after Major Henderson, a USMC pilot killed at Midway. This airfield was to attain an immortal name in American history.

It was expected that a critical situation would develop, since Japanese forces would react immediately. Operating from secure bases, they could dominate the area, and continuous air protection would be needed during the build-up of forces. The pivot of the whole operation was Henderson Field, and the Seabees, the

United States Marines landed virtually unopposed on Guadalcanal on 7 August 1942, and work began at once to complete the airfield which was to become known as Henderson Field. However, the Japanese reaction was immediate and it seemed that the American forces faced disaster.

Naval Construction battalion, got to work at once. Although taken completely by surprise, Japanese reaction from the air was swift and several attacks were made. These were beaten off with the loss of one transport, the *George E. Elliott,* which burned throughout the night.

Japanese reinforcements in six transports from Rabaul put to sea at once. One was torpedoed by US submarine S-38, and the remainder turned back. It was a lucky break for the troops ashore. However, Admiral Mikawa had already sailed with all available gunpower in the area. This comprised the heavy cruisers *Chokai* (flag), *Aoba, Kako, Kinugasa* and *Furutaka,* with two light cruisers and one destroyer. Their orders were to destroy all shipping off Guadalcanal and Tulagi. To accomplish this required an immediate night action.

Through a series of bad communication failures by air reconnaissance, Admiral Turner had no precise information of the whereabouts and course of the Japanese forces. He knew they were at sea, that they would probably attack, but when, where and how he did not know.

Rear-Admiral Fletcher, who was commanding the support force with its carriers, had been cruising to the south of Guadalcanal, but in view of the likely presence of Japanese submarines, Admiral Fletcher decided to withdraw his carriers from the area. They were priceless and he was not prepared to lose them in this way, or to subject them to mass air attacks from land-based Japanese aircraft. The disconcerting news that there would be no air cover at all reached Admiral Turner during the evening of 8 August and he had not yet finished unloading. As a protection, the escorting cruiser screen

was split into three. Between Guadalcanal and Tulagi lies the large cone shaped island of Savo. To the west and north-east of the island patrolled two destroyers, *Blue* and *Ralph Talbot,* and the three sections consisted of a southern force under the command of Rear-Admiral Crutchley RAN in the cruiser *Australia* with HMAS *Canberra* and USS *Chicago* and two destroyers patrolling in a box formation to the south of Savo Island and therefore blocking the entrance to the unloading area. The northern force to the east of Savo comprised the American cruisers *Vincennes, Astoria* and *Quincy* together with two destroyers under the command of Captain Riefkohl in *Vincennes.*

The last section covering the approach to Tulagi consisted of the cruisers USS *San Juan,* HMAS *Hobart* and two destroyers commanded by Rear-Admiral Norman Scott. The transports were to continue unloading all night.

This was a hastily conceived defensive plan which was necessary to block the expected Japanese attack.

At 20.30 Admiral Turner called an urgent conference on board his flagship, the transport *McCawley.* Admiral Crutchley left immediately with the heavy cruiser *Australia,* leaving Captain Bade of *Chicago* in command of the southern force. Due to the departure of the carriers Admiral Turner recommended the withdrawal of the transports next morning, and the dismayed General Vandegrift was left without adequate supplies for his 18,000 Marines.

It was not expected that a surface action would occur that night but that a mass attack from the air would take place at daybreak.

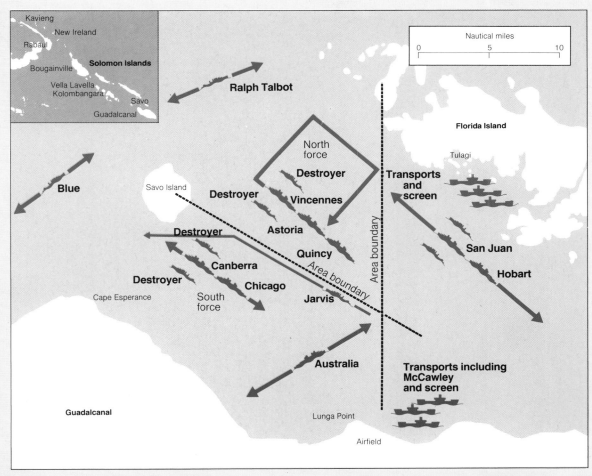

Battle of Savo Island, 9 August 1942.

At 23.30 a heavy rain squall drew a curtain between the cruiser groups, and aircraft were heard heading into the sound. The significance of this was not grasped and Admiral Turner did not receive any signal.

By the time Admiral Crutchley returned to his flagship the night was well on and he decided to patrol seven miles to the west of the transports and not rejoin the southern force.

Meanwhile Admiral Mikawa was eagerly assimilating the reports of his scout planes which were circling the beachheads unrecognized, unopposed and ready to illuminate the area for his attacking cruiser force. He knew where the Allied cruiser force was patrolling and he therefore planned to brush through them to the south of Savo Island in order to get among the transports.

Approaching in line ahead at 26 knots he sighted the destroyer *Blue*. All guns were trained on her, but she failed to see the Japanese force and warn the cruisers. In minutes she was left well behind.

Soon the southern force was in view on a collision course. The destroyer *Patterson* saw the loom of a ship 5,000 yards ahead and broadcast a radio alarm — but it was too late. Japanese float planes dropped brilliant flares over the transports at Lunga Point which silhouetted *Chicago* and *Canberra*. Admiral Mikawa opened fire at 4,500 yards just as the first of a spread of torpedoes had reached its mark. Two torpedoes hit *Canberra* on the starboard side and the first of twenty-four shells crashed into the unsuspecting cruiser, her main armament still trained fore and aft. Within minutes this fine ship was out of the war.

Chicago following behind took a torpedo on her bow, and by the time her main armament opened up, the Japanese cruisers were disappearing into a rain squall on a north-easterly bearing. Admiral Mikawa ordered his one destroyer *Yunagi* to reverse course and block the south-west entrance to the sound. The main target was the illuminated area thick with transports, but Admiral Mikawa decided to attack the northern force first. Heavy rain clouds and squalls blanketed the area. No word had been passed to *Vincennes* of the northern group, and no gun flashes had been seen, although there had been sounds of gunfire.

Hitherto Mikawa's cruisers had been steaming in a single column. Now, having glimpsed *Vincennes*, the Admiral changed course to east-north-east. The ships following lost contact and at high speed the force divided into two groups;

a western one of three cruisers and an eastern one of four cruisers led by flagship *Chokai.* The three American cruisers were between them. Such was the speed and complete surprise of the attack that the *Astoria, Quincy* and *Vincennes* were literally overwhelmed. In *Astoria* no one had reacted to the flares or to *Patterson's* warning, when within a minute a searchlight from the light cruiser *Yubari* lit the cruiser and shells began to fall around her. *Astoria* replied but an 8 inch shell ripped into her superstructure, turning the midships section into a flaming torch. From a range of 5,500 yards she was hit again and again until fires spread throughout the length of the ship. One remaining gun continued to fire and hit the forward turret of *Chokai,* but it was only a matter of minutes before this too was silenced and *Astoria* was so badly damaged that she sank the next day.

Quincy next ahead of *Astoria* was lit by searchlights from *Aoba,* and one of the first shells to land on her set fire to the plane resting on the catapult. From then on no other lights were needed. Caught in a cross-fire between the two groups of Japanese cruisers she was hit repeatedly. But her main armament went into action and scored three hits on *Chokai's* chartroom, forward turret and catapult. One by one her guns were blasted apart, and finally a torpedo crashed into her port side amidships and the ship slowly came to a stop, sinking rapidly. She was an inferno, drifting and out of control. She finally sank at 02.35 with great loss of life.

The last ship to be engaged was *Vincennes.* She opened fire and illuminated a target on the port side, her second salvo hit *Kinugasa* but without causing much damage. Then her aircraft on the catapult was hit and again the flames made further illumination unnecessary. The concentrated fire from both Japanese groups was so intense that there was no means of escape. Torpedoes opened up her port side and a minute later she was again torpedoed. No guns remained in action and the ship came to a stop with a heavy list to port.

Suddenly all firing stopped as the Japanese forces withdrew from the scene, but *Vincennes* could not be saved and she sank at 02.50. The destroyer *Ralph Talbot,* patrolling to the north of Savo Island, encountered the Japanese force and was set upon. Although badly damaged she was saved by a rain squall.

Admiral Mikawa's objective had been the transports off Lunga Point, but he continued on a northerly course and returned from whence he came. He missed a golden opportunity, but having lost control of his force in the furious action he felt he would not have time to return to the beachhead, destroy the transports and be clear of the area before the expected air attack from Admiral Fletcher's carriers at dawn. In any case he had done great damage.

Heavy cruisers *Canberra, Astoria, Quincy* and *Vincennes* had been sunk and *Chicago* badly damaged. There was also some damage to the Japanese force but very few casualties. However, the US submarine S-44 on patrol sighted the returning cruisers on 10 August and closing to 700 yards put four torpedoes into IJN *Kako* which sank within four minutes.

The invasion force was in a desperate position without air cover. Unloading went on throughout the day, despite bombing, but by nightfall the transports were obliged to withdraw, leaving the Marines on their own with insufficient stores for the job in hand. By a remarkable effort Henderson Field was ready to accept aircraft by the 20 August. Tropical rainstorms turned the airstrip into a sea of viscous mud but it was still operational. Major-General Roy Geiger USMC was appointed commander of all Allied planes flying from Henderson Field, and the Seabees (Naval Construction battalion) worked right round the clock to keep the airfield operational.

One thousand Japanese troops under Colonel Ichiki landed unopposed from six destroyers on the night of 18 August and attacked the Marines' position at once.

The Japanese Command in Rabaul had underestimated the American strength which was now 16,000 and after a fierce and bloody battle near the Tenaru River they were halted with very few survivors. The United States Marines had gained a toehold on Guadalcanal.

The first intimation of the presence of a Japanese naval force was the destruction of the Australian cruiser Canberra *and the disabling of* Chicago *within minutes. The Japanese light cruiser* Yubari *then illuminated a further American cruiser force and Admiral Mikawa opened fire at once.*

147

The United States cruisers Astoria, Vincennes *and* Quincy *were now subjected to a torpedo attack and devastating shellfire from the Japanese cruisers. Each was set on fire within minutes and all had sunk by next morning. The transports and supply ships lying off Lunga Point, Guadalcanal, were now in the greatest danger.*

The Battle of the Eastern Solomons

The American landings in the Solomons had generated further immediate Japanese reaction. The Battle of Savo Island had given them the initiative, though the first Japanese troop landings had been unsuccessful and a far greater confrontation was needed. This took place on 24 August at the sea battle of the Eastern Solomons. Admiral Yamamoto, Commander-in-Chief, decided that the reinforcement of Guadalcanal would be supported by the Combined Fleet. His forces consisted of three carriers, three battleships, ten cruisers and twenty-three destroyers. Against this, Admiral Fletcher's carriers — *Enterprise, Saratoga* and *Wasp*, with their escorting cruisers and destroyers, and the battleship *North Carolina*, were patrolling well south of Guadalcanal, out of range of Japanese search-planes. A big engagement was coming and Admiral Nimitz was deploying everything he had to meet it.

Meanwhile both sides were busy supplying their forces. The nightly run by Japanese destroyers carrying reinforcements was unopposed. On 21 August the destroyer *Kawakaze* torpedoed the American destroyer *Blue* which was protecting two supply ships. Command of the sea at night belonged to the Japanese.

The first intimation that a Japanese fleet was at sea was a sighting of surfaced submarines and troop transports with their escorts at 09.30 on 23 August. A strike was launched from *Saratoga* and Henderson Field. Nothing was found for the commander, Admiral Tanaka, guessing that he had been spotted, reversed course and succeeded in confusing the pilots. Intelligence reports suggested that the main attack would not come for a few days and Admiral Fletcher detached *Wasp* and her escort to refuel.

The Japanese tactical plan was to detach one light carrier *Ryujo*, a heavy cruiser and two destroyers to act as a diversionary group ahead of the main body and tempt Admiral Fletcher to make an all out strike on them. When this strike was committed, the full weight of the Japanese carrier air power would be concentrated on the American carriers.

As a further diversion, on 24 August a heavy raid was made on Henderson Field. This was broken up by defending Marine fighters, but United States reconnaissance planes had sighted the *Ryujo* force within range of the American carriers. Admiral Fletcher took the bait and sent thirty-eight aircraft from *Saratoga* into the attack. He now had sixty-six aircraft committed to the air strike and on air reconnaissance, when shore-based reconnaissance planes reported the fleet carriers *Shokaku* and *Zuikaku* only 198 miles from his carriers. Then came news of four Japanese cruisers and several destroyers 260 miles away.

As radio reception was very bad, he could not alert his aircraft aloft to this new danger and *Wasp* was away refuelling. Reinforcements from Pearl Harbor and elsewhere were still hundreds of miles away. This was exactly what Admiral Nagumo wanted. Admiral Fletcher still had a small strike force to send against *Shokaku* and *Zuikaku* but the aircraft would have had to land after dark. Instead, he decided to stack extra fighters above his two carriers to augment the combat air patrol and wait. But two of his reconnaissance aircraft had sighted *Shokaku*

If the American naval forces and in particular the carriers could be destroyed, then Guadalcanal would fall. At the Battle of the Eastern Solomons Japanese aircraft tried to sink USS Enterprise, *seen here with her escort of cruisers and destroyers.*

and attacked immediately scoring near misses which did little damage. Fifty minutes later *Saratoga's* air strike found the *Ryujo* force and the dive-bombers went in, scoring four hits. This was followed by torpedoes from either beam from the Avengers and the courageous little carrier had no chance. She was crippled and sank that evening. No American aircraft were lost on the raid. But Admiral Nagumo's aircraft were already on the way from the two big carriers in two groups spaced an hour apart. *Enterprise* was surrounded by her escort, as shown in the diagram, while *Saratoga* was more than ten miles distant, also surrounded by her escort. They awaited the attack and at 16.18 Japanese aircraft were picked up on radar 101 miles distant.

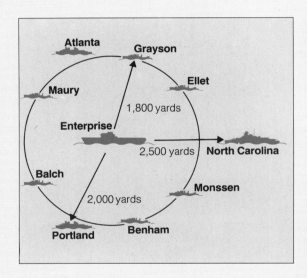

The Enterprise *group, 24 August 1942.*

Combat air patrol was raised to fifty-three aircraft and the remaining strike aircraft were ordered aloft. Everything that could fly was flown off, the fighters in an all out bid to defend the two carriers from the forthcoming attack, and the SBD Dauntless dive-bombers and TBF Avenger torpedo aircraft to attack the Japanese fleet carriers.

Radio reception was bad due in part to overloaded radio frequencies and also to poor radio discipline. When the Wildcats saw the Japanese strike splitting up into positions for their dive they went for them and a wild dog-fight ensued. In some cases the protecting fighters followed the bombers down through their own intense anti-aircraft fire. The air battle between the escorting Zeros desperately trying to defend their 'Val' dive-bombers and the Wildcats, fighting them off and trying to intercept the bombers before they began their dive, was the fiercest of the war so far. The anti-aircraft barrage put up by the battleship *North Carolina,* the anti-aircraft cruiser *Atlanta* and destroyers was intense but most of the 'Vals' did get through. *Enterprise* was hit three times and was soon in danger with 170 killed or wounded. As the Japanese planes turned for home, the fight

began to save the ship. Gradually fires were extinguished and by 01.00 on 25 August the damage was made good.

Admiral Fletcher turned south in an attempt to prevent a night gun action which the Japanese were trying hard to effect by closing at high speed. Just before midnight Admiral Kondo gave up the chase and returned north. Throughout the battle *Saratoga* had not been sighted or attacked but her aircraft certainly had helped to save the *Enterprise*.

At first light on 25 August, Marine and Navy pilots from Henderson Field found and attacked Admiral Tanaka's reinforcement force. His flagship, the light cruiser *Jintsu*, was hit and the largest troop transport sunk, as was the destroyer *Mutsuki* as she was taking survivors on

board. There was just no chance that Admiral Tanaka could land his troops in daylight, and he turned back.

It was an inconclusive battle. Admiral Fletcher had responded to the 'bait' and left himself wide open to an all out attack, without being able to mount a similar attack. *Enterprise* had been damaged and seventeen planes had been lost. The Japanese casualties, about seventy aircraft with their experienced pilots, had been much higher. A light carrier had been sunk together with a transport and a destroyer; and a light cruiser, a seaplane carrier and a destroyer had been seriously damaged.

In retrospect the first round seemed to have been a strategic defeat for the Japanese. For six weeks following the Battle of the Eastern Solomons there was a period of continuous movement of supplies on both sides. It was a curious tactical situation. Mastery of the area round Guadalcanal changed every twelve hours. By day the Americans controlled the area from the air, and supplies of all kinds were discharged from ships under the protection of the Marine fighters from Henderson Field.

As dusk came on they withdrew fast and left the way clear for Japanese surface forces. The 'Tokyo Express' in the form of fast destroyers led by Rear-Admiral Tanaka dashed in to discharge cargo and reinforcements, and after a short sharp period of shelling the American positions, returned north at high speed.

The range of the Dauntless dive-bombers was such that Tanaka's destroyers could be nearly out of range by the time the dive-bombers had located them after dawn next morning. Added to this, fuel for the Americans was desperately short, and with the build-up of forces it was impossible to keep pace with the very considerable supplies needed.

Then on 31 August *Saratoga* was torpedoed by a Japanese submarine. She survived but was out of action for three critical months.

Jungle warfare was new to the Marines, and they learned the hard way. On the Japanese side the position was worse. They suffered from a total lack of essential stores and the nightly arrival of hundreds of reinforcements brought only men and weapons and the bare necessities for survival, with a lack of even the most rudimentary medical supplies.

Japanese troops landing on Guadalcanal from destroyers at night. Mastery of the area around Guadalcanal changed every twelve hours. By day the Americans maintained control from the air and supplies of all kinds were landed under the protection of the Marine fighter aircraft from Henderson Field. At night, however, the Japanese held control of the sea and were able to land reinforcements at will, at the same time preventing all American movement.

There were a handful of Australian and British civilian planters and colonial officers who had stayed behind in the Solomons area after the invasion. They were provided with wireless sets and lived alone in the jungle, in many cases on the same island as the Japanese. These devoted and brave men gave consistently accurate early warning of the movements of ships and aircraft. Some were captured and killed, all were hunted. The courage of these 'coast watchers'

was matched by that of the Solomon Islanders. Despite capture and torture they remained loyal to the Allies, gathering information about shipping at great risk and rescuing downed aviators in the jungle. With this invaluable network it was possible to set up an early warning system which allowed fighter aircraft on Henderson Field to take off in time to gain height and meet the oncoming Japanese bombers before they reached their targets.

The United States Marines were new to jungle warfare, and the sickness rate rose alarmingly. None the less vigorous patrolling was undertaken by both sides, resulting in clashes deep within the jungles of Guadalcanal.

The 'coast watchers'. A handful of Australian and British officers remained in Japanese-held territory supported by loyal Solomon Islanders. They reported on the movement of aircraft and ships. This valuable early warning given to Guadalcanal enabled fighter aircraft to intercept Japanese air raids.

In a despatch sent to Admiral Nimitz, Admiral Halsey wrote of the 'coast watchers,' 'The Intelligence signalled from Bougainville by Read and Mason saved Guadalcanal, and Guadalcanal saved the South Pacific.'

Although this may be a slight exaggeration, there was certainly truth in his remark.

The Battle of Bloody Ridge

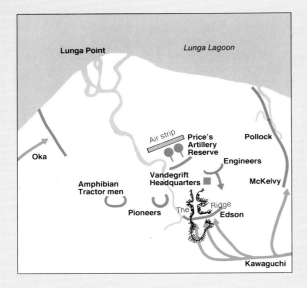

The crucial battle for the high ground.

The American position was still extremely precarious, and the situation was not to improve, for another crisis was on the way. General Kawaguchi had landed to the east of the Marines' position, at Taivu, and his engineers began hacking a path through the jungle to enable his forces to attack from a point southeast of Henderson Field. Allied native scouts and aerial reconnaissance caught occasional glimpses of the main body of troops, but the Marines grossly under-estimated their numbers. General Vandegrift still had insufficient troops to hold off an imminent major attack from all sides. He therefore constructed a series of mutually supporting strong points to cover the airfield and his flanks for a distance of up to two miles inland from the sea. The vital high ground, commanding the whole area, he gave to Colonel Edson and the Raider and Parachute Battalion USMC. This ridge, to be called Bloody Ridge, was to become an immortal name in United States Marine Corps history. Finally he held in reserve one battalion with all available artillery. These dispositions were to prove correct. The Japanese plan was to make an encircling movement and General Kawaguchi had decided to attack this ridge of high ground, capture it and so control the whole plain and Henderson Field.

The attack began on the night of 12 September with the Japanese probing for weak spots and infiltrating between them. By morning Edson's Raiders were worn out, but the position had been held, though General Kawaguchi had not yet launched his main attack. This was to take place the following night. During the day the Raiders dug in and got what rest they could. As night fell on 13 September a red rocket flared over the jungle and heavy mortar fire enveloped the Ridge. At 22.30 the main attack came in, resulting in furious hand-to-hand fighting. Edson's flank was exposed and he pulled his centre company of sixty men back to the last knoll of the Ridge. In the swirling darkness lit up by Japanese coloured rockets, the Marines 105 mm howitzers fired furiously all night, their shells falling in the undergrowth from which Japanese attackers poured. At times shells fell perilously near the defenders who clung desperately to their positions. The Japanese forced their way through a wall of steel emanating from artillery, mortars, machine guns and grenades right up to the bayonets of the exhausted

Raiders. Time and again the attackers rallied to supremely brave and bloody action. Time and again they were driven back. Bodies piled up on the wire in front of the Marines' position and still the Japanese seemed unstoppable. As night wore on ammunition was dragged up to the defenders and in the ghastly light from flares and shell bursts the Japanese attacks slowly

dwindled. It was an area of devastation and death with the corpses and wounded of both sides intermingled in the trenches on the Ridge. Day broke silently over the shell-torn and repulsive scene, but soon the roar of aircraft engines broke the stillness as every aircraft took to the skies and with their strafing machine guns forced General Kawaguchi's weary survivors

back into the jungle. One fifth of all the American forces engaged that night on the Ridge were killed or wounded, but of the 3,450 troops under General Kawaguchi's command, only half remained. The Battle of Bloody Ridge was one of the crucial ground actions of the Pacific war. It was won by the courage and discipline of individual Marines under inspired leadership against a force of fanatically brave Japanese troops who had marched for many miles through thick jungle without sufficient food or medical supplies. Had the battle been lost, Henderson Field would have been lost, and with it the island itself could well have fallen to the Japanese.

The desperate attempt by Japanese forces to capture the high ground overlooking the airfield on Guadalcanal. Throughout the night of 13 September 1942 fierce and bloody hand-to-hand fighting took place. As the sun rose again over the shattered hillside what remained of the Marine forces were still in control of the ridge.

The Battle of Cape Esperance

The essential decision to reinforce Guadalcanal was made with the knowledge that Japanese carriers and battleships were at sea in the northern Solomons, and that the waters to the south of Guadalcanal held nearly a score of submarines. Admiral Ghormley committed his two sound carriers *Hornet* and *Wasp* together with the battleship *North Carolina* as distant escort, and the convoy moved toward the island. Admiral Turner, commanding the convoy, realized that he had been spotted and took the difficult decision to withdraw temporarily, well knowing how badly these reinforcements were needed. On 15 September, surrounded by destroyers and cruisers, with *Hornet* five miles to the north, *Wasp* had just turned into wind to recover and launch aircraft. No one realized that the Japanese submarine I-19 was lying in wait, and her presence had not been detected by the destroyers. At 14.35 the submarine fired a spread of four torpedoes at the carrier *Wasp* of

A Japanese cruiser force approaching Guadalcanal to bombard the airfield on 11 October 1942 was met by American naval forces. Despite surprise they failed to inflict a decisive defeat on the Japanese.

which three hit simultaneously with enormous explosions. One hundred and ninety-three of the ship's company were killed and 366 were wounded. Despite all efforts to save her this gallant ship which had served the Allies so well in the relief of Malta, was abandoned at 15.20 and sunk by torpedoes about three hours later.

Meanwhile I-15, keeping company with I-19, attacked the *Hornet* group, sending a torpedo into the battleship *North Carolina*, and opening up a hole 32 feet long by 18 feet high. Nevertheless she was able to keep her station, maintaining 25 knots. At 14.45 *O'Brien*, one of the escorting destroyers, was hit, blowing off her bow. It was a daring attack and none of these ships could be spared easily. In the seven weeks since Guadalcanal had been occupied, the effective United States Pacific Fleet Carrier Force had dwindled from four to one, but the Japanese still had two fleet carriers and a number of light carriers in the area. The damage to *North Carolina* left only one new battleship, *Washington,* operating in the Pacific. It was a time of crisis. If the United States lost the ability to force convoys through, Guadalcanal would fall. Admiral Turner's convoy of transports with

the vital Marine Regiment was still at sea, and the admiral decided he had to take the risk of closing Guadalcanal. The transports arrived off Lunga Point in hazy weather without further incident and the Americans received their much needed men and supplies.

Throughout September the air action over Guadalcanal was increased. Japanese aircraft swarmed over the area daily but resistance to them mounted and their tactics then changed to dropping flares and single bombs at night.

The arrival of the 7th Marine Regiment gave General Vandegrift an opportunity for 'active defence', but his first sorties were repulsed with 170 casualties. Both sides prepared for a major attack on 7 October. The Marines plan was to force the Japanese back, and the Japanese plan was to secure the Matanikau River and overwhelm the Marines from the west. A fierce battle in heavy rain ensued with hand-to-hand fighting but the Marines held their positions.

A further and final Japanese attack led by General Hyakutake was to take place after a large and heavily escorted Japanese convoy had

arrived, including two seaplane carriers, bringing with it heavy artillery. The convoy reached its destination but in doing so ran into Admiral Norman Scott's cruisers which resulted in the night battle of Cape Esperance.

The opposing forces approached Guadalcanal for the same reason. The Japanese convoy arrived and the covering heavy cruisers proceeded to close the island for a bombardment. However, the Americans were in the process of landing the 164th Infantry Regiment and the escort proceeded to block the entrance to the roadstead at Savo Island while the reinforcements disembarked. Neither side knew of the other's intentions.

The Japanese heavy cruisers *Aoba*, *Kinugasa* and *Furutaka* together with two destroyers, *Hatsuyuki* and *Fubuki*, were commanded by Rear-Admiral Goto. Barring his approach was Admiral Scott's blocking group consisting of heavy cruisers *San Francisco* and *Salt Lake City*, the light cruisers *Boise* and *Helena* and five destroyers, *Farenholt*, *Laffey* and *Duncan* in the van and, bringing up the rear, *Buchanan* and *McCalla*.

The American force moved up the west coast of Guadalcanal at high speed, turned east round the north end of the island and then slowed to patrol between Savo Island and Gape Esperance. At 22.35 Admiral Scott ordered a countermarch. It was pitch dark, and to add to the problem of control, destroyer *Duncan* had seen suspicious indications on her fire control radar just before the countermarch and had gone off alone to investigate. *Farenholt* and *Laffey* were still abreast the cruisers steaming hard to take station ahead of the column when Admiral Scott's flagship *San Francisco* made her first radar contact at only 5,000 yards? Were these Japanese or his own destroyers? There was no doubt in the minds of *Helena*'s gunners who had been tracking the advancing ships for some time. The ships were now visible to the naked eye and at 23.46 *Helena* opened fire.

Admiral Goto, oblivious of the reception ahead, was preparing to carry out his bombardment and his first intimation of danger was *Helena*'s opening salvoes which hit *Aoba*, leading the column. The other American cruisers were only seconds behind *Helena* and fantastic as it may seem, Admiral Goto thought he was being fired on by friendly ships. He ordered an immediate reversal of course, before being mortally wounded on *Aoba*'s bridge. His ships were trapped because by good fortune Admiral Scott had achieved the classic crossing of the 'T' formation, enabling all his guns to bear on an oncoming enemy who was unable to retaliate as all but his forward guns were masked. As each ship approached the turning point of churned up water it was plastered by the overwhelming fire power of the American ships.

Aoba had turned right followed by *Furutaka*, both burning and lighting up the sky, but *Kinugasa* turned left and in so doing was saved. The American destroyer *Duncan*, which had gone off on her own, now found herself less than a mile from the Japanese cruiser *Furutaka* and in the line of fire from her own friends. She twisted and turned to escape a cascade of shells, firing all her guns and launching torpedoes. But she was hit repeatedly by both sides, and uncontrollable fires led to her being aban-

doned. Her sister ship *Farenholt*, still between the two cruiser forces, was also hit but continued firing until a further hit shut down her engine room. This also was probably fired from a friendly cruiser.

The destroyer *Fubuki* was caught in the beams of *San Francisco*'s searchlight and subjected to overwhelming fire. She exploded, rolled over and sank at 23.53. Two minutes later Admiral Scott ordered a turn to the north-west to place his ships parallel with those of the retiring Japanese, of which *Aoba* and *Furutaka* were still clearly on fire. *Aoba* somehow managed to extract herself and struggled out of the battle. Wrecked but still floating, and remarkably with her guns still firing accurately, this fine ship made her escape. The unfortunate *Furutaka* was the target for more hits and one torpedo. She slowly came to a stop and sank twenty-two miles west of Savo Island. But the remaining Japanese cruisers fought back hard. After a shattering surprise they responded by firing fast and accurately. The light cruiser *Boise* was hit repeatedly, having flashed her searchlight on to a suspicious object and in so doing given her position away. As shells rained down on her a brilliant sheet of flame lit up the sky and she was only saved by the action of *Salt Lake City*, the next ship astern, who turned right deliberately and gallantly interposed herself between *Boise* and her enemy.

One Japanese cruiser and one destroyer had been sunk and two further destroyers were sunk next day by aircraft from Henderson Field, as against one American light cruiser badly damaged and one destroyer sunk. The Japanese had received artillery, reinforcements and badly needed supplies and the Americans were reinforced by the units of the Americal Division.

Despite the initial unexpected and overwhelming fire power of the American force in the early stages, the Japanese bombardment force had not been destroyed. More serious was the tactical use of the long single column formation by the Americans which made the ships difficult to control and was to prove how dangerous it was in the major sea battle that was yet to come.

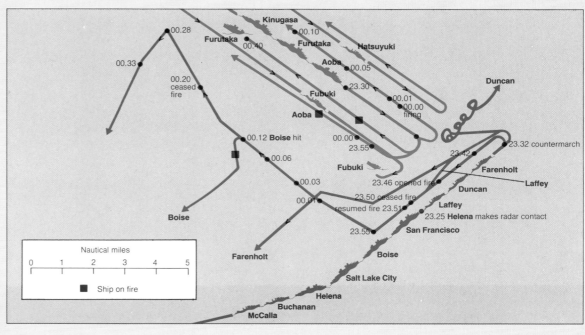

The confrontation at the Battle of Cape Esperance, 11 to 12 October 1942.

The Battle of Santa Cruz Islands

The Japanese naval bombardment of Henderson Field on 13 October 1942.

Henderson Field now had ninety operational aircraft, and also General Vandegrift had more troops, but optimism was premature. Vice-Admiral Kurita, with the battleships *Kongo* and *Haruna* and destroyers sweeping ahead, was descending on Guadalcanal. Shortly before midnight on 13 October a Japanese observation plane lit the airfield, to be followed by sixteen 14 inch guns opening fire with a monstrous thunder that reverberated through the hills. Over 900 14 inch shells crashed down on to Henderson Field in a devastating bombardment for which there really was no adequate response. For eighty minutes this overwhelming assault rained down on the Marines and their newly arrived Army reinforcements. The whole area was in flames. Aircraft, stores and fuel were tossed into the air in an inferno of exploding ammunition. Hardly an aircraft escaped some damage and out of the ninety planes on the airfield only forty-two were salvaged. In addition the aviation fuel supply was all but destroyed.

The only bright side to this disastrous night action was the fact that four motor torpedo boats had arrived at Tulagi the day before. They immediately put to sea, heading for the sound of the guns. A spirited action with the destroyer screen followed and while no hits were made this intervention probably helped Admiral Kurita in his decision to break off the engagement and retire.

The next night Admiral Mikawa himself entered the roadstead with two heavy cruisers and fired 752 8 inch shells at the beleaguered forces. Dawn on 15 October saw Japanese transports supported by destroyers and aircraft discharging men and stores at Tassafaronga in daylight. By now Japan had some 29,000 troops on the island. The surrounding area was scoured for aviation gas and enough was scraped together to enable the pilots to take off in any aircraft fit to fly to attack this tempting target. Three large transports had to be beached at the cost of seven American aircraft.

That night a further visitation from the cruisers *Myoko* and *Maya* pumped 1,500 8 inch shells into the area. There was no doubt that the Japanese Navy was making an all-out bid to blast the island into complete submission, and had undisputed control of the sea at night.

There now followed a massive airlift by the Americans to make good the losses in planes and supplies. Every possible plane was pressed into service together with supply barges and fast destroyer escorts.

It seems remarkable that considering the vast might of American resources, the situation on Guadalcanal remained critical for so long, but it must be remembered that on the other side of the world the huge 'Torch' convoys had set sail for North Africa. The South-west Pacific theatre was still designated a holding operation and the Allied weakness lay in not having overall superiority in modern fast carriers and capital ships.

While this was to be remedied and the tables were to be turned, the immense distances that lay between the United States and the Solomon Islands required an enormous number of supply ships — and these were just not available if the needs of the North Atlantic were adequately to be met.

On 18 October 1942 Admiral Halsey replaced Admiral Ghormley and took command of the South Pacific area and South Pacific forces, setting up his headquarters at Noumea. In Washington the decision was made to hold Guadalcanal at all costs. In Tokyo the Japanese High Command reached the same conclusion; Guadalcanal was to have top priority and Port Moresby and Papua were to take second place. Henderson Field had to be taken. The ground attack started on 21 October when Major-General Sumiyoshi made a frontal attack on General Vandegrift's western defences along the Matanikau River. In intensity the battle

Japanese naval forces made a last desperate but unsuccessful attempt to destroy the American carriers in the Pacific. During the battle USS Hornet *was set on fire and had to be abandoned despite the efforts of her ship's company to save her.*

came very near to the desperate encounter on Bloody Ridge the month before, but the American line just held. Flying conditions in the pelting rain were as difficult as they could be, but even so the Marine pilots broke up one air assault after another, with losses in the ratio of seven to one against the Japanese. The second battle for the airfield had been repulsed, and Japanese losses after an exhausting trek through the jungle were measured in thousands, whereas the Americans suffered only 500 casualties.

Admiral Yamamoto's forces were now at sea waiting for certain news of the capture of Henderson Field. The Admiral was confident that he could destroy the American naval presence because he had no less than five carriers, five battleships, fourteen cruisers and forty-five destroyers, although these were dispersed over a wide area of the Solomons.

The morning after a Japanese naval bombardment. This nightly shelling by battleships and cruisers destroyed aircraft, fuel and ammunition dumps and caused some casualties. However, the airfield was never completely out of action for long.

Admiral Halsey had at his disposal the carriers *Enterprise* (repaired after the battle of the Eastern Solomons) and *Hornet*, the battleship *South Dakota*, together with six cruisers and fourteen destroyers.

The first signs of activity occurred when reconnaissance aircraft spotted one Japanese carrier 650 miles north of Espiritu Santo on 23 October and two more on 25 October. Admiral Kinkaid commanding the task force sent out a combined search and strike force which failed to find the carriers and on returning at night lost six aircraft.

The next day a further search and strike sortie was flown from *Enterprise* covering a wide area. Individual attacks were made on units of the Japanese fleet when sighted, including successful hits by a pair of Dauntless dive-bombers on the light carrier *Zuiho* at 08.40 on 26 October which put her out of action for the day. The opposing forces were only a critical 200 miles apart when an immediate strike by sixty-five Zeros, 'Kates' and 'Vals' left the Japanese carriers at 07.30. Between 07.30 and 08.15 the American carriers replied with a strike of twenty-seven dive-bombers and twenty-three Avenger torpedo-bombers in three separate waves escorted by twenty-three Wildcats.

The hostile forces passed one another *en route* to their destinations and Admiral Kinkaid was warned of what was to come. His two carriers were operating ten miles apart, each with its tight circle of supporting gunfire and with a combat air patrol of thirty-eight fighters. At about 09.30 the approaching Japanese forces were picked up at a distance of seventy miles and at 09.57 the Wildcats saw the first wave of 'Val' dive-bombers at 17,000 feet. At about 10.00 *Enterprise* entered a local rain squall which hid her, but *Hornet* was clearly visible and an attack on her went in at 10.10. The 'Vals' dived and the air was blackened by shell bursts while the fighters, flying through their own flak, destroyed the first wave, but lost height in doing so. More 'Vals' followed and *Hornet* was hit. One aircraft, crippled by a shell burst, dived deliberately into *Hornet*'s flight deck, doing her great damage. Simultaneously, torpedo-carrying 'Kates' flew through murderous fire to drop torpedoes, two of which tore into the engineering compartments. The carrier, in a thick cloud of smoke, slowed to a stop and lost all power and communications. Three more bombs hit the flight deck and detonated inside the carrier. Within ten minutes the attack was over. *Hornet* was in a very bad way and throughout the morning the fight went on to save her. Meanwhile the Japanese submarine I-21 fired a salvo of torpedoes at 11.02 sinking the destroyer *Porter*. At 16.15 a further torpedo attack by six 'Kates' made for the stricken *Hornet* — now being towed by the cruiser *Northampton* — and by 17.02 the ship's company had been taken off by destroyers and the blazing carrier was abandoned. *Hornet* had lived for a year and had ferried the first aircraft to raid Japan, but she was now lost, although her aircraft had found the opposing fleet carrier *Shokaku* and the still smoking *Zuiho*.

American Dauntless dive-bombers dived on *Shokaku* fighting off the protecting Zeros and flying through a hail of flak. Between three and six 1,000 pound bombs hit the carrier, but the

Avenger torpedo aircraft failed to find her and finish the work begun by the dive-bombers. She was once again saved by the fast efficiency of her ship's company's damage control parties, although she was out of the war for nine months. One of the escorting cruisers *Chikuma* was also badly damaged by bombing but she survived. Meanwhile the *Enterprise* group had been covered by a local rain squall. Her aircraft only managed to attack the battleship *Kirishima* and without success. However, she was intact and could mount another strike. *Shokaku* and *Zuiho* could no longer operate aircraft but still *Zuikaku* and *Junyo* were unscathed. One bomb could cripple *Enterprise* and the Japanese were determined to drop it. The carrier was now exposed in sunshine.

The first strike by forty-four Japanese dive-bombers was picked up on radar at twenty-six miles and a veritable wall of steel met them. Twenty-three bombs were dropped between 11.05 and 11.35. *Enterprise* shot down seven planes close to the ship while the guns of *South Dakota* manoeuvring at speed about 1,000 yards from *Enterprise* accounted for others. But about twenty-four aircraft got through to hit the carrier twice with one near miss.

As the damage control parties were coping with the considerable destruction, the first wave of 'Kate' torpedo-bombers came in low. Nine were destroyed before the Wildcats began to run out of ammunition. About fourteen of the torpedo planes succeeded in reaching Admiral Kinkaid's

A Dauntless dive-bomber landing in mud and rain at Henderson Field, Guadalcanal.

Task Force 61 and *Enterprise* was the target. Five more were shot down but the nine remaining aircraft bore bravely on and dropped four torpedoes to port and five to starboard. All were avoided by the twisting and turning carrier, manoeuvring within the close ring of her protecting force. One last torpedo-bomber heavily on fire deliberately crashed into the destroyer *Smith*. The entire forward part of the ship was enveloped in flames. The skipper conned his ship smartly through the formation, nuzzling the burning ship's bow close under *South Dakota*'s quarter, where the battleship's foaming wake quenched the fires.

For the American forces this was a critical moment. Aircraft were anxious to land, as the damage control parties feverishly mended the torn deck and cleared off the debris. There was a providential few minutes' lull in the fighting before a strike from the light carrier *Junyo* was detected at 12.00 at fifty miles. The aircraft came out of low cloud which forced them to make shallow runs. Eight were shot down at about 12.25 and there was only one near miss on *Enterprise*. A last attack came in minutes later. This time the attackers made for *South Dakota* which took a bomb on Number 1 turret with no damage, and the anti-aircraft cruiser *San Juan* where a bomb did considerable damage.

Both these ships lost steering control for some minutes and careered through the formation, luckily without any collisions.

The battle, the fourth big carrier action in six months, was over. Measured in combat tonnage actually sunk, the Japanese had won a tactical victory at sea despite the damage to *Shokaku* which forced her to return to Japan. However, the land assault against the Marines having been repulsed, there was now an important breathing space in which to reinforce Guadalcanal and regroup forces at sea. Priceless time had been gained by the Americans but the biggest showdown was yet to come.

The naval battle of Guadalcanal

At the end of October 1942 there was a feeling of frustration on all sides. The American forces were unable to seal off Guadalcanal and to prevent the Japanese gaining reinforcements. In fact both sides were pouring in troops and supplies without much hindrance and Henderson Field was being lengthened to take heavier aircraft. But something had to give. Naval Intelligence and the coast watchers' reports all pointed to a further Japanese attack from the sea. In fact eleven high speed transports were intended to reach Guadalcanal on 14 November, and the airfield was to be put out of action by bombardment by two battleships on the two previous nights.

On the American side a reinforcement convoy had arrived and unloaded. The Japanese bombardment group had been sighted from the air and Rear-Admiral Callaghan who commanded the cruiser and destroyer escort for this last reinforcement operation moved to block the northern entrance to the Sound. With this, the only American naval force in the immediate vicinity, it was a desperate decision, and was to be a one-sided encounter.

Admiral Callaghan kept a tight control of his force in column, the van consisting of the four destroyers Cushing, Laffey, Sterett and O'Bannon, each of which had orders not to act independently. In the centre were the anti-aircraft cruiser Atlanta, the heavy cruisers San Francisco (flag) and Portland, with the light cruisers Helena and Juneau. Bringing up the rear were the destroyers Aaron Ward, Barton, Monssen and Fletcher. Few of these ships had operated together before, and in the short time available no battle plan had been issued to commanding officers.

On the Japanese side, the advance guard headed southward planning to pass west of Savo and bombard Henderson Field for two nights. Under the command of Vice-Admiral Abe they consisted of the battleships Hiei and Kirishima, the light cruiser Nagara and fourteen destroyers. Their job was to smash Henderson Field completely, and the battleships were all crammed with thin-shelled, quick-fused bombardment projectiles with flashless powder. Admiral Abe believed that the American cruisers would have left the Sound and that opposition would be minimal.

It was at the very start of Friday 13 November, at 01.24, that American radar picked up the approaching bombardment group at 27,000 yards. Admiral Callaghan turned to starboard to meet his enemy head-on but slightly on the port bow. The opposing forces were approaching each other at over 40 knots. The American admiral in San Francisco had inadequate radar and wild confusion of talk over the voice radio gave him scant information on what was ahead.

At 01.41 the lead destroyer Cushing sighted two Japanese destroyers at only 3,000 yards and immediately turned to port to unmask her torpedo tubes. The column followed, but surprise was lost in the near pile-up and indecision that followed the abrupt turn. Admiral Callaghan in the sixth ship of the line neither knew of the Japanese presence, nor the reason for the turn, as the voice radio (TBS) channel was a confused medley due to the inexcusable lack of signal discipline. The Japanese were

caught offguard by the American ships but reacted swiftly. At 01.50 their searchlights swept the area and came to rest on Atlanta. The cruiser and her consorts opened fire and counter-illuminated at a range of only 1,600 yards but shells soon smothered Atlanta. She stopped dead in the water with many casualties, and was scuttled next morning.

Immediately after Atlanta had been immobilized, the Japanese and American ships mingled at high speed and at point-blank range in the darkness, so it is impossible to reconstruct accurately what happened. Cushing in the lead engaged a destroyer to starboard but was hit amidships by a heavy calibre shell from a battleship which severed all power lines and reduced her speed. The battleship Hiei loomed out of the darkness on a near collision course less than 800 yards away. Six torpedoes were fired using local control but none were effective as they were too close for the torpedoes to become armed. A probing searchlight picked out Cushing. Within minutes she was reduced to a sinking wreck and gradually flames took over. At 03.15 with her magazines blowing up she was abandoned and remained a burning pyre until the following afternoon, when she sank.

Laffey, next behind Cushing, also nearly collided with the huge bulk of Hiei. Her torpedoes were also launched at too short a range, failed to arm and bounced off the battleship's sides, while her machine guns sprayed the huge pagoda type bridge as Hiei swept past.

Two large calibre gun salvoes and a torpedo put Laffey out of action for all time. She was abandoned and the burning hull exploded. Sterett following behind took on a ship to starboard and started fires, but a Japanese salvo at point-blank range disabled her steering and radar. Manoeuvring with her engines only, she fired four torpedoes at Hiei at 2,000 yards but scored no hits.

Seriously on fire by now she engaged other targets but became separated in the hideous mêlée of battle. Next came O'Bannon firing furiously and scoring hits while trying to avoid a collision with Sterett and with the huge Hiei only 1,200 yards away and closing rapidly. O'Bannon fired two torpedoes, but at too short a range and neither torpedo exploded. The battleship's 14 inch guns could not depress

sufficiently to take on the diminutive O'Bannon and shells tore over the top of the ship. Hiei was now badly on fire from numerous hits and the sheets of flame from her salvoes together with the enveloping smoke and thunderous roar of her big guns all but stunned O'Bannon as she tore by. Admiral Abe realized that there would be no question of a bombardment of the Marines that night. The American column had penetrated his destroyer screen and was between his two battleships. He therefore ordered a retirement. Throughout all this, Kirishima had been firing at close range and scoring hits but was herself untouched.

Admiral Callaghan in San Francisco (next behind the blazing Atlanta) was in no position to control the battle. At the start of the engagement she had illuminated and taken under fire a vessel on her port beam, and then a searchlight held her in its glare. She found and hit Hiei repeatedly but Kirishima had pinned down the brightly illuminated flagship and dealt out heavy punishment. A Japanese destroyer darting down her port side added to the devastation topside. Steering and engine control were temporarily lost and as she slowed down she suffered an avalanche of shells which killed Admiral Callaghan and nearly everyone on the bridge. At this juncture, cruisers astern of San Francisco rallied to her aid. The cruiser Portland immediately behind her took on the ships illuminating the flagship and lashed out at them with her turret guns. In the glare of the searchlights, confused by the flash and roar of guns and the burning ships around her, Portland was unable to avoid a torpedo which tore into her stern. The torn plates acted as a rudder and she made an involuntary complete circle. As she came out of it Hiei loomed up in her sights at 4,000 yards and inflicted more damage. But Portland with her warped stern continued to steam in tight circles throughout the night, counting nine burning vessels around her at one time.

Helena, next astern of Portland, had opened fire with the other cruisers. Weaving her way through damaged ships ahead of her she shifted from target to target, in an attempt to silence the ships tormenting San Francisco. Ships loomed out of the darkness or were silhouetted against burning vessels. The range was so short that machine guns were able to add to the din of battle while smoke hung in the air, partly obliterating the scene of carnage.

The last of the cruisers was Juneau. During the hectic quarter of an hour between 01.50 and 02.03 she had difficulty in identifying targets but took on anyone she could distinguish. A torpedo crashed into her forward fireroom with a shock which put the ship out of action and she lay dead in the water and out of the fight. Throughout the remainder of the night she struggled to effect repairs and by morning was able to raise steam.

Bringing up the rear of the American squadron were the destroyers Aaron Ward, Barton, Monssen and Fletcher. They were handicapped by lack of information and the almost impossible task of distinguishing friend from foe. Aaron Ward took on a target on her starboard side and continued attacking until she saw it explode and sink. But her hull had been pierced by nine medium calibre shells and she lay dead

The Guadalcanal action on 13 November.

The destruction of Japanese transports carrying reinforcements for Guadacanal. Navy and Marine Corps aircraft attacked throughout the day, sinking seven ships and drowning thousands of Japanese soldiers. Admiral Tanaka's destroyers bravely went alongside to rescue survivors despite the onslaught.

in the water. For the rest of the night she repaired damage and was only able to get under way next morning. *Barton*, next in line, had a total combat life of exactly seven minutes. She opened fire, launched four torpedoes to port, stopped to avoid collision and received two torpedoes. She broke in half and sank in a matter of seconds, taking with her all but a handful of her crew. *Monssen*, following on, fired a full salvo of torpedoes at a battleship and another vessel on her starboard beam, firing every gun on the ship as targets loomed up at close quarters. Starshells began to burst over and round her. Two blinding searchlights held her like a vice and she was deluged by some thirty-seven shell hits before becoming a blazing hulk. She was abandoned during the night and finally sank next day.

Fletcher was the very last ship in the squadron and after firing five torpedoes at an enemy ship she threaded her way through the chaotic scene and at full speed found herself ahead of the retiring Japanese forces. She had a charmed life and received no hits — though torpedo wakes and gun salvoes followed her.

During those fifteen minutes, a wild and an infernal scene was witnessed by the participants. The blinding light of starshells and searchlights dimmed the stars overhead. Elongated red and white trails of shell tracers arched and criss-crossed. Magazines exploded and oil fed conflagrations sent up twisted yellow columns, while the horizon was dotted with the dull red glow of burning hulls. The sea itself,

fouled with oil and flotsam, and tortured by underwater upheavals, rose in geysers from shell explosions. Gradually the action died down and so ended one of the most desperate sea actions of all time.

Hiei steered an erratic north-westerly course having taken over eighty topside hits. Destroyer *Akatsuki* had been sunk and *Portland*, still steaming in circles, sank the motionless *Yudachi*. Three more Japanese destroyers were badly damaged but were able to return to their base. Meanwhile three of *Hiei*'s destroyers stood by her. Mercifully for the Americans the bombardment of Henderson Field did not take place. It was reprieved by the savagery of the night battle, and in the morning aircraft took off to attack the slowly moving battleship. She took more and more punishment but fought back gallantly throughout the morning. Finally her crew were taken off and she slipped below the surface at dusk.

There was to be a final postscript to this action, the first part of the great naval battle of Guadalcanal. The surviving American ships had worked throughout the night to raise steam and as dawn broke *Helena* took charge of the badly damaged *San Francisco, Portland, Juneau, O'Bannon, Sterett* and *Fletcher*, slowly setting course for the New Hebrides. The depleted squadron now entered an area covered by Japanese submarines. One of these, I-26, lay in wait and fired a spread of torpedoes. *Juneau* was hit at 11.00 and completely disintegrated. Seeming to be in the centre of a submarine

attack the squadron continued on and failed to alert the rescue services. Out of about 100 survivors who escaped miraculously from the eruption of *Juneau*, all but ten perished. Their suffering through privations and rapacious shark attacks is one of the grimmest stories of the war at sea.

The Japanese objective was to eliminate Henderson Field, and Admiral Abe's failure to do this in no way softened Admiral Kondo's determination to land troops and supplies on the island. Vice-Admiral Mikawa in *Chokai* with four heavy cruisers, two light cruisers and six destroyers was ordered to make an immediate bombardment of Henderson Field, and this took place during the night of 14 November, doing considerable damage but not putting the airfield completely out of action.

On their return the Japanese squadron was savaged by the pilots from Henderson Field, sinking the heavy cruiser *Kinugasa* and damaging the heavy cruiser *Chokai*, a light cruiser and a destroyer. The score was just beginning to even out.

It will be remembered that the original Japanese plan was to land troops on Guadalcanal on the 14 November following the massive bombardment by *Hiei* and *Kirishima*. The bloody night action of the 13 November prevented the bombardment but Rear-Admiral Tanaka with his eleven destroyers guarding eleven large troop carrying transports was already heading for Guadalcanal. Meanwhile Admiral Kinkaid's Task Force 16 with the carrier *Enterprise* and two new battleships *Washington* and *South Dakota* had departed Noumea on the 11 November and was moving up to Guadalcanal as fast as possible.

The Battle of Guadalcanal. In the night action of 13 November 1942 eight American destroyers and five cruisers fought against two Japanese battleships and twelve destroyers at high speed in confined shoal waters. It was all over in twenty-five minutes of wild confusion and was probably the most desperate sea action of the whole war.

164

At 08.30 on 14 November 1942, Rear-Admiral Tanaka's reinforcement group was sighted just 150 miles north-west of and approaching Guadalcanal and a strike was launched against the transports, which were also attacked by search planes from *Enterprise*. Thus a combined attack was launched including fifteen Flying Fortresses from Espiritu Santo. Throughout the day the slaughter of the transports and their human cargo went on. Seven ships were sunk while Admiral Tanaka's destroyers courageously went alongside the burning transports, despite the continuous air attacks, and saved what troops they could. It was a massacre made all the more horrible by the proximity of land. Survivors in the water could have reached the beaches, and to prevent this the aircraft made repeated runs, machine gunning anything that moved in the water. By nightfall four transports were left and it was decided to run them on the beach, and for the destroyers to retire. This was done and next morning the luckless transports were attacked with the same ferocity and blood-soaked decks were littered with dead and dying Japanese soldiers. It had been a disastrous reinforcement operation. However, for sheer tenacity Admiral Tanaka stands out as a very courageous commander and a fine seaman. In the face of that tremendous onslaught, with the sea stained red by the bloodshed, he stayed with his transports and undoubtedly saved many hundreds of lives.

While this action was taking place, Admiral Lee was commanding the battleships *Washington* and *South Dakota* which were steaming hard for Guadalcanal. With him he also had the destroyers *Walke, Benham, Preston* and *Gwin.* Intelligence reports showed that Admiral Kondo had collected a further bombardment group including the undamaged *Kirishima,* the two heavy cruisers *Atago* and *Chokai,* a light cruiser and six destroyers. It was fortunate for the Marines that Admiral Lee would be able to reach Guadalcanal first. Accurate information was provided by the submarine *Trout* which had attacked the force without success.

Early in the evening of 14 November, Admiral Lee was off the northern coast of Guadalcanal. Leading his column were the destroyers followed by the battleships. It was indeed a risk to commit two new 16 inch battleships to an area as restricted as these shoal-studded waters round the island, but Admiral Halsey knew the crisis was so grave the chance had to be taken.

Just in time at 22.52 Rear-Admiral Lee was patrolling between Savo and Cape Esperance when Admiral Kondo's forces approached in three sections. At 23.00 *Washington*'s radar picked up the cruiser *Sendai* due north of his force. Fire was opened and *Sendai* doubled back under cover of smoke. Admiral Lee's lead destroyers spotted the Japanese destroyers *Ayanami* and *Uranami* which had been detached from *Sendai* and were making their sweep round the western side of Savo. They

The Japanese battleship Hiei *had been sunk in the first action. The remaining Japanese battleship* Kirishima *returned two nights later to bombard the airfield; she was met by two American battleships and after another night engagement was sunk by USS* Washington.

opened fire while *Gwin* the rear destroyer-sighted Admiral Kondo's advance guard of the cruiser *Nagara* and four destroyers, and opened fire. The Japanese replied at once taking all four destroyers under fire and launching a torpedo attack. *Walke* was struck and was soon ablaze. *Preston* was hit by heavy calibre shells and rolled over and sank and *Benham* was torpedoed in the bows. The American battleships were striving to protect their

destroyers, when suddenly *South Dakota* lost all power throughout the ship due to a circuit break. It was a critical moment.

At 23.35 Admiral Lee altered course to pass south of the burning destroyers. *South Dakota* started to follow her but had to turn to starboard to avoid *Benham* and became silhouetted by the burning *Preston* and *Walke*. Luckily the power flowed back into the battleship and

she opened fire, for silhouetted against the fires of the destroyers she attracted a spread of thirty-four torpedoes, all of which missed. At 5,000 yards searchlight shutters were snapped open to expose *South Dakota* clearly to the combined fury of the whole bombardment force.

She replied with everything she had but was in a very tough spot, and found herself the primary target of three heavy ships.

Admiral Lee in *Washington* had 'lost' *South Dakota* from his radar screen and was unsure of her position. However, when she was silhouetted by the Japanese searchlights he opened fire on a large target he had been tracking on radar. It was *Kirishima* at 8,400 yards, unaware of *Washington*'s presence. Lit by starshell she was hit by nine out of seventy-five 16 inch and some forty 5 inch shells. Within seven minutes she was in flames. Destroyers closed her and at

03. 20 she was scuttled north-west of Savo. Of the American destroyers *Gwin* was the sole survivor of this devastating action.

The three day naval battle of Guadalcanal was one of the most furious of naval engagements. Fought in shoal waters, the early stages at point-blank range, it resulted in the now still waters becoming known as Ironbottom Sound.

Tassafaronga and the Japanese evacuation

A sharp defeat was inflicted by eight Japanese destroyers commanded by Rear-Admiral Tanaka on a cruiser and destroyer force sent to intercept them. Japanese 'long lance' torpedoes sank one cruiser and severely damaged three more.

The great naval battle of Guadalcanal was the turning point in the struggle for control of the island. The Marine and Navy pilots retained ascendancy in the air and it became more and more difficult for Japanese reinforcements to land while American reinforcements of all kinds poured in.

Admiral Halsey heard from the coast watchers that eight Japanese destroyers were heading for Guadalcanal on 29 November, and he ordered a cruiser force to intercept. Rear-Admiral Wright proceeded to sea at once with a much larger force consisting of heavy cruisers *Minneapolis, New Orleans, Northampton, Pensacola* and

the light cruiser *Honolulu.* He also took with him six destroyers. On the Japanese side Rear-Admiral Tanaka had been ordered to supply the beleaguered ground troops by making high speed dashes in and out of Guadalcanal every four days. The method was to jettison drums of supplies under cover of darkness which would be retrieved next day.

Shifting his flag to one of his destroyers he set out with 1,100 drums and gave strict orders that action was to be avoided if possible and gunfire was not to be used. Admiral Tanaka knew from intelligence reports that an American force was on its way. Balanced against this was the desperate plight of the Japanese ground forces. Literally starved Jof food and medical supplies and with ammunition running low, the troops were suffering untold miseries. They had to be supplied somehow and Admiral Tanaka was by far the best Japanese commander to undertake this very dangerous task.

At 22.25 on 30 November the American force was slowly moving up the eastern shore of Guadalcanal in the pitch dark and Ironbottom Sound was like a black mirror. There were no picket destroyers ahead, but radar contact with the approaching Japanese force was made at 23,000 yards.

Admiral Tanaka, with no radar and no means of monitoring American radio circuits, was blind to the approaching cruisers. The disposition of his destroyers on a southerly course opposite Savo Island was in the following order: *Naganami* (the flagship), *Makinami, Oyashio, Kuroshio, Kagero, Kawakaze* and *Suzukaze* in line ahead with *Takanami* on the port bow of the flagship. This vessel and the Admiral's flagship carried no supplies and were prepared to fight on instant warning. On entering the Sound and prior to releasing the floating drums, speed was reduced to 12 knots on a course parallel to and two miles from the shore.

spreads of torpedoes, but within the first few moments of the battle, twenty fast-running torpedoes were on their way to American targets. The first two warheads struck flagship *Minneapolis,* the van cruiser, and some sixty feet of her bow dangled down in the water like an immense scoop with the deck awash to Number 1 turret. She came to a stop.

New Orleans, next astern, had to take violent avoiding action as she swept by the flagship. In so doing she was put in the track of a torpedo which hit her port bow, triggering off two forward magazines and blowing off the whole forward section of the ship, back to Number 2 turret. *New Orleans* slowed to 5 knots spouting flame from her truncated nose. *Pensacola* was silhouetted as she turned away to avoid a collision. A torpedo caught her directly below the mainmast, knocking out all power and rupturing oil tanks. She was ablaze and out of the fight but still afloat while *Honolulu* turned hard right and at 30 knots, zigzagged her way out of the mêlée sustaining no hits.

Northampton was the last cruiser in the line and took the worst hammering of all. She was hit by torpedoes from the destroyer *Oyashio* which had now reversed course. Two warheads detonated, at once igniting oil, and the entire ship became a mass of flames. Her list increased and *Fletcher* and *Drayton* closed to take off the ship's company, and she rolled over and sank.

The battle was over. Hardly any of the 1,100 drums of precious Japanese supplies had reached shore, and the destroyer *Takanami* had been sunk. Against this the Japanese had inflicted a sharp defeat on an alert and superior cruiser force, sinking one ship and very badly damaging three. The credit for this remarkable feat must go to Admiral Tanaka, a superb tactician and a great destroyer leader. The fact that he was without his flagship *Jintsu* and his squadron's decks were cluttered up with supplies makes it all the more remarkable. The well disciplined crews, properly briefed, reacted immediately to a very difficult situation and having fired their torpedoes withdrew to avoid further damage.

This was the last of the great sea battles fought to protect Guadalcanal, but the island would

At 23.16 the leading American destroyer held the Japanese on her radar at 7,000 yards on the port bow and approaching. Permission to fire torpedoes or for the destroyers to act independently was withheld, and it was not until the leading Japanese destroyers were abaft the beam that the order was given. Thus surprise was lost. At 9,200 yards Admiral Wright opened fire and the whole squadron joined in, selecting targets by radar and illuminating the scene by starshell. The broadsides of eleven vessels shattered the velvet darkness. Admiral Tanaka's ships had trained and fought together and the order to fire torpedoes and retire at speed was acted upon at once. Destroyer *Takanami* acting independently fired a full salvo and reversed course to the right. She was clearly visible on the American radar screens and became the main target. As she caught fire more heavy shells poured into her until she was ablaze. The other destroyers, hampered by deckloads of drums of supplies, took longer to fire their deadly

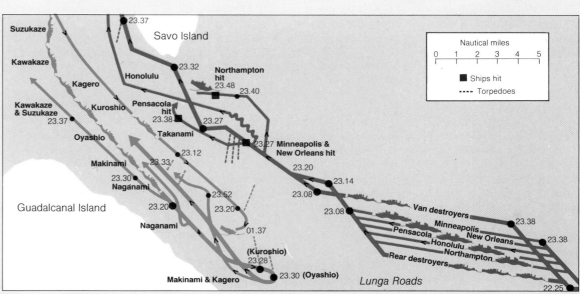

The Battle of Tassafaronga, 30 November 1942.

169

American troops and pilots had no idea that this was in fact an evacuation, and every effort was made to thwart what was thought to be a reinforcement. On the night of 7 February the final evacuation took place. It was to be a brilliantly executed operation achieved with complete secrecy. But to so many of those starved and disease-ridden Japanese soldiers it was the end of a nightmare. They had fought with fanatical courage, while being deprived of food and medical comforts. The toll of dead and missing makes grim reading. The true numbers will never be known. Some 14,800 had been killed or were missing, and perhaps 9,000 died from disease or starvation, with 1,000 more being taken prisoner. Many thousands more had died in sinking transports on the way to war. On the naval side the figures will never be known.

Ironbottom Sound is the resting place of more warships sunk in action against each other in such a small area than anywhere else on earth. They lie there as a result of some of the most concentrated and vicious fighting that the world has known. Guadalcanal has passed into legend and perhaps the most fitting monument is that jagged cone of Savo Island. It stands forever brooding over the still, calm waters of Ironbottom Sound. To the west, and only six miles away, it watches over the beaches and jungle-covered shoreline behind which lies Henderson Field.

American aircraft dominated Guadalcanal to such an extent that it was only possible to supply the Japanese garrison by destroyers carrying hundreds of drums of food and materials which were jettisoned off shore and picked up before dawn.

not be secured until the Japanese troops had been defeated, and they were still being reinforced. Nightly runs by Japanese destroyers were now the main target of the fliers from Henderson Field and of the PT (torpedo and gunboat) Boat Squadron which had been based at Tulagi. It became ever more difficult and dangerous to sustain the Japanese garrison and even submarines were used to bring in vital stores and supplies. Reconnaissance aircraft spotted ships in Rabaul Harbour at the end of December, and United States submarines took some toll of this shipping, but against this the heavy cruiser *Chicago* was torpedoed on 29 January 1943 during a series of determined twilight attacks by Japanese aircraft. She was taken in tow but had to be abandoned.

It seemed yet again as though there was to be a further build-up of Japanese troops early in February but this activity had nothing to do with reinforcements: Tokyo had finally decided to evacuate the island. In all nineteen destroyers reached Guadalcanal and the evacuation began under cover of darkness. The second evacuation run was undertaken by one light cruiser and twenty-two destroyers. At the time the

Finally, in a brilliantly executed move, the Japanese evacuated the island in such secrecy that the Americans were totally unaware of the fact until all had been taken off.

New Guinea

While the battle to hold Guadalcanal against the Japanese onslaught was in progress, another and equally serious situation had developed in New Guinea. The Japanese assault on Port Moresby had been turned back at the Battle of the Coral Sea and Japan could not sustain another attempt to capture the town with its important harbour facilities without air cover and this was no longer available. Thus on 22 July 1942 11,430 Japanese troops landed at the small village of Buna on the north coast of New Guinea. It was an unopposed landing and a glance at the map will show its position exactly opposite Port Moresby and only a hundred miles away.

The Owen Stanley Mountains, a jagged and precipitous barrier of rain forest, mist and spongy moss, rose to a pass 6,500 feet high. The Japanese chose this, the Kokoda Trail, for their assault. It was an appalling task to manhandle equipment, ammunition and food up to this tortuous pass and the troops suffered dreadfully from starvation and disease as they inched their way forward against a stubborn rearguard action by Australian troops, fighting in the same near impossible conditions.

After six weeks, the Japanese troops had reached Ioribaiwa, just thirty-two miles from Port Moresby and only twenty miles from General Kenny's USAAF airfields. It was here

In New Guinea, Japanese troops were supplied in part by barges, and this resulted in nightly clashes with American PT boats. These encounters were fiercely disputed with losses on both sides.

that General Blamey's Australians held fast and on 26 September they began to force the advancing Japanese back down the trail.

This narrative is concerned with naval and amphibious operations and thus it is impossible to describe in detail the heroic defence of Port Moresby by Australian troops and the equally fierce determination of Japan to capture it.

At the eastern end of the Papuan Peninsula lies Milne Bay. Whoever held it could command the

sea passage round to Port Moresby and it was ideal as a forward airfield. Australian and United States troops got there first. An attempt by the Japanese to follow them was successful and fierce fighting ensued before the defenders finally forced the Japanese to withdraw, and they never attempted another assault. But the Japanese were constructing defences round Buna and the whole coastline was studded with reefs, making any approach other than by small ships with local knowledge impossible. The Allies formed a small flotilla of assorted ships,

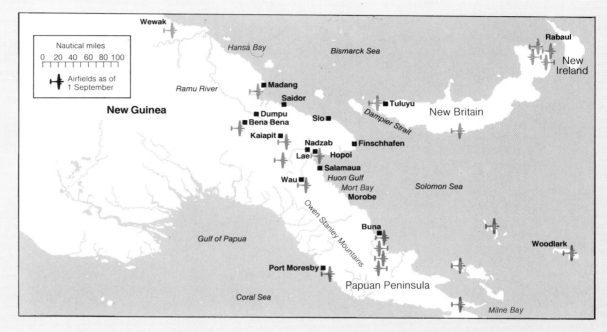

Eastern New Guinea and New Britain saw some of the fiercest fighting of the whole war.

and this was aided by hydrographic surveys. It enabled the Allies to take supplies in by sea and land between Cape Nelson and Oro Bay. They survived the hazards of the reefs and bombing by Japanese aircraft, but not without loss.

The Allied troops, moving over the Owen Stanley Mountains or being ferried into newly constructed airstrips, kept up pressure on the Japanese positions round Buna. It had all the problems of the Guadalcanal conflict without the ability to bring large convoys in by sea or the benefit of a Henderson Field. Certainly this area produced some of the toughest fighting anywhere in the world at that time. It was to be a long and desperately hard struggle. American PT boats were stationed in Milne Bay. From there, and from forward bases, they attempted to cut off Japanese supplies and reinforcements to Buna. The Japanese constructed hundreds of barges; moving them by night and working close inshore. As night fell they ran the gauntlet of the PT boats, but it was by no means a one-sided affair. Fierce machine gun battles took place nightly with heavier support from field guns on shore to protect the inshore barges.

On land the battle for Buna raged with men living, fighting and sleeping in the mud and slime of malaria-infested swamps. It was bad enough for the Allies who were able to evacuate and reinforce by air, but for the Japanese the situation was quite desperate. Gona was taken in December and Buna in January 1943. The Allied casualties were higher than in Guadalcanal: the Australians had 5,698 killed and the Americans lost 2,959.

The reason for this long drawn out and bloody campaign was the lack of sea power on either side. If the campaign had had all the necessary landing craft, air cover and sea bombardment, it would have been over in a matter of a few weeks. If supplies could have reached the Japanese under an umbrella of carrier air power and reinforcements by air and sea, they could have remained against determined attacks. As it was their losses were far higher than the Allies.

But there was no let up. Japanese forces landed to the north at Lae in Huon Bay in January to be followed by 9,400 men at Wewak 382 miles north-west of Lae. Meanwhile Allied reinforcements of PT boats and a build-up of naval stores proceeded at Milne Bay.

The Japanese decided to reinforce their garrison of 3,500 troops at Lae by a further 6,900 soldiers from Rabaul in New Britain. Sixteen ships (eight transports and eight destroyers) under the command of Rear-Admiral Kimura departed from Rabaul on 28 February. They were combat loaded and even if some ships were lost, the remainder would bring much needed assistance to the garrison. The escort was provided by those ships that had fought so hard at Guadalcanal and they were certainly a formidable force.

Meanwhile General Kenny's air strength in Papua had increased to 207 bombers and 129 fighters. New tactics for attacking ships at sea had been evolved. The B-25 Mitchell bombers were modified by the inclusion of six machine guns mounted in the nose, and they carried 500 pound bombs with a five-second delay fuse.

The aircrews had been trained to approach at masthead height, strafing as they came in, dropping their bombs and climbing away before they exploded.

The convoy was sighted on 1 March and again picked up at 08.30 on 2 March at the western end of New Britain and approaching the Dampier Strait. The first strike from 5,000 feet by B-17 bombers sank one ship and damaged two more. Two destroyers picked up some 950 survivors and raced into Lae after dark. Next day, as the two destroyers rejoined the convoy, the B-25 aircraft arrived under a cloudless sky. They were escorted by fighters who kept the forty Zeros away and the attack went in. The bombers approached at sea level and the ships turned to face them. As they approached, the machine guns strafed the crowded decks and the bombs exploded under the ships. When they completed their runs, Beaufighters of the RAAF swept in, strafing the decks of the ships as they slewed round or scattered. All eight transports were sunk together with four destroyers. The sea was littered with rafts and ships' boats and as darkness fell the four remaining destroyers loaded with 2,734 survivors steamed north at high speed. Ten PT boats set out to sweep the area after dark. Next morning planes and PT boats again attacked the survivors in the water, machine gunning anything on the surface until nothing was left alive. The Japanese losses in addition to their ships exceeded 3,000, the majority shot in the water. Such was the disaster that no further convoys were despatched and in future reinforcements had to come by barge from Cape Gloucester or by submarine.

On the Allied side progress was slow but none the less effective. Though starved of equipment, the beginnings of an Amphibious Training Command was set up by Rear-Admiral Barbey USN. Additional small craft and destroyers began to arrive to form the basis of the Seventh Fleet. A small American reinforcement was landed in the Huon Gulf at Nassau Bay at the end of June 1943 to ease the logistics problem. Before this, Australian troops were supplied by air to the airstrip at Wau and thence overland. The Japanese meanwhile had consolidated at Salamaua and Lae.

In order to take the north coast of Huon Gulf and so push the Japanese back along the coast of New Guinea it was essential to maintain superiority in the air. The daily dogfights between General Kenny's Allied fighters and the Japanese Army Air Force were resulting in losses on both sides, but gradually the Allies attained parity and then superiority. An airstrip near Wau was constructed and by the end of July was operational. This was strategically placed to support the assault on Lae and Salamaua. Meanwhile PT boats attacked barges on their nightly run along the coast to supply

Japanese garrisons. Such was the vigilance of Allied aircraft that little could move in daylight. Japanese submarines were also used to bring in much needed supplies. The Japanese decided that a large scale air attack on American airfields and positions would stabilize the position for them, but on 14 August Allied bombers destroyed nearly half the attacking force on the ground and it was therefore cancelled.

During this time the Navy had done little in comparison to the support it had provided in the Solomons. Part of this was due to the reef-strewn coastline and part to a lack of air cover, but in September the assault on the north coast of the Huon peninsula took place. A seaborne force comprising the Australian 9th Division was ferried from Milne Bay to positions seventeen miles to the east of Lae. On 6 September a bombardment by five destroyers preceded the

The Battle of the Bismarck Sea. Eight Japanese transports escorted by eight destroyers departed from Rabaul for New Guinea on 28 February 1943. Extra machine guns were placed in the nose of the B-25 Allied bombers. As they approached at masthead height they opened fire on the crowded decks, dropping delayed action bombs which exploded beneath the ships as the aircraft climbed away.

landing which met little opposition, except from a bombing raid, and by nightfall the division's 7,800 men were ashore and 1,500 tons of stores had been landed. This landing formed the right hook and next day there was an airborne landing to the west by American paratroops who captured the small airstrip to the north of Lae. In just twenty-four hours, Australian and American engineers had prepared the strip for transport planes.

In the following week several thousand of Major-General Vasey's Australian troops had been flown in and were at the outskirts of the town. Bombardment from the sea by destroyers and a continuous supply of food and ammunition from down the coast, coupled with the pressure by the Allied troops, finally led to the withdrawal of the Japanese garrison. They faced gruesome conditions as they retreated across

the peninsula to Sio. Constantly harassed by the Australians, they hacked their way through the pitiless terrain and while some 1,500 out of 2,000 reached Sio, less than 400 were in any condition to fight. It was a terrible ordeal.

General MacArthur kept up the momentum and Rear-Admiral Barbey was equal to the challenge. Supplies were loaded at Buna and the Australian 20th Brigade was embarked at Lae and landed before dawn on 22 September, six miles north of Finschafen. The Japanese had prepared for an overland assault and were taken by surprise and by 2 October the town was captured.

Vigorous patrolling offshore by PT boats kept the Japanese barge traffic to a minimum but a destroyer sweep attempting to trap supply-carrying submarines ended with the loss of the

US destroyer *Henley* hit by torpedoes, without damage to the submarines.

Finally, General Kenny's air force made the heaviest Allied air strike of the campaign so far against Rabaul in early November, with 349 aircraft. This did considerable damage to the port but destroyed few ships. What it did do was to ease pressure on the Solomons campaign which was being fought simultaneously with that taking place in New Guinea.

The Japanese had three offensive campaigns to deal with — in New Guinea, the northern Solomons and now one over Rabaul itself. We will now turn to the second of these.

The Solomons campaign

The battle for Guadalcanal took place at the same time as General MacArthur's New Guinea operations. It may appear that the battle to hold Guadalcanal has been covered in far greater detail than the New Guinea campaign and that the heroism of the Australian troops with the American Allies has been brushed aside. Similarly, the Japanese defence of this area has not been fully described. However, this narrative concerns the war at sea with naval and marine forces, and we must confine ourselves to this sphere of the hostilities.

With the evacuation of Guadalcanal by Japanese forces an immediate consolidation and build-up of American stores then took place. Air superiority was the key to the whole operation and the Wildcat fighter had been overtaken by the far heavier F6F Hellcat and the gull-winged F4U Corsair which could climb faster than any Japanese aircraft and had a range double that of the Wildcat. Above all the training of American pilots had been thorough and in such numbers that they were able to keep up with aircraft production. The Japanese had no such advantages, either in men or machines. The doctrine of squadrons fighting to the last man meant it was no longer possible for veterans to be sent home to instruct the pupil pilots. But the Japanese did have one delaying tactic. With airfields and naval bases stretching north to Rabaul they had garrisoned the Solomons so that there was no alternative but to assault each island in order to protect the new base on Guadalcanal and to relieve pressure on New Guinea. From the American point of view, Tokyo was still a very long way away and the Japanese had the benefit of a series of well defended islands in depth stretching all the way back to the Homeland.

Little has been said of the Allied advance in signal intelligence, but efforts to read the Japanese codes and to evaluate signal intelligence were producing dividends. One such example will suffice. The Commander-in-Chief Combined Fleet, Admiral Yamamoto, had flown south to visit establishments in the Solomons. His visit was monitored by intelligence and the arrange ments for his visit to Bougainville were read. It was decided to intercept. Such was the accuracy of the information that his exact time of arrival was known. On 18 April 1943 sixteen USAAF P 38 Lightnings took off from Guadalcanal and arrived as the planes and escorts carrying the Commander-in-Chief were preparing to land at Buin. The fighters opened fire and the 'Betty' bombers flamed into the jungle, killing the admiral and his chief of staff. To avoid suspicion there was no announcement of this incident, but the loss to Japan was grievous.

The first priority for the Americans was the capture of Munda, a collection of islands to the north-west of Guadalcanal and an important Japanese base. As a preliminary, Admiral Halsey ordered offensive sweeps up the 'Slot' to disrupt the Japanese build-up of defensive stores and reinforcement of their garrison. A cruiser and destroyer force under Rear-Admiral Merrill sank two Japanese destroyers on 6 March while a newly laid minefield accounted for three more. Plans were now complete for the first amphibious landings and Munda airfield was to be the target. It was a considerable undertaking under the command of Rear-Admiral Kelly Turner, involving landings at four points. At Rendova it was virtually unopposed, although Japanese air attacks badly damaged the command ship *McCawley*.

At Viru, there was little resistance, and none at Wickham Anchorage, although there was confusion in the rain and swell. The position was thus ready for the assault on Munda, and a landing was soon made, preceded by a naval bombardment. Rain and wind hampered an already chaotic scene but by daybreak on 5 July it was under control, nine battalions of troops were ashore, and the transports had departed, the only casualty being the destroyer *Strong* sunk by a torpedo fired with uncanny accuracy by Japanese destroyers which were retiring after bringing in more reinforcements.

The Japanese were determined to hold Munda — reinforcing the island by nightly destroyer

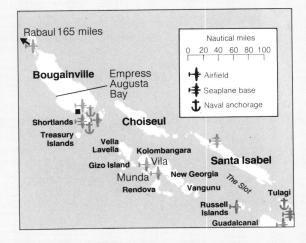

Bases in the Solomon Islands in June 1943.

runs, and getting clear before daybreak. Signal intelligence and the coast watchers were feeding Admiral Halsey with information about the troop movements — and one such destroyer convoy was discovered moving down the 'Slot' on 5 July.

Rear-Admiral Ainsworth with a force of cruisers and destroyers proceeded to intercept. By midnight his force was off the north coast of Kolombangara and a Japanese force of ten destroyers, (three being escorts) were picked up on radar at 24,700 yards. American cruising dispositions changed to a destroyer van of *Nicholas* and *O'Bannon,* cruisers *Honolulu, Helena* and *St Louis* with destroyers *Jenkins* and *Radford* in the rear. This had ominous similarities to the tight formations which were characteristic of earlier battles. There had been no time for a conference or for the issue of detailed orders for this, the Battle of Kula Gulf. The range had decreased to 7,000 yards to the nearest group when gunfire was opened but surprise had been lost. Admiral Akiyama in *Niizuki* had already sighted the force and had ordered a torpedo attack as the American guns opened fire. The first salvo put *Niizuki* out of action, killing the admiral. Here was a case where an immediate torpedo attack by the American destroyers would have paid off, but no such permission was given. Over 2,500 rounds of gunfire smothered the Japanese screening force with very little damage except for the sinking of *Niizuki*. Both the remaining destroyers turned north at speed making smoke to reload, having fired sixteen 'long lance' torpedoes. At 49 knots these lethal weapons were approaching the American squadron. At 02.03 on 6 July the torpedoes arrived, three hitting the cruiser *Helena* and breaking her back. She sank fast, only her bow remaining above water. It was only then that destroyers *O'Bannon* and *Radford* fired torpedoes, but they were now chasing the retreating Japanese destroyers and no hits were made.

The Japanese Commander-in-Chief, Admiral Yamamoto, was ambushed and killed by American fighter aircraft when visiting naval establishments in Bougainville by air. The interception took place as a result of signal intelligence and the attack was made by sixteen Lightning fighters from Guadalcanal. The flight was one of the longest made, arriving just as the Japanese aircraft were preparing to land.

It is interesting to digress for a moment. The two remaining Japanese escort destroyers had reloaded empty torpedo tubes. Their 'long lance' torpedo was superior to anything the Allies possessed and their ability to reload from a store of torpedoes moved into position on a carriage running on rails was unique. No Allied navy had this facility and it paid off on a number of occasions, but this time little further action took place except that destroyer *Nagatsuki* hit a reef and was destroyed next day from the air; her brave crew fought off the attack by twenty-one bombers until every gun was knocked out.

For the Americans it had been an unsatisfactory action. One thousand six hundred Japanese troops and stores had been landed at Vila for the loss of two destroyers, while *Helena* had been sunk and the superior weight of American gunfire had failed to stop the Tokyo Express.

The advance had got bogged down and was disorganized on land as Japanese reinforcements were still arriving. At sea HMNZS *Leander* had been sent to make good the loss of *Helena,* and at sea intelligence gave Admiral Halsey the departure time of another Japanese reinforcement group led by the veteran light cruiser *Jintsu* (without Rear-Admiral Tanaka).

Five destroyers were to escort four destroyer transports to Vila. Admiral Ainsworth sailed to intercept with five destroyers in the van, the cruisers *Honolulu, Leander* and *St Louis* in the centre and five destroyers in the rear. The sea battle of Kolombangara, which took place on 12 and 13 July 1943, began when a PBY Catalina aircraft reconnaissance reported the Japanese force of one cruiser and five destroyers twenty-six miles distant and closing.

Admiral Ainsworth formed his one column battle disposition as shown on the map and at 01.09 ordered the van destroyers to attack with torpedoes. The Japanese knew exactly where the approaching Americans were and at the same moment launched their torpedoes and

turned away north. The Allied cruisers concentrated on the largest blip on their radar, the cruiser *Jintsu,* and by 01.17 had fired over 2,600 six inch shells at her. *Jintsu* exploded after receiving two torpedoes from the American destroyers. That fine old veteran of Guadalcanal sank, taking with her nearly all hands, together with Rear-Admiral Izaki.

While this furious gunfire action was taking place, the Japanese torpedoes were running with unerring accuracy. By quick ship handling they were avoided by all except *Leander* which was hit by one and was now out of the battle.

The Japanese escort force had retired north into a rain squall and reloaded their torpedoes and

The Japanese Navy was unique in its ability to reload destroyers' torpedoes at sea, and Japanese torpedoes led the world.

by 01.57 had turned south again to attack the much superior American force which had become scattered. *St Louis* was hit at 02.08, followed in quick succession by *Honolulu* and the destroyer *Gwin* which exploded in a sheet of flame. Thus the highly disciplined and compact Japanese escort group had damaged two cruisers and sunk one destroyer from a numerically stronger force in a matter of minutes.

Air cover was needed urgently by the Americans and this arrived just in time to break up a dawn attack by eighteen 'Vals' protected by twenty Zeros, while the damaged squadron made its way back to Tulagi.

The struggle to capture Munda was going badly for the Americans. Conditions were atrocious and the troops disorganized and dispirited, with parties of Japanese filtering in among them at night, resulting in hand-to-hand combat in isolated spots. The Japanese had been successfully reinforced and now supplies were urgently required for the American troops ashore.

Commander Arleigh Burke took in six destroyers, landing stores and evacuating wounded. There then followed a series of bombardments and gradually the troops inched forward, destroying pill boxes one by one and forcing back the fanatically brave Japanese. There were many acts of heroism on both sides until finally the weight of American support enabled the troops to enter Munda unopposed.

The battle for control of the Solomon Islands was a long and bitter struggle. American aircraft made repeated bombing attacks on shipping of all kinds engaged in supplying Japanese positions. One casualty was the cruiser *Kumano* which was damaged.

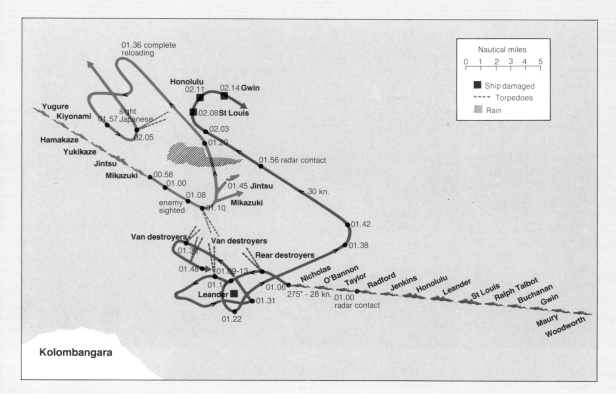

The Battle of Kolombangara, 12 to 13 July 1943.

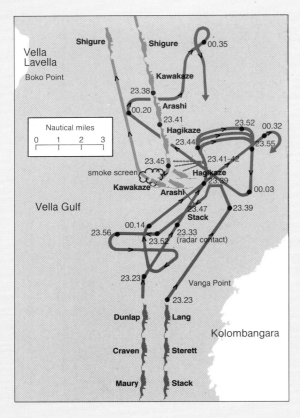

Vella
Lavella
Boko Point

Shigure   Shigure   00.35

Kawakaze

23.38
00.20   Arashi
23.41
Hagikaze   23.52
23.44   00.32
23.55
23.45   23.41-42
smoke screen   Hagikaze
23.09
Kawakaze   Arashi   00.03
23.47
Stack   23.39
00.14
23.56   23.33
23.52   (radar contact)

Nautical miles
0   1   2   3

Vella Gulf

23.23   Vanga Point

23.23

Dunlap   Lang

Craven   Sterett   Kolombangara

Maury   Stack

The Battle of Vella Gulf, 6 August 1943.

These attacks from the air forced the Japanese commanders to rely on barge traffic and to counter this, four PT boat squadrons comprising some fifty-two boats were brought up. Their nightly attacks on barges resulted in fierce hit-and-run actions.

In order to relieve pressure, Admiral Samejima ordered a destroyer sweep with a bomber attack on the Rendova base. In the close action skirmishes that ensued PT 108 (Lieutenant John F. Kennedy) was cut in two by a destroyer. Lieutenant Kennedy gathered his crew together and they swam to land. Then setting off alone with a battle lantern, Kennedy swam out to attract the attention of the expected PT boats but none came, and he returned exhausted. He was picked up by natives who took him to the nearest PT boat base and he guided the rescue boat to where the survivors were hidden, and returned with them to base.

Japanese destroyers had long operated independently while American tactics dictated the rigid positioning of destroyers in the van and rear of the cruisers, instead of allowing them a much freer hand to attack with torpedoes. Commander Moosbrugger discussed this with Admiral Wilkinson and when next a Tokyo Express was announced leaving harbour, he was ordered to take his destroyers up the 'Slot' and attack, without cruisers, and thus the Battle of Vella Gulf took place on 6 August 1943.

The Japanese force consisted of four destroyers — *Hagikaze, Arashi* and *Kawakaze* carried 900 troops and fifty tons of stores, while *Shigure* with no encumbrance acted as escort.

Commander Moosbrugger divided his force of six destroyers into two divisions, consisting of *Dunlap, Craven* and *Maury,* and *Lang, Sterett* and *Stack.* As the Americans rounded the north coast of Kolombangara and sailed into Vella Gulf, their radar showed four blips at 20,000 yards converging.

For once the Japanese were relaxed, as they were expecting only PT boats, and the three American destroyers fired twenty-four torpedoes and immediately turned 90 degrees to starboard. Meanwhile the other three ships were on the starboard quarter. Within minutes *Hagikaze* and *Arashi* were hit in the engine rooms while in *Kawakaze* a torpedo struck the forward magazine with a huge explosion. *Shigure* alone was unscathed, and withdrew. The Americans then opened fire on the stricken destroyers, all of which sank. It was a vindication of the destroyer men's tactics.

American forces had landed in strength at Empress Augusta Bay in the Solomon island of Bougainville on 1 November 1943. Japanese naval forces moved south to destroy the transports off shore and were intercepted by American cruisers. In the fierce engagement Japanese aircraft lit the American squadron with flares and the Japanese broke off the engagement thinking that the shell splashes were torpedo hits.

In late September the strongly held island of Kolombangara was evacuated by the Japanese garrison very successfully. Considering that the American forces had superiority both at sea and in the air, the Japanese did very well to evacuate 5,400 men by barges and another 4,000 by destroyers. Although the island was now in American hands, the garrison had escaped to fight another battle.

On another occasion a support group of six Japanese destroyers was formed to cover the evacuation from Vella Lavella on 6 October 1943. This was intercepted by a routine patrol of three American destroyers which sank the Japanese destroyer *Yugumo*. However, the superior Japanese force had also fired torpedoes, badly damaging destroyer *Selfridge* and finally sinking *Chevalier*.

During these exchanges the Japanese evacuation force slipped in and took off the garrison safely. Admiral Ijuin's object had been to rescue his troops. Not only had he achieved this but he had sunk one destroyer and badly damaged another for the loss of *Yugumo*.

The most formidable of the Solomon Islands was undoubtedly Bougainville, where at the southern end was the Japanese naval base at

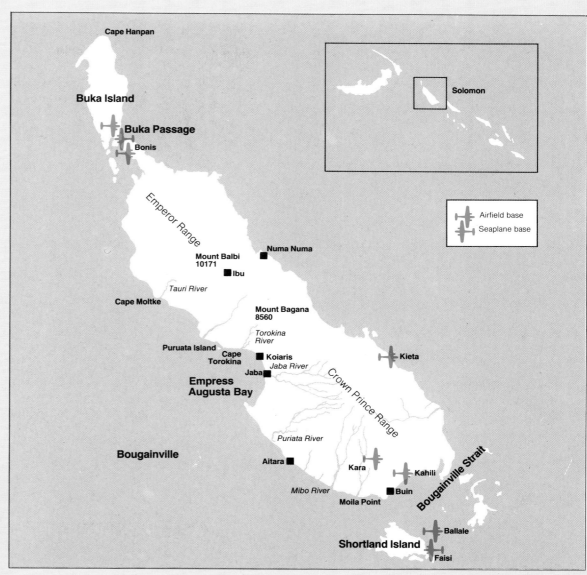

A section of the Solomons showing Bougainville and adjacent islands.

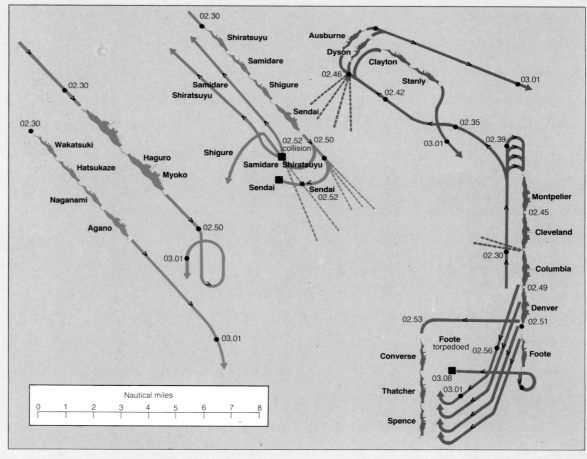

The Battle of Empress Augusta Bay, Bougainville, 2 November 1943.

Shortlands with its numerous airfields. While no further Japanese troop reinforcements were sanctioned, it was nevertheless considered vital to hold the island and its garrison was expected to do so by defending the southern area where the assault seemed most likely. It therefore came as a complete surprise when a large amphibious force landed at Empress Augusta Bay half way up the island on the west side.

A bombardment force shelled the Shortlands and its nearby airfields and every available American aircraft was used to prevent opposition to the landings which were so close to Japanese air and sea bases. The assault force under Lieutenant-General Vandegrift was brought up in large transports, making them easy targets, and 14,000 Marines and 6,000 tons of stores were landed without serious mishap just north of Cape Torokina on Bougainville on 1 November 1943.

It came as no surprise when Admiral Samejima, Commander of the Japanese Eighth Fleet, received word of the landings and reacted at once. The naval forces at Rabaul were to sail immediately and to destroy the transports off the beaches - exactly as Admiral Mikawa had been ordered to do at Guadalcanal. The heavy cruisers *Myoko* and *Haguro* together with two-light cruisers and six destroyers were available and set sail under the command of Rear-Admiral Omori. Reconnaissance aircraft kept Rear-Admiral Merrill informed of the movements of the Japanese force coming south. He had carefully placed his forces well to the west of Empress Augusta Bay. They comprised four destroyers under Captain Arleigh Burke in the van, the leading destroyer three miles ahead of four cruisers (operating 1,000 yards apart) and

another four destroyers 3,000 yards behind the rear cruiser. This time the destroyers were to have freedom of action.

At 01.30 on 2 November 1943 an American plane damaged cruiser *Haguro* and reduced the squadron's speed to 26 knots and at the same time a plane from the *Haguro* reported Admiral Merrill's position, but underestimated the size of his support group. The Japanese force altered course to intercept.

At 02.27 cruiser *Montpelier* (flag) made radar contact which showed Admiral Omori to have two heavy ships in the centre with a screen of a light cruiser and three destroyers on either flank. The range was 40,000 yards and closing from the north-west.Admiral Merrill turned north and despatched the van destroyers to attack independently with torpedoes. He then turned 180 degrees south, ordering the rear destroyers to countermarch to become the van. They were to move off to the south flank as soon as a target appeared.

Meanwhile Burke's four destroyers fired twenty-five torpedoes but they all missed due to Admiral Omori altering course in order to close. The light cruiser *Sendai* leading the forward column was engaged by the full fire power of four American cruisers. Her rudder jammed and she was seen to be on fire. The last two destroyers in her column, *Samidare* and *Shiratsuyu*, collided as they tried to avoid the concentrated shell fire. But the initial American torpedo

A lone dinghy — the fate of so many airmen until lifeguard submarines could be stationed in sufficient numbers to rescue them when their aircraft were shot down.

attack had failed. The Japanese heavy cruisers opened fire and illuminated the targets. Admiral Merrill made smoke and opened the range, deciding to engage the opposing forces at long range to avoid torpedoes which he well knew were dangerous. Both sides now made some violent manoeuvres at high speed and both obtained hits. Meanwhile to the south the destroyer *Foote* became detached and she was hit by one of the torpedoes meant for the cruisers, blowing off her stern.

Japanese aircraft appeared overhead and dropped flares which illuminated the American cruisers in a brilliant light, showing up huge shell splashes which Admiral Omori thought were torpedo hits. He calculated he had destroyed three of the cruisers and then ordered a withdrawal. Now the American destroyers sank the damaged *Hatsukaze* and the flaming *Sendai* which was still active.

The Japanese had failed to disrupt the landings and had been driven off with losses. One hundred aircraft attacked the American forces at dawn but little damage was done due to efficient fighter cover and the combined fire power of the squadron. None the less, the Japanese had no intention of allowing matters to remain as they were and from Truk Admiral Koga sent seven heavy cruisers south to Rabaul. These were *Takao, Maya, Atago, Suzuya, Mogami, Chikuma* and *Chokai* together with destroyers and a fleet train of oilers. There was nothing in the area that could possibly stop this heavy concentration of gun power had they attacked at once. The only forces available were aircraft from Rear-Admiral Sherman's fast carrier Task Force 38, built around *Saratoga* and *Princeton* which had been covering the Bougainville operations. But the Japanese cruiser force had to be stopped somehow. Admiral Nimitz took a very real risk in deciding to attack the heavy cruisers in Rabaul harbour using the carrier aircraft, which could have been wiped out by the heavily defended port. It was indeed a risk and speed was vital.

On 5 November Task Force 38 proceeded at best speed under heavy cloud to a launching point 230 miles from Rabaul. Twenty-three Avenger torpedo-bombers and twenty-two Dauntless dive-bombers, protected by fifty-two Hellcat fighters, all concentrated in one wave. They were flying into the most strongly defended Japanese-held area in the South Pacific. The bombers kept together in a tight formation until nearing the target, when the Avengers dropped to sea level unseen through scattered clouds, planning to attack immediately after the SPD Dauntless aircraft had made their dives.The Hellcat fighters took on the seventy Japanese fighters which came up to meet them and every gun opened up from the shore batteries which ringed the harbour, augmented by the fire power of the ships that were at anchor.But the Japanese had been surprised and only five American fighters and five bombers were lost, in this attack which was over almost before it began. Although not one Japanese ship was actually sunk the destruction was considerable. *Maya, Takao, Atago, Agano* and *Mogami* were all damaged and were under repair for some time. Three destroyers were also damaged. All except *Maya* and *Agano* were able to withdraw back to Truk and they did not return.

Admiral Halsey received the loan of the new carriers *Essex* and *Bunker Hill* together with the light carrier *Independence* and with this force proceeded to attack Rabaul again on 11 November. Rain obscured the harbour and made both the attack and defence difficult. The light cruiser *Agano* was again hit by a torpedo and her stern was blown off. A destroyer was sunk and others damaged. The Japanese then counter-attacked the carriers and another wild dogfight ensued. No damage was done to the ships but the attacking force was badly mauled and their losses were heavy.

It is quite fair to say how fortunate the carrier force was to come out of that action unscathed. It only takes one bomb or one torpedo to do irreparable harm, and while superior ship handling and the courage of the fighter screen contributed mightily to their escape, equally the courage of the Japanese pilots could well have resulted in a disaster to the new and precious American carriers.

On land at Empress Augusta Bay, the position was consolidated. The Japanese still retained their main force at Shortlands waiting for an attack which never came. The construction of Allied airstrips now took precedence and by the end of December two were ready, one being able to take heavy bombers. The conditions inland were horrible; mud and swamp made road and airstrip building a nightmare, but by the end of the year the Allies had made considerable progress and had consolidated their position. Word reached Admiral Halsey through signal intelligence that troops from Buka were

to be transported to Rabaul on the night of 24 November in three transport destroyers and two screening destroyers. Captain Arleigh Burke with Destroyer Squadron 23 was ordered to intercept, with air cover provided for the following dawn.

The destroyers were in two divisions. Captain Burke in *Charles F. Ausburne* with *Claxon* and *Dyson* leading, *Converse* with *Spence* 5,000 yards on his port quarter. The Japanese destroyers had disembarked their troops and were returning when at 01.41 Burke's destroyers picked them up on radar at eleven miles to the east and closing. He headed direct for the contact and at 6,000 yards the division fired fifteen torpedoes, promptly turning 90 degrees right to avoid any torpedoes from the Japanese destroyers. Without radar the Japanese only sighted Burke's ships withdrawing half a minute before the torpedoes arrived. *Onami* (leader) seemed to explode in a sheet of flame while *Makinami,* just behind her, also exploded and seemed to break in two. A chase to catch the transport destroyers ensued, the American destroyers reaching 33 knots. As they closed, both adversaries opened fire and the Japanese fanned out. Burke's destroyers concentrated on *Yugiri,* hitting her until she started circling and sank as the destroyers approached. *Converse* and *Spence* of the second division meanwhile concentrated on the still burning *Makinami* and she was sunk by gunfire at 02.45. Burke was now dangerously close to Rabaul and hauled round under the protection of fighter cover. This Battle of Cape St George had been a classic action.

The Battle of Cape St George — Thanksgiving Day 1943. American Destroyer Squadron 23 led by Captain Arleigh Burke sank three Japanese destroyers without loss.

In summing up, Bougainville had not been retaken, although Allied troops were well established on the island. Rabaul was to be subdued by air attacks alone, but it was essential to stop Japanese supplies leaving Rabaul for their beleaguered troops in New Guinea and to neutralize the airstrips at the western end of New Britain. Thus it was decided to invade the west end of the island at Cape Gloucester and thereby to control the Dampier and Vitiaz Straits. This was effected in the closing days of 1943, but a much greater build-up was in progress to the north-east which was to require everything the Allies could muster. It was to be the beginning of a series of operations to capture one island chain after another, culminating in the recapture of the Philippines and eventually leading to the invasion of Japan.

The assault on Tarawa

While the Solomons campaign was being waged with ferocity by both sides at sea, in the air and in the rain-sodden jungle on land, preparations for the largest amphibious landing to date in the Pacific were nearing completion. The Gilbert Islands lie 1,200 miles to the north-east of the Solomons and it was on the islands of Makin and Tarawa that the first assault was to be made in November 1943.

On the other side of the world Operation 'Torch' — the invasion of North Africa — has been described and was indeed a vast armada. Considering the way in which the Pacific had taken second place in ships, aircraft, supplies and men, this was also a truly remarkable feat of logistics which carried 27,600 assault troops, 7,600 garrison troops, 6,000 vehicles and 117,000 tons of cargo to their destination in the Gilbert Islands in 200 ships. This huge fleet converged on the area from Pearl Harbor, from New Zealand and the base at Efate in the New Hebrides. Ahead of them went no less than eleven battleships, nine heavy cruisers, five light cruisers and a host of destroyers. The air power was no less impressive and consisted of six fleet carriers and thirteen light and escort carriers. In addition there were over 100 Liberator bombers and twenty-four PBY Catalinas with twenty-four medium bombers stationed at Funafuti 700 miles to the south.

Makin and Tarawa were to be assaulted simultaneously. The former is a lagoon surrounded by small islands linked by coral reefs with an entrance at the south-west corner. Considering the overwhelming American fire power the occupation of Makin was an anti-climax, taking three days to overcome the garrison of 800 Japanese soldiers who fought to the last man alive. At sea on 21 November (the day after the initial landing) sixteen bombers attacked the American carriers at dusk about thirty miles west of Tarawa. Six Japanese aircraft survived this brave attack which badly damaged the light carrier *Independence*.

Japanese submarines also tried to attack the transports and were driven off, but not before I-175 had torpedoed the light carrier *Liscome Bay* which blew up, killing 642 of her crew.

We now turn to Tarawa. The garrison consisted of more than 4,500 tough and seasoned men, many of whom had been on Tarawa for months and were concentrated on the small island of Betio, not far from the only deep water entrance to the lagoon. Surrounding the string of coral islands are reefs, and surf gets up when the trade winds blow.

The Japanese were determined to hold Betio — an area less than two miles long, no more than 600 yards wide, tapering to a point. In the centre and widest part of the island was an airstrip of over 4,000 feet with triangular taxi-ways.

The defence was ingenious and methodical, with interlocking fire lanes. The outer barricade at the water's edge consisted of coconut logs stapled together, over or through which light and heavy machine guns covered the beaches at point-blank range. Some of these guns were embedded in concrete or armour plate. At various points along the shore, fourteen coast defence guns of up to 8 inch calibre were sited to fire out to sea. These had elaborate and strong bomb-proof underground storage facilities. Interlocked in the defensive position were twenty-five field guns mostly in concrete pill boxes and well protected against anything but a direct hit. The garrison could be accommodated in a series of bomb-proof shelters with baffle compartments, so thick that they could withstand anything except heavy calibre AP delayed action shells. Finally the island was relatively flat, not rising more than a few feet above sea level.

Probably its greatest natural protection lay in the vagaries of the tide and the lack of accurate tide tables. This is very important to the story which follows.

Admiral Turner was in command of the assault, and the troops disembarked from their transports into LVTs (Amtracs or lightly armoured tracked personnel carriers) for the first assault waves, and into landing craft for the subsequent waves. The dawn pre-assault bombardment was made by three battleships followed by four cruisers and a number of destroyers from ranges of 15,000 yards to 2,000 yards, continu-

ing for two and a half hours. Three thousand tons of naval projectiles were hurled at this coconut-covered island which was now a mass of craters and fireswept undergrowth under a pall of smoke rising into the early morning sky. Yet it was not enough to silence the defenders, as the flat trajectory of the shells did not wreck the low, flat island.

The initial landing was to be made on a three-battalion front on beaches Red One, Two and Three, using the 100 Amtracs (LVTs) available. The state of the sea and the strong westerly set put the timetable back an hour. Naval gunfire was resumed but had to stop when the pall of smoke prevented accurate spotting, and the Japanese had time to transfer troops from the southern shore to the lagoon site.

The entrance to the lagoon had been swept by two mine-sweepers protected by two destroyers as the first waves followed and then turned sharp right to square up for the final run to the beaches. The leading waves of LVTs hit the coral reefs ringing the beaches, climbed over them and prepared to land. But events did not continue to go smoothly. This smashed island with its supposedly punch-drunk garrison poured merciless fire into the approaching LVTs. Beach Red One was the most fiercely defended area. Waiting until the assault craft were 100 yards from shore the Japanese opened up with every weapon in the arsenal. Amtrac drivers were killed, the vehicles slewed round and Marines were killed before they ever reached the beach.

As they ran up the sand a hail of bullets met them. To become established and to maintain momentum it was essential to have a steady flow of reinforcing waves, but the untracked landing craft which followed the stalled first wave were stuck fast on the reef due to the vagaries of the tide. As the men leapt into the water and waded ashore for some 700 yards they were met by a hail of bullets. After the initial hold up, the landing craft carrying the artillery which was urgently required ashore waited until dark. The Sherman tanks, so vital to the attack in the early stages, crawled ashore. Eleven made it and proved to be invaluable.

Between Red Two and Red Three beaches was a stone and wooden pier which could provide some shelter, but the area around it was strewn with obstacles. None the less the Marines of the Second Division inched their way inland, finding small arms fire useless against pill boxes. They had too few flame throwers, but those they did have were put to good use.

Fire support was called for and promptly given but by midday the regimental reserves and half the divisional reserve had been thrown in. The issue was critically in doubt and was very dangerous for the Americans. Communications with the command post in the battleship *Maryland* were poor as most of the Marines' radios had been knocked out.

A strict timetable in an operational plan is difficult to halt once it gets under way. All men, guns, ammunition and stores required for the assault had been loaded into landing craft and had proceeded towards the lagoon entrance on time. Thus the area became badly congested and provided prime targets for the defenders' well-sited guns.

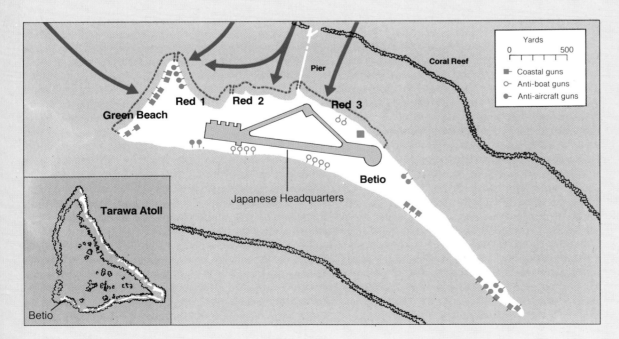

The attack on Tarawa in the Gilbert Islands.

The assault on Tarawa, seen from inside a Japanese bunker.

By the end of D-Day about 5,000 Marines had been landed but it is estimated that 1,500 had been killed or wounded. Navy fire control parties ashore called for air strikes and gunfire and they gave much needed relief to the troops. As daylight faded the Marines had a toe-hold from the centre of Red Two to the centre of Red Three and a further area on the corner of Red One. There they dug in and during the night inched forward, particularly on the corner of Red One, moving across the end of the island along Green One and Two.

From the Japanese angle it had been a terrible day. A counter-attack through the gap down to the beach which could have cut off the Marines could not be mounted as Rear-Admiral Shibasaki, commanding the defence, was out of contact with his troops. Half of his men had been killed already and naval gunfire had severed communications. It was left to small units acting on their own initiative to move forward as best they could. The Marines tackled each party as it came on. Some Japanese swam out to wrecked vehicles off shore and sniped all night adding confusion to the desperately tired Marines, who were now short of water, food and ammunition.

As dawn broke the divisional reserves began to assault the eastern end of Red One to close the gap. They were met by murderous fire as they waded ashore and their losses were greater than those of any battalion on D-Day. But gradually the situation improved for the Americans. Marines landed on Green Beach and pushed inland and by the afternoon others had fought their way across the airfield and had reached the southern shore. Tanks now rumbled up to

the pill boxes and fired point-blank into them, taking one after another. To prevent a Japanese withdrawal to the north, a force including artillery was sent to hold Bairiki, which was the next island to Betio.

There were signs that the Marines were overcoming the fanatically brave defence of this tiny coral island and with the arrival of a fresh battalion the bridgehead was pushed right

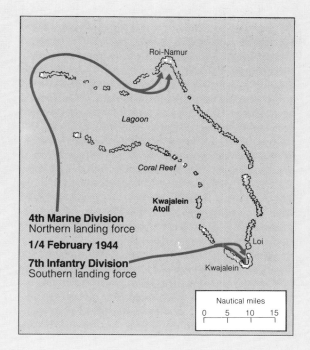

Kwajalein, the largest of the Marshall Islands.

across the island at the eastern end of Red Three. While this was going on, the Seabees had already begun to repair the airstrip and at noon on the fourth day a carrier plane landed.

The defence was desperate as each strongpoint was attacked, but Betio was finally secured. The Japanese garrison had literally been obliterated, with the men dying at their posts. In fact, only one officer and sixteen enlisted men actually survived to be taken prisoner, which can only be considered a truly horrendous statistic.

On the American side, the total number of personnel engaged in the action — Marines and Navy personnel ashore — was 18,313, and the total casualties were 3,110, or 17 per cent of the attack force. During the next few days the rest of the small islands that make up the atoll were occupied with little opposition.

Running north from the Gilbert Islands of Tarawa and Makin lie the Marshall Islands, which are dominated by Kwajalein, 550 miles from Tarawa and the largest coral reef in the world. Japanese air power was distributed in an interlocking series of airfields throughout a series of atolls. If the Americans were to take the Marshall Islands without very severe casualties to their men and ships, Japanese air power would have to be overcome.

Two major and sustained air strikes by Admiral Mitscher's fast carrier groups attacked the whole network of airfields during the assault on the Gilbert Islands to such an extent that Japanese air power was virtually destroyed either on the ground or in the air. Thus when Kwajalein was assaulted the defenders were unable to call for significant air support.

As a prelude to the assault, the undefended island and lagoon of Majuro was occupied, affording a magnificent anchorage and supply base for the operation.

The map on page 181 shows the two main defended areas of Kwajalein. In the north lies Roi-Namur with its airfield and in the south Kwajalein Island. One of the lessons learned at Tarawa was that the pre-assault bombardment had been insufficient and not accurate enough to destroy strong points before the assault was made. This time a concentrated and prolonged bombardment by heavy calibre shells and a series of air strikes took place at Roi-Namur. The objectives were literally taken apart, and a large proportion of the 3,700 defenders of Roi-Namur were killed before the 4th Marine Division reached the shore on 31 January 1944. They attacked from inside the lagoon, and with an unexpectedly high wind and surf there was much confusion before the Marines finally reached the shore, but the result was never in doubt. The remaining Japanese garrison held out until they were overwhelmed by the strength of the American build-up of Marines and armour.

Kwajalein Island in the south was then assaulted by the 7th Army Infantry Division. The pre-assault bombardment was again massive, and after capturing the small islets at the entrance to the lagoon, the waves of assault craft made for the shore. For two hours the troops encountered little resistance, but from then on they were forced to fight every inch of the way. Strong points were defended to the death and as the troops inched their way forward the guns of the support ships off shore concentrated on reinforced concrete gun emplacements. By 7 February Kwajalein Atoll had been captured. Over 41,000 troops had been committed and the total casualties were 372 killed and 1,582 wounded. Against this overwhelming strength it is estimated that the Japanese garrison was only 8,675 men of which 7,870 were definitely killed. The fury of the bombardment and the tenacity of the defence are shown in these terrible figures.

American Marines landing on Tarawa, which was the first major atoll to be assaulted. The pre-assault bombardment failed to break the defences and casualties were very heavy. The Japanese garrison of 4,500 was completely destroyed, with only about seventeen soldiers surviving after terrible hand-to-hand fighting.

Air strike on Truk

Truk lagoon has one of the finest anchorages in the South Pacific and the Japanese Combined Fleet was stationed there from 1942. It was not heavily defended but its capture would require a highly complicated assault. Aerial reconnaissance on 4 February 1944 showed the Japanese presence convincingly, but as a direct result of that particular aerial reconnaissance the fleet was moved to Palau.

Ten American submarines stationed off Truk in early February 1944 torpedoed the light cruiser *Agano,* while preparations were made for three fast carrier groups to attack the airfields and harbour. The tactics involved firstly a fighter strike of seventy-two aircraft from five carriers. Over the target they were met by the island's protective fighters and in a wild dogfight thirty Japanese aircraft were shot down and more aircraft were destroyed on the ground before the American fighters turned for home. As soon as they had left the area, eighteen Avenger aircraft arrived and attacked the airfields and dispersal areas on the three main islands. At the end of the day fewer than 100 of the 365 aircraft stationed at Truk were still serviceable.

Next day, dive-bombers and torpedo-bombers with protective fighters were launched in succession and were then met by some fighter opposition and a heavy anti-aircraft barrage as they concentrated on shipping in the harbour. One light cruiser and two destroyers were sunk together with some small craft, but the main disaster for Japan was the destruction of six tankers and seventeen merchant ships making a total tonnage of about 200,000, though some were beached or left burning. During the night twelve aircraft from USS *Enterprise* made the first night bombing attack from an American carrier, selecting targets at masthead height in the lagoon and accounting for nearly one third of the tonnage destroyed in this operation. It was a very severe blow, for these ships carried war material, and the loss of so much supply shipping handicapped the movements of the Combined Fleet.

Japanese retaliation was in the form of a small successful strike on the carriers at night, torpedoing USS *Intrepid* and putting her out of action for some months.

Meanwhile Admiral Spruance had sailed two battleships, two cruisers and four destroyers round the atolls to intercept any escaping Japanese ships. The light cruiser *Katori,* already damaged by aircraft, was attacked and in the unequal fight she fought until she actually sank. Similarly the destroyer *Maikaze* was engaged by battleships and destroyers and she too continued firing to the end.

As a result of the air strikes Admiral Nimitz decided that an assault from the sea could be avoided. With their supply ships gone, the Japanese were forced to withdraw the Combined Fleet, first to Palau and then to Singapore, where it was badly placed to intervene against the American offensive moves now under way in the Central Pacific.

American carrier-borne aircraft struck at the major Japanese naval base at Truk on 17 and 18 February 1944. While the actual damage done to warships was not decisive, the vulnerability of the anchorage forced the Japanese High Command to withdraw major units further south for greater security. During this raid Japanese aircraft suffered a crippling blow but the lasting result was the sinking of 200,000 tons of shipping laden with fuel and war materials of every sort required constantly by a fleet at sea.

Aircraft from the escort carrier USS Card *sinking U-117 on 7 August 1943.*

5

The Western Oceans

October 1943 to May 1945

The British Submarine Service

The story of the British Submarine Service in the war at sea has been brought together into one chapter to consider its contribution to the successful outcome of the war.

At the outbreak of war in September 1939, Britain possessed fifty-six submarines (Germany owned a similar number) although less than forty were fully effective. They varied in size from the large Thames Class of 1,850 tons down to the small H Class of 410 tons — twenty years old and intended for the shallow waters of the North Sea and the Baltic. The 2nd and 6th Flotillas were based in Britain, the 1st in the Mediterranean and the 4th in China.

Although few survived the war, and in total, seventy-seven were lost, Britain built no less than 164 boats. The mine was the greatest danger to British submarines, operating in many cases in shallow water, and it may have been the reason for about one-third of the losses. While German U-boat losses to Allied aircraft attack were nearly 50 per cent (354, with aircraft assisting surface forces in another forty-six cases out of a total of 783), British losses were only five, and of these three were bombed to destruction in Malta harbour. Axis submarines probably sank five, but remarkably, British submarines destroyed no less than thirty-five German, Italian and Japanese boats.

During the conflict at sea, British submarines sank 1,257 Axis merchant ships of 1,800,000 tons. No capital ship was actually sunk by a British submarine, and the opportunities to do so were rare, though two were torpedoed and

survived. However, six cruisers were sunk and another twelve were torpedoed but survived. Seventeen destroyers were sunk as were more than 100 minor war vessels.

After the subjugation of Europe: Dutch, Polish, French and Norwegian submarines arrived in British ports and operated alongside British boats. Early losses were severe as operations were mostly confined to the shallow waters of the North Sea and the entrance to the Baltic, to report on the movement of German shipping. But in particular the patrol of HMS *Salmon* in December 1939 was remarkably successful. She was a small boat of only 670 tons and sank the German U-36 from a range of 5,000 yards. A few days later she sighted the huge German liner *Bremen* of 51,700 tons returning to Germany. At this early stage, International Law forbade the sinking of merchant ships without first ensuring the safety of the passengers and crew — although Germany disregarded this in the sinking of the *Athenia*. *Salmon* surfaced and prepared to stop the liner when a German aircraft arrived and she was forced to dive. Two days later she intercepted the German cruisers *Leipzig* and *Nürnburg* and torpedoed both, putting them out of service for months, in fact *Leipzig* never put to sea again.

In the same month *Triumph* was mined but survived, though *Oxley* was sunk in error in September being out of her correct position. 1940 opened with a number of losses in the shallow and extremely hazardous waters round Heligoland between the Netherlands and Denmark.

The invasion of Norway saw the despatch of nineteen boats to that area but they achieved limited success. The German light cruiser *Karlsruhe* was torpedoed and sunk, and a number of supply ships were also sunk but in no obvious way was the progress of the German advance really hindered, and British losses had again been severe. By the end of June 1940 twelve boats had been lost including *Seal* which was captured in shallow water after prolonged depth charging, and by the end of the year the total had risen to twenty-five. Submarine operations off Norway were restricted by the German minefields which are thought likely to have been the cause of some losses.

With the entry of Italy into the war in June 1940 and the removal of French naval forces from the area, reinforcements were sent to the Mediterranean. The boats on the China Station had been recalled to Alexandria, but lack of foresight in peacetime was to have the most serious consequences for Malta.

The cost of constructing bomb-proof pens in the rock had been denied to the Royal Navy and with the arrival of German dive-bombers from January 1941, the ordeal of Malta began, and with it the almost impossible task of operating submarines from the island. At the height of the air bombardment it was necessary for the boats to remain submerged in harbour. Added to this, the reinforcements from the Far East were all large boats unsuitable for the shallow waters in which they were to patrol. The restrictions on attacking merchant ships still applied in the Mediterranean until July 1940, and mines

HM submarine Trident *on Arctic patrol. British submarines spent many months blockading the ports of northern Norway. The threat of operations in the Arctic or a break out into the Atlantic by German heavy units was always a danger to the Allies.*

claimed more boats in the early months with meagre successes to compensate for their heavy losses.

In northern waters HM submarine *Clyde* had damaged the battlecruiser *Gneisenau* but the situation for the submarine service was as desperate as it was for the rest of the Royal Navy in those dark days of 1941. A considerable number of boats were tied down in mounting a blockade of Brest where *Scharnhörst, Gneisenau* and *Prinz Eugen* were holed up. In the Mediterranean, Axis forces were sent to North Africa in heavily escorted convoys partly following a route through shallow waters from the Italian mainland. They were difficult to attack, due to the short crossing,but the cruiser *Armando Diaz* was sunk along with a number of supply ships. *Upholder* caused serious damage to the Axis reinforcements by sinking four transports, followed by a tanker and the 18,000 ton *Conte Rosso* in a series of skilful attacks ending with the inevitable depth charging which was nearly fatal. By the end of June 1941 forty Axis ships had been sunk, some in the very difficult shoal waters off North Africa. Malta now came under the most intense air bombardment and to supply the island became almost impossible. Submarines assisted in this duty — *Porpoise* making no less than nine trips.

Operations in the eastern Mediterranean brought success and in September 60,000 tons of shipping were sunk, with the invaluable assistance of intelligence from Ultra and with Lieutenant-Commander Wanklyn in *Upholder* responsible for two thirds of the sinkings. Three submarines were sent to intercept three large liners which had left Taranto escorted by six destroyers. *Upholder* attacked on the surface, despite the fact that her gyro compass was out of action. The sea was very rough. Firing by eye in the wildly swinging boat Lieutenant-Commander Wanklyn hit two of the liners, one of which began to settle, while the other was only damaged. *Upholder* went deep to reload, and passing under the damaged ship she rose to periscope depth and with two torpedoes she managed to sink it.

British submarines were now causing the most serious problems to General Rommel and the Afrika Korps and while seven were lost in the Mediterranean in 1941 their achievements were remarkable. The numerous minefields and heavily escorted convoys sailing through shallow waters made every attack extremely hazardous. British submarines sank five Axis submarines throughout 1939 and 1940, four in 1941, nine in 1942, and nine in 1943, and with Britain's fortunes at the lowest ebb in the Mediterranean at the end of 1941, *Urge* put three torpedoes into the great Italian battleship *Vittorio Veneto* which, although failing to sink her, helped to redress the balance of power.

Returning to the north, the submarine blockade of Brest failed to stop the German squadron from making a dash back to Germany and this added an extra threat to the Arctic convoy route. The submarine *Trident* torpedoed the *Prinz Eugen* off Trondheim *en route* to northern waters but failed to sink her. These northern patrols which stretched as far as the northern tip of Norway were just as unpleasant for the British submarines as they were for the U-boats operating against convoys to Russia. A blockade of the fiords within which *Scharnhörst* and *Tirpitz* were lying meant a period of cold and unrelieved monotony, but was vital to allow early warning of the battleships' movements even though a torpedo hit might not be feasible.

Minelaying was an extremely important function of the Submarine Service, and probably the most successful was the Free French *Rubis*, which laid 683 mines in twenty-eight patrols resulting in the sinking of fourteen supply ships of 21,410 tons, and damage to eight small warships and a U-boat. British minelayers included *Rorqual* and *Narwhal* as well as *Seal*.

Returning to the Mediterranean, *Torbay* entered Corfu harbour and destroyed two large merchant ships, but against this on 4 April 1942 *Upholder* was lost. At this time the 10th Flotilla and two naval air squadrons from Malta were the only Allied Naval force in the central Mediterranean to dispute the passage of Axis reinforcements to North Africa, but due to bombing it was impossible for the submarines to remain in Malta. They were therefore withdrawn, and the highly successful *Urge* was lost on passage to Alexandria. Repeated supply runs were made to assist in the defence of Malta, although this prevented their use in an offensive role. With the arrival of the 'Torch' convoy to North Africa, eighteen submarines were

deployed to protect and guide the assault forces to the beaches. Continuous patrolling and the sinking of supply ships — and a notable patrol by *Unbroken* — inevitably resulted in losses, for in 1942 twelve boats failed to return from operations and three were sunk in Malta harbour. But in 1943 success returned with some remarkable patrols — one in which *Turbulent* sank a convoy of four ships and its escorting destroyer in one devastating attack, and one in which Commander Bryant in *Safari* also sank four ships including an armed merchant cruiser. Then came Italy's surrender. The effect of these operations is borne out by the testimony of General Rommel's Chief of Staff who said 'we should have taken Alexandria and the Suez Canal if it had not been for your submarines attacking our lines of communications.'

In the Indian Ocean British submarines were based in Ceylon, and at one time eighteen boats were operating from Trincomalee. The operational areas were mostly in the Malacca Straits, off Java, and in the South China Sea. The boats did not have the range of the American boats to cruise long distances in the Pacific, and the areas selected were often necessarily in shallow waters. Japanese anti-submarine warfare was not of a high standard, particularly in the case of their smaller vessels. *Tally Ho* surfaced and sank her adversary by gunfire rather than be caught in shallow water in the Malacca Straits. This boat had a particularly successful record, her largest victim being the Japanese cruiser *Kuma* on 11 January 1944. Two other submarines had notable successes, the first being *Trenchant* which sank the cruiser *Ashigara* on 8 June 1945 off Sumatra with a 4,000 yard run in flat calm conditions in daylight. The other, *Shakespeare,* was hit during a gun battle which prevented her from diving. Throughout the day she fought off twenty-five air attacks, shooting down one aircraft and eventually returning to Trincomalee with assistance. At the end of the war there was a very successful attack on the cruiser *Takao* by midget XE craft — to be described later.

The losses in the Far East were three British and four Dutch submarines but against this must weigh the sinking of two cruisers, two destroyers, five U-boats, thirteen minor naval vehicles and forty-seven merchant ships with a total of about 130,000 tons. While not achieving the same tonnage sunk as the German U-boats or the American submarines, the British boats operated from the Arctic to the Pacific and particularly in the Mediterranean where conditions were exceedingly difficult due to shoal waters and the clarity of the sea. This produced disproportionate losses and underlines the courage and determination of their crews which matched in every way the exploits of their foes and their allies.

Mines in the fairway. The convoy route down the east coast of Britain carried millions of tons of food, fuel and materials for the prosecution of the war. German aircraft, surface ships and light coastal forces laid mines necessitating continuous sweeping operations.

191

HMS Wallace, *a V and W class destroyer from the First World War on escort duties in the Western Approaches to Britain.*

With the fall of France in 1940, an invasion of Britain appeared to be imminent. As we have seen, the control of air space above an opposed landing assault from the sea was an absolute necessity. Despite serious bombing of airfields and cities, British fighter planes denied this control to Germany. To counter the invasion thirty-two destroyers and five corvettes were withdrawn from the Home Fleet and Atlantic escort duty to dispute the passage of the many hundreds of landing craft and barges which would have been required to cross the English Channel. One of the consequences was that losses in the Atlantic rose alarmingly, despite the few U-boats that were operational.

While the invasion of Britain was first temporarily and then finally deferred, the bombing of the south and south-western ports, and the long range guns mounted on the coast of France, meant that all major convoys had to be routed round the north of Scotland to reach London and east coast ports. But the port of London had to be kept open at all costs, and protection of these inshore convoys throughout their journey down the east coast was essential. German light forces were stationed in French, Belgian and Dutch ports. Aircraft laid magnetic mines at night in the swept channels of the coastal routes, dive-bombers attacked from the air, and E-boats from the sea. Losses mounted until each convoy had its own minesweeper and destroyer escorts with air cover provided by the RAF. The acoustic mines in the early years were a major hazard, while the nightly attacks by E-boats, many of which laid mines, were a constant threat.

The E-boat offensive was countered by the production of motor gunboats (MGBs) to patrol outside the convoy routes and intercept E-boats proceeding to or returning from operations. Many fierce engagements were fought in the North Sea or off the Dutch coast, where British Coastal Forces would lie in wait.

Activity was not confined to defence of the convoys and there were regular sweeps across the Channel to intercept German coastal traffic. In 1942 motor torpedo boats (MTBs) were coming into service in large numbers, and as the war progressed British Coastal Forces did extract a serious toll of German inshore convoys. Gradually the MGBs gained a parity with the E-boats but it was to be a very long time before they were able to defeat this strong arm of the *Kriegsmarine*. The fact remains that had Hitler not invaded Russia and instead unleashed his air power on British ports and inshore convoy routes in 1941, sustaining this attack over a long period by bombing ports and carrying out intensive minelaying from the air, then it is very probable that Britain would not have survived.

Of the many calls upon British naval and air forces, those of watching the sea ports of the Bay of Biscay and countering the activities of the long range Focke Wolf Condor aircraft tied down a lage number of units. Fierce engagements were fought by all arms in this restricted but dangerous area. Meanwhile aircraft of the RAF Coastal Command gradually extended their activities to offensive sweeps along the coasts of France and Holland. Flying at sea level they attacked with delayed action bombs at masthead height until German inshore convoys were forced to proceed only at night.

Offensive minelaying disrupted German sea traffic and gradually the earlier situation was reversed. In the summer of 1942 offensive sweeps by destroyers and Light Coastal Forces were routine and extended from the coast of Norway to the Bay of Biscay. This is not to say that British losses were negligible, especially in

British Coastal Forces first defended the east coast convoys, and then expanded into a major force in the war at sea. They sought out German coastal shipping and lay in wait for returning E-boats. The picture shows boats listening for the tell-tale noise of approaching shipping on a still night off the coast of Holland.

aircraft, and until a rigorous training programme was completed, air attacks against shipping resulted in quite unacceptable losses.

Between 19 July 1942 and February 1943 (eight months) German shipping losses from all causes in Home Waters amounted to 250 ships (261,154 tons). The RAF flew 4,659 sorties and made 849 direct attacks but in fact they only accounted for eighteen ships (28,566 tons) and lost seventy-eight aircraft, which amounts to 4.3 aircraft per ship sunk. However, this state of affairs was to change.

The build up of MTBs and MGBs coincided with far better air co-operation and from now on this integrated offensive, including minelaying, became a source of worry to Germany. Her mercantile building programme was small and there was an acute shortage of ships while the escorts and flak ships built in greater numbers

became special targets for attack. These attacks, while gaining in momentum, fell far short of stopping German coastal traffic, and her coastal forces were still in a position to strike back hard at any point they might choose along the south and east coasts of Britain. In attack the E-boats showed the same dash and determination as their British counterparts, while along the coast of Europe the defending flak ships with excellent armament were formidable adversaries to the aircraft and coastal forces that sought to attack them.

In 1944, as the time for the Allied invasion of Europe approached, more intensive anti-U-boat minelaying was undertaken by British Coastal Forces to prevent interference with shipping required for the Channel crossing. This coincided with intensifying the sweeps against German shipping and there were considerable losses on both sides, but the increasing Allied strength and the decreasing German resources began to tell. The German light forces fought back and there were numerous occasions when E-boats boldly attacked convoys and caused casualties among ships that were heavily escorted. But with the invasion of Europe came complete Allied domination of the invasion area and the virtual elimination of interference from Germany's naval forces in that sector, although fierce engagements were still being fought in the approaches to the English Channel to deny U-boats access to the vast armada of shipping that lay just out of reach. These attacks remained a threat right up till the end of the war.

In addition to the U-boats, the remaining German E-boats attacked shipping in lightning strikes and while some damage was done the numerous escorts drove them off. British Coastal Forces continued to seek out a diminishing number of targets, but the mine became the real power of destruction. Minelaying by air and sea particularly in the Baltic had resulted in the loss of German shipping out of all proportion to the cost in laying these lethal devices. In the early years of the war the German mine was the most serious danger to coastal shipping and towards the end of the conflict the tables were turned and Germany was virtually paralysed by the mining activities of the Allies.

Coastal warfare had begun in May 1940 with the invasion of the Low Countries and continued to the last day of the war. It was a very serious aspect which in the early days came near to disrupting completely the routes upon which Britain depended for her survival. The struggle for the mastery of the seas round Britain is a story of heroism and tenacity in which the Allies and Germany fought with every possible means and defeat was not conceded until the very end.

The final defeat of the wolf packs

At the end of the last chapter on the Atlantic in May 1943, Admiral Dönitz had suffered such losses that he was forced to withdraw his U-boats temporarily from operations. Three major factors contributed to the problems facing Germany's vital U-boat arm. Firstly, reinforcements had enabled the Allies to provide far stronger escorts and far more air cover round the convoys, and escort carriers accompanied them during the most dangerous sector of their passages. Secondly, Coastal Command aircraft, with their 10 centimetre radar, not only closed the gap in mid-Atlantic but also patrolled an area of the Bay of Biscay through which most U-boats proceeded to and from their home ports. The third factor was intelligence, and it was crucial. The German ciphers were read and then passed to the Submarine Tracking Room directed by Commander Rodger Winn RNVR. U-boat sightings and direction finding following a U-boat's wireless transmission at sea all gave a deadly accurate picture of German offensive dispositions.

It was the combined use of these three arms of the service, welded by training and experience, that together produced a shattering effect on Germany's U-boats when they ran the gauntlet of the Bay of Biscay.

On the German side, the immediate addition of more close range anti-aircraft guns meant that the boats could fight it out on the surface with the aircraft which appeared without warning out of fog or at night, guided to the scene by their new radar sets.

The survivors of Germany's U-boat fleet were formed into a new group operating in quieter waters to the west of the Azores. It was not long before the Admiralty directed countermeasures to that area. In the North Atlantic no convoys were attacked in June but three U-boats were sunk. To protect his boats from air attack on the outward and return journeys in the Bay of Biscay, Admiral Dönitz appealed to Hitler for more *Luftwaffe* protection. Had there been full co-operation between these two arms then the situation could again have favoured the U-boats, as the Allied search aircraft were vulnerable to attack. Certainly some co-operation was given and the results gave added protection to U-boats in this dangerous area, but it was not long before long range fighter bomber aircraft provided interception patrols which hampered the activities of the *Luftwaffe's* JU 88 aircraft.

The months of June and July 1943 had been disastrous for Germany, for in addition to the countermeasures in the Atlantic and Azores, where the islands were occupied by the Allies, aircraft intercepted and sank four boats on the northern transit route round Scotland.

The table on page 195, provided by *War at Sea* Volume III by Captain S.W. Roskill, gives a list of Allied merchant ships and U-boat sinkings in the period from June to August 1943.

Despite these clearly quite unacceptable losses, German U-boat crews continued to fight their way out to operational areas with determination and courage. They either beat off air attacks with their own anti-aircraft guns or were sunk. On the Allied side, sightings brought air and surface forces on to the scene and U-boats were attacked relentlessly, backed by improved

German U-boats caught on the surface, particularly in the Bay of Biscay, used close range armament to defend themselves. Either they shot down their attacker or faced the probability of being sunk. The long range bomber also faced destruction far from land, and many lone bomber versus U-boat actions took place.

training and inter-service co-operation. Of the Escort Groups, the 2nd, commanded by Captain F.J. Walker RN, was outstandingly successful.

At the end of July, eleven U-boats, including two 'Milch Cow' replenishment boats, were sighted and attacked. They fought off their air attackers, badly damaging two aircraft for the loss of two boats. The 2nd Escort Group now arrived and two more boats were sunk. Further sightings resulted in the sinking of another boat and the remainder being recalled.

This period, covering July 1943 and the first week in August, saw eighty-six U-boats crossing the Bay of Biscay. Of the fifty-five sighted, sixteen were sunk by aircraft and one by surface ship — six others were forced to return, while air patrols off Cape Finisterre and the coast of Portugal sank three more boats and damaged a fourth. Fourteen Allied anti-submarine aircraft, however, were shot down as a result.

It was the climax of the Bay of Biscay offensive and a blow to German hopes of winning the Battle of the Atlantic, but the U-boats fought back. Admiral Dönitz now altered the route. By keeping close to the Spanish coast U-boats had a relatively safe passage under the protection of the *Luftwaffe* which destroyed seventeen bombers and six fighters. The new glider bomb, directed on to its target by a parent bomber, sank one frigate and damaged another. The great problem facing Admiral Dönitz was to extend the period of operations at sea and so avoid the dangerous Biscay areas. Of the Type XIV 'Milch Cow' supply U-boats only ten were built and eight had been sunk. This was an extremely serious blow to Germany. The value of these large boats was out of all proportion to their numbers, and the period from June to August 1943 showed the following sinkings:

Date	Boat	Area
12 June	U-113	Operational area
24 June	U-119	Bay of Biscay (in-bound)
13 July	U-487	Operational area
20 July	U-457	Bay of Biscay (out-bound)
30 July	U-461	Bay of Biscay (out-bound)
30 July	U-462	Bay of Biscay (out-bound)
4 August	U-489	North transit area (out-bound)
7 August	U-117	Operational area

We can see that four of the boats never reached their operational area. Of the two boats remaining at sea out of the original ten, none being in harbour anywhere, U-460 was sunk on 4 October and U-488 was lost on her next patrol.

Aircraft from the escort carrier USS *Card* had sunk the supply tanker U-117 on 7 August and damaged U-66 which was being refuelled from her, and within a week two more emergency supply boats were sunk by aircraft from the same carrier. Shipping in the Atlantic enjoyed a quiet August and the pressure against U-boats was maintained by air attacks which were accounting for more and more German losses.

In the East, a relatively small number of boats (no more than seven German and eight Japanese) which made the long passage into the Indian Ocean, sank fifty-seven ships of 337,169 tons between June and December 1943. They caused considerable dislocation since they all carried vital cargoes. Some of these U-boats were refuelled from the few remaining surface blockade-running tankers which had not been sunk, and others received fuel at Penang, where the Japanese had arranged base facilities for their Allies.

Allied merchant ships and German U-boats sunk between June and August 1943

	Allied ships	German U-boats			
		In Bay of Biscay	On northern transit route	On North Atlantic convoy routes	In other theatres*
June	10	4	2	8	2
July	38	16	0	8	10
August	10	5	2	8	9
Total	58	25	4	24	21

*includes Caribbean, East Coast of USA, Brazil, West Africa, South Atlantic and Indian Ocean.

During the first ten days of September 1943, no ships were sunk in the North Atlantic. However, it was not long before the *Kriegsmarine* began to deploy its forces once again. Twenty-eight boats arrived on station, having proceeded across the Bay of Biscay submerged by day and so managing to elude the ever-present reconnaissance aircraft.

Convoys ONS 18 and ON 202 left the United Kingdom between 12 and 15 September 1943, consisting of twenty-seven and forty-two ships respectively, with two escort groups of fourteen ships. Across the line of the approaching convoys were nineteen U-boats which were strung out north to south in the mid-Atlantic. Aircraft from Iceland sank one U-boat on 19 September well to the north, while against this two ships of the convoys were sunk on 20 September, the frigate *Lagan* also being damaged by the new acoustic torpedo which homed on to the noise of the ship's propellers.

Allied aircraft continued to support the convoys throughout the day, one of them sinking U-338, also by an acoustic torpedo similar in principle to those used by the U-boats. The two convoys had by now joined up and a further escort group was diverted to join the defence of this very large collection of ships, but eight more U-boats had also closed the area. A battle of wits ensued and the U-boats made every possible attempt to attack in the face of the powerful surface and air escort. One U-boat was damaged, and as night closed in three attacks were launched on the convoy. The frigate *Escapade* had been damaged by an accidental explosion and left the convoy, and during the night the Canadian corvettes *St Croix* and *Polyanthus* were sunk by acoustic torpedoes. The next day fog shielded the convoy and no ships were lost, but intelligence provided evidence that a further attack was imminent. It was mounted against the convoy on the night of 21 September. The escorts attacked U-boat contacts as they tried to get at the merchantmen and despite their determined efforts they were kept at bay. U-229 was rammed and sunk by HMS *Keppel* in the early hours of 22 September and the following night was one of wild activity. Asdic contacts were continuous and the roar of depth charges reverberated around the convoy as the U-boats made desperate and courageous attempts to attack. The frigate *Itchen* was sunk by an acoustic torpedo with the loss of virtually her whole ship's company, together with the survivors of the two Canadian corvettes which had been sunk earlier on. The U-boats had pierced the screen during the night and sunk four merchant ships. During the following day the action was broken off.

As a U-boat offensive it had proved to be a disaster. Six merchant ships (36,422 tons) had been sunk but three German boats had been lost and three more badly damaged. Admittedly four escorts had been sunk but it was actual war materials tonnage that was so vital to Admiral Dönitz and during the battle no less than nineteen boats had been involved. The new acoustic torpedoes used against the escorts had initially caused losses but when an antidote was introduced, the new torpedo failed to be the battle-winning weapon that Germany had hoped for.

The next convoy was diverted away from the re-formed line of U-boats, through intelligence supplied to the commander of the escort. On 2 October aircraft from Iceland were deployed in strength and sank three U-boats without the loss of any merchant ships. At the end of September convoy SC 143 had sailed from Halifax and was attacked by eighteen boats. The Polish destroyer *Ookan* was torpedoed and sank, but three U-boats were sunk by aircraft, again without loss to the convoy.

There is no doubt that the training of air crews and the tactics of immediate low level attacks had contributed greatly to the increasing success of the air escorts. The U-boats had to stay on the surface to maintain the speed necessary to be in position for a night attack and thus became very vulnerable. But the main reason for the Allied success was that Ultra's decrypted signals arrived in time for the Allied forces to be positioned to attack the U-boats. Although Ultra itself was not the cause of the successful actions, it was responsible for the dispositions being made correctly.

Far to the south in the area of the Azores, the United States escort carrier *Card* had sunk two U-boats in August including supply boat U-489, and this had been followed by another boat, U-117. Now reinforcements in the shape of two American escort carriers, the *Core* and *Block Island* sank a further three boats, forcing the remainder to operate in the south-west away from the activities of these lethal escort carriers. The sinking of the supply boats meant that outward-bound U-boats were called upon to replenish one or two which were virtually stranded in the Atlantic with insufficient fuel to return to their bases.

The pressure on the attacking U-boats never let up. Conditions in the North Atlantic were atrocious and the escort groups were at sea for long periods. These little ships rolled and pitched to an alarming degree and at action stations throughout the night the crews were soaked and in their exhaustion came near to breaking point. However, it was their vigilance that saved the convoys from the equally determined massed U-boat attacks.

It was again a case of which side was able to keep up the almost impossible pressure the longest and the U-boats had no respite. The courage of the lone bomber's air crew, hundreds of miles away from land, as they swept in at 100 feet to face the U-boats' gunfire was equally matched by that of the submariners who faced certain death if the lethal depth charges were dropped before they could destroy the bombers or at least deflect their aim.

As an illustration of the improved position on the convoy routes in September and October 1943, twelve merchant ships were lost out of 2,468 which had sailed in sixty-four convoys. Twenty-five U-boats had been sunk, of which five were by surface escorts, six by American carrier aircraft and thirteen by shore-based aircraft, with one shared by aircraft and surface vessels. As a result Admiral Dönitz immediately dispersed his forces more widely.

It seems hard to credit this change of fortune for the Allies in the late autumn of 1943. In 1940, 1941 and 1942 under-strength escorts were vainly trying to protect some thirty to forty ships against a U-boat pack which seemed to hold all the cards. The numbers of U-boats increased, but gradually, very gradually, not only did the convoys gain more escort vessels, but they were manned by highly trained and battle hardened crews. Aircraft with equally well trained crews were capable of giving air support throughout the convoys' voyages. The continuous and up-to-date flow of decrypted messages from Ultra also laid bare the tactics of the U-boat offensive, and played such an important role in its defeat. This information, training and co-operation combined with an increasing supply of ships and aircraft, new weapons and improved detection equipment was to achieve Allied victory in the Atlantic.

Looking back we may allow ourselves to ponder on Professor Trevor Roper's remark, 'History is not merely what happened: it is what happened in the context of what might have happened.' This is nowhere more evident than in Air Marshal Goering's contribution to the defeat of his country in refusing to give all out co-operation to the German Navy in the days after the conquest of Europe. It seems probable that he could have tipped the scales and rewarded the courage of the U-boat crews with victory had he thrown the full weight of the *Luftwaffe* behind Admiral Dönitz.

It was now certain that Germany would not win the Battle of the Atlantic, but this change of fortune was by no means the end of the story. Certainly the grip was tightening and October 1943 produced an agreement between the British and Portuguese Governments to allow Allied aircraft to use bases in the Azores. This greatly increased the air coverage on the West African and Carribbean-Gibralter convoy routes, as well as denying the replenishment area which had been used previously by the U-boats.

U-boat sinking increased without any commensurate destruction of merchant ships in convoy. The now massive escorts with their inner and outer ring of protecting vessels and continuous air support from escort carriers and shore-based aircraft made interception almost impossible. Captain Walker's 2nd Escort Group led the way in developing new tactics. On picking up a U-boat contact, a set drill went into operation. A 'directing ship' was positioned about 1,000 yards astern of the submerged U-boat to keep in contact all the time by Asdic, while another ship not using Asdic steamed very slowly (at about 5 knots) up the U-boat's track trying to remain undetected.

Thus the U-boat commander had no knowledge of his attacker, feeling that he was only in contact with one vessel astern of him. When the attacking vessel had passed slowly over the U-boat, and proceeded to a spot sufficiently far forward to allow time for the depth charges to sink to their detonating depth, she began to drop or fire about twenty-six charges in pairs at nine second intervals to explode at between 500 and 700 feet. Thus a carpet of depth charges would fall along the U-boat's course. If the boat had been taking evasive action, three attacking ships would steam close abeam together and the same creeping barrage of what was now possibly eighty depth charges would fall on the unsuspecting U-boat. It was devastating and it was lethal.

In the last four months of 1943, Germany lost sixty-two of her U-boats, and in November and December in the North Atlantic seventy-two convoys, totalling 2,218 ships, reached their destination without suffering any loss. By comparison in March of the same year, the Allies lost 108 ships of 627,377 tons to U-boat attacks.

The Arctic and the sinking of the Scharnhörst

HMS Duke of York *opens fire on the German battlecruiser* Scharnhörst *in freezing weather on 26 December 1943.*

The German battleship *Tirpitz* had been badly damaged in Altenfiord by the X craft submarines in September 1943, and convoys to Russia had been resumed but with heavier close escort. In the Arctic, better direction finding equipment enabled U-boat transmissions to be pinpointed and the convoys re-routed, while the darkness hindered *Luftwaffe* air reconnaissance. When convoy RA 55A set sail for home from the Russian port of Kola on 22 December, it was in the knowledge that the winter gales had done more damage to the two preceding convoys than air or surface action. The cruisers *Belfast, Norfolk* and *Sheffield* were to remain to the east of Bear Island in order to shield an outward-bound convoy JW 55B on the dangerous last leg of its journey.

These convoy movements were known to the German Group North, but air reconnaissance had failed to detect any heavy units of the Home Fleet or the cruiser force. Thus it seemed that it was a favourable situation in which to sail the *Scharnhörst* to intercept. An attack on the convoy at night by destroyers assisted by the big guns of the *Scharnhörst* could well inflict such damage as to cause it to scatter before the arrival of heavier escorts; by which time *Scharnhörst* would be heading for the protection of her anchorage. The need to relieve pressure on the Eastern Front where events were going badly

for the German Army prompted Admiral Dönitz to sail the battlecruiser. Signal traffic from Alten Fiord to Germany usually went by land line and was thus secure, though *Scharnhörst* was not connected to the land line. With the forthcoming operation an increase in wireless traffic was monitored by Bletchley Park. One signal was decoded by 20 December. It stated 'Urgently request air reconnaissance against heavy group which is probably at sea. Battlegroup is at three hours notice.' This could only mean that *Scharnhörst* was to put to sea.

As the signal traffic increased, this vital information was fed to the Commander-in-Chief, Home Fleet, Admiral Sir Bruce Fraser, in the battleship *Duke of York* and to Admiral Burnett commanding the cruiser force. The executive signal that *Scharnhörst* was to sail was sent at 17.00 on 25 December and was in the hands of the British commanders early the next day.

At sea the position was as follows:

The eastbound convoy JW 55B (consisting of nineteen ships) had sailed from Scotland on 20 December with an escort of ten destroyers, and the usual distant cover was provided by the battleship *Duke of York,* the cruiser *Jamaica* and four destroyers. The convoy had been sighted two days later by German reconnaissance aircraft and U-boats were despatched to form a line south of Bear Island. Since it was thought probable that *Scharnhörst* would attempt to intercept and as the convoy was only 400 miles

from Altenfiord, orders were given for it to reverse course for three hours to enable the *Duke of York* and the *Jamaica* to be in a better position to cover it.

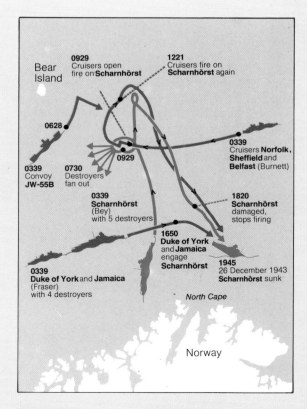

Scharnhörst is caught in a trap.

HMS Northern Pride. *She and many like her accompanied convoys to Russia on anti-submarine and rescue duties.*

The westbound convoy RA 55A was ordered to proceed further north and four fleet destroyers were detached to join JW 55B since it seemed that this was the convoy which would be attacked. As we have seen, the Commander-in-Chief was informed early on 26 December that the *Scharnhörst* was at sea. The position at 03.39 is shown on the map on page 197. The U-boats had been detected and forced to submerge and the convoy had passed over their patrol line. There was to be some daylight between 08.27 and 15.34, but otherwise darkness covered the stormy seas as the convoy kept station as best it could in the Arctic conditions. Convoy RA 55A, well to the north-west, was now out of danger and proceeded without incident to reach port on 1 January 1944.

JW 55B was fifty miles south of Bear Island, making 8 knots with its augmented close escort. Admiral Burnett with the three cruisers had altered course to the south-west, making an interception with *Scharnhörst* possible, as she was now known to have left Altenfiord and was presumed to be heading north. Finally, Admiral Fraser's heavy squadron was 210 miles south-west of the convoy, steaming at 24 knots. There was a gale blowing from the south-west with a heavy following sea, which made life very unpleasant indeed for the escorting destroyers.

Admiral Fraser now broke wireless silence to give his position and ordered Admiral Burnett and the convoy to give theirs. Thus each of the British forces knew where the others were.

At the same time the convoy was ordered further north and the cruisers were directed to close it to provide added protection.

At 07.30 Admiral Bey in *Scharnhörst* ordered his destroyers to search to the south-west. He lost touch with them and they never rejoined the flagship. This order and a failure to maintain signal contact had a bearing on the events which followed.

At 08.15 Admiral Burnett with the three cruisers hauled round to the north-west towards the convoy and at 08.40 *Belfast* picked up *Scharnhörst* on her radar at 25,000 yards. She was heading direct for the convoy only thirty miles away. The range closed rapidly and at 09.20 *Sheffield* reported 'enemy in sight at 13,000 yards'. *Belfast* fired starshell, but because of the line of bearing only *Norfolk* was able to open fire at that moment. *Scharnhörst* received at least one hit as she altered course immediately to the south and at full speed rapidly drew away. At 09.55 Admiral Bey again altered course, hoping to work round to attack the convoy. The German battlecruiser was

The Scharnhörst *sinks. It is probable that her radar was damaged early in the battle and she was thus blind to the approach of the overwhelming British forces. She sank in a freezing gale with very few survivors.*

tracked by radar but in the prevailing sea was drawing away from the cruisers. Admiral Burnett altered course to close the convoy immediately as he could see the danger looming on his plot.

At 09.30 the Commander-in-Chief ordered the convoy still further north and detached four of his escorting destroyers to join the approaching cruiser squadron. It was *Musketeer, Opportune, Virago* and *Matchless* who joined the cruiser squadron which was now coming between the convoy and the *Scharnhörst*.

By now radar contact had been lost and unless his target could be located, Admiral Fraser would either have to proceed to Kola direct or return home, as his destroyers were running short of fuel. For some moments the situation was in the balance. *Scharnhörst* could either be searching for the convoy or more probably heading for home at speed. In that case the Commander-in-Chief could not overtake her without the fuel situation becoming critical.

However, at noon *Belfast* regained radar contact and at 12.21 *Sheffield* reported 'enemy in sight at 11,000 yards', and the cruisers opened fire. The destroyers were disposed in a bad position to attack as *Scharnhörst* had turned south for home. One or two hits were probably scored, but *Norfolk* had one turret and most of her radar put out of action by 11 inch shells and

Sheffield suffered slight damage. Fire was checked and the cruisers shadowed by radar as the battlecruiser headed south into the arms of the battleship *Duke of York*. Starshell from *Belfast* illuminated the *Scharnhörst* and she was taken completely by surprise when the main armament of the *Duke of York* and *Jamaica* opened fire at 12,000 yards. It seems that in the earlier engagement her radar had been put out of action for obviously she had no idea of the presence of the British battleship. Admiral Fraser now conformed with the erratic movements of his adversary as she tried desperately to break out of the trap. The cruisers to the north opened fire to prevent her making an escape in that direction.

The German battlecruiser's superior speed opened the ranges, but she had been badly damaged and her speed was now dropping. A gun duel ensued between the two big ships and *Scharnhörst*'s position was desperate, her speed dropping still more and her guns falling silent for a time.

The British destroyers had been struggling to gain an attacking position in the heavy seas but this was impossible until *Scharnhörst*'s speed had been checked. By 19.00 *Savage* and *Saumarez* had approached from the north-west under heavy fire, while *Scorpion* and the Norwegian *Stord* came in unobserved from the south-west. Torpedoes were fired by all four

HMS Belfast *at the Battle of North Cape. With the rest of the cruiser squadron she shadowed the* Scharnhörst *until the arrival of the battleship* Duke of York.

destroyers and it seems likely that three hit. The destroyers drew away while *Duke of York* and *Jamaica* came up from the south-west and opened fire at 10,400 yards. They were joined by Admiral Burnett's cruisers and the resulting devastating fire enveloped the now almost stationary crippled *Scharnhörst*. The cruisers and destroyers then closed in and the German ship was subjected to a mass torpedo attack by the cruisers and destroyers. She was covered in a pall of smoke and probably sank at about 19.45. The British force searched the heaving icy and wreck-strewn waters for survivors, but only thirty-six were found alive.

Scharnhörst had proved to be a remarkably fine ship whose career as a raider caused consternation when in the Atlantic. Her presence in Arctic waters had been a constant threat and in her final action she had fought against overwhelming odds, blind without the benefit of radar.

The invasion of Europe

All the trials and tribulations of the Allies for the last four years had been endured for one single goal — the invasion of Europe. Hitler could not be beaten solely by bombing the great cities of the Ruhr or by a sea blockade. Germany realised that the Allies would attack the continent of Europe and that a final showdown would have to come, though each side was making feverish attempts to perfect the design of secret rockets or more deadly weapons, to bring the other to its knees.

The invader had the choice of where to land and the defender the disadvantage of having to protect all possible areas of assault. To this end the Allies played a giant game of deception. Hitler was obsessed with the idea that Allied forces would land in Norway and this erroneous idea was allowed to develop. The Balkans was another fruitful area for rumour and large numbers of German troops were held in these distant countries to ward off a non-existent Allied plan. But the great deception had to be in northern France. The decision to invade the Normandy coast and Cherbourg Peninsula had been taken long before the detailed planning of

The invasion fleet for Normandy was spearheaded by assault landing craft heading for five beaches, and this was followed by a mass of fighting and supply equipment in every form of craft.

Operation 'Overlord', the assault on Europe, and its naval counterpart 'Neptune', had begun. What was essential was to feed information to Hitler and his generals that the assault thrust was to come in the Pas de Calais, the shortest route across the Channel. Thus it was that even after the build-up of forces ashore in the Cherbourg Peninsula, the German High Command considered the invasion in that area to be no more than feint and believed that the real thrust would come in the area of Calais. Here the German 15th Army was on full alert to hurl back an assault. Had General Rommel sent a number of divisions, and particularly armour, down to Normandy before D-Day, the outcome might have been different. In the event they were not moved until after the Cherbourg Peninsula was in Allied hands. This deception played a vital role in the events to come.

The southern half of Britain was flooded with troops and equipment so that it became an almost total training and assembly area. The ports round the coast of Great Britain were jammed with every conceivable vessel, each one allocated a vital task and each one tied into the most elaborate logistical plan ever devised.

It was upon the Allied navies that the burden rested for the safe and timely arrival of the assault forces at the appointed beaches, for the covering of the landings, and the subsequent

support and maintenance of the rapid build-up of the Allied forces ashore.

The main features of the assault were the dropping of two airborne divisions inland shortly before the assault from the sea, and the landing of five divisions and Commandos and Rangers along a front of fifty miles between Caen and the Cherbourg Peninsula followed by a rapid build-up of forces through D-Day and D+1. Thereafter the plan called for the seaborne landing of one and one-third divisions on each successive day.

Admiral Sir Bertram Ramsay was appointed to organize this enormous force with its need for continuous supply under the overall command of General Eisenhower and while at sea all military forces were under naval command. The Eastern Naval Task Force (British) was under the command of Admiral Vian and his responsibility was to land the British Second Army in three areas named Sword, Juno and Gold, along a thirty mile front. The Western Naval Task Force (American) was under the command of Admiral Kirk whose responsibility was for the landing of the United States First Army in two areas at Omaha and Utah beaches on a twenty mile front. Thus the threat of congestion of shipping in the sea lanes was a real possibility. Each Task Force had a very powerful bombardment group for close support.

German naval forces available for action in this area included forty-nine U-boats, a large number of small surface craft (mine-sweepers etc.), five destroyers and thirty-nine E-boats. German strategy relied on these forces to disrupt and hinder any invasion, but the real defence was the massive line of fortifications and coastal defences which were to contain any attempted Allied landing until a large and balanced mobile force could be rushed to the area and the invaders thrown back into the sea.

To counter any threat from either end of the Channel, and particularly from the Bay of Biscay, Allied forces mustered an overwhelming force of 286 destroyers, sloops, frigates, corvettes and trawlers — 79 per cent being British, 17 per cent American and 4 per cent other Allies. Their duties were to seal off the approaches to the Channel and to escort the assault forces across.

For the assault phase, 1,213 naval ships were involved, including seven battleships, two monitors, twenty-three cruisers, 100 destroyers and escort destroyers, 130 frigates and corvettes. To this must be added the prodigious figure of 4,126 landing ships and landing craft of every conceivable design.

Another vital aspect was the preliminary air offensive to disrupt Germany's land communic-

ations. In order to deceive, equal attention was paid to communications in the Pas de Calais area, the suggested target of a mythical and non-existent 'First US Army Group' under General Patton, which was supposedly about to cross the Channel.

The assembly of ships was spread over every possible southern port and harbour, and minute instructions were given to each vessel as to its combat loading, succession of sailing etc. Every square mile of sea from Cornwall to the French coast near Ushant, stretching back up the Channel, was covered by air reconnaissance every thirty minutes day and night.

The convoy routes and the whole area of the invasion beaches were to have massive air support. Two thousand aircraft ensured that there was complete mastery of the skies.

The assault area had no protective harbours at all, and it was open to the swell and surf on its sloping beaches. It was therefore necessary to construct a prefabricated artificial breakwater.

It was made of steel and concrete units each 200 feet long, placed end to end and sunk to form a harbour and sheltered water. Fifty-five old merchant ships and four obsolete warships were to be sunk in position to add to the sea defences of the area. Finally, centrally placed inside these Mulberry harbours were main stores piers, connected to the shore by two floating roadways, each half a mile long. Nearer in were two piers for unloading barges and landing craft, and these were also connected to the shore.

The requirements for petrol would obviously become enormous. In order to overcome this problem an ingenious flexible pipe — 'Pluto' — was rolled across the Channel sea bed, to provide a continuous supply of fuel.

All these preparations would become impracticable unless sea lanes were kept swept free of mines. Indeed, the assault could not begin before the mine-sweepers had cleared and marked the Channel. To undertake and maintain this sweeping, 287 vessels were employed almost constantly.

LSTs (landing ship tanks) on Omaha beach three days after the assault landing. The build-up of stores was continuous and once ashore they were taken inland to large dumps, ready to supply the forward troops.

It was only after the successful capture of the beaches, their consolidation and the holding of any German counter-attack measures, that the harbours and terminals could be secured and the actual invasion and the liberation of Occupied France could take place.

The German defences were massive and sited in depth so a pre-invasion air bombardment was essential. This consisted of a heavy night bomber attack on ten principal targets during the night preceding D-Day. Medium bombers were to follow and make pinpoint attacks at dawn on six battery positions which were known to be vital to the German defences. The actual beach defences were to be subjected to an air bombardment of 4,200 tons of bombs in the last forty-five minutes before the first wave of assault troops hit the beaches. At sea, rocket launching craft supporting the landing were given the job of plastering the beach defences just ahead of the first waves approaching the shore, while finally a sustained naval bombardment at first light was to be delivered from ships at sea. The enormous strength and deployment in depth of the German defences were such that it was essential to engage carefully allocated targets. Fighter spotter aircraft were allocated to observe and report the fall of shot, and since this was of critical importance eight squadrons were specifically trained to this work, including one American squadron which flew Spitfires. Battleships, monitors, cruisers and destroyers each had their allotted targets.

Experience in the Mediterranean and in the Pacific had shown how essential it was to have a strong beach party to co-ordinate the arrival of the assault forces and to set up signal communications. These parties landed with the first waves, and their job was to ensure the fast turn round of the assault craft and the rapid clearance of stores and men from the immediate landing area.

It is hard to credit the size of the armada required to carry and maintain this huge invasion force right down to small but essential water tenders, cable laying vessels, inshore colliers and oilers.

While the approach was to be in darkness, the actual assault was planned to take place in daylight for accuracy of pilotage and bombardment — three hours before high water. In each month only three or four days occurred with these conditions and the weather was unpredictable. Assault training was carried out all along the south coast of Britain and the date was fixed for 5 June. Security was absolute and no communication of any sort was allowed after sealed orders were opened on 28 May. The vast armada prepared to set sail from ports all over the British Isles but the weather predictions for 5 June were so bad that D-Day was postponed for twenty-four hours.

In a force 5 wind and a choppy sea, the armada set out on the afternoon of 5 June. It was not until 03.00 on 6 June that Admiral Kranke's Group Command West was informed of the presence of large ships in the Normandy area. Air bombing and jamming had made much of the German radar inoperable, so visual sighting was the first intimation of the impending battle.

From midnight until 05.00 1,056 British heavy bombers attacked ten of the most important coastal batteries and prime defensive positions, dropping 5,000 tons of bombs. This was followed by 1,630 Liberators, Fortresses and medium bombers, which attacked the actual beach defences. However, low cloud resulted in most of the bombs falling too far inland.

For the last twenty minutes, fighters and medium bombers attacked the actual beach area, while at 05.30 warships' guns opened up along the whole fifty miles length of the assault area. Never before had such a heavy rain of shells poured on land targets from sea and air.

As the first assault landing craft wave reached the beaches, rocket firing landing craft blanketed some of the assault sectors. The sea was choppy and great difficulty was experienced in controlling the landing craft as they attempted to avoid obstacles. Despite this, landings on the British sector were effected without much initial opposition although many landing craft were damaged on the beach defences.

On the American sector at Utah beach, accurate bombing meant that most of the shore batteries had been silenced and landings were successful, despite the fact that they took place about a mile to the south-east of the intended spot. This proved providential as the defences along the high-water line were lighter in that area. Rapid progress was made inland and by 18.00 on 6 June, 21,328 men, 1,742 vehicles and some 1,695 tons of stores were ashore. This was made possible due to the previous capture of the causeways leading inland by the earlier drop of parachute troops.

In contrast, the Omaha beach assault came up against very strong opposition. The initial bombardment had failed to neutralize the heavy guns, which had in fact been moved further inland, and of the thirty-two American supporting tanks which had been launched 6,000 yards off shore, only five reached land. The landing force was thirty-five minutes late which gave the German defenders time to take up their positions and to open accurate and concentrated fire on the beaches where the first assault wave was pinned down. Much of the artillery had been swamped in their landing craft and the beach defences claimed many more in the choppy sea. The situation was serious, with a confused mass of assault craft trying to reach the shore under heavy fire, despite the fact that destroyers came in very close to fire at point-blank range. Losses mounted and it was not until 17.30 that the beaches had been secured and troops began to move inland and consolidate their positions.

Despite some setbacks, by the end of the first day the assault had succeeded, with far fewer casualties than had been feared except on Omaha beach. The German defences had been subjected to intense shelling and bombing, and in most instances these attacks had an uncanny accuracy. However, the slowness of the German High Command to react to the initial assault contributed to its success.

As night fell, the naval forces took on the task of defending the beaches. No serious attacks were made, but pressure mines were laid and dropped and these caused casualties over the next few days until countermeasures largely nullified these complicated and lethal mechanisms. Determined attacks by E-boats were contained by the surface screens round the beachhead areas and a destroyer action off Le Havre prevented an assault on the mass of shipping. While weather was always the greatest hazard, a major cause of worry was still the U-boats. Because of security and surprise, the

The Mulberry harbour. This harbour was constructed in Britain and towed across the Channel in sections. Together with block ships it formed an artificial barrier through which craft of all sizes were able to go alongside piers to unload their cargoes.

The scene on D-Day +2. The wind has dropped and the sea moderated as the heavy swells from the battleships Warspite *and* Ramillies, *together with the monitor HMS* Roberts, *bombard distant heavy batteries. Nearer in are the cruisers and destroyers on call from the troops ashore, while landing craft move to and from the beaches.*

thirty-six boats earmarked to disrupt the invasion were still in port at the critical moment. There now followed a mass attack on any U-boat moving north from the Biscay ports. In this area eleven boats were sunk between 7 and 25 June, mostly by air attack, despite the loss of a number of aircraft to the light calibre guns of the U-boats who elected to fight it out on the surface. The air and sea activity protecting the shipping was intense, with U-boats trying every possible means of breaking through the cordon of ships and aircraft which barred their way. In the event the U-boats were unable to do significant damage, though a courageous attempt was made to penetrate the defence.

In the assault area the sea was still choppy and a mass of wrecked and stranded craft littered the beaches. While the convoys of reinforcements and stores continued regularly across the Channel, the stream of block ships and the component parts of the Mulberry harbours were being towed across and sunk in position, and within ten days the harbours were taking shape.

Hard fighting was taking place ashore and the bombarding ships were in action in support. The very long range of the 15 inch guns caused surprise and consternation to the build-up of German counter-attacking armour seventeen miles inland.

As more and more men poured across the sea they reinforced the battle-weary troops who were encountering strong resistance from the German Army, and more and more stores were required. At that moment, on the night of 19 June, a gale struck the Channel and for eighty hours the vast armada struggled to survive. The beaches were littered with assault craft, coasters and parts of one Mulberry harbour which had broken up and was driven ashore. In all, some 800 craft littered the beaches. Unloading almost came to a standstill and with the build-up of German resistance a crisis arose. However, flexibility and initiative gradually restored order and as the wind dropped supply convoys resumed and the chaos on the beaches was straightened out. But the U-boat threat was not yet over. The new 'schnorkel' fitted boats could remain submerged for long periods and were difficult to sight from the air. Their determined attempts to attack shipping caused some losses but eventually, despite their almost suicidal courage, they were prevented from gaining the initiative over the Allies.

As the troops moved inland the port of Cherbourg was captured on 26 June and the bombarding ships gradually withdrew leaving smaller warships to convey troops and stores across the Channel. It is here at the end of June 1944 that we must hand over to the military historians, for Operation 'Neptune', the Allied navies' task of safely conveying troops and stores for the invasion of Europe had been completed, though the Army needed to be maintained ashore right up to the end of the war and was constantly taxing naval resources.

Final victory in the Atlantic

As the Allied forces advanced into France the continuous supply convoys were subjected to nightly German minelaying and attacks by E-boats. U-boats attempting to enter the Channel were driven back and the strain on their crews was almost unbearable. The sheer numbers of Allied anti-submarine vessels and aircraft made their task virtually suicidal and the U-boat fleet was moved to ports further south as the Allies advanced on their bases. They were followed by Allied naval and air forces. Anything that moved was subjected to attack. Brest was occupied on 18 September and all U-boats not fitted with schnorkels were transferred to Norway. The schnorkel boats continued to operate wherever the chance occurred in the Channel or Western Approaches, and never gave up. Those based in Norwegian waters operated against the Arctic convoys and one or two ships were sunk. The great battleship *Tirpitz* was still at anchor in northern Norway and while damaged both by the Royal Navy's Fleet Air Arm and by Bomber Command she was still afloat. She had been immobilized but her big guns were still serviceable. On 12 November 1944 an RAF raid finally sank the battleship whose very presence, without even firing a gun, caused such havoc in the war at sea in the Arctic. With her went 1,000 of her crew.

During the second half of 1944, 159 ships made the Arctic passage without loss and of the 100 returning ships only two were sunk. The balance of power was certainly in the Allies' favour.

From June 1944 until the end of the war eleven British and seven United States escort carriers operated in the Atlantic. In addition to attacking surfaced U-boats, their aircraft directed surface vessels to the scene and prevented boats from positioning themselves to attack ships in convoy. The German U-boats stationed in Norway had to make the long passage round the north of Scotland before arriving in operational areas. Allied aircraft with anti-submarine forces patrolled this area continuously, but in September 1944 twenty-five U-boats made the passage successfully. This was followed in October by

a further forty-nine. The use of the schnorkel whereby a boat could recharge her batteries while at periscope depth undoubtedly assisted in this operation. The arrival of these boats saw the start of an inshore campaign round the coast of Britain. While some dozen ships were sunk, the losses in U-boats were a heavy price to pay. Air raids on Hamburg destroyed a number of boats then building and the Norwegian bases were also attacked by heavy bombers. None the less the inshore campaign was fought with sustained bravery by the U-boats, for the sighting of each one drew out the full quota of air and sea countermeasures. During the last four months of 1944 only fourteen ships were sunk in coastal waters out of some 12,000 sailings.

Despite overwhelming Allied superiority in every branch of anti-submarine warfare, the U-boats continued their attack.

The battle for control of the seas continued right up to the end of the war. German aircraft continued to lay mines in constricted waters without causing much dislocation and E-boats clashed with Allied coastal forces in a series of operations at night — but the overwhelming strength of Allied air and naval forces made these attacks little more than brave gestures, for the end was in sight. The map showing U-boat sinkings from August 1944 to May 1945 tells its own tale. On 4 May 1945 Admiral Dönitz ordered all U-boats to cease hostilities and

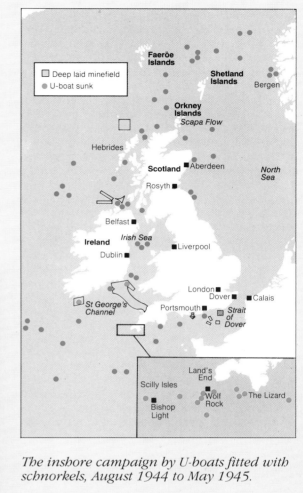

The inshore campaign by U-boats fitted with schnorkels, August 1944 to May 1945.

return to base. Even at that time there were forty-five in the Atlantic area and twelve were actually in British inshore waters. Between 1939 and 1945 Germany built 1,162 U-boats of which 719 were lost at sea and sixty-three in harbour. Out of 695 sunk by Allied action, 521 were sunk by British or Commonwealth forces, and the Royal Canadian Navy and RCAF contributed mightily to this figure.

The German U-boat arm accounted for 2,775 ships of 14½ million tons, the greater part of the 4,786 merchant ships of 21,194,000 tons sunk during the war. This is only part of the story, for a very large number of Allied ships were damaged and limped into harbour. In addition German U-boats sank 175 Allied warships, the great majority being British.

This loathsome war at sea, in which 30,000 merchant seamen died (13 per cent of all who sailed), claimed the lives of over 70 per cent of the operational crews of U-boats of the *Kriegsmarine,* while the Royal and Commonwealth Navies lost 51,500 dead or missing in the war, some 47,000 of them in the war with Germany. May these horrendous statistics coupled with the courage of the young men who flew above the oceans and fought on or below the seas be echoed in the words used by Admiral Arleigh Burke in his Foreword — 'God help any nation which neglects to study its past.'

Swordfish aircraft with which Britain entered the war were still in use in 1945. This aircraft, fitted with rockets, sank U-752 in the Western Approaches.

6

The Pacific
January 1944 to August 1945

USS Laffey *on picket duty on 16 April 1945 off Okinawa. This destroyer survived twenty-two kamikaze aircraft attacks over a period of eighty minutes.*

Submarine warfare in Japan

The Japanese submarine I-19 operating south of Guadalcanal on 15 September 1942 penetrated the destroyer screen and in a daring attack fired a spread of torpedoes which sank the American carrier Wasp. This left only one serviceable carrier in the South Pacific at a time when heavy units of the Japanese fleet were known to be in the Solomons area. At the same time submarine I-15 torpedoed and damaged USS North Carolina, again leaving only one serviceable battleship in the area. Finally the American destroyer O'Brien was torpedoed and later sank.

At the outbreak of war Japan had a well balanced force of submarines, ranging from the 20 ton midgets to the huge 400 feet transport boats, a number of which carried seaplanes for reconnaissance. The fleet submarines of over 1,000 tons were the I-type and the remainder were the smaller RO-type,

The midget submarines failed in nearly every case, but in one respect the Japanese submarines led the world and that was in their highly efficient torpedoes. While the 24 inch 'long lance' torpedoes were not fitted to submarines, the 21 inch oxygen enriched type 95 that they did use were extremely efficient. It was slower and had a shorter range than the 22,000 yards of the long lance but there were few failures, and it was a potent weapon.

The fact that Japan did not have more success with her fleet was due in part to its deployment by High Command. Twenty-seven submarines were placed round Pearl Harbor, but too far out to be of use. However, it was I-156 which first sighted HMS *Prince of Wales* and HMS *Repulse,* and in the early days air reconnaissance from submarines was valuable. The brief appearance of Japanese boats off the American coast (and the torpedo hit on USS *Saratoga*) resulted in a form of convoy system being introduced, but the Japanese did not persevere and withdrew submarines from these profitable waters. This proved to be a mistake. Had there been an all out attempt to interfere with shipping from the west coast of America on the route to Australia and to Hawaii, it would have meant tying up a large number of anti-submarine escorts at a time when they were in very short supply, and the Battle of the Atlantic was at its height.

Another reason for the apparent lack of success at the outset of hostilities stemmed again from High Command directives. Commanders were restricted by a rigid centralized control, and personal initiative was much inhibited. For the Japanese there was no Admiral Lockwood to revitalize a service which suffered from a lack of spontaneous decision-making.

This centralized control failed to exploit submarines in the Indian Ocean, and thus deprived Japan of some easy pickings in the early days. This is not to say that there were not significant sinkings in that theatre. Over twenty Allied merchant ships were sunk and the British battleship *Ramillies* seriously damaged. The lightning conquest of key bases in the South Pacific within months of the outbreak of war gave Japan an unrivalled opportunity to make use of new forward bases in Singapore and Java, and to paralyse the Indian Ocean.

At the Battle of Midway submarines on both sides failed to achieve any real results, and this was at a time when their intervention could have been decisive. The only Japanese success was in the sinking of USS *Yorktown,* but by that time she was a smouldering wreck lying dead in the water, and from America's viewpoint only *Tambor*'s sighting of Admiral Kurita's cruisers off Midway had any tangible outcome.

In the bitter struggle for Guadalcanal, Japanese submarines played a major part. Their presence in the restricted waters of the Solomons resulted in pinning down a large number of American warships on convoy duties, and their successes included the sinking of the carrier *Wasp,* the cruiser *Juneau* and two destroyers. They also damaged one carrier and two battleships and attacked and damaged some vital supply ships. However, this was over a period of six months of critical naval engagements, and with the force at their disposal the results in terms of supply ship sinkings were not commensurate with the opportunities that were afforded. There was a reason for this: the Japanese ground forces were becoming hemmed in for lack of supplies due to the activities of the American Marine Corps pilots who made it difficult for ships to approach the island in daylight. Submarines were being used in ever increasing numbers to act as carriers of essential supplies. It was not a job the Japanese Submarine Service relished, but it was vital to the beleaguered garrisons. More and more they were put at the disposal of the Army for sending in supplies, evacuating and transporting troops and for a variety of other operations. So many boats were used in this way that the effectiveness of the Service dwindled.

This occurred at a time when American anti-submarine countermeasures had not been perfected, and the opportunity for the Japanese to do lasting damage had been lost for ever. With the close of the Guadalcanal campaign the position had changed, and Japanese boats faced a far more formidable enemy. Few of their boats were fitted with suitable radar or sonar and by the end of 1943, fourteen had failed to return from operations in the Solomons. It was during the Marianas campaign that the greatest defeat was inflicted upon the Japanese submarine fleets. The assault on Saipan caused a huge concentration of American warships and transports in the area, and no less than twenty-five RO boats were sent to intercept. They brought back no information of value and failed to sink or damage a single ship. The strength of American countermeasures can be seen by the fact that seventeen out of the twenty-five failed to return. They were in a desperate plight, not unlike the position in which Admiral Dönitz found himself when trying to send his boats across the Bay of Biscay. In the Japanese case the actual physical number of United States aircraft in the sky and the number of destroyers and destroyer escorts protecting the fleet and convoys made it virtually suicidal to remain on the surface or to attack at periscope depth.

Japan probably built more midget submarines than any other nation in the Second World War. While there were many gallant attempts to strike at the opposing forces, very little success was achieved. This may well have been due to the suicidal nature of the operations. It is easier to point an aircraft at a ship below it, and to dive on to that ship, than it is to manoeuvre a slowly moving and detectable midget submarine towards its target from some miles out to sea. The Japanese trained hundreds of young men to drive human torpedoes against the mass of shipping congregated off invasion beaches, but in almost every case they were detected and did not survive.

The last major success for the Japanese Submarine Service was the sinking of the United States heavy cruiser *Indianapolis* in the very closing weeks of the war, when the operational strength of the Service was down to four boats.

Submarine warfare by the United States

USS Sandlance *was an outstandingly successful submarine. On her first patrol she encountered typhoons and icebergs as well as sinking a number of merchant ships. On 13 March 1944 she surfaced to find herself among a heavily escorted convoy. With her last torpedoes she sank the light cruiser* Tatsuta *and three merchant ships, and survived heavy depth charging.*

The United States Submarine Service began as a largely ineffective and somewhat frustrated force which transformed itself into a highly competent machine and, towards the end of the war, achieved devastating results. United States submarines were responsible for nearly one-third of all Japanese warships destroyed and nearly two-thirds of merchant shipping sunk. The boats were well equipped except for the old S boats which were withdrawn as new models came off the production lines. But in the early days American torpedoes were thoroughly defective. Time and again boats fired salvoes of torpedoes at prime targets only to see them bounce off or pass beneath their quarry. Little wonder there was frustration. There were command weaknesses ashore and afloat also. The background of poor training, and the sparing use of torpedoes for training in peacetime, meant that material deficiencies were not fully realised. Over-cautiousness and insufficient aggressiveness by boat commanders were also shortcomings that could be laid at the door of the force commanders and their pre-war

predecessors. Throughout 1942 the total tonnage sunk in the Pacific was 72,500 tons.

A radical change occurred with the appointment in May 1942 of Rear-Admiral Lockwood as Commander Submarines South-west Pacific with headquarters in Australia. This dynamic commander took the situation in hand. He established the inadequacy of the torpedoes and put the situation right, appointed a number of new skippers and imbued a sense of aggressiveness into his men, which resulted in their attaining such success later. In 1943 he was promoted to Commander Submarines Pacific Fleet (based on Pearl) and his leadership continued to inspire the Service.

The Americans had the benefit of Ultra's secret code breaking and signals analysis work. As the war progressed so decrypted messages flowed into the submarine headquarters in time for boats to intercept convoys or individual warships with startling results.

The Submarine Service was a potentially lethal arm of the Imperial Japanese Navy, but it was blunted without adequate radar or sonar. Its deployment tactics were rigidly controlled by the High Command, as we have seen, and opportunities to effect real damage were lost, especially when it was being used to supply isolated garrisons. The United States had far superior radar and the priceless ability to read Japanese ciphers and so to direct boats to

known convoy routes. Thus Japan was denied the full use of a potentially crucial arm of her Navy, and the United States was spared many damaging losses.

But in the early days, as with the Japanese, many Allied submarines were used on special missions to evacuate or land vital personnel and equipment. The Pacific submarine fleet at Pearl Harbor had not been touched by the air raid in December 1941 but the loss of the Asiatic fleet headquarters at Manila Bay when it was bombed to destruction, and where twenty-seven boats had been stationed, was a severe blow, for now patrols had to start from Freemantle or Brisbane in Australia. Another serious aspect was the loss of the complete store of torpedoes at Cavite. The Dutch had a number of submarines in the East Indies, but repair facilities were disorganized and many boats were lost. At the start of the war the United States submarines had no radar, but carried up to twenty-eight torpedoes and were able to cruise for sixty days. This was far longer than British boats, which were generally nearer home bases, while the Germans extended their cruises by supply boats at certain periods during the Battle of the Atlantic.

The Battle of Midway saw the first mass concentration of US submarines and the results were disappointing; only *Nautilus* fired torpedoes at the Japanese carriers, and these missed! The newly acquired oilfields in the East Indies were

absolutely vital for the Japanese war effort, but in the early days American submarines were singularly unsuccessful in hindering the passage of the tankers that moved in these waters.

The Battle of Savo opened the struggle for Guadalcanal and the first major Japanese warship, the heavy cruiser *Kako,* was torpedoed and sunk as she returned to her base at Kavieng on 10 August 1942 by the elderly submarine S-44. Submarines operating in these areas were not really successful and seemed unable to prevent the Japanese reinforcements reaching the island. In February 1943 there were only forty-seven fleet submarines in the Pacific, but at the end of the year the total had risen to 104.

Successes mounted too, and the Brisbane boats during the next fifteen months sank 204,000 tons of shipping including one light cruiser, three destroyers and a submarine, while in total the American submarine fleet sank 286,000 tons between July and October. The number of submarine versus submarine actions in the war was impressive. Thirty-nine German and Italian

USS Harder *achieved fame in action with Japanese destroyers off Tawi Tawi where the Combined Fleet was stationed. In four days she sank three and damaged two Japanese destroyers. The painting shows the sinking of IJN* Tanikaze. Harder *was herself sunk by depth charges on 24 August 1944.*

boats were sunk by Allied submarines and twenty-five Japanese, while the number of Japanese successes in this field are thought to be small. American submarine losses through all causes were two in 1941, eight in 1942 and sixteen in 1943.

The American losses in 1943 mostly occurred at a time when the war in the Pacific was concentrated in the New Guinea and the Solomons areas. Patrolling off Rabaul was dangerous and targets were not nearly as plentiful as in the Atlantic. Nevertheless, the results were still impressive. One of the most successful boats during these months was *Silversides* which sank four ships in January, four in October and three in December. Vigorous patrolling in the China Seas resulted in success for *Tarpon* in February with the sinking of two liners (total 28,000 tons) and *Wahoo* sank nine ships (95,000 tons) in March, while *Trigger* sank two tankers and two cargo ships (27,000 tons) in September. As the year ended the United States submarines were being welded into a remarkably efficient arm of the Navy which was really to come into its own in 1944.

Orders stated that Japanese destroyers were to be given priority, although continuing pressure was to be maintained on the convoys that they protected. January had been a good month for the American submarines, (fifty ships of 241,000 tons were sunk), and February was better with fifty-four of 257,000 tons. A particularly successful first patrol was made by USS *Sandlance.* After sinking three freighters and a passenger cargo ship (and encountering both a typhoon and icebergs which rendered one periscope inoperable) she sank another freighter. On 13 March she surfaced in the centre of a convoy with a light cruiser and two destroyers as escort. She sank the cruiser *Tatsuta* and three merchant ships before diving deep for sixteen hours during which time 102 depth charges were dropped.

The question of oil tankers should again be raised. In the first eighteen months of the war only nine Japanese tankers had been sunk by submarines, but in the latter part of 1943 the total rose to fourteen. In January 1944 eight

were sunk by submarines, and the air raid on Truk on 17 February cost Japan five tankers in a day. In the same month USS *Jack* sank four in one day out of a convoy and turned the sea into a holocaust of burning oil, and during the last four days of February a further three were sunk.

So twenty oil tankers were sunk in the first eight weeks of 1944. These facts alone show how damaging this course of action was to Japan, for in the first six months of 1944, a total of forty-three oil tankers were sunk (twenty-three by submarines). The figures below show the critical position of oil imports into Japan in 1944.

January	1,000,000 barrels
February	900,000 barrels
March	900,000 barrels
April	700,000 barrels
May	600,000 barrels
June	600,000 barrels

In order to be nearer to the supply of oil, the majority of the Japanese fleet was now stationed at Singapore.

As in all other theatres of war, there were never enough destroyers to go round, particularly for convoy work. In this field the most successful United States submarine was USS *Harder.* On her fourth patrol she sank destroyer *Ikazuchi* and damaged another on 14 March. On her next patrol out of Freemantle at the end of May 1944, *Harder* attacked at close range and blew up the destroyer *Minatsuki.* On 7 June she was spotted and waited until the Japanese destroyer was only 650 yards away, when she fired three torpedoes. Fifteen seconds later destroyer *Hayanami* was hit and sank. *Harder* went deep and accepted heavy depth charging. On 9 June she surfaced to see two destroyers. At 1,000 yards, when the destroyers were overlapping, four torpedoes were fired. The first destroyer was hit and burned furiously and as the second destroyer turned to avoid the wreck, she ran into the fourth torpedo.

These attacks were made by *Harder* off Tawi Tawi in North Borneo, where the Japanese Combined Fleet was now stationed. As a result, movement of Japanese warships in this area was restricted, particularly in the case of carriers where much needed flying training for new pilots was seriously curtailed. This definitely affected forthcoming operations. The sighting reports sent off by *Harder* when the Combined Fleet sailed north towards Saipan for what was to be the Battle of the Philippine Sea were of vital importance in the days ahead. On her next patrol *Harder* sank two Japanese destroyer escorts on 22 August 1944 but never returned.

The assault on Japanese merchant shipping was relentless. 'Wolf packs' on the lines of the German U-boats were formed and as a pack they were just as lethal. On 13 August 1945 one tanker, one escort carrier, one cargo ship and one transport, a total of 47,928 tons, were sunk on one night.

A sinking Japanese freighter seen through the periscope of an American submarine.

Towards the end of the war American submarines were sent on lifeguard duties to rescue airmen who had landed in the sea. Five hundred and four aircrew were rescued by submarines.

USS *Tang* operating off Formosa on 11 October 1944 sank two heavily laden freighters. On 23 October she sighted a large escorted convoy and attacked on the surface at night. As she entered the convoy, a ferocious battle ensued. Three ships were sunk and possibly three others were badly damaged. She was boxed in with three burning vessels on one side and a freighter, a transport and a destroyer on the other. She extricated herself and twenty-four hours later, having reloaded, found another heavily escorted convoy including a tanker with aircraft on her deck. Another night attack took place on the surface. *Tang* was credited with two definite sinkings but fate then stepped in. Her very last torpedo was aimed at a damaged transport but it malfunctioned, swerved to the left and came round in a circle, hitting and sinking the submarine. Very few of the boat's company survived to be taken into captivity.

In the early hours of 21 November submarine *Sealion II* was operating in the East China Sea when radar contact was made with two battleships, two cruisers and three destroyers. In a surface attack at 3,000 yards range two sets of explosions lit the night sky, and later a further

huge explosion resulted in the battleship *Kongo* (31,000 tons) being sunk. It was later discovered that destroyer *Urakaze* had been the second victim of the earlier attack.

The oil situation was now desperate for Japan. Submarine contacts with tankers were not accidental, for Ultra decrypts were now flowing in fast, and a convoy's composition, destination, speed and position were often known in time to be acted upon.

The year 1944 ended with a total sinking of 2,451,914 tons of shipping, and while Japan's merchant fleet began the year with a total of 4,947,815 tons it ended with only 2,847,534.

The total number of Japanese warships sunk in 1944 was equally impressive, and consisted of one battleship, four aircraft carriers, three escort carriers, two heavy cruisers, eight light cruisers, thirty destroyer escorts and seven submarines; in all, fifty-five vessels.

The US Submarine Service now became an unassailable team guided with consummate skill by Admiral Lockwood. Fast decoding of

Ultra signals was the major reason for the submarines' ability to be in the right place at the right time, but it was the submarine commanders and their crews who caused such havoc and literally brought disaster to Japan.

As an example, a wolf pack of submarines *Parche, Hammerhead* and *Steelhead* were off Formosa at the end of July 1944. At 03.00 on 31st *Steelhead* attacked a convoy and a freighter and tanker were hit. Rockets soared up into the night and in the glare *Parche* saw several ships in silhouette. Three escorts were between the submarine and the convoy. *Parche* swung away at full speed and arrived at a position directly ahead of the convoy which was approaching fast. The submarine passed the leading freighter with 200 yards to spare. Two tankers were to starboard. A stern shot hit the freighter, while four torpedoes were fired at the leading tanker and three at the second. The first tanker sank at

Japan relied entirely upon imported oil and the American submarine offensive largely destroyed the means of bringing it from the East Indies to the Japanese mainland. Here a burning tanker lights up the night sky.

once but the second, although hit, continued on. *Parche* flung herself into the middle of the convoy with shells and tracer criss-crossing around her, and fired torpedoes at one ship after another. A small fast cargo vessel turned to ram and *Parche* scraped by with full right rudder. She was hemmed in by approaching ships and fired three torpedoes at an advancing passenger cargo vessel at very close range. Two torpedoes hit her in the bow and she stopped as if hitting a sandbank; the next torpedo sank her immediately. As *Parche* pulled clear further explosions were heard as the wolf pack continued the attack. It was one of the most furious attacks of the war and performed in the same style as Otto Kretschmer in U-99 in early 1941 in the Atlantic.

The United States did not achieve this success without losses. Sixteen boats failed to return in 1943 and seventeen in 1944.

Finally we come to the submarine lifeguard operations. Several boats were placed strategically to be vectored on to the last known position of a pilot who had crashed or jumped. Admiral Lockwood agreed to release submarines for this purpose and they did well. The figures speak for themselves. In 1943 there were seven rescues, 117 in 1944, and in 1945 380 pilots and crewmen were saved from the sea by submariners.

One such rescue is of contemporary interest. USS *Finback* was on lifeguard patrol off Chichi Jima during air operations in September 1944 when a plane was reported to have splashed. The pilot was rescued and the navigator was seen to be near an island held by the Japanese, who were firing at the little rubber raft close inshore. *Finback* dived and came to periscope depth alongside the navigator who held on to the periscope and after some difficulty was gradually pulled out to sea and out of range of the gunfire, when the submarine surfaced and took the crewman on board. The pilot who had been rescued was a Lieutenant (junior grade) George Bush who was destined to do great service for his country and the world.

In this summary of the submarine service of the United States Navy we should end with a note about Japan's position. Her merchant fleet, and in particular her oil tankers, had been completely decimated and starvation of the war effort, and indeed of the country itself, was a distinct possibility.

Although similarly afflicted, Great Britain, with the enormous help of the United States in supplying war materials and particularly aircraft, was able to produce countermeasures to check and then to destroy the submarine campaign being waged against her. Japan was unable to do this. It is perhaps right to stress the fact that in the Royal Navy, training in anti-submarine warfare was brought to a pitch of perfection never even approached by Japan. Her never-strict convoy system only started when sinkings became intolerable and her depth charges were virtually unchanged throughout the war. This can be seen in the relatively small number of United States submarines destroyed by this weapon, since Japan only possessed primitive sonar and radar, whereas she lost virtually all her fleet from the combined assault of aircraft and explosive devices.

214

*During the campaign to isolate Japan, United States submarines
penetrated minefields to attack inshore shipping. This painting shows
USS* Tang *during the last week of October 1944. She engaged two
large Japanese convoys sinking six ships and damaging a number of
others. These actions were very similar to those of Captain Kretschmer
in U-99 in the Atlantic. The night sky was lit by burning tankers and
transports. On 25 October 1944* Tang *fired her last torpedo which
malfunctioned and came round in a circle hitting the submarine in
the stern. She sank with the loss of all but four of her crew.*

The assault on Saipan

Troops of the 2nd Marine Division transferring from a transport to landing craft before assaulting Saipan on 15 June 1944.

Moving north from the New Guinea campaign we reach the Marianas, a group of some fifteen islands which stretch for over 400 miles in an arc running north and south. Since the First World War, Japan had held a mandate over these islands (except for Guam) and Japanese nationals in 1944 outnumbered the local population by two to one.

The map of the Pacific on page 268 will show the strategic position of the Marianas. By mounting an expedition to capture them the United States could create bases from which Japan could be bombed by long range aircraft, and they would afford an all-round springboard for further operations, including the capture of the Philippines.

The naval force under overall command of the Commander-in-Chief Admiral Nimitz was in the form of a huge task force under the operational command of Admiral Spruance which included the Joint Expeditionary Force under Vice-Admiral Turner. Admiral Halsey who had come up from the Solomons area began planning the moves to take place three months ahead. But Saipan presented special problems to the Americans. It was thickly populated and the coral limestone caves afforded excellent defensive positions from which to command the landing beaches. Detailed information about the beaches was scarce and air photo reconnaissance necessitated flying over 4,500 mile round trips. Although this was accomplished, it was hardly a satisfactory basis on which to plan an invasion. The assault on Saipan was scheduled for 15 June 1944 and estimates of the strength of the Japanese garrison were wildly short of the truth, for it consisted of a grand total of some 31,500 men under General Saito.

The defences of the island had not been completed, and had the assault been made three months later there would have been even more formidable an opposition.

The northern attack force (Task Force 52) comprising the 2nd and 4th Marine Divisions with escorts departed Pearl Harbor on 29 May, while the 27th Infantry Division (reserve) sailed two days later. They arrived on 7 and 8 June at Eniwetok lagoon 1,000 miles to the east of Saipan, and a southern attack force (Task Force 53) left the Solomons on 4 June and moved up to the north.

Admiral Mitscher sailed from Majuro on 6 June 1944, and the force comprised seven fleet carriers and eight escort carriers. They attacked air bases within range of Saipan, destroying aircraft on the ground and damaging airfields, between 11 and 13 June. They also sighted and attacked a convoy of twelve ships, sinking ten totalling over 30,000 tons. Land based aircraft contributed by striking at the Palaus. The object was to isolate Saipan from any reinforcement aircraft reaching the island from the string of airfields within range.

The seven new battleships attached to the fast carrier groups commenced the bombardment of Saipan and Tinian on 13 June. This, however, achieved very little, since the crews were inexperienced in this highly specialized form of naval warfare.

The next day the bombardment was taken over by the more experienced and 'older' battleships *Maryland, Colorado, Pennsylvania, Tennessee, California, New Mexico, Mississippi* and *Idaho*. This was more successful but in no way did it destroy the defences which were sited to cover the beaches. During the bombardment underwater demolition teams were reconnoitring the beaches, blasting a way through the coral and taking depth soundings. This priceless information was obtained with great skill and courage, but the fact remains that the assault forces were denied the precise information which was essential to a landing if it was to be effected without heavy casualties.

General Saito (and Admiral Nagumo of Midway fame, whose job it was to command the small naval presence in the Marianas) were confident

This assault presented vast logistical problems on a scale unheard of before because of the distances involved. Saipan, the first island to be attacked, lies 3,500 miles from Pearl Harbor, from which the majority of the 127,000 troops, over two-thirds of whom were Marines, were to be embarked. Over 700 warships and auxiliaries would also be involved and the entire expeditionary force was to be at sea at the same time. The ships allotted were thus tied up for at least three months, and every item that would be needed, including fuel, provisions, ammunition and stores had to be guaranteed for every day of the operation. Once Saipan had been secured, first Tinian, then Rota and finally Guam were to be liberated.

The first counter-attack by Japanese troops defending Saipan. American Marines had a precarious hold on the beaches, and there was a serious gap between the 2nd and 4th Divisions. At this point Japanese troops made a desperate attempt to reach the shore and the attack was only held when Marine Corps tanks gave support. Destroyers out at sea illuminated the area with starshell.

that they could hold Saipan until Admiral Ozawa and the Mobile Fleet could arrive and launch one devastating air and sea battle to break up the armada of ships and landing craft which were just visible in the dawn. The Japanese Mobile Fleet had already sailed on 13 June and was duly reported by USS *Redfin;* American Intelligence had also flashed the news to Admiral Spruance.

As the assault on Saipan went in it was met by devastating fire from the shore. The landings on 15 June were made on a broad front to allow for fast deployment inland. Despite some dangerous congestion on the left flank caused by two units landing on the same beach, it seemed that all was going well, but it wasn't. In fact the preliminary naval bombardment had been insufficient, for as it lifted, Japanese troops left their protecting trenches and manned their guns which had not been destroyed. Further inland well concealed field guns and mortars had registered on the reefs, beaches and roads

inland. Machine gun posts, well stocked with ammunition, enfiladed the beaches. After the first wave of 700 LVTs had landed, carrying 8,000 Marines to shore in the first twenty minutes, the Japanese laid down such a barrage on the beaches that it seemed as though the whole area had erupted in spray. It was a deadly and devastating fire.

Some of the first assaulting Marines had pushed inland to a depth of 700 yards, but the remainder were pinned down. Fire control parties in contact with the ships lying off were unable to obtain satisfactory radio contact. Thus at a critical moment the most powerful naval fire support ever seen in the Pacific was unable to assist the troops because they could not make their wants known.

The Japanese troops just behind the beaches and further inland stood their ground and fought from well concealed positions with great courage. Behind them in camouflaged and cleverly sited positions, the guns and mortars poured accurate fire on to the beaches controlled by forward observation posts which pinned the Marines to the ground. By nightfall a little more than half the planned beachhead had been occupied and there was a dangerous gap between the 2nd and 4th Marine Divisions. Some 20,000 assault troops were ashore but casualties were in the region of 2,000. During the night Japanese troops counter-attacked.

The battlefield was illuminated by starshell from the destroyers as the attackers threw themselves on to the Marines. Each time they were thrown back, more took their place, and hand-to-hand fighting broke out in the dangerous gap in the American lines. Finally the arrival of five Sherman tanks stopped this determined attempt to drive the Marines into the sea. On both sides that night 'uncommon courage was commonplace'. As dawn came the Marines were still there, though battered and exhausted, and the Japanese forces were ready to face another day of bombardment.

The reserve 27th Army Division was ordered to land at dusk on the second day of the assault. Meanwhile under continuous artillery fire the beachhead was consolidated with stores and the whole of the divisional artillery. That night the Japanese made a further counter-attack in strength. The attack began at 03.00 and lasted until 07.00. The destroyers were called upon to illuminate the area and night was turned into day, as forty-four Japanese tanks supported the attack. They were stopped by every weapon available and were finally destroyed by the 75 mm guns on the Marines' half tracks. The Americans' success in holding off this counter-attack was in no small degree due to the massive artillery support they received from newly landed artillery regiments. By the morning of 17 June Saipan beachhead was secured, but the island itself was by no means captured.

The last surviving Japanese troops on Saipan broke out of the ring of encircling American forces in a desperate attack on 7 July 1944. They overran one army unit and were finally held by the guns of Battery H of 3/10th Marines whose shells exploded seventy-five yards forward of the muzzles. In the battle which followed over 4,000 Japanese troops died. In Saipan over 3,400 American troops were killed and 13,000 wounded, while the staggering total of nearly 24,000 Japanese were buried.

News had reached Admiral Spruance that a submarine had sighted a Japanese carrier force emerging from the San Bernardino Strait in the Philippines, and a further Japanese carrier strike force was steaming north towards Saipan. To meet this threat some of the cruisers and destroyers supporting the land fighting were detached to augment the fast carrier screen. Unloading was to cease at dusk next day and the transports were to withdraw to a safe position until recalled. Finally the fire-support battleships were to move twenty-five miles to the west to cover Saipan in case surface units of the Japanese Mobile Fleet eluded the fast carriers and fell on the thinly protected assault forces. For close air support the Marines would have to rely on the escort carriers alone.

While the battle to wrest away the island of Saipan from the stubborn and fanatically brave

Japanese continued, preparations were taking place to the westward to meet the Japanese Mobile Fleet which was coming to the rescue of the beleaguered island garrison. The Battle of the Philippine Sea was soon to take place, and regretfully it is not possible to follow step-by-step the two weeks of tough fighting on land which now followed.

Progress was slow and casualties mounted on both sides as the Japanese troops became holed up in caves and were attacked by flame thrower and explosive charges. It was a bitter battle. Finally General Saito gathered his remaining troops for one last attempt to break out of the encircling forces which were driving him into an ever smaller perimeter. This last effort by the remaining garrison, many of whom were wounded and some of whom had no weapons, was a desperate sacrifice of life. They inflicted as much damage as they could before perishing in what has now become known as the Great Banzai Charge. At 04.45 on 7 July some 4,500 Japanese troops, all that were left, fell upon units of the 27th Division. They poured through a gap left between two of the Army battalions and overwhelmed a number of units.

They then advanced down the railway line and the Marine gunners were unable to fire forward as they knew that units of the 27th Division were ahead of them. As the Japanese attacked the Marine positions, only Battery H of the

3/10th was able to fire. Fuses were cut to just four-tenths of a second and shells exploded seventy-five yards ahead of the gunners. Gunners were killed at their posts as they fought to the last against the despairing bravery of the remnants of General Saito's garrison. The attack was held after bloody hand-to-hand fighting during which the gunners were forced back until the line was re-formed.

The staggering number of 4,300 Japanese dead was counted after the battle. Saipan had been taken at a prodigious cost to human life. The total American casualties were 3,426 killed and 13,099 wounded, making a total of 16,525 out of 67,451, 24 per cent of those who participated in the operation. Japanese losses were appalling. In all 23,811 were said to have been buried and 921 were made prisoners of war.

The Battle of the Philippine Sea

For Japan the only way in which the relentless pressure on her defensive line could be halted was in a fleet action to destroy or cripple the United States fleet. The question was where would the Americans strike next? The Japanese settled on a Palau and Western Carolines area, and the secret Z plan was entrusted to Admiral Ozawa, to strike and destroy the carrier force when and where it was sighted. The oil problem continued to be a crucial factor. The Mobile Fleet was sent south to Tawi Tawi, North Borneo, to be near oil supplies, since American submarines were regularly sinking tankers and producing a critical shortage in Japan. Admiral Ozawa's own Cardiv 1, consisting of the new carrier *Taiho* with *Shokaku* and *Zuikaku* was training in the area, and at the same time Cardiv 2, which comprised the carriers *Junyo*, *Hiyo* and *Ryujo*, along with Cardiv 3, composed of light carriers *Zuiho*, *Chitose* and *Chiyoda*, had also sailed from Japan to join the Mobile Fleet at Tawi Tawi. With them went the giant battleship *Musashi*.

Two problems faced the Japanese High Command: the poor quality of their new young pilots and the fact that Tawi Tawi was not secure against submarine attacks. The young replacements for the aircrews shattered at Rabaul and during the Solomons campaign had had no more than two to six months training, and they were needed to fly the improved D4Y 'Judy' dive-bombers and B6N 'Jill' torpedo-bombers as well as the new Zero 52 fighters. They lacked time, combat experience and training as a group. Courage alone could not make up for these defects and they were unprepared for the forthcoming battle.

American Intelligence pointed to the concentration of warships in the area of Tawi Tawi, and Japanese forces coming south were spotted and reported heading for Tawi Tawi by USS *Harder*. Further submarines were ordered to ring the anchorage and one important result was that Japanese sea and air training was seriously impaired, at a time when it was most needed.

Meanwhile more Japanese submarines were deployed in all areas where American operations were taking place or were considered probable. At least twenty-five submarines were used with disastrous repercussions for Japan. No less than seventeen were sunk during the next month, without any useful information being obtained, and with not one American ship being damaged. Aircraft accounted for two submarines, and destroyers and destroyer escorts sank the remainder. The most successful was destroyer escort USS *England,* with only about ten weeks' sea experience, for in thirteen days she sank six submarines which was a feat unequalled in World War II.

Japanese submarines were deployed to destroy American forces engaged in the assault on Saipan. They achieved no success and in the many engagements the destroyer escort USS England *sank no less than six Japanese submarines in twelve days, a feat not exceeded in any other theatre of war.*

These successes were greatly assisted by accurate information supplied by Signal Intelligence (Sigint), which now reached the stage where a steady flow of decrypted messages was being passed to commanders on the spot in time for them to take action.

The Japanese planners were convinced that the next American thrust was to be against the Palau Islands, and air units were moved to airfields further south to be in a position to assist in the destruction of American forces. Thus at a crucial moment Japan was taking air strength from the very area where the next assault was to be made, and so depriving herself of possibly 25 per cent of available land-based aircraft.

It must have been a devastating blow when American aircraft struck at the Marianas on 11 and 12 June 1944, destroying aircraft on Saipan, Guam and Tinian and as far north as Iwo Jima. When this was followed by the full-scale invasion of Saipan it seemed that the Z plan (Operation A-GO, the destruction of the American fleet) must be put into action. Admiral Toyoda, the Japanese Commander-in-Chief, felt that he would have some added benefit from airfields in the area, and land-based aircraft could add weight to the attack. What he did not know was the extent of the damage done by Admiral Mitscher's air strikes and he had by then moved a significant number of aircraft out of the area anyway to prepare for the anticipated action in the Western Carolines.

Admiral Ozawa's Mobile Fleet sortied out from Tawi Tawi on 16 June at 09.00. The news was flashed to Admiral Nimitz by the submarine *Redfin* that evening. After refuelling, the Mobile Fleet proceeded north, entering the San Bernardino Strait, and was spotted by coast watchers and by the submarine *Flying Fish*, positioned for just that purpose. At the same time another boat — USS *Seahorse* — was closing to cover the Surigao Strait and was just able to make out a powerful force of battleships, carriers, cruisers and destroyers. This was the force comprising *Zuiho*, *Chitose* and *Chiyoda* together with the four battleships *Yamato* and *Musashi*, *Kongo* and *Haruna*, eight cruisers and a destroyer escort. Meanwhile Japanese shore-based aircraft had attacked the American carrier force off Saipan, but the protective fighters drove them off without loss to the fleet.

A comparison of the strength of the opposing fast carrier fleets is shown in the chart below. This shows that, except for heavy cruisers,

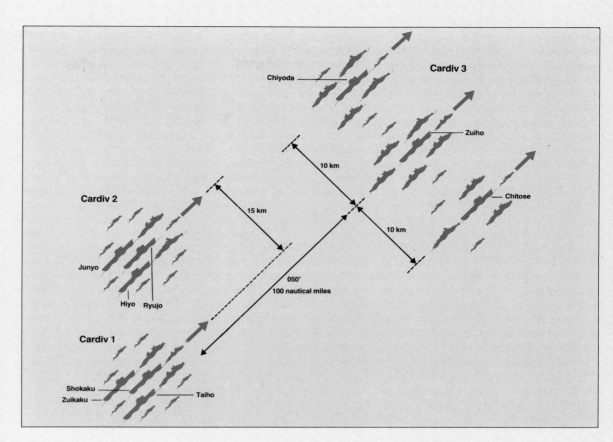

The Japanese forces in position for the Battle of the Philippine Sea at 04.15 on 19 June 1944.

Admiral Ozawa's force was at a major disadvantage, and the disparity in aircraft strength was even greater, compounded by the Japanese pilots' lack of combat experience.

The numerical superiority was further compounded by the fact that the leading American pilots were veterans of many air strikes and all pilots had had nearly two years training with at least 360 hours flying experience before joining their carriers.

However, in three respects the Japanese admiral had some advantage. Firstly, the easterly trade winds enabled him to launch and recover aircraft unhindered as he approached the American fleet, whereas Admiral Mitscher had to reverse course to head into wind and had little chance of making headway to close the Japanese forces. Secondly, the Japanese aircraft (without armour and therefore lighter) had a search range of up to 560 miles, against the American 450. They could strike from 300 miles, whereas the American range was about 260. Thirdly, and most important, Admiral

Ozawa counted (mistakenly) on the available support of a large number of land-based planes. There were in fact 484 Japanese aircraft in the Marianas on 10 June, and the airfields could be used for refuelling. In this way the range would have been extended and re-arming speeded up. If Admiral Ozawa could attack and slow up the American forces, causing damage and destruction of aircraft before the carriers began their attack, then the serious disadvantages under which he laboured would be redressed. He had not been told of the crippling losses sustained by his land-based planes during the raids of 11 and 12 June, and was under the impression that they were at near full strength.

With the sighting reports relayed by the submarine *Redfin*, it was plain to Admiral Spruance that the Japanese Mobile Fleet would not be in a position to join the attack until 17 June. He therefore sent a strong task group comprising three fleet and four light carriers to attack the Bonin Islands of Iwo Jima, Chichi Jima and Haha Jima. These would make useful staging posts for reinforcements from the Japanese mainland, but they also held aircraft which would probably be used to attack his task force in the forthcoming battle. The results, in fact, further damaged Admiral Ozawa's prospects.

Despite searches Admiral Spruance failed to locate Admiral Ozawa's forces and the only information available had come from submarines. Further searches by Admiral Mitscher's aircraft on 19 June still could not pinpoint the Japanese forces, but Admiral Ozawa's planes had caught sight of the American task force at 15.14 the previous day. He decided to keep his main body about 400 miles from the last reported position of the American forces and to push his van strike force a hundred miles nearer. Next morning he would be in a position to attack. He had the advantage of knowing where his enemy was.

	Carriers	Light carriers	Battleships	Heavy cruisers	Light cruisers	Destroyers
Japanese	5	4	5	11	2	28
United States	7	8	7	8	13	69

	Fighter/bombers	Dive-bombers	Torpedo-bombers	Float	Grand total
Japanese	234	99	99	43	475
United States	470	233	192	65	960

On the American side Admiral Spruance had two obligations. He had to protect the invasion fleet and the Marines ashore on Saipan who were engaged in a bloody conflict. He also had to destroy the Japanese Mobile Fleet. There was an inherent danger that Admiral Ozawa could slip by him in the night and be in a position to attack the ships anchored off Saipan. He therefore withdrew eastwards to be closer to Saipan, and from Japanese reconnaissance planes seen over the fleet it was obvious that an attack on him was going to be made that day.

The American Task Force 58 under Admiral Mitscher was disposed in four carrier groups each with their cruiser and destroyer escorts, together with a battleship group. They were some twelve miles apart and could operate independently, but give mutual support.

The Japanese forces consisted of a vanguard and a main body. The vanguard consisted of the light carriers *Zuiho, Chiyoda* and *Chitose,* with four battleships including the mighty *Yamato*

and *Musashi,* four cruisers and nine destroyers. These were positioned so as to give massive mutual fire support. One hundred miles astern was the main body of one light and five fleet carriers with one battleship, two cruisers and nineteen destroyers. The map on page 221 shows the situation at 04.15 on 19 June.

The scene was set for the greatest air battle in the world's history. It opened with an air battle over Guam. Land-based fighters and bombers were taking off and landing and fierce fighting took place. The Japanese pilots were unable to shake off the American fighters sent to prevent their reaching the task force, and none did.

At 10.00 the first Japanese air strike was detected by radar at a distance of 150 miles, and the entire American task force flew off a very strong fighter group, together with deckloads of bombers, under orders to orbit to the east on call. The carriers' decks and the likely combat area were thus cleared of all aircraft which would not contribute to the defence of Task

Force 58. The Japanese pilots were to be met by 140 Hellcats while eighty-two others were ranged on combat air patrol at between 18,000 and 23,000 feet. Into this mass of aircraft flew the van force's first wave of sixteen Zero fighters escorting forty-five Zero fighter bombers, each carrying a 550 pound bomb, and eight torpedo laden 'Jills'. They had no chance against the more experienced and heavily armed and armoured American Hellcats who far outnumbered them. Each squadron was controlled from its parent carrier by experienced fighter directors and the flagship *Lexington* had a Japanese speaking officer who listened into the Japanese radio frequency. He was able to give the fighter directors a running commentary on the instructions given to the Japanese squadrons by their controller, who was orbiting outside the area of action. The resulting devastation was predictable.

The Hellcats dived on the rigid Japanese formations and one after another the unarmoured and vulnerable aircraft burst into flame or

The air battle of 19 June 1944 over the Philippine Sea was the greatest air combat to take place in aviation history. The Japanese pilots who had replaced earlier combat losses had had insufficient training to face the experienced American fighter pilots operating from the carrier groups. On that day alone over 300 Japanese aircraft were destroyed in action as against twenty-three American fighters.

themselves to attack the massed Japanese aircraft as they wheeled into formation. There were 111 aircraft — eighty bombers and torpedo-bombers escorted by forty-eight Zero fighters had set out from the main body but seventeen had fallen out for various reasons. These young men, with a smattering of more experienced pilots as leaders, were no match for the American Hellcat pilots. Once again they were cut to pieces as they approached the task force. Flaming and exploding aircraft in individual combat filled the sky. The gunners of the task force made their contribution but again it was the fighter pilots who caused most of the destruction. For mile upon mile behind the fleet the wreckage of Japanese planes littered the sea, giving a last resting place for the shattered remains of many a courageous but virtually untrained Japanese pilot. Ninety-seven failed to return to their carriers, and no damage had been done to the American fleet.

Miles away and unaware of the disaster which had befallen his aircraft, Admiral Ozawa was aboard his new carrier *Taiho.* At 09.10 the submarine *Albacore,* which had been stationed to report and intercept, found herself in a position to attack the oncoming Japanese carrier. After firing six torpedoes she went deep and was heavily depth-charged. The attack was made at the moment when *Taiho* had turned into wind to fly off her aircraft for the third raid. A torpedo was seen approaching by one of the aircraft which had just taken off. To protect his carrier the pilot immediately dived on it and a huge explosion detonated the torpedo and blew the aircraft to pieces. However, this brave act did not save the ship because one other torpedo made a hit. It did little to slow her speed and for some hours all was well. Damage control parties tried to isolate the ruptured gasoline lines, and clear the inflammable fumes. In doing so a mistaken order was given to turn on the ventilator fans which had the effect of blowing the heavy vapour throughout the ship.

The inevitable happened at 15.32 when the fleet carrier's armoured flight deck was lifted off by a huge explosion. Admiral Ozawa transferred his flag to the cruiser *Haguro.* The *Taiho* was a blazing wreck. She heeled over and sank stern first just after 18.30, taking with her 1,650 men out of a crew of 2,150, plus thirteen aircraft.

Three hours after *Albacore* made her attack, another American submarine, the *Cavalla,* stationed sixty miles away raised her periscope to find the veteran carrier *Shokaku* only 1,000 yards away, flanked by two destroyers. Six torpedoes were fired and of these four hit. *Cavalla* now had to withstand a heavy attack as depth charges exploded all around her for the next three hours. Above her the veteran of Pearl Harbor was doomed. Flames raged throughout the ship and as she settled three explosions tore

her apart and she rolled over and sank. Her losses were nearly as dreadful as those of the *Taiho,* 1,263 officers and men out of a complement of about 2,000 lost their lives, and with them went nine aircraft.

Returning to the carrier battle and the third raid on the American Task Force: the time was 10.00 as thirty-seven aircraft took off. Owing to a mistaken course only twenty approached the carriers and were set upon by forty Hellcats. Although outnumbered and outmanoeuvred, only seven were shot down and the remainder made their escape.

The fourth and final raid of the day consisted of eighty-two aircraft from Admiral Ozawa's main body. They approached an area in which United States carriers had been reported, but they found nothing and headed for Guam, although some sighted ships *en route* and attacked. They failed to make any direct hits and were themselves attacked. The remainder, forty-nine aircraft bound for Guam, were set upon by Hellcats which had been stationed over the island for just that purpose. As the aircraft circled to land they were attacked; out of the eighty-two aircraft which had set out seventy-three were either shot down or destroyed on the ground. Sporadic fighting continued until dusk as aircraft tried to land on Guam, but the air patrols intercepted them as they came in.

As dusk fell the air battle was over. 'The Great Marianas Turkey Shoot', as it was called, had started at 06.00 and continued for twelve hours. More planes had been flown off from both carrier forces than ever before, or ever would be again during the war.

The bare statistics in themselves are terrible enough. At the start of the action on 19 June, Admiral Ozawa had 475 aircraft in all. On the morning of 20 June, the Japanese admiral had only 126 operational aircraft. Further aircraft losses that day brought the figure for the two days to the staggering total of 426 together with about fifty land-based planes.

On the American side the losses were extremely light. Twenty-three aircraft had been shot down in combat or by anti-aircraft fire from the ground. Three had been lost on search missions and six others operationally. Out of this number only twenty-seven aircrew had been killed in action on 19 June.

This victory for the task force had been aided by the valuable work done by the fighter directors who guided their fliers to their targets, with the vital information gleaned from the lone Japanese linguist on board *Lexington.* The victory was made possible by the experience and training of the American pilots, their overwhelming numbers and the strong offensive capabilities of their aircraft. It was without doubt the greatest defensive victory in the air in history. Had the Japanese pilots been of the same quality as the Americans it is equally certain that the results would have been different. The failure of the Imperial Japanese Navy to train pilots to replace those lost in action during two and a half years of war to anything like the same standard as their predecessors was a fundamental mistake. They sent relatively untrained but equally brave young men to attack a numerically superior and better trained force.

exploded. In many cases the attacking Hellcat pilots flew through the debris of the explosions as they took on the next target. At one moment seventeen Japanese aircraft were seen to be on fire and diving towards the ocean, or to have hit the sea with a momentary flash and splash followed by a pall of smoke. Of the sixty-nine aircraft that comprised the raid, forty-two were destroyed and only twenty-seven set course to return to their carriers. No serious damage was done to the American task force. *South Dakota* received the only direct hit of the day which did not affect her efficiency and one or two other ships had near misses. While the defensive fire from the ships accounted for a number of Japanese aircraft, at least twenty-five out of forty-two were shot down by the fighters. The first raid was over and American aircraft began to land to refuel and rearm. Four American pilots were killed in action and a number of aircraft were badly damaged.

The second raid was detected at 11.07 giving time for the Hellcat squadrons to position

Admiral Spruance did not have sufficient information upon which to order a strike against the Japanese forces, and despite having a number of night fighters with long range tanks in his fleet, he waited till early on 20 June before resuming his searches. They flew to a limit of 325 miles but were seventy-five miles short of the position where Admiral Ozawa was preparing to refuel.

All through the morning of 20 June, air searches went on by both sides, but no sightings were made. Admiral Ozawa was still unaware of the enormity of his aircraft loss, since Guam was making exaggerated claims of success.

It was not until 15.57 that the voice of one of the American searching aircraft was heard. 'Enemy fleet sighted time 15.40. Long. 135.25 E, Lat. 15.00 N, course 270 and speed 20 knots'. It was

The Japanese fleet was not sighted until the following day (20 June) and despite the inevitability of a night recovery of aircraft, an all-out strike was ordered immediately. The attack was at maximum range and due to the lack of preparation, unco-ordinated. Against heavy gunfire the pilots only sank one carrier and faced a long flight back to their carriers.

Despite the probable presence of Japanese submarines the sky was illuminated and deck lights were turned on to assist the returning American pilots. Twenty aircraft had been lost in action but 100 were lost either from deck crashes or ditching due to lack of fuel, though in this case the majority of the aircrew were rescued by destroyers.

over 275 miles away from Task Force 58. This was a very long way and recovery would have to take place at night. However, Admiral Mitscher took a calculated risk and the order was given to launch every available aircraft for what could be a final knock-out blow to cripple the Japanese Mobile Fleet so that the battleships could attack the next day.

At 16.21 the task force turned into wind and soon eighty-five fighters and seventy-seven dive-bombers with extra fuel tanks and sixty-four torpedo-bombers were heading into the west as the sun began to sink lower in the sky. To reach their targets the American strike force had to fly nearly 300 miles at a speed of 130 — 140 knots to conserve fuel. They flew in independent carrier formations and there was no time to organize a rendezvous from which to deliver a set piece attack. First to be sighted were the six oilers escorted by six destroyers. These were attacked and two were disabled and had to be abandoned.

The Mobile Fleet was spread out over an area of thirty miles and the sunset provided a brilliant backdrop in a spectrum of colours. The sky was rapidly becoming filled with anti-aircraft shell bursts, adding even more colour as the sun sank below the horizon. In this wild and desperate battle with aircraft diving from every angle and being met by every gun in the Japanese fleet, it was remarkable that American losses were so light. The carrier *Hiyo* was sunk and the *Zuikaku* very badly damaged. As she was attacked the pilots flew through the protecting barrage put up by the battleship *Nagato* as she manoeuvred close to the carrier.

At noon on 20 June Admiral Ozawa had about 100 carrier planes available and operational but during the evening he had lost sixty-five of them in air combat. The Japanese fighter pilots had been airborne in time to meet the attack but had been overwhelmed by the numbers of escorting Hellcats (though they destroyed eighteen American aircraft.) The battle lasted barely twenty minutes and then all was quiet. Both sides were exhausted, and none more so than the American pilots who now turned wearily to the east on the long flight back to their carriers after darkness fell at 19.45.

Admiral Mitscher opened out his three task groups to give them manoeuvring room for the very difficult task of recovering the aircraft. At 20.45 the returning planes began to circle the carriers and he now made the decision to illuminate the carrier decks and direct searchlight beams vertically into the sky as a beacon on which the pilots could home in, disregarding the danger of submarines or Japanese aircraft which might be in the vicinity. The recovery took two hours. Deck crashes occurred and planes now desperately short of fuel had to wait aloft while the crashed aircraft were thrown over the side. As the carriers had headed into wind, and so increased the distance for the returning aircraft, a trail of ditched planes stretched for many miles. All night, and during the next days, destroyers searched for survivors, and when it was all over eighteen aircraft with their crews had been shot down in combat, but eighty-two aircraft with 209 aircrew crashed on landing or ditched. Out of that number only forty-nine pilots and aircrew were lost.

The Battle of the Philippine Sea was over, and there was no serious attempt to pursue the Mobile Fleet which was now retiring. It is possible that a further, final attack could have been made but Admiral Spruance decided at the time that his overall responsibility was to stand guard over the critical land battles on Saipan. Admiral Ozawa had fought the battle with sound tactics which should have given him a greater reward had his young men been better trained. The result was that never again did the Japanese fleet seek combat in a full-scale carrier action. However, the events in the Marianas were by no means over.

While the battle in the air was taking place, USS Cavalla *came to periscope depth to find the veteran Japanese carrier* Shokaku *1,000 yards away flanked by two destroyers. Four torpedoes set the ship ablaze. She sank with much loss of life.* Shokaku *had been part of Admiral Nagumo's strike force at Pearl Harbour and had taken part in nearly every carrier engagement since, though she missed the Battle of Midway having been badly damaged during the Coral Sea action.*

The securing of Tinian and Guam

The air battle sealed not only the fate of Saipan and the rest of the Mariana Islands, but Japan itself. For no matter how bravely the Japanese Army fought, the United States Navy had command of the sea and the air. The Battle of the Philippine Sea took place in the middle of the assault on Saipan, which was finally secured on 10 July 1944. American forces now proceeded to plan their assault on the other major islands in the Marianas.

The island of Tinian lies just five miles south of Saipan separated by the Saipan Channel. The 2nd and 4th Divisions of the United States Marine Corps who had fought through the Saipan battles were selected to capture the island, and air bombing began on 11 June and continued for six weeks. Fire support ships started bombarding on 14 June and continued until the assault day on 24 July.

The island held a garrison of just over 9,000 men. Their position was hopeless from the start, and in normal circumstances they would have surrenderd — but the Japanese commander Vice-Admiral Kakaji Kakuta decided to hold the island to the last man. Suitable beaches for the assault were almost non-existent and the decision to use two beaches at the north end, one 60 yards and the other 160 yards long, was only possible if the preparations were minutely planned and executed by a highly trained assault force.

On 24 July, the leading units of the 4th Division USMC landed on the two tiny beaches at first light. Perfect co-ordination resulted in a continuous flow of Amphtracs followed by larger landing craft (LCTs and LSTs) with pre-loaded guns, tanks, ammunition and stores passing through the bottle-necks of the tiny landing beaches, to fan out into dispersal areas. By nightfall 15,614 troops were ashore with only fifteen killed and 200 wounded, though two 6 inch guns concealed in emplacements damaged two support vessels — the destroyer *Norman Scott,* and the battleship *Colorado.* Japanese reaction to the surprise landing was slow as the bombardment had smashed road and telephone communications. However, during the night of 24 July determined counter-attacks were made, but the Marines had overwhelming fire power support and by morning 1,250 of the attackers lay dead. Marine casualties were less than 100.

The momentum of the advance continued and there was no way in which the defenders could have succeeded in stopping it. At sea Admiral Mitscher's fast carrier group had already pounded the airfields of Iwo Chichi and Haha Jima, and there was no interference from Japanese aircraft.

The island was secured by 1 August, but not until every yard had been fought over, and for weeks after that the surviving Japanese troops gave their lives in futile attacks. It had been a near perfect amphibious operation which had cost the lives of 389 USMC and Navy personnel with 1,816 wounded. From Japan over 5,000 were buried and 252 were taken prisoner. No one will ever know what happened to the remaining 4,000.

Guam is the largest and the most important of the Mariana Islands. It had been wrested from the Americans in December 1941, and its recapture had been planned to begin a few days after the Saipan assault. This was delayed because of the unexpectedly dogged resistance of the Japanese on Saipan and allowed for the most meticulous and the most devastating pre-assault bombardment of the Pacific War. There were about 19,000 fighting men on Guam together with coast defence, anti-aircraft and field guns, all cleverly sited and protected. Every suitable beach was protected by formidable underwater defences which would have to be blown up before landing craft could reach the shore.

All Japanese aircraft on the island had been destroyed, and on 8 July the systematic pre-assault bombardment began, and lasted until the landings on 21 July. During these thirteen days, 6,258 rounds of 16 and 14 inch shells were fired. Spotter and strike aircraft reported every movement on the ground and every Japanese defensive area was subjected to the same merciless bombardment.

The naval Underwater Demolition Teams (UDTs) began to destroy the beach defences by demolition on 17 July under cover of a naval bombardment and in three days had blown up over 300 large coral and cement filled blocks linked together by wire. The landings were to take place on two beaches on either side of Apra Harbour on the west of the island. The northern beaches were to be assaulted by the 3rd Marine Division and the southern by the 1st Provisional Marine Brigade, with the 77th Division USA as reserve. The assault was to be commanded by Major-General Roy Geiger USMC.

At 06.00 on 21 July 1944 the assault began. Despite the naval bombardment, the Marines attacking in the northern sector were subjected to intense mortar and small arms fire on landing. Over 25,000 tons of cargo were moved from the beach to dumps inland as the Marines increased the perimeter during the first week, and it was here that a large number of the casualties occurred, with 753 being killed and 3,147 wounded.

Throughout the war the inhabitants of the island, the Chammoras, had remained loyal to the United States and every precaution was made by dropping leaflets to ensure that they took to the hills and were spared as much of the bombardment as possible.

The 20,000 Marines ashore were dug in and awaited the counter-attack which came in at daybreak on 22 July and was repulsed. By 24 July the Marines had captured most of the high ground overlooking the beaches. On the night of 25 July the Japanese delivered their most serious counter-attack. It had been well planned and hard fighting took place right into the centre of the Marines' position, but it was thrown back eventually, and the Marines advanced immediately under the protection of a very heavy bombardment from the sea to link up with the southern beachhead.

In the south the Marines came under heavy mortar and artillery fire. Twenty-four Amphtracs were disabled although the old battleship *Pennsylvania* moved into Agat Bay within 1,000 yards and fired a main battery salvo every twenty-two seconds, and thousands of rounds of 5 inch and 40 mm ammunition at the cliff which overlooked the landing. Without that kind of support, the landing would have been thrown back. Unloading of supplies was difficult, but by nightfall the Marines and GIs were dug in preparing for a counter-attack which started at 22.30. Tanks were used in this assault but the position was held.

Throughout the whole period covering the assault on Guam troops ashore were able to call for air support from the escort carriers. They kept planes in the air ready to strike at targets pointed out to them, and there was never a time during daylight hours when air support was not immediately available. In contrast to this, the Japanese had no air support, and knew that there was to be no rescue, and no reinforcement. They fought where they stood.

Next day, 22 July, saw a further advance inland, yard by yard towards Mount Alifan which was honeycombed with caves, every one of which had to be captured or sealed by demolition. By nightfall the Americans had captured the ridge from which the Japanese had overlooked the landing. At daybreak on 23 July a further Japanese attack was repulsed and during the day the rest of the high ground covering the beach was taken. Despite the enormous fire power of the battleships, cruisers and destroyers, the Japanese still withstood the advance of the Marines and GIs and Orote Peninsula still remained in Japanese hands although it was sealed off. It was from there that a final attack was launched on the night of 25 July when the defenders, having been issued with all the liquor from the stockpile, made a crazed sacrificial and fanatical attack. At dawn on 26 July, over 400 bodies lay in front of the Marines' positions, and after further heavy fighting Orote Peninsula was in American hands once again.

During the next three days the assault forces from the northern and southern beaches joined up and moved inland cutting the island in half. The Japanese had withdrawn from the southern half and were now concentrated around Mount Santa Rosa for a last stand. In order to capture the island the American forces literally had to destroy every Japanese soldier and sailor who barred the way. Intensive naval bombardment continued to support the Marines and Army troops as they fought their way to the north of the island. The Japanese Command Post fell on 12 August and the island was then finally announced secure.

Thus three weeks after landing, the battle of Guam was over. But at least 9,000 Japanese remained in the jungle and fighting continued right up to the end of the war.

The casualties were very high. American forces lost 1,335 killed or missing and 5,648 wounded, but the Japanese losses constituted the whole of the force defending the island — 19,000 less 1,250 prisoners, the rest killed, including some 8,500 killed or captured after 10 August.

Operation Forager, to recapture the Marianas, was completed in exactly two months, as a result of three land campaigns and the greatest air battle in the history of the world.

Leyte Gulf — logistics

The problems of maintaining a fleet the size of the United States Task Force in the Pacific were immense. It was at sea for many weeks at a time and was wholly dependent on the At Sea Logistics Service Group. This consisted of oilers, ammunition ships and store ships of every kind. In addition replenishment aircraft were carried on escort carriers together with all the spares needed to keep the aircraft in action. Thus the whole of the naval operation depended entirely on supplies being instantly available on call. In this painting USS Intrepid is refuelling while a carrier approaches a fleet oiler already refuelling a destroyer.

The problem of logistics — the supply and maintenance of a huge American fleet at sea and an army either in transports or fighting — was one which dominated every decision made by the force commanders. The speed with which the American forces moved from Guadalcanal through the Solomons, up the coast of New Guinea, to the Gilbert, Marshall and Mariana Islands, was breathtaking.

For Japan it was one body blow after another. The Japanese were trying desperately to hold a defensive outer ring which was broken by one attack after another, and they could never be sure where the next blow would fall. It was certain that the Philippines would be attacked, but the American submarine offensive was destroying the merchant ships which were required for the supply and defence requirements of their garrisons.

The industrial output of America was vast, but it had to be fed to bases in the Pacific across thousands of miles of ocean. To maintain the momentum of advance, sufficient fuel of all grades, ammunition of all calibres, provisions and stores of every conceivable nature had to be available as soon as they were required. Between 6 October 1944 and 26 January 1945 the Fast Carrier Forces of the Pacific Fleet were at sea for thirteen out of sixteen weeks. The vital supply link was provided by a unique product of war — the At Sea Logistics Service Group. It was a fleet in itself, comprising thirty-four fleet oilers, escort carriers with replacement aircraft and pilots, supply ships, destroyers and destroyer escorts and tugs to assist in towing damaged combat ships. The squadron carried in addition every item the fighting forces needed while at sea. A staggering 110,000 tons of ammunition were issued to the fleet between September and the end of November 1944.

Overcoming the problems of logistics and the protection of this vital arm of the United States Navy was of the utmost importance. A breakdown would jeopardize the whole Pacific operation and the fact that services were sustained should rank equally with the operational successes of the combatant ships. If in this narrative this area is sometimes seemingly overlooked, it is worth reminding ourselves that it was, in fact, in the forefront of every planning move and every decision which was made by the force commanders.

For Japan supply logistics were an escalating nightmare. Her outposts and garrisons were denied replenishments due to attack from the air, from submarines and from surface action. The fact that the morale and courage of her soldiers, sailors and airmen was able to be sustained during such adversity lies in the very nature of the Japanese people.

The final battles in this ghastly war continued to be fought with the utmost ferocity, though there could only be one outcome, but the overwhelming superiority of the American forces at sea and in the air was made possible only by the continuous quality of the support they were given.

Peleliu and Ulithi

Saipan, Tinian and Guam in the Marianas had been wrested from the Japanese and further south in a series of lightning moves General MacArthur had advanced a thousand miles in four months. The whole of the north coast of New Guinea was in Allied hands and now the question was where to strike next. The guiding concept for Pacific strategy was to 'obtain bases from which the unconditional surrender of Japan could be forced'. But which? The final decision was for General MacArthur's forces to occupy Morotai and for the Central Pacific forces to take Peleliu, with Ulithi as a main anchorage, and then to land at Leyte in the Central Philippines.

Meanwhile Admiral Halsey's Task Force 38 had sailed from Eniwotek on 28 August, and carried

out a wide ranging attack on airfields which might interfere with the forthcoming operations. Entering the Visayan Sea to the west of Leyte, he was under threat from eight major and six secondary operational Japanese airfields. From 12 to 15 September he proceeded to attack them all, flying 2,400 sorties in which about 200 Japanese aircraft were shot down or destroyed on the ground. At the end of the strike, Admiral Halsey realised that Japanese air power in the area was considerably less than was thought, and as a result of these strikes was still further reduced. He suggested the bypassing of Peleliu and reducing it by sea and air bombardment with a direct and immediate assault on Leyte, as a means to establishing American forces on the Philippines. However, it was decided not to alter the plans, except for

the important decision to bring forward the Leyte landings by two months.

It was vital to have a thoroughly well protected anchorage and forward base for the many hundreds of ships of all kinds which were operating in the Pacific. Ulithi was the chosen site and was occupied in September 1944. It was decided to launch the assault on Peleliu on 15 September coinciding with the Morotai landings. The plan was for a pre-assault bombardment on 13 and 14 September, with underwater demolition teams to enable the landing craft to cross the coral reefs. Over 2,000 tons of 16, 14, 8 and 5 inch shells crashed on to the beaches, causing devastation to the undergrowth and revealing numerous caves. Here, as at Tarawa and Saipan, little or nothing was known about the island or

On 15 September 1944, American Marines landed on the small island of Peleliu in the Palaus. This was considered necessary in order to support the forthcoming battle for the Philippines and was preceded by a three day bombardment. The Japanese defenders were sited well back from the beaches and were able to pour a concentration of gunfire as one wave of Marines followed another. The particular strong point seen here was sited to enfilade the whole of one beach, and honeycombed with mortars and machine guns. This caused a confusion and pile up which threatened the whole operation. A company of the veteran 1st Marine Division finally overcame the defenders, who fought to the very last man.

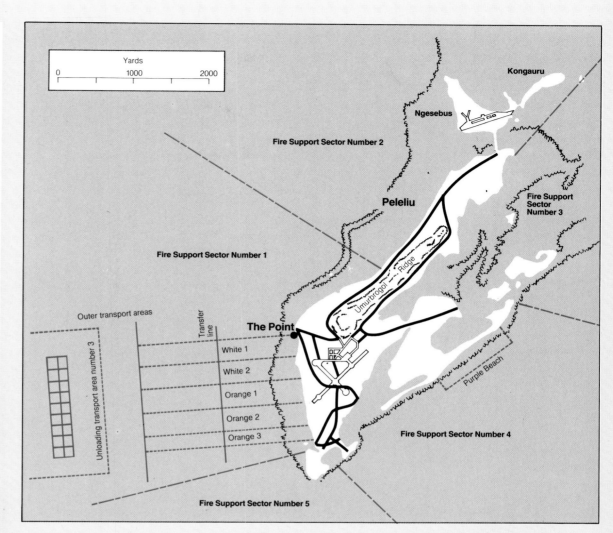

Peleliu showing the landing beaches. The fortified caves can be clearly seen.

its defences, and the erroneous idea that naval bombardment would enable troops to walk ashore was again to prove a costly and tragic error. The Japanese tactics were now to hold a line well back from the beaches and so escape the bombardment, to site mortars and artillery inland to cover the beaches with sustained fire, and to organize defensive positions from which swift counter-attacks could be mounted.

The assault was to be made by the veteran 1st Marine Division (which must surely be classed as one of the finest divisions serving in the whole of the Second World War) on five beach areas opposite the airfield. From there they were to advance across the airfield and northwards through to the Umurbrogol Ridge and consolidate. LSTs brought the Marines to the assault area and launched them in their LVTs supported by LVT tanks. These amphibious vehicles were able to negotiate the reefs and with them went Sherman tanks with flotation bags which were to be of crucial importance.

The pre-assault bombardment successfully exposed the presence of caves and none were more lethal than those in the area of White One and White Two beaches, and they had not been destroyed. Although no more than a large outcrop of coral, the area was honeycombed with passages and well sited with guns, anti-tank guns and machine guns. The Marines were forced to seek what cover they could as one by one their LVTs were hit. It was not for some hours that the position was taken after hand-to-hand fighting, and the critical danger to the beachhead was eliminated.

Defensive fire from concealed caves plastered the beaches with mortar shells and gunfire, but the Marines pressed on to the edge of the airfield. Here they were met by a counter-attack including thirteen light tanks, but after heavy fighting and the assistance of every gun and tank ashore the attack was held, with the destruction of the Japanese tanks and many of those who attacked with them.

The island was by no means taken and Japanese troops held out in the intense heat, disputing every inch of the way for another month, mainly in the mass tunnels inside the Ridge. In fact the last Japanese was not killed in action until 25 November and of the Marines 1,950 were killed and 8,500 were wounded. The Japanese garrison of about 13,000 men stood where they were and fought to the last man, only 301 surviving to be taken prisoner.

In contrast, the neighbouring island of Angvar, six miles to the south-west of Peleliu, was assaulted and captured without much resistance, and the occupation of Ulithi had been unopposed. Here was an ideal anchorage and construction began at once. Airstrips, an advanced fleet base, a boat pool and a 100 bedded hospital were soon established, as were recreation centres. At one time no fewer than 617 ships were anchored in the lagoon which was to become the main base for Pacific operations until the end of the war.

It provided every sort of facility and store required for a fleet constantly at sea, needing continuous replenishment and at times repair.

Leyte Gulf – the air battle over Formosa

As a prelude to the landings on the Philippines at Leyte Gulf, the fast carrier force of the Third Fleet undertook a series of air strikes between 10 and 20 October 1944. The force comprised nine fleet carriers, eight light carriers, six battleships, four cruisers, ten light cruisers and sixty destroyers. This huge force sailed into the Japanese-held waters and carried out a series of crippling air strikes with the loss of just one light carrier and severe damage to only two cruisers. The damage it inflicted was serious enough to result in a complete halt to the reinforcement of aircraft during a critical period. However, reinforcements were able to be flown in later.

On 10 October 1944, 1,396 sorties were flown against Okinawa and nearby islands far to the north and under 400 miles from the Japanese

As a preliminary to the assault on the Philippines, Task Force 38 with nine fleet carriers and eight light carriers supported by six battleships, fourteen cruisers and fifty-eight destroyers struck at Japanese airfields on Formosa. On 12/13 October 1944 the Japanese losses were crippling and this had a material effect on their ability to reinforce their defence of the Philippines. The following week the task force moved south to attack airfields on the Philippine mainland with equally devastating results. The Japanese counter-attacks involved nearly one thousand aircraft but the American losses were slight and much of the attacking force was destroyed.

loss of stores, dumps, hangars and workshops was equally serious. The Japanese replied with a counter-attack by nearly 1,000 sorties in a series of raids on the carrier force, beginning late into the evening of 12 October, which scored no hits, and forty-two aircraft failed to return.

It was the largest Japanese attack made on a carrier force. The American losses in these operations were not light, seventy-six planes failed to return to the carriers. On 13 October at dusk a further attack by Japanese 'Betty' bombers disabled the cruiser *Canberra* and on 14 and 16 October the light cruiser *Houston* was hit twice by aerial torpedoes. Both these ships were saved and arrived eventually still under tow at Ulithi 1,000 miles away.

The concentration of air power over Formosa was increased by B29s of the Army Air Force in China dropping 1,290 tons of bombs. The whole object of the operation was to prevent air reinforcements reaching the Philippines and in this it succeeded.

The assault ships for the landings at Leyte were only three days away and on 17 October Admiral Halsey began his planned direct support. This was repeated the next day when airfields in northern Luzon were pounded, the airfields round the capital, Manila, including the old American Clark Field, were also attacked. There then followed attacks on every known airfield in the central Philippines. The main weight of this operation fell to the escort carriers, the fast carriers being preoccupied with Formosa.

Between 20 and 24 October the air strikes were supported by American and Allied bombers and fighters from all over New Guinea, the Solomons and from China. Every possible staging post or reserve area from which aircraft could attack the assault forces at Leyte was hammered. From Hong Kong to Borneo airfields were pounded by every available unit that could reach them and as a result fewer than 200 combat planes were able to take to the air during the first few days of the landings. However, the destruction of aircraft was not in itself final. The factories in Japan were still untouched and from them poured a succession of new aircraft, many of which were allotted to a special attack corps to become better known as the kamikazes.

mainland. A number of ships were sunk in the harbour and over 100 planes destroyed. The cost was twenty-one USN aircraft with five pilots and four crewmen. Refuelling and the supply of replacement aircraft was completed next day and the task force proceeded to a position fifty to ninety miles off the coast of Formosa. For the next two days the airfields were pounded. Aircraft were destroyed in combat or on the ground and enormous quantities of fuel, stores and ammunition were also destroyed. It is estimated that Japan lost some 500 aircraft, but the

The sea battles of Leyte Gulf

The 'return to the Philippines' so dear to the heart of General MacArthur was the culmination and coming together of two great campaigns. The long campaign in the New Guinea area, fought under horrible conditions by Allied troops against a doggedly determined defence, and the assault up the Central Pacific which started at Guadalcanal. The landings at Leyte were a huge amphibious operation, though on a smaller scale than the invasion of Europe. None the less, the 738 ships of the Seventh Fleet with the addition of the Third Fleet of seventeen fast carriers, six battleships, seventeen cruisers and sixty-four destroyers was the most powerful naval force ever assembled up to this date. It set out from Manus in the Admiralty Islands, gathering units as it proceeded, and rendez-voused to the east of Leyte Gulf on 17 October. During the next two days a considerable mine-sweeping operation was undertaken and the underwater detection teams then pronounced the beaches clear of obstacles. The destroyer *Ross* hit two mines, however, and was badly damaged. The assault on Leyte went in on 20 October 1944, preceded by a naval bombard-ment. The Navy had transported and covered the landing and provided air strikes and patrols over the area. As a preliminary, every Japanese airfield was again attacked to deter interference with the landings. Thus Japanese aircraft did not appear in any large numbers but one aircraft evaded all obstacles and attacked the cruiser *Honolulu* with a torpedo and put her out of action. Next day a Japanese plane crashed into the foremast of HMAS *Australia*. This fine ship had covered most of the operations in the Pacific since the assault on New Guinea, but she was not out of the war for long.

The assault had gone well. Within five days, 133,000 men and 200,000 tons of stores were landed. Casualties were light and the main portion of the invasion fleet had left. The three amphibious force flagships remained, with twenty-five LSTs and twenty-eight Liberty ships with a support force of battleships and escort carriers. The Philippines campaign on land was an Army operation and is outside the scope of this narrative and so we turn to the forthcoming battle off Leyte which ranks with the greatest sea battles of all time.

The Japanese Commander-in-Chief could not put into operation his plans to attack and destroy the United States fleet and to dispute the landings until he knew exactly where the invasion was to take place. He now knew, and the fleets sailed immediately to intercept. The general outline of Admiral Toyoda's plan ('SHO-1') was as follows.

The Mobile Fleet under Admiral Ozawa was divided into three sections, the Northern, and the First and Second Striking Forces.

The Northern Force commanded by Admiral Ozawa himself was based in Japan's Inland Sea and consisted of the two old battleships *Ise* and *Hyuga* partly converted to carry aircraft and the

large carrier *Zuikaku* with the light carriers *Zuiho*, *Chitose* and *Chiyoda*.

As there were insufficient trained air groups available, these carriers proceeded to sea purely as a bait to lure Admiral Halsey's Third Fleet to the north and away from Leyte. They were to proceed south to the north-east coast of the Philippines escorted by three light cruisers and eight destroyers, and were supplied with no air strike capability.

The other unit based in Japan (but moved to the Formosa area during the big air strikes) was known as the Second Striking Force under Admiral Shima. This was to join up with the southern contingent of the First Striking Force and consisted of one light and two heavy cruisers and about nine destroyers.

The main portion of the large and powerful Japanese battle fleet was stationed far to the south in Lingga Roads off Singapore to be near the oil supply. This was the First Striking Force, divided into Centre and Southern Force and was made up of the two largest battleships in the world, the new and mighty *Yamato* and *Musashi* with five old battleships, eleven heavy cruisers, two light cruisers and nineteen destroyers. In considering what follows we must keep in mind the lack of air support at the disposal of the Japanese Commander-in-Chief. The Battle of the Philippine Sea had smashed the carrier-borne air arm and the devastating raids on Formosa and the airfields in the Philippines before the assault had seriously denuded him of air strike capability. However, despite this, 400 Navy and Army aircraft were flown into the Philippines on 21 and 22 October and some 200 had managed to survive the air assault on Formosa.

Admiral Toyoda gave the order 'Execute SHO-1' on 18 October and the First Striking Force moved out of its anchorage near Singapore. The Northern Force under Admiral Ozawa sortied from the Japanese Inland Sea on 20 October and made for an area to the north-east of Luzon as a bait to draw the American Third Fleet north to meet it. The forces coming up from the south left in two echelons and after refuelling at Brunei, Admiral Kurita's Centre Force moved up along the Palawan Passage. Its composition was as follows: battleships: *Yamato*, *Musashi*, *Nagato*, *Kongo* and *Haruna* with the heavy cruisers: *Atago*, *Chokai*, *Myoko*, *Kumano*, *Chikuma*, *Takao*, *Maya*, *Haguro*, *Suzuya* and *Tone*. With them went two light cruisers and fifteen destroyers.

Their directive was to break through the San Bernardino Strait and then to move south round the coast of Samar to enter the Leyte Gulf and destroy the shipping on which the invasion so much depended.

The Japanese reacted at once to American landings at Leyte Gulf in the Philippines by sailing the fleet from their southern bases to attack and destroy the American invasion forces. On 23 October 1944 US submarines Darter *and* Dace *were on patrol off Palawan and, in addition to reporting their presence, torpedoed and sank two heavy cruisers —* Maya *seen in the distance and* Atago, *the flagship of Admiral Kurita.*

The Southern Force under Admiral Nishimura was made up of the battleships *Yamashiro* and *Fuso* with the heavy cruiser *Mogami* and four destroyers. Their orders were to force a passage through the Surigao Strait and move north to join Force 'A' in a pincer movement to complete the annihilation of the shipping in Leyte Gulf. This would be possible because the Northern Force would have lured Admiral Halsey's Third Fleet to the north with the almost irresistible temptation to destroy the carriers. It was certainly a desperate expedient, but in keeping with previous Japanese tactics.

The small Second Striking Force under Admiral Shima was ordered south to join Force 'C' and consisted of the heavy cruisers *Nachi*, *Ashigara* and *Aoba* with two light cruisers and twelve destroyers and destroyer escorts carrying reinforcement troops for the Philippines.

The first notification that this large fleet was at sea was the sighting of the Centre Force 'A' on the morning of 23 October, as it was proceeding through the Palawan Passage, by the submarines *Darter* and *Dace*. At 06.32 on 23 October *Darter* was only 980 yards from the leading cruiser of the port column. She fired her six bow torpedoes at the heavy cruiser *Atago* which happened to be Admiral Kurita's flagship, and four hits were made. Fires spread rapidly as the cruiser came to a halt. Immediately after firing the bow tubes *Darter* swung round and fired the four stern tubes at the next cruiser — *Takao*. Two torpedoes hit at 06.34, damaging her severely.

Meanwhile *Dace* had managed to get into position to fire at the third cruiser in the starboard column, and the heavy cruiser *Maya* exploded. As the smoke subsided nothing could be seen of her.

When *Darter* returned to periscope depth after being depth charged she saw *Takao* dead in the

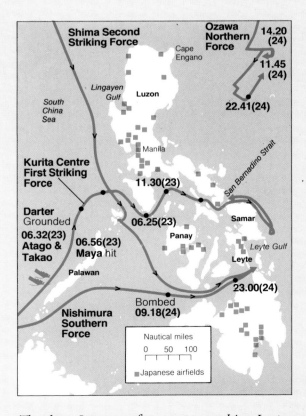

The three Japanese forces approaching Leyte Gulf on 23 October 1944.

Part of the Japanese Southern Force consisted of the battleships Fuso *and* Yamashiro *with one cruiser and four destroyers. Their orders were to force a passage through the Surigao Strait and attack the invasion forces. Barring their way was an overwhelming force of six American battleships, eight cruisers and twenty-eight destroyers. As the Japanese force approached it was deluged by gunfire and torpedo attacks and all but one destroyer perished in this unequal fight.*

water with two destroyers and aircraft nearby. For five hours she tried to get at her and finally surfaced, with *Dace,* to try to shadow her. The area contains many coral shoals and *Darter* ran on to one at 17 knots. Efforts to refloat her were unsuccessful and she was abandoned.

During 24 October information was received in Admiral Halsey's flagship that two Japanese forces were closing in on Leyte Gulf, one from the west and one from the north-west. This was correct, except that Admiral Ozawa's Northern Force (the bait) had not been seen. Admiral Halsey pulled his task groups in towards the coast to the east of southern Luzon for air searches and strikes later that day.

Japanese aircraft based on Luzon counter-attacked. In three separate raids determined attempts were made to get at the carriers and one aircraft bombed the light carrier *Princeton.* Fires raged and most of her crew were taken off. The cruiser *Birmingham* went alongside to give assistance and help to fight the fires, when a huge explosion ripped the carrier's stern apart

and over 600 of *Birmingham*'s crew were killed or wounded. *Princeton* could not be saved and was sunk by torpedoes.

Meanwhile the American air strikes had begun. Forty-five aircraft attacked the Centre Force followed by a further strike of equal strength and at 19.35 on 24 October, fifty-four more aircraft joined the strike. In all 226 aircraft were involved. Admiral Kurita had no combat air patrol (after the first strike at 10.26) but he put up an impressive barrage. Each battleship had 120 anti-aircraft guns of various calibres, and with that enormous fire power eighteen American aircraft were shot down. The giant *Musashi* was sunk after nineteen torpedoes and seventeen bombs had hit her. The attack had concentrated on this one ship and the cruiser

being provided by sixteen escort carriers with a screen of twenty-one destroyers and destroyer escorts. They were operating in three groups, thirty to fifty miles apart, to the east of Leyte Gulf, flying combat air patrol over the Gulf, anti-submarine patrols and ready to give what support was called for. Up to the north and under surveillance were one Japanese fleet carrier and three light carriers, two converted battleship-carriers, numerous light cruisers and destroyers. Admiral Halsey decided to annihilate this force, but it must be said that this decision was taken even after night air reconnaissance had reported Admiral Kurita's force had reversed course once more and was heading for the San Bernardino Strait, and was definitely not retiring.

We return to the Southern Force under Admiral Nishimura which had been shadowed, and consisted of the battleships *Fuso* and *Yamashiro* with the heavy cruiser *Mogami* and four destroyers. Following them some forty miles astern was Admiral Shima's force of two heavy cruisers and a light cruiser. They were all proceeding through the Mindanao Sea in a position to clear the Surigao Strait by dawn on 25 October, unaware that a trap lay ahead through which it would be quite impossible to pass. Lying in wait was an advance guard of thirty-nine PT boats on either side of the passage. Further up were three destroyer squadrons waiting in the shadows of the narrows and, finally, concentrated off the exit to the Strait was the American battle line. Seven cruisers steamed back and forth across the mouth of the Strait and behind them were the veteran bombarding battleships *California, Tennessee, Mississippi, West Virginia, Maryland* and *Pennsylvania*. This vast array of gunfire was stationed in such a way as to cross the T of the approaching Japanese Southern Force. This meant that all American guns could fire while only the forward guns of the approaching force could bear.

The action opened with an attack by the PT boats at 23.00 and lasted intermittently until 03.00. No torpedo hits were made and they were driven off by the destroyer escort. Their main contribution was to plot the advance of Admiral Nishimura.

Next in line, and far more deadly, were the destroyers. The sea was calm, with no wind, and the night very dark. The First Destroyer Squadron (54) was divided into two groups with two destroyers on the western side and three on the eastern side of the narrows. As the Japanese force approached, the destroyers went in to attack, fired twenty-seven torpedoes at about 03.00 and retired making smoke. The Japanese dispositions were a van of four destroyers followed by flagship *Yamashiro,* then battleship *Fuso,* and finally cruiser *Mogami.* In this destroyer attack *Fuso* was hit by torpedoes, and slowed down. The second attack at 03.23 by Desron 24 was assisted by a blinding flash as destroyer *Yamagumo* blew up after receiving a hit from the first torpedo attack. After the American destroyers had fired their torpedoes and were retiring, hits were seen on two other destroyers which sank, leaving only *Shigure*. The flagship was known to have been hit by two torpedoes but at that moment did not slow down. However, *Fuso* was a burning pyre, drifting apart in two halves and only *Mogami,* the flagship and the destroyer *Shigure* remained.

Myoko which took a torpedo and was ordered to return to base. With all surprise gone, Admiral Kurita now reversed course to await a more opportune moment to cut through the San Bernardino Strait. The retiring Centre Force was reported to Admiral Halsey at the same time as news came of the sighting of the Northern Force with its carriers. Admiral Halsey's orders had been explicit. If the opportunity occurred or could be created, he was to destroy the Japanese fleet or a major part of it while giving protection to the ships lying in Leyte Gulf. His pilots returning from their strikes had given over-optimistic reports of their successes and reported that Admiral Kurita was definitely retiring. He was not — he had only reversed course. Halsey knew that Admiral Nishimura's Southern Force 'C' was approaching the Surigao Strait

and that the entrance was blocked by Admiral Kinkaid's powerful battle line of modernized battleships, cruisers and destroyers. Surely this was now the time to go north and destroy Admiral Ozawa's carriers once and for all. He therefore made this fateful decision: Task Force 38 was to move north at full speed to engage and to destroy this Northern Force.

Task Force 38, less one group which was refuelling, comprised five fleet carriers, five light carriers, six battleships, one heavy and seven light cruisers and thirty-eight destroyers. If they had remained where they were there would have been little for them to do for the moment. The Surigao Strait was blocked and Admiral Kurita was thought to be in retreat. Support for the land forces and combat air patrols was

The Battle of Samar, in which a vastly superior Japanese force penetrated the San Bernardino Strait and attacked a small force of American escort carriers, sinking two together with three destroyers. However, two Japanese cruisers and one destroyer were sunk in a spirited defence. The painting shows a smoke screen protecting the carriers which Admiral Kurita mistakenly took to be the large fleet carriers. In the sudden confrontation, made all the more dangerous by the presence of torpedoes fired by American destroyers, the Japanese force became separated and thus failed to destroy the lightly armoured escort carriers.

As *Yamashiro* continued into the mouth of the battle line, sinking and burning ships could be seen behind her. On the American side one destroyer had been badly hit but was afloat and was towed out of action.

The final action began at 03.53 when the battle line opened fire and a monstrous eruption descended on the Japanese battleship. It was utterly one-inesided. She could only reply with her forward turrets since the rest of her armament was masked as she advanced towards the continuous flashes of gunfire. With her consort *Mogami* she absorbed hit after hit from the overwhelming fire power of the battleships and cruisers. As she came on, zigzagging and reeling under the hits which were illuminating her as the shells started fires throughout the ship, she still continued to fire doggedly ahead. *Mogami* was being hit too and began a slow turn to reverse course. At 04.19, her guns still firing, the brave *Yamashiro* slowly came to a stop, capsized and sank. As *Mogami* turned away she

was seen to fire a salvo of torpedoes. The American battle line checked their fire to avoid the torpedo attack, and in the respite that followed, the blazing cruiser limped out of action.

Admiral Shima's Second Striking Force of three cruisers and four destroyers now came up. PT boats had attacked this force, and PT 137 damaged the light cruiser *Abukima*. Seeing the devastation ahead Admiral Shima reversed course. In doing so the heavy cruiser *Nachi* collided with the burning *Mogami* and sustained severe damage to her stern. The battle of the Surigao Strait was over. Of the force which was to attack the shipping at Leyte, only *Mogami* (which by superhuman efforts had controlled the fires) and the lucky destroyer *Shigure* returned to the west. With them were Admiral Shima's two heavy cruisers, the damaged light cruiser and four destroyers.

A pursuit by cruisers and destroyers followed. The destroyer *Asagumo,* whose bow had been

blown off in the earlier destroyer attack, was steaming slowly west with her forward section awash when she came under fire from two light cruisers and three destroyers. She returned the fire gallantly, her last shot being fired as her stern went under. The pursuit was now taken over by aircraft which found the still burning *Mogami*. After the attack her crew were taken off and that fighting cruiser which had been in so many actions was despatched by a Japanese torpedo. The damaged light cruiser *Abukuma* was bombed and sunk by USAAF aircraft.

This operation and the pursuit sank all the remaining ships of the Southern Force except two cruisers and four destroyers. The dispositions and the overwhelming strength of the American forces made it inevitable that the Japanese forces would be destroyed. It was the last engagement in sea warfare in which a battle line was employed, but it was only one part of the great naval engagement which made up the Battle of Leyte Gulf.

The defensive battle of Samar. American aircraft attack and sink the Japanese cruiser Chokai.

As we have seen, Admiral Kurita's Centre Force had reversed course after the sinking of the giant *Mushashi* and this had helped Admiral Halsey to decide to go north to engage the carriers under Admiral Ozawa. However, at 17.14 on 14 October (the same day on which he had been seen to withdraw), he reversed course again, and passed through the unguarded San Bernardino Strait, turning south along the east coast of the island of Samar (a fact that had been reported to Admiral Halsey). His force consisted of a destroyer squadron on each flank with six heavy cruisers in the centre and two and a half miles astern were the four battleships *Yamato*, *Nagato*, *Kongo* and *Haruna*. Their object was to proceed direct to Leyte Gulf and destroy the shipping. As dawn broke no opposing forces could be seen.

On the American side the battle group was some way to the south, in the mouth of the Surigao Strait with its cruiser and destroyer force intent on pursuing the remnants of the Southern Force. The only United States naval forces in the area were the escort carrier Task Group 77.4 under Rear-Admiral T.L. Sprague, divided into three groups, named Taffy 1, Taffy 2 and Taffy 3, from their voice radio call signs. They were thirty to fifty miles apart. Taffy 1

(Rear-Admiral T.L. Sprague) was to the south, off northern Mindanao, Taffy 2 (Rear-Admiral Stump) was off the entrance to Leyte Gulf and Taffy 3 (Rear-Admiral C.A.F. Sprague) was to the north, off Samar.

Each escort carrier had a complement of twelve to eighteen fighters and eleven or twelve Avengers, and Taffy 3 had launched twelve aircraft at dawn to cover the ships in Leyte Gulf.

Taffy 3 consisted of six escort carriers, *Fanshaw Bay*, *St Lo*, *White Plains*, *Kalinin Bay*, *Kitkun Bay* and *Gambier Bay*. Her screen was made up of the three destroyers *Hoel*, *Heermann* and *Johnston* with destroyer escorts *Dennis*, *J.C. Butler*, *Raymond* and *S.R. Roberts*. At 06.45 on 25 October look-outs observed anti-aircraft fire from the north and surface radar contact was made. The pilot of an Avenger reported four Japanese battleships, eight cruisers and a number of destroyers twenty miles from Taffy 3. Look-outs then saw the tall pagoda type masts of the battleships. At 06.58 the mighty Japanese squadron opened fire, the shells falling around the carriers and rising like great geysers. It was Admiral Kurita's Centre Force and it had arrived completely undetected. The wind direction was such that Admiral Sprague had to turn toward

the Japanese threat to launch his remaining aircraft when his only means of escape was to turn south at his best speed of 17½ knots. The formation turned together sufficiently to launch as the huge 18.1 inch guns of the *Yamato* thundered out at the colossal range of 35,000 yards. The escorting destroyers raced round the outside of the carriers making funnel and white chemical smoke. There were no direct hits. The formation now ran into a rain squall and the carriers turned unseen on a southerly course.

Admiral Kurita was as surprised as the Americans. He was under the impression that he had fallen upon at least some of Admiral Halsey's fleet carriers. All serviceable aircraft from Taffy 3 were being flown off and these were augmented by planes from Taffy 2. The Japanese cruisers had headed out to the east to cut off the carriers as they turned to fly off their supposed deckloads of aircraft, and the Admiral lost tactical control of his force.

The destroyers escorting Taffy 3 made smoke and then turned to attack. *Johnston* launched

237

torpedoes but was hit and badly damaged by heavy calibre shells. After sustaining further damage in repelling a Japanese destroyer attack on the escort carriers, she finally sank at 10.10. Destroyer *Hoel* was also sunk at the same time after firing torpedoes which forced the battleship *Kongo* to turn away to avoid them, and thus to open the range. *Johnston* had achieved the same effect with the battleships *Yamato* and *Nagato* at a crucial moment. Destroyer escort *S.R. Roberts* was sunk soon afterwards. The objective of the Japanese Strike Force was to

destroy shipping off Leyte, but the sighting of the escort carriers, which Admiral Kurita took to be fleet carriers, upset his plans and he lost control of the action after the immediate counter-attack by the destroyers and aircraft commenced. However, the escort carrier USS *Gambier Bay* was sunk by shell fire, and *Fanshaw Bay* and *Kalinin Bay* were badly damaged. The swift action by the destroyers undoubtedly threw the Japanese force into some confusion and distracted its attention away from the carriers at a critical time. How

ever, the carriers were saved from complete destruction by the action of the carrier aircraft. Co-ordinated attacks were mounted from 08.30 by the other light carriers in Task Group 77.4, and it was these aircraft that drove off Admiral Kurita's vastly superior gunpower. Every aircraft that could be made operational took part and the well controlled attack from the air was decisive. The two Japanese heavy cruisers *Chikuma* and *Chokai*, veterans of almost every action in the war to date, were sunk by torpedoes and bombing, as was *Suzuya* while

After ensuring that there was sufficient air cover and fire power to protect the beach-head at Leyte and the supply ships lying off shore, Admiral Halsey with his very powerful task force, turned north. A Japanese carrier force had been sighted off the north-east corner of the Philippines, and he was determined to destroy it. The Surigao Strait was covered and Japanese forces known to be in the area of the San Bernardino Strait had been attacked and had reversed course. It was a calculated risk, for he would be too far away to intervene if strong Japanese forces came upon the scene. The Battle of Cape Engano followed in which one Japanese fleet carrier, three light carriers, one light cruiser and three destroyers were sunk, all without significant American losses. The painting shows carrier aircraft attacking IJN Zuikaku, *the last veteran of Pearl Harbor while the converted battleship* Ise *endeavours to protect her.*

The air chase of Admiral Kurita's force did not result in him sustaining further major damage, and it was called off on 27 October, after he had withdrawn through the San Bernardino Strait and made good his escape.

There now occurred the first of the hundreds of attacks which were to be made by Japanese aircraft diving to their death with deliberation and supreme self-sacrifice in the kamikaze suicide missions. This new aspect of the war will be discussed later, but at this moment, on 24 October 1944, a kamikaze aircraft was diving on light carrier *Santee* of Taffy 1, crashing through her deck and exploding in the hangar deck. Fires were started and extinguished and the ship survived, although she was also torpedoed by the Japanese submarine I-56 at 07.56. *Suwannee* was hit next but was also back in operation within two hours. At 10.50, just when the escort carriers of Taffy 3 were recovering from their ordeal, five more kamikaze aircraft attacked. As a result, *Kirkum Bay* was damaged but *St Lo* was also hit and after an enormous explosion at 11.25, she foundered.

While the hectic action of the morning of 25 October was taking place, signals for help were reaching Admiral Halsey 300 miles away to the north. He despatched Admiral McCain's group, which had been oiling and was nearest, to go to the rescue; but his aircraft could not reach the scene for three hours. Admiral Oldendorff's battleships were also at least three hours away. Admiral Halsey's determination to sink the remaining Japanese carriers seems to have become an obsession. Despite the report at 17.14 that Admiral Kurita had reversed course again, and with his main responsibility the protection of the army at Leyte, he nevertheless took this overwhelming force 300 miles to the north. It was fortunate that Admiral Kurita should choose this moment to vacillate and lose control, both for the United States Forces and for Admiral Halsey. The Americans had three groups with the overwhelming strength of five fleet carriers, five light carriers, six battleships, one heavy and seven light cruisers and thirty-eight destroyers. Opposing him was one fleet carrier — *Zuikaku* — and three light carriers, the converted battleships *Ise* and *Hyuga*, nine destroyers and two light cruisers. At the time of the forthcoming battle the Japanese air strength

was only twenty-nine. This was due to the lack of a sufficiently intensive training scheme for Japanese pilots. Their losses at the Philippine Sea battles had been enormous, and few replacements of anything like the American calibre of pilots were available. Their carriers were thus purely bait — but to lure Admiral Halsey northwards would give the rest of the Japanese fleet a slim chance to reach Leyte Gulf and thus destroy the shipping upon which the landing depended.

The American groups rendezvoused at 23.45 on 24 October, but Admiral Ozawa had sent his two battleships south at 14.30 and they were seen at 15.30 and the rest of the Japanese forces an hour later.

The first strikes were made the next day, 25 October, at 08.10. Hellcats preceded the Avenger torpedo-bombers and a number of hits were made. Helldivers dive-bombed the Japanese ships which then put up a fierce anti-aircraft barrage, but the light carrier *Chitose* was hit by bombs and sank at 09.37, and one destroyer sank instantly with all hands. By now the Japanese force was strung out, *Zuikaku* and *Zuiho* also having been hit. The second strike arrived at 09.45 and *Chiyoda* was attacked leaving her stationary in the water from 10.12 until she was sunk by gunfire at 16.30. But fourteen ships were still afloat. Two hundred aircraft comprised the third strike, which began at 11.45. *Zuikaku* took three torpedoes and finally rolled over and sank. Throughout the attack she was protected by the battleship *Ise* but the veteran carrier could not be saved. Strike number four arrived on the scene at 14.45 and the crippled *Zuiho* was finally sunk. The battleship *Ise* was the main target for the next two waves, but although she received thirty-four near misses she was not severely damaged. This ship was saved by her expert manoeuvring tactics and the anti-aircraft fire she threw up. The last strike of the day inflicted no further damage to the widely dispersed remnants of the Japanese force.

There now came the question of pursuit by the battleships of the Task Force. The pleas for help from Samar were insistent and with reluctance Admiral Halsey withdrew at 11.15, in the hope of returning in time to bar the way through the San Bernardino Strait. For he was obviously too late. Before withdrawing with all his forces, Admiral Halsey's cruisers sank the damaged carrier *Chiyoda* and the destroyer *Hatsuyuki*. Finally a patrol line of United States submarines was placed in the path of the retreating Japanese forces, and the light cruiser *Tama* was sunk by submarine *Jallao*.

This battle, the largest naval action ever fought, was decisive in one way. It was the last time that the Imperial Japanese Navy sortied as a major force. It was fought with great bravery by sailors and airmen from the moment that the trapped Japanese Southern Force was faced with an impossible penetration of the Surigao Strait, and with equal and inspired bravery by the Taffy 3 formation of escort carriers and their dedicated escorts. It also saw the introduction of yet another aspect of the war at sea — the coming of the kamikazes.

Kumano was torpedoed and damaged by destroyer *Johnston*.

There was now no question of attacking the support ships off the Leyte beachhead, and Admiral Kurita ordered a withdrawal at 09.11 to save his strike force, for he now realised that his force was probably the only surviving part of Operation SHO-1 in the area. He also believed that it would not be long before the full weight of Admiral Halsey's carriers and battleships would descend upon him.

Securing the Philippines

The Battle of Leyte Gulf may have ended, but the Navy was asked to continue to give all-round air support to the Army until the end of the month, and then throughout November. This coincided with the start of a new phenomenon in air warfare — the kamikaze. While individual acts of suicide had taken place since 1942, it was only in 1944 when Japan's position was so desperate that the Kamikaze Air Corps was organized. The name 'kamikaze' means Heavenly Wind and is derived from an event in 1570 when a Chinese invasion of Japan was brought to a halt by a typhoon.

American fighter planes and their highly trained pilots held an overwhelming superiority over the less experienced apanese airmen. To this must be added the British invention of the proximity fuse which was used in anti-aircraft shells. The shells exploded automatically when close enough to their target, and were lethal. The value of this secret mechanism was a major factor in the destruction of aircraft. For the kamikaze pilot with little training, any obsolete plane could be used. He was only required to aim the aircraft with its bomb at an enemy ship. Even if the plane was hit, the momentum often carried it on to the target where blazing fuel would cause the ship to catch fire. The suicide of hundreds of young men using these devices caused far more damage than conventional air strikes. While Task Force 36 was operating in support of the Army, no less than seven hits were made on United States carriers, and destroyer *Abner Read* was sunk on 1 December. New tactics were introduced in the form of picket destroyers which were stationed some miles from the fleet to give early warning of the arrival of the kamikaze air strikes. These ships suffered grievously in the months to come.

The situation on Leyte had now become serious for the American forces. Despite the air strikes made before landings took place, the main reinforcements of Japanese aircraft were arriving on Leyte and Luzon and they had begun to recover control of the air. The Army Air Force was unable to give effective air support to General

MacArthur due to the condition of the airfields in the monsoon period, and the Navy was forced to remain in the area. On 2 November Admiral Nimitz released units of Task Force 38 for operations against airfields in Luzon. *En route* the light cruiser *Reno* was hit by a torpedo from submarine I-42 but survived. The air strikes were successful and a large number of Japanese aircraft were claimed destroyed on the ground and in the air, for the loss of thirty-six aircraft and one kamikaze hit on USS *Lexington* causing 182 casualties. The Japanese air pressure on Leyte had been eased, but their troops were arriving nightly via Ormoc Bay on the west coast and close to the American positions — seemingly without much opposition. By 12

Kamikaze aircraft attacking HMAS Australia off Lingayen, to the north-west of the Philippines.

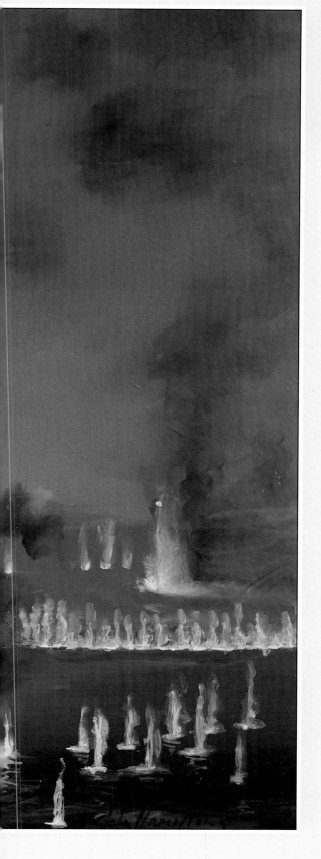

A young kamikaze pilot prepares to crash deliberately into an American warship which is defending itself with every available close-range weapon.

November there were 45,000 Japanese troops on Leyte, an increase of about 23,300 since 20 October. Although outnumbered by the 101,000 American troops, they also had 365,000 troops elsewhere in the Philippines. Air attacks on Japanese convoys were stepped up and on the days of 8, 9 and 11 November, Task Force 38 launched 347 aircraft in an operation which destroyed five or six transports with 10,000 men, together with six destroyers. Japan could ill afford these losses and their destruction shortened the Leyte campaign considerably.

Shipping strikes off Luzon followed on 13 and 14 November during which one light cruiser and seven merchant ships were sunk and an estimated eighty-four aircraft were destroyed for the loss of twenty-five American planes. Such was the enormous increase in America's ability to prosecute the war that these two events can be described almost in passing, while the Battle of the Bismarck Sea less than twenty-one months before had had a highly significant effect on the whole of the New Guinea campaign.

In a series of sweeps west of Manila on 25 November the heavy cruiser *Kumano* already damaged during the Battle of Samar was sunk, but kamikazes made determined attacks on the carriers and these resulted in the curtailing of imminent operations. On land the Japanese put up strong resistance, and even with the superior equipment available to General MacArthur, it was a very difficult and arduous campaign for both sides in the appalling weather. General MacArthur asked for the loan of four night fighter squadrons of the US Marine Corps from the Solomons to take over protection of the area, and this produced an immediate and significant lessening of Japanese attacks.

At sea, PT boats and destroyers sought to close Ormoc Bay to Japanese reinforcements and a number of night actions were carried out.

As the American forces advanced and the Japanese forces were squeezed into a smaller perimeter it was decided to make an American landing at Ormoc Bay. As dawn broke on 7 December the 77th Infantry Division which had been conveyed in landing craft and destroyers waded ashore without opposition and by nightfall was established, although a furious attack by sixteen Japanese aircraft sank the destroyers *Mahan* and *Ward*. Owing to the mud and impassable tracks the division needed to be supplied by sea. There followed a series of small but fierce actions as both sides sought to supply their troops. It was not until 18 March 1945 that Leyte was pronounced reasonably secure; and events elsewhere in the Philippines must now claim our attention.

The American Joint Chiefs of Staff had decided on the liberation of Luzon and Manila — the capital of the Philippines — as the next operation. In order to achieve this, the large island of Mindoro was to be taken, followed by a landing at Lingayen. Both these were ambitious projects, and as the timetable was 15 December for Mindoro and 9 January for Lingayen, it created a vast and complicated logistics problem. Hundreds of ships had to be available at short notice at the right place, with the right cargoes, at the right time. Facing the Americans were 260,000 Japanese troops in Luzon, while in the general area of the Inland Sea of Japan six battleships (including the *Yamato*) four carriers, four heavy cruisers, about thirty-five destroyers and some forty-three submarines were in position. There were numerous air bases with about 400 Japanese aircraft still operational at the time that the Mindoro convoy sailed. Many of these aircraft were within easy striking distance and the

241

decision to take the island held risks. The landings themselves presented very little difficulty, and units of the 24th Infantry Division and the 503rd Parachute Regiment USA landed safely on 15 December. The real problem for the Americans was to come from the air. As the large LST landing craft approached the shore two were hit and set on fire by kamikaze aircraft which penetrated the air patrols; both vessels sank. The Army were unable to provide sufficient air cover and fighters from the escort carriers off shore together with Marine fighter squadrons were required to assist in the protection and supply of this very vulnerable operation. Within a week an airfield had been constructed on the island, which was of great assistance, although it did not stop the brave young Japanese suicide pilots from throwing themselves at targets in an attempt to make the beachhead untenable. Admiral Kimura had gathered a small force of one heavy cruiser, one light cruiser and six destroyers for a bombardment of the American positions on 26 December. The squadron was attacked by night from the air, and after a token bombardment it withdrew, destroyer *Kiyoshio* being sunk by torpedoes from PT-123.

Although Mindoro was consolidated and a base was being built up, supply problems were still considerable, and in almost every convoy the Americans sustained losses from Japanese air attacks. When the invasion convoy passed on its way to Lingayen the Japanese air activity moved north with it, and Mindoro was secured.

Vice-Admiral McCain had taken over command of Task Force 38 from Vice-Admiral Mitscher on 30 October, and to cope with the serious threat from kamikaze raids, the fighter complement on board his carriers was increased. He had been at sea during the Mindoro operations and it was because he had blanketed the airfields in northern Luzon so heavily that the invasion had been accomplished without serious losses.

On the completion of these strikes, the task force proceeded to refuel from tankers on 17 December some 300 miles to the east of Luzon. The weather began to deteriorate, but oiling went on for as long as possible, and this proved to be too long. Within hours a typhoon that had been building up all day hit the task force, and on 18 December the fleet was scattered, battered and disorganized. The terrifying ordeal of individual ships resulted in the drowning of 790 officers and men from the destroyers *Hall, Monaghan* and *Spence,* all of which foundered. Much damage was done and the task force put into Ulithi for repair. They sortied again on 29 December to render air support in the liberation of Luzon at Lingayen.

The Lingayen landings took place on 9 January under the protection of heavy and widespread air strikes on Japanese airfields during the approach and at the beaches. The landings were to be made by four Army divisions with

The typhoon of 18 December 1944 caused the loss of three destroyers and the drowning of 790 officers and men. This natural disaster did considerable damage to ships and aircraft. The painting shows Admiral Halsey's flagship USS New Jersey *at the height of the storm.*

243

one in reserve and they were drawn from New Guinea and other areas far to the south, as well as from Leyte itself. The problems of transporting this force were obviously immense. Admiral Oldendorff took command of all operations *en route* to Lingayen with a fleet of 164 warships. They were attacked heavily at intervals and despite the strong combat air patrol, the escort carrier *Ommaney Bay* was hit and sunk by a kamikaze aircraft, and a number of other ships were damaged.

This large naval force was in a position to cover and protect the assault force which was following and stretched over a distance of forty miles. Mine-sweeping the approaches to Lingayen Bay had been completed, and it was the kamikaze aircraft that caused the greatest concern as the assault force approached the area.

Very little Japanese resistance was encountered and the landings went ahead on 9 January despite air attacks. HMAS *Australia* was hit for

the fifth time by kamikazes but by nightfall American forces were well established ashore, when the Japanese unleashed a new weapon, the suicide boat. Seventy of these craft attacked, each with two 260 pound depth charges. They were only 18 feet long and after closing a ship at anchor would drop the charges with shallow settings. A number of ships were damaged, but the suicide squad lost a high proportion of their boats. Within two days of arrival the airstrip at the beachhead was operational, and the assault

convoys now departed, but not before further damage had been inflicted by kamikaze aircraft.

While these operations were taking place, Admiral Halsey ordered Task Force 38 into the South China Sea for a major strike. This huge force consisted of eight carriers, six light carriers, eight battleships, three heavy and thirteen light cruisers and seventy-four destroyers. In addition, twenty-nine oilers and a large fleet of supply vessels were in support. Escort carriers

with replenishment planes, ammunition ships and scores of other vessels made up the service force. The first and by far the most successful strike was on 12 January 1945 on the coast of Indo-China when forty-four ships totalling 132,000 tons were sunk. Of this number, fifteen were combatant vessels of 16,700 tons and at least twelve of the merchant ships were tankers. Eight hundred and fifty aircraft took part in what was one of the heaviest blows to Japanese shipping on any day of the war. Because

Admiral Nimitz had sanctioned the use of United States submarines in this area for life-guard duties, and with the assistance of friendly locals, very few of the pilots were lost from the twenty-three planes shot down.

Further operations continued against Hainan and Hong Kong, but none of the heavy war-ships of the Japanese fleet were found. A tornado built up in the South China Sea, and with bad visibility and the need to seek shelter for oiling, the earlier successes were not repeated. However, the sorties allowed the most powerful naval strike force in the world to cruise at will in an area hitherto considered Japanese territory, although a brave attack was launched by kamikaze aircraft. With oiling completed and the bad weather subsiding Task Force 38 headed back to Formosa which was heavily attacked and ten merchant ships were sunk, including five tankers and up to 100 aircraft claimed destroyed. Japanese pilots flew through some of the fiercest flak imaginable and penetrated the fighter cover over the fleet. All the kamikaze pilots died — but not before they had succeeded in severely damaging and setting on fire the carrier *Ticonderoga* and had sunk the picket destroyer *Maddox*.

The liberation of the Philippines under the command of General MacArthur was an Army operation supported by the Navy who transported all supplies, furnished landing craft and gave close support bombardment. Navy and Marine Corps pilots provided invaluable back-up to forward troops particularly in their dash for Manila. Each of the many islands in the archipelago, and further south the East Indies and Borneo, all required the active participation of the Navy in their support of Allied forces. This was particularly so in the case of escort carriers which acted as floating airfields and allowed an air umbrella to cover each landing.

We must now move north-east to the Bonin Islands — one of which, Iwo Jima, was to be the cause of nightmare action for all involved. However, before this the role played by the British Navy must be recounted.

Always at sea and within reach of the Pacific Fleet were American supply vessels of all kinds and sizes. It was a vital and often unrecognized contribution to Allied victory in the Pacific.

245

The British Navy in the Pacific

By the summer of 1944 it was possible to release major units of the British fleet from Home waters and in late December Admiral Sir Bruce Fraser, commanding the Eastern Fleet in the Indian Ocean, was appointed Commander-in-Chief of the enlarged British Pacific Fleet. Rear-Admiral Sir Philip Vian, as Flag Officer Carrier Squadron, was Officer in Tactical Command of Operations.

Owing to the logistical problems involved it was agreed that the British task force would be self-supporting and have a fleet train of its own. Thus Task Force 113 came into being with Task Force 112 becoming the Royal Navy Service Squadron. Due to the vast size of the Pacific conflict the provision of an independent British Service Squadron may seem to be of small importance. However, despite the generous American, Australian and New Zealand support, much of the equipment required to maintain the fleet at sea had to come from the other side of the world. These logistical problems were immense but none the less were overcome successfully. Finally, *en route* to the Pacific, carrier aircraft were to attack the major oilfields and refineries at Palembang in Sumatra.

Leaving Ceylon on 16 January 1945 were the carriers *Indomitable* (flagship), *Illustrious, Indefatigable* and *Victorious,* the battleship *King George V (Howe* having gone on ahead to Australia), the cruisers *Argonaut, Black Prince* and *Euryalus* with two destroyer flotillas. After refuelling at sea the force approached the position for flying off. Combat air patrols covered the task force while fighter groups were despatched to attack Japanese airfields in the Palembang area. The attack was made on two refineries on 24 and 29 January 1945. On 24 January the strike force was made up of forty-three Avengers, sixteen Hellcats, twenty-four Corsairs and twelve Fireflies. Fierce aerial combat ensued and the targets were bombed with considerable precision. The attack was successful and flames from burning oil tanks mingled with black smoke reaching high up into the sky. Key distillation plants had been taken apart and much of the refinery was unusable.

After refuelling, the repeat attack took place on 29th. Heavy anti-aircraft defence again greeted the strike, but the refinery was hit with such accuracy that output was cut by half during the next crucial three months.

The fleet then set sail for Sydney, Australia, now renamed Task Force 57. Sydney was to be the main base, but as it was 3,500 miles from Okinawa, intermediate facilities were needed at Manus with advanced bases at Ulithi and Leyte. To maintain the task force at sea now required a minimum of 100 ships, and at the end of the war this had risen to 123.

After a period of training the British Pacific Fleet moved up to Manus, and on 16 March, Task Force 57 reported to Admiral Nimitz and came under his command for operations in support of the assault on Okinawa. One of the problems facing the Americans was to prevent the reinforcement of Japanese aircraft from Formosa via the chain of islands which form a link with Okinawa. The main cluster form the Sakishima Gunto Islands to the south-west of Okinawa, and these were to be the target of the British Pacific Fleet.

On 23 March Task Force 57 weighed anchor from Ulithi and headed north. Although in size the British ships were only the equivalent of one of Admiral Mitscher's four groups that made up Task Force 58, none the less they made an imposing force. Commanded by Vice-Admiral Sir Bernard Rawlings the force comprised the battleships *King George V* (flagship) and *Howe,* the four fleet carriers *Indomitable, Victorious, Illustrious* and *Indefatigable,* five light cruisers and eleven destroyers. Embarked were 142 fighters and sixty-five torpedo-bombers. Strikes against runways and parked Japanese aircraft were now made daily. However, on 2 April the

Japanese returned the assault, one kamikaze getting through and crashing down on to *Indefatigable*'s flight deck. Because the deck was armoured in contrast to the American wooden decks, only temporary delays were experienced and the ship soon became operational again. Air strikes were now switched to

Formosa, from where the Japanese kamikaze aircraft were making direct attacks on the American forces. Sixteen Japanese aircraft were destroyed for the loss of one British. Further strikes took place whenever the weather permitted, and after almost a month of continuous action the force withdrew to Leyte.

En route to the Pacific, units of the British Pacific Fleet struck at the oilfields of Sumatra in two highly successful raids which destroyed installations and halved production. This was at a time of acute shortage for Japan. Aircraft are seen in action over the Pladjoe refinery.

By 4 May Admiral Rawlings was back in the Sakishima Gunto area, HMS *Formidable* having relieved *Illustrious*. A naval bombardment of the Japanese airfields was carried out, during which some twenty kamikazes approached the carriers, and one broke through the fighter screen. It crashed on *Formidable*'s flight deck, but again the steel deck proved its worth. Fourteen Japanese aircraft were destroyed that day. After refuelling on 6 May and returning to the area on 9 May, both *Victorious* and *Formidable* were hit by kamikazes, without irreparable damage. Air strikes continued in the same pattern until 25 May when the fleet returned to Sydney. With the arrival of the carrier *Implacable*, the battleship *Howe* was detached to refit in Durban, and the new carrier with five cruisers and an escort of one light carrier and five destroyers, sortied to attack the Japanese base at Truk in order to neutralize its potential as a staging post, or anchorage. On 14 and 15 May an air strike and surface bombardment inflicted little extra damage on a fortress already nearly destroyed and depleted of aircraft.

On 28 June the British Pacific Fleet left Sydney for the north, joining up with Admiral McCain's fast carrier task groups, *King George V* taking part in the bombardment of Hitachi, while aircraft from the British carriers attacked Tokyo. Within days, the news of the dropping of the atomic bomb reached the fleet, and operations were suspended with the capitulation of Japan.

Having described in outline the involvement of the major British naval forces in the Pacific, it is time to end with two incidents in the south. At Singapore, British midget submarines (XE craft), an improved type but similar to those which attacked the German battleships in north Norway, were used for the last time. Two damaged Japanese cruisers, veterans of the war at sea were lying in Singapore. Two XE craft negotiated the forty mile passage of the Jahore Strait on 30 July. Charges were laid under *Takao* by XE-3, but delays due to Japanese patrols precluded the attack on *Myoko*, and those of XE-1 were added to those already under *Takao*. They exploded and she settled on the sea bed. The XE Craft returned safely after a very difficult and dangerous operation.

The last destroyer action of the war occurred in the Straits of Malacca off the Malay Peninsula, thousands of miles away from where Task Force 57 was operating. As a result of decrypted messages it appeared possible to intercept the cruiser *Haguro* which was at sea. Armed with ten 8 inch guns with a range of 31,600 yards, and a secondary armament of eight 5 inch guns together with two quadruple torpedo tubes, she was a formidable veteran of almost every campaign and could maintain a speed of 30 knots. Against her were ranged five British destroyers with their 4.7 inch guns. She was picked up on radar at the extreme range of 68,000 yards on 15 May 1945.

As night drew on the British destroyers, which were ahead of *Haguro* and her escorting destroyer *Kamikaze*, formed a position round her. *Haguro* opened fire and *Saumarez* was hit in the boiler room just after firing a spread of torpedoes. A mass torpedo attack by *Verulam*, *Vigilant*, *Venus* and *Virago* now took place and the Japanese heavy cruiser seemed unable to hold off the smaller destroyers. The night skies were lit by starshell as three torpedoes hit in quick succession. Although *Haguro* fought back she was unable to locate her adversaries in the smoke-laden air, and further attacks slowed her down until she was seen to be sinking. One by one her guns became silent and she rolled over and sank.

For the Royal Navy the cessation of hostilities in the Pacific was the end of a very long road. Before the defeat of Germany a large and balanced fleet had been sent to the Far East and it was only the forerunner of the whole weight of British sea power which was prepared to continue the fight, together with the Army and RAF. After six long years of continuous action at sea by the Royal Navy in every ocean of the world, the last enemy of the Allies had been defeated.

On 15 May 1945 five British destroyers engaged and sank the heavy cruiser Haguro *which was off Malaya in company with one destroyer. It was a simultaneous torpedo attack from all quarters and no British ships were lost.*

The assault on Iwo Jima

```
(anp)
SA TE KO 4 : Any or all ships or Stations
DE
& SI TI TE   Singapore Comm Unit IO
SI 0 700 -NA I W53

- - - - - - - - - - - - - - - - -  Any or All Ships or Stations
From:     SA TE KO              ??
Action:   SO WI YA 3            ??
          MA MU KI 0
                        Air Group 936
Info:     FU O MU I
          NU MA K08    Comdr/\ Minesweep Div 44
          SI    E RO 5
          S  E YUFU 6  Comdr Spl Base force# 11, Saigon
                          Garble
04/I4I043/I  I945           (TOI 04/I4I42I) ga

From: Captain #2 TOSHI Maru.
          Section #2 schedule changed as follows:
I.        Depart at I400 on the I4th. Arrive PHUQUOC Island at I030
on the I6th. Rendezvous with Convoy SA  SI  45 (KITAGAMI /HOKU/UE/Maru,
TENCHOO /AME/NAGAI/ Maru). Depart at I200. Anchor in east entrance
SINGAPORE Straits at 2I00 on the 20th. Scheduled to arrive SINGAPORE
at I400 on the 2Ist. Speed 8.5 knots.
          Noon positions:
          17th 9-25 North, I0I-40 East
          18th 7-12 North, I00-44 East
          19th 5-23 North, Io3-II East
          20th 2-30 North, I03-52 East
          Leave SAIGON Communication Zone and enter I0th Communication
2.
Zons at I400 on the I4th.


JN-5  3587-F  (Convoy)      (Japanese)  (hltm) Navy Tr 04/I4/45/Q
                                                      04/I4I043/I
```

In the autumn of 1944 it was assumed that the Allied invasion of Japan would take place within twelve months, and that the island of Iwo Jima would be required as a staging post and forward base. Plans for its capture were nearing completion as General MacArthur's troops were fighting in Luzon. Roughly four and a half miles long and two and a half miles wide, the island is covered with a fine volcanic ash. At the south end and dominating the whole island is Mount Suribachi, a dormant volcano. The ash has one virtue: when mixed with cement it makes rock-hard concrete. The defender of Iwo Jima was Lieutenant-General Kuribayashi and he knew that once the Americans struck he would receive no reinforcements and no support. The garrison numbered 23,000 including engineers who had designed the most elaborate underground fortifications behind solid concrete walls. With a command post 75 feet below ground, the general had over 360 field guns, thirty-three larger naval guns and 100 large anti-aircraft guns. Sixty-five heavy mortars

were also hidden behind reinforced concrete, amongst which were 320 mm mortars capable of throwing a 700 pound bomb on to the invasion beaches. Interconnecting passages with numerous entrances, all camouflaged by the fine dust, lay silent and waiting. Although documents captured elsewhere showed that Iwo Jima was being fortified, the full extent was unknown to the Americans.

To coincide with the invasion, and also to stop air reinforcements, Admiral Spruance sailed the 5th Fleet into the Sea of Japan, and arrived at his launching position 125 miles south-east of Tokyo on 16 February. His targets were airfields and aircraft factories, but as the weather closed in the task force retired towards Iwo Jima. The largest force of US Marines ever assembled under one command was now approaching the island. The 3rd, 4th and 5th Divisions were under the command of Major-General Schmidt, while Vice-Admiral Kelly Turner once again commanded the amphibious forces afloat.

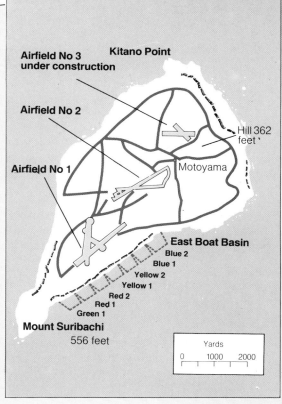

Iwo Jima, 19 February 1945. US Marines assaulted the eastern side of the island.

Experience should have shown that heavy salvoes, carefully controlled by spotter aircraft, would destroy the strong points already discovered by aerial photographs. Instead the island was subjected to the most intense indiscriminate two-day pre-assault bombardment of the Pacific war so far; 38,000 shells from 16 inches to 5 inches were fired at the island before the Marines touched down on the beaches on 19 February 1945.

The only satisfactory area for the assault was at the south end of the island on either side of Mount Suribachi. The eastern shore was chosen — extending to a length of about 3,500 yards to form a beachhead. Two Divisions, the 4th and 5th, were to land simultaneously — the 5th Division on the left, to force its way across the island, capturing Mount Suribachi and then turning north along the western shore, while the 4th Division on the right made for Number One Airfield ahead of them, and then wheeled north to cover the right flank. The 3rd Division was held in reserve.

General Kuribayashi and his troops had withstood the intense two-day bombardment by staying deep inside the fortifications. Although a number of gun positions had been destroyed and casualties to the defenders had not been light, the men were rather more dazed and choked with dust than seriously depleted. The defence was still generally intact as the final pre-assault bombardment lifted.

The assault was headed by twelve support landing craft (LCS-L) firing a salvo of 120 4.5 inch rockets just behind the shoreline and raking the area with cannon and machine-gun fire. This was followed by a mass air strike over the heads of the Marines in the 68 LVT(A) amphtracs which approached in line abreast, arriving

Mount Suribachi at the southern tip of Iwo Jima, seen from the air. Its capture by the US Marines was vital to the whole operation, since it overlooked the whole island.

exactly on time at H Hour, 09.00. The next series of assault waves followed, and by 09.44 the first waves of Sherman tanks were ashore. Previously the underwater demolition teams working under fire had cleared the beaches of obstacles, giving the landing craft a clear run in.

All went well for a few moments. The trouble started when tracked vehicles and particularly tanks tried to climb the fine volcanic ash and became bogged down. Mortar fire now descended on the beaches, pinning down the Marines and the assaulting troops and causing congestion. This was compounded by smashed landing craft broached to and the beaches became impossibly cluttered with the approach of each successive wave. As the troops moved inland the defenders came up from their underground dug-outs and manned their guns, which in some places were barely visible slits in the uneven ground.

Out to sea, with liaison officers on board, gunfire support was well co-ordinated, but only a direct hit on an actual gun would silence it. In some cases this necessitated the use of 15 inch armour-piercing shells registering a direct hit on an emplacement very close to the troops on the ground.

The tanks eventually made their way up the beaches with great difficulty, though many were knocked out by land mines, and cleverly sited anti-tank guns destroyed others. One unit reached the sea at the western neck of the island only to find that the defenders had allowed them through and then fired on them from the rear. The whole area was filled with dust from the shell fire, and a rising surf added to the chaotic problems on the beaches, where there was no protection. Unloading wave after wave of landing craft under a hail of mortar and gunfire resulted in heavy casualties, many of whom were wounded a second and third time before they could be evacuated. The Marines fought their way inland with courage and the defenders stuck to their posts until they were literally

blown apart by demolition charges or burned to death by flame throwers. It was a hell on earth.

By nightfall on 19 February, 30,000 Marines were ashore with 2,420 casualties in an area only 3,500 yards long and 700 yards deep. This area contained six regiments, six artillery battalions and two tank battalions. They dug in for the night awaiting a counter-attack which never came. It was no part of the Japanese plan. Instead they were subjected to shelling throughout the night — for the plan was to fight for every yard of the island from well prepared permanent positions.

At first light on 20 February the Marines began the assault on Mount Suribachi while the remainder of the two divisions wheeled to the right to begin inching their way north. Suribachi was a mass of fortifications and from the summit Japanese observers could view the whole scene and direct artillery and mortar fire where required. To capture the mountain meant assaulting one strong point after another using flame throwers and demolition charges. The Japanese positions were so sited as to give all-round interlocking covering fire, so each assault had to be co-ordinated.

It took three days of hard fighting to capture the position, and eventually a small American flag was to be seen fluttering from the summit.

The desolation and horror of abandoned assault beaches on eastern Iwo Jima.

The capture of Suribachi was important but marked only the beginning of the hard slog, as the defenders fought to the last, and each strong point was blasted apart. Every morning battleships and cruisers moved in to fire on pre-selected targets. This huge concentration of fire power day after day undoubtedly wore down the defenders, and in many cases sealed them inside the caves and fortifications. They literally died in their thousands where they stood, and, without doubt, sold their lives dearly.

Ship to shore co-operation is well illustrated by the following incident. The US battleship *Washington* was informed that 300 strong points with gun emplacements giving all-round support were set into the rocks in a space of 500 by 1,000 yards facing the Marines at one point. The air spotter directed *Washington*'s main armament with salvoes of three 16 inch shells directly into its face at 50 yard intervals. Those direct hits ate into the cliffs and, with secondary armament included, firing deliberate rounds, started landslides that sealed off most of the mouths of the caves. This went on for ten hours and twenty minutes on 20 February.

At about noon that day the wind changed, producing a surf which increased the chaos of broached landing craft until the whole beach was cluttered with materials of war, and clearing this under mortar fire resulted in more casual-

ties. At sea kamikaze aircraft attacked the protecting task force and *Saratoga* sustained seven hits, killing 123 and wounding 315. On the same night the escort carrier *Bismarck Sea* was hit by a kamikaze and sank with the loss of 218 of her crew.

By 24 February the 3rd Division USMC which had been held in reserve had landed and taken up a position in the centre of the island with the 4th and 5th on the right and left.

Continuous ground fighting in all weathers, with rain and squalls at times, brought the Marines towards the north end of the island. It was a familiar pattern. Pinned down by accurate Japanese fire, the troops called for naval or artillery support. Under cover of the bombardment the troops rushed forward to positions from which flame throwers and demolition teams could attack the slits through which the Japanese were fighting to the last, killing everyone inside the bunker.

Supplies for the Americans were coming ashore from both sides of the island whenever conditions allowed, and by 12 March it was possible to release the heavy bombardment ships. By 26 March the island was virtually in American hands, although for long afterwards isolated groups of Japanese troops held out. One such group managed to blow up 6,000 cases of

dynamite, and another to rush an infantry command post, all 200 of whom were killed. The Marines had paid dearly for this volcanic island. Nearly 6,000 of their number had been killed and 17,272 wounded, while the Navy and all other personnel who were not Marines lost 881 killed and 1,917 wounded.

From the Japanese point of view the picture was one of total destruction. They realised that there would be no evacuation, and no support. One thousand one hundred and eighty-three of the Japanese survived as prisoners of war, and the remainder of the garrison of over 23,000 must have been killed. For both sides it was a dreadful slaughter but even so was eclipsed by the air raids on the Japanese mainland which were taking place.

Iwo Jima now became an air base, and B-29 bombers returning from air raids on Japanese cities landed there when they were unable to reach their own airfields due to battle damage, but the Americans had paid a very heavy price for this facility.

Okinawa – logistics, preparations and landing

While preparations were in hand for the assault on Okinawa, the last staging post before the assault on the Japanese mainland, massive air raids were carried out on the large urban areas of Japan. The B-29s carried mostly incendiary bombs and the mainly wooden houses of light construction suffered horribly. One particular raid on 9 and 10 March destroyed 250,000 homes, rendering more than a million people homeless and burning 83,793 people to death.

From 18 to 31 March Task Force 58 sortied from Ulithi for Japan and made the first strike on airfields in Kyushu. The force was attacked and the carrier *Wasp* was hit on 19 March by a dive-bomber, with 370 casualties, but the carrier continued in action. The worst damage was done to *Franklin* which was hit by two bombs. Huge fires left 724 dead and 265 wounded, but the carrier was taken under tow, and eventually, under her own power, she made the 12,000 mile trip to New York. Task Force 58 bombed strategic targets, damaging sixteen warships including the massive *Yamato,* but their main assault was against the airfields. The Japanese agreed that the losses were 'staggering' — possibly up to 500 aircraft in all — and this loss was to interfere with Japanese support for the forthcoming operations on Okinawa, where over 100,000 troops were preparing a last ditch defence. In addition the island had a population of over 400,000 Okinawans.

Before turning to the assault, let us consider the logistics. Firstly the distances: Okinawa to Pearl Harbor is more than 4,000 miles and to San Francisco is 6,200 miles. Fuel for the fleet was positioned at a number of points and from 4 April to 27 May, 8,745,000 barrels of fuel oil were issued together with 259,000 gallons of diesel and 21,477,000 gallons of aviation fuel.

Four escort carriers were used to ferry replacement planes from Ulithi and Guam and seventeen more escort carriers shuttled these replacements between the west coast and the forward bases. Some 845 planes and 207 pilots and crew were sent to the fleet. These escort carriers often transported many different kinds of spares, some 10,000 different items being necessary on a large carrier.

Strict shipping control was vital. Provisioning was on a huge scale and much was done at sea, but the many hundreds of thousands of tons of items to be consumed, smoked or worn came from Australia or America to staging depots or direct to the front line.

Finally we come to ammunition. For the Okinawa operation the naval expenditure of ammunition (in rounds) was as follows:

12 to 16 inch	23,760
6 and 8 inch	81,200
5 inch	502,770

In addition Task Force 58 was issued at sea with 34,773 rockets and 62,216 aircraft bombs.

Task Force 58 was the largest naval force ever to be at sea on extended operations. This was only possible because the support squadrons fuelled and maintained the fleet continually. They provided replacement aircraft, ammunition, food and the thousands of items required by ships in action. It was a remarkable achievement.

The B-29 bombers of the Strategic Air Force were based on Saipan and Tinian. Each of these aircraft made some eight missions per month and each plane consumed 6,400 gallons of aviation gasoline and carried eight tons of bombs. Over 100 ships were required to support the Super Fortresses alone.

The assault force for Okinawa was to consist of three Marine divisions (1st, 2nd and 6th) and four infantry divisions (7th, 96th, 77th and 27th). A fifth – the 81st – was to be held in reserve. This expeditionary force constituted the Tenth Army and was under the overall command of Lieutenant-General Buckner.

The assaulting Marine divisions were commanded by Major-General Geiger. In all some 180,000 combat and 115,000 service troops would be landed. Against them 77,000 Japanese troops were carefully positioned to fight where they stood with no chance of being evacuated or reinforced. This expeditionary force was under the command of Admiral A.K. Turner whose experience of previous operations was second to none.

The actual landings were planned on a four division front over five miles of beaches on the west coast of southern Okinawa.

In the battle to capture Okinawa, the difficult part of the exercise turned out to be easy, and what was considered to be a relatively easy part of the operation was extremely difficult.

The pre-assault bombardment lasted a week and the fire support group (Task Force 54) was massive, consisting of nine elderly battleships, backed by cruisers and destroyers. The beaches

which had been selected for the assault were smothered, and the underwater demolition teams cleared the approaches to the shoreline under cover of protecting shellfire. In the air, the kamikaze pilots attacked Task Force 54 despite the strong air patrols and battleship *Nevada,* and cruisers *Biloxi* and *Indianapolis* and four destroyers were hit.Despite the aerial bombing of the island and the strikes by Task Force 58, Okinawa was still ringed by airfields from which kamikaze aircraft could drop out of the skies. This was no atoll or extinct volcano, it was an island sixty miles long, well wooded,

with towns and villages, and the assault was planned in the southern half, starting from the west along a five mile strip of beaches.

In the air the training of kamikaze pilots continued despite the air raids, and it was upon these young pilots that the responsibility for breaking up the assault ship armada rested. This vast armada of ships assembled for the assault comprised 1,213 in all. This did not include the Allied Naval task forces or the logistics and service ships for the fleet. A vitally important part of the expeditionary force were the mine-

Units of the 1st Marine Division USMC in LVT assault craft pass the battleship North Carolina *during the run in to the beaches of Okinawa. Although the actual landing and the first few days were not seriously disputed by the Japanese defenders, yet every yard of the final battle to capture Okinawa was bitterly contested. The enormous firepower and overwhelming strength of the American forces overcame the last fanatically brave stand by the Japanese Army.*

sweepers. They had been present in all the invasion assaults and with destroyer escorts they swept and buoyed the channels.

To the south-west of Okinawa lie the Kerama islands. The need for a protective anchorage for refuelling and front line repairs was important and it was decided to capture these islands. This was successfully completed by 26 March when the small garrison was overwhelmed. The scene was set for this vast invasion force to make landings scheduled for 1 April.

The big attack transports hove to in position and troops disembarked in landing craft, proceeding to a start line 4,000 yards off shore. The bombarding battleships closed to 1,900 yards

Few warships have been called upon to withstand such ferocious attacks as the kamikaze inflicted. The picket destroyers off Iwo Jima and Okinawa were positioned up to ninety miles off shore; they gave early warning of approaching Japanese raids, and were themselves the first targets. Here USS Hazelwood *is seen battered but still afloat.*

and the bombardment opened at 06.40 on 1 April 1945, continuing until 07.35. Then the massed carrier borne aircraft swept in over the advancing landing craft with an earsplitting roar. The landing craft in perfect line extended as far as the eye could see, climbing over the reefs for their last dash to the shore. Wave after wave followed with Sherman tanks ready to float off for the final assault.

After this preliminary bombardment and last-minute bombing, the Japanese made absolutely no reply, for their main defensive positions were miles away in the south, and the landings were unopposed. General Ushijima, who commanded the defending troops, had decided that he could not forestall the invasion on the beaches, neither could he defend the whole of the island. He therefore withdrew to the centre of the island, abandoning two important airfields at Kadena and Yontan. Instead his 32nd Army established a series of very strong interlocking defensive positions, centred on the town of Shuri. The caves in this area were tunnelled and a complex maze of linked fire points were developed which were considered to be

almost impregnable. To General Ushijima a vitally important aspect of the defence was to be the mass assault of kamikaze aircraft upon the support ships that were anchored off the beaches, because without the continuous supply of fuel and ammunition the invasion could not possibly be sustained.

By nightfall on 1 April, 50,000 American troops were ashore and a bridgehead had been secured. Unloading went on all night and the troops pushed inland. Empty transports withdrew, and the build-up continued, despite being broken off for three days due to bad weather, but there were no signs of major resistance from the Japanese. The role of the Navy was to transport the troops and to supply them, as well as protecting the armada from possible air attacks. Despite one or two brave attempts to pierce the air patrol, the skies were relatively clear and in fact only two supply ships were badly damaged on the first day.

The troops ashore made rapid progress, the Marines heading north and east and the Army to the south. Marine fighter squadrons were based on the newly acquired airfields, and were able to give immediate support to the troops on the ground. At the start of the second week ashore the advance slowed down and then halted. The Army had approached the heavily fortified area round Shuri while the Marines, having advanced in the direction of Nago by 6 April, found themselves in very heavy fighting in the hills of the Motobu Peninsula. This was not taken for another two weeks by the 6th Marine Division, units of which had moved towards the north end of the island, by the 13 April. The main fortifications and the concentrated fire power of the Japanese defence, however, lay in the Shuri area, and fighting continued, the Army and Marines forcing their way southward inch by inch. The situation at sea had changed too, so it is to the shipping lying at anchor, and the protecting warships that we must now return.

The kamikaze attacks of 6 and 7 April came as a shock to the Americans. Admiral Toyoda began Operation Ten-Go, in which 700 aircraft (355 of which were kamikaze) were used. Destroyers *Newcomb* and *Leutze* were crashed several times and narrowly avoided total destruction. The radar pickets, destroyers stationed up to eighty-five miles from Okinawa in a position to give early warning, were set upon. Destroyers *Bush* and *Colhoun* were sunk after taking enormous punishment from the Japanese pilots whose flaming aircraft bore down on them constantly. By nightfall the destruction was considerable, three destroyers, one LST and two ammunition ships had been sunk, while ten ships, including eight destroyers had been seriously damaged with many casualties. It was the first of the massed raids. The 355 kamikaze planes never returned to base and well over half the remaining bombers were destroyed. This was a ratio that Japan could not withstand for very much longer.

Okinawa was the last major Japanese stronghold to be assaulted before the invasion of mainland Japan could be attempted. While the Army and Marine divisions were locked in fierce combat in the south of the island, huge supply dumps were being built up for the next assault. Meanwhile, out at sea a fleet of supply ships waited to be unloaded.

257

Okinawa – the last sortie of the Imperial Japanese Navy

Okinawa could not be reinforced, nor could its garrison be evacuated, but the assault could be hindered by a heavy attack from the sea which would sink the transports and dislocate the supply of materials ashore. With the overwhelming Allied fire power concentrated off Okinawa the only outcome would be the certain annihilation of the attacking force. It was a hopeless concept, but none the less it was attempted. To conserve oil the Japanese naval commander took on board sufficient fuel for a one-way trip. There would be no return.

The massive battleship *Yamato* was to sortie from Japan and, in company wih the light cruiser *Yahagi* and eight destroyers, make a final bid for Okinawa. This was a direct parallel with the kamikaze attacks from the air and the force set out from Bungo Suido on 6 April. It was to follow up with the massed kamikaze attacks just described, and would finally destroy any ships in the assault anchorage not already sunk or damaged in the air attack.

All ships had enough food for five days and their magazines were crammed with shells. *Yamato* was spotted by the submarines *Threadfin* and *Hackleback* positioned off the coast, and her course and speed were relayed at once to Admiral Spruance. She had no air cover after 10.00 on 7 April to meet the vast strength of Task Force 58's air power. Air reconnaissance picked up the Japanese force and shadowed it until the first air strike at 12.10 on 7 April.

In all nearly 300 aircraft attacked the squadron. Due to lack of practice *Yamato*'s gunners were inaccurate and wave after wave of aircraft dived on her. By 13.44 five torpedoes had hit her port side and one by one her guns were knocked out. This, the largest warship ever built, was all but defenceless against the ceaseless rain of bombs from the squadrons of American aircraft which attacked. Further torpedoes found their mark and bombs hitting her decks eventually reduced them to a shambles. The slowly moving and helpless giant was then subjected to a final attack. As she gradually rolled over, her battle flag touched the water and at 14.17 she slid under the waves, taking with her 2,496 men.

Her consorts fared nearly as badly. Light cruiser *Yahagi* put up a tremendous fight taking twelve bombs and seven torpedoes in a merciless attack before she sank. Of the eight destroyers, four were sunk and four were badly damaged, although they managed to escape to bring the news back to Japan. It was to be the last sortie of the Imperial Japanese Navy and it had cost only ten aircraft and twelve American lives.

The sinking of IJN Yamato, *the world's largest battleship. She had sortied from Japan with an escort of one light cruiser and eight destroyers on 6 April 1945. She had insufficient fuel and food for the return voyage, and her orders were to attack and sink Allied forces off Okinawa, before she herself was sunk. She was shadowed and attacked by no less than 280 aircraft.* Yamato *sank after numerous torpedo and bomb hits as did light cruiser* Yahagi *and four destroyers, all of which fought to the end.*

The mud of Okinawa. Stretcher bearers bringing back wounded pass a mortar squad of K Company 3rd Battalion Fifth Marine Regiment on 1 June 1945.

The troops ashore required constant fire support and a huge amount of supplies. They required protection from air attack as did the ships that supplied them and this the Navy undertook. This huge armada was attacked with incredible bravery by the young pilots who flew the kamikaze and conventional bombers. It cannot be stressed too often how these pilots flew into murderous anti-aircraft fire with its close proximity fuse, although in comparison with the American fighter pilots who intercepted them, they were virtually untrained; their courage certainly made up for their lack of combat experience.

So while troops ashore were locked in battle, the second attempt to destroy shipping off Okinawa took place. Between 7 and 11 April, eleven US warships had been hit, including the battleship *Maryland.* The radar picket patrols had been attacked constantly, but their presence enabled patrol aircraft to be vectored on to attacking Japanese planes in time to prevent them breaking through into the anchorage. In the brilliant sunshine of 12 April 1945, Admiral Toyoda's second mass attack was launched. It consisted of 185 kamikaze aircraft with 150 fighters and forty-five torpedo aircraft. Few returned to their bases that night, but 12 April proved a bad day also for the ships which were attacked. The radar picket destroyers again took the brunt of the punishment, and that day saw the first successful attack by 'baka' bombs. These weapons were 20 feet long with a wingspan of $16\frac{1}{2}$ feet and were slung beneath a twin-engined bomber. Released in the combat area, the suicide pilot inside the bomb then took control and guided it on to the target. These very lethal weapons could attain a speed of 500 mph with the help of booster rockets. Their weight with a warhead of 2,645 pounds of explosive made the parent aircraft unwieldy and an easy target unless well protected by fighters. It was extremely fortunate for the Americans that the Japanese had so few of these bombs. USS *Mannert L. Abele* on picket station was the first ship to be sunk by this weapon.

As the day progressed the American squadron was steaming in a circle formation with an outer diameter of 9,000 yards, and an outer screen of destroyers. Japanese aircraft came in, skimming just above the water at 14.50. Destroyer *Zellars* was hit but survived, and an attack on the battleship *Tennessee* followed. Three planes were shot down close to the ship and a fourth ahead. The fifth aircraft scraped the side of the bridge, crashing into the ship and scattering flaming gasoline as it finally disintegrated and its bomb exploded. Fires were contained but *Tennessee* sustained 129 casualties. The attack was over in ten minutes but eight further ships had been hit.

The attempt by the Japanese to destroy the American support fleet failed, but the toll of ships and aircraft was considerable. Ten mass attacks each involving twenty to 300 aircraft were mounted, and possibly some 1,900 young Japanese pilots drove their aircraft to a flaming death from April to June 1945. One such attack was on the destroyer *Laffey*, on picket duty at 08.27 on 12 April. Probably no ship has ever survived a barrage of such intensity. Kamikazes came in from all quarters over a period of eighty minutes and twenty-two separate attacks were made. *Laffey* was hit by six aircraft and four bombs, and near missed by one aircraft and one

261

The Shuri Barrier on Okinawa. This was the main Japanese defensive position and was defended literally to the death. Flame throwers and explosive charges were the only means of destroying each determined pocket of resistance.

bomb — and survived. The battle for Okinawa at sea went on for week after week. Aircraft appeared over or in sight of the anchorage daily when the weather was fit to fly and after the on-slaught of 12 April, eighty further ships were hit and seriously damaged. These included the carriers *Enterprise, Intrepid* and *Bunker Hill,* the battleship *New Mexico* and the cruiser *Birmingham* together with destroyers, mine-sweepers, the ammunition ship *Canada Victory* and landing craft of all types.

While the battle at sea was going on, and Japanese aircraft were being flown in only to be destroyed with their pilots in a violent explosion, the battle on land was mounting in fury.

The speed with which the Marines had been able to reach the north of the island enabled the 77th Division to assault and capture the island of Le Shima off the northern coast of Okinawa on 20 April. This occurred after a naval bombardment and some hard fighting to capture the high ground at a cost of 1,074 casualties. Further south XXIV Corps — the 7th and 96th Infantry Divisions — came to a standstill on 14 April. This was followed by an earth shattering bombardment by battleships and destroyers, together with twenty-seven battalions of artillery, all firing 19,000 rounds in forty minutes.

Then 650 Navy and Marine aircraft with bombs, rockets and napalm attacked, and the troops moved forward. Instead of stunning or even destroying the Japanese defenders, the Army was stopped cold when relatively untouched troops came up from caves and bunkers deep in the rock to man the defensive positions. The Japanese again fought and died where they stood. After five days of the bitterest fighting with progress measured only in yards, the American forces slowly began to overcome the Japanese outer defences. This gradual advance continued throughout May.

The lst and 6th Marine Divisions moved south to the right of XXIV Corps, and on 4 June, units of the 6th Division assaulted the Oroku Peninsula from the sea. By 13 June it was in

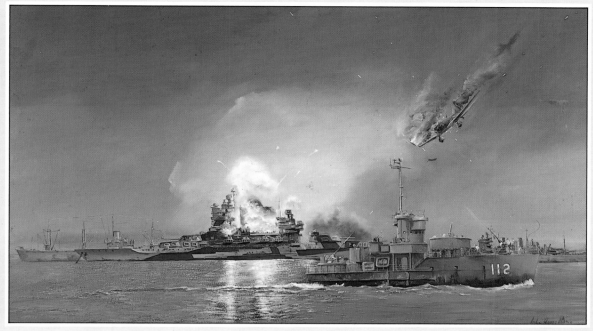

A kamikaze attack on USS New Mexico on 12 May 1945 at dusk. Two aircraft dived deliberately on the battleship doing considerable damage and causing 173 casualties.

American hands. The fortress of Shuri, shattered and wrecked, was abandoned by General Ushijima on 29 May.

The size of the land operation and the number of troops involved on both sides were such that a detailed account is not possible here. Sufficient to say that the capture of Okinawa came about after the most violent and vicious fight, in which parts of the island were literally torn apart, and the trapped Japanese garrison stood, fought and died until all organized resistance came to an end on 22 June and the campaign was declared to be over on 2 July. It was a campaign where the contribution of the Navy was crucial, for had the kamikaze aircraft got in among the transports the battle on land could not have been sustained.

The Japanese losses in the land fighting are hard to gauge accurately. The total of Japanese dead is more than the 77,000 garrison, for to this must be added between 15,000 and 30,000 Okinawans who were caught up in the land fighting. In all, American losses were 7,374 killed and 31,807 wounded and 230 missing. During the eighty-two days of ground operations thirty naval ships were sunk and 368 damaged. Seven hundred and sixty-three carrier-based aircraft were lost in action or operational accidents. Four thousand, nine hundred and seven naval personnel were killed in action and 4,824 wounded. The Japanese lost about 7,500 aircraft. These are only the bare figures. Behind them lie the desperate actions by the defending garrison and the bravery and loss sustained by the United States Marines and Army Divisions as they literally took the island apart. The Japanese aircraft losses tell their own tale of burning aircraft with the pilot strapped in, guiding his plane towards its target unless blown to pieces by a direct hit. Of the ships sunk (none of which was a fleet carrier though some were very badly damaged) the list of killed and wounded bears testimony to the tremendous fight that went on to save the ships or quench the fires and to salvage the lives of those who were so brutally burned and battered. Iwo Jima and Okinawa together were but a small foretaste of what was to come if the invasion of mainland Japan was to take place.

The Allied Navy turned towards its next objective. As has been seen the British Pacific Fleet as Task Force 57 was an integrated part of Admiral Spruance's Task Force 58, and when Admiral Halsey relieved him on 27 May, Halsey took over the supporting role off Okinawa. He was soon to be subjected to another typhoon. Task Force 38 headed towards it on 5 June and the cruiser *Pittsburgh* lost her bow in winds which reached 97 knots sustained for over a minute, and seas which exceeded 60 feet. While considerable damage was done to many ships including *Hornet* (where the forward 25 feet of her flight deck collapsed) and other carriers, no ships were lost.

After making good storm damage, Task Force 38 sortied from Leyte Gulf and set course for Japanese waters where it remained until the end of hostilities. On 10 July Tokyo was attacked, and after refuelling, the fleet proceeded north to northern Honshu and southern Hokkaido where on 14 July a mass attack on shipping took place. In all one thousand three hundred and ninety-one sorties were flown in which one destroyer, two destroyer escorts and eight auxiliaries were sunk as were twenty merchant ships, including seven car ferries; twenty-one were damaged. Next day the ferries were again attacked. These were important since much of the coal trade southwards was carried in railway trucks on these ferries. Out of twelve, eight were sunk, two were beached and two were damaged. Seventy sailing colliers and ten steel freighters were also sunk. This raid probably reduced the coal carrying capacity by half. At the same time a bombardment of shore targets — including an iron works — was carried out by three battleships, two cruisers and nine destroyers. This resulted in the iron works coming to a standstill.

Further bombardments were carried out next day at Murroran, Hokkaido, where the second largest coking and pig iron plant in Japan was situated. Very substantial damage was done, and the pressure was kept up, for on 17 July a bombardment by five battleships, cruisers and destroyers sent 1,238 16 inch shells into Hitachi, some eighty miles north-east of Tokyo. HMS *King George V* and two British destroyers added to the destruction of other plants nearby, and the result in conjunction with B-29 raids was to halt production completely. With an improvement in the weather the carriers struck Tokyo Bay and succeeded in damaging the battleship *Nagato*. Allied losses in aircraft had been light, but at sea the cruiser *Indianapolis* was torpedoed by submarine I-58 on 29 July. Two torpedoes struck her starboard side at night, and owing to loss of power her SOS messages were not received. The ship was abandoned, but its non-arrival was not questioned. Eighty-four hours later an aircraft happened upon an oil slick and spotted survivors. A total of 883 of the ship's company died and 316 were rescued.

Task Force 38 carried out a massive replenishment on 21 and 22 July involving the transfer of 6,369 tons of ammunition and 379,157 barrels of fuel oil, 1,635 tons of stores and ninety-nine replacement aircraft. From 24 to 28 July the task force struck at targets in the Inland Sea with some of the heaviest raids of the war. The battleships *Haruna*, *Ise* and *Hyuga* were so damaged that they settled on the bottom in shallow water. These veterans of much fighting were joined by the cruisers *Tone* and *Aoba*. Three aircraft carriers were destroyed and at this point bad weather halted the attack. No Japanese aircraft had been involved.

The last major American air strike of the war occurred on 9 August. A concentration of 200 Japanese bombers was reported to be preparing to crash land 2,000 suicide troops for an attack on B-29 bases in the Marianas. As a result of the raid nearly all the Japanese aircraft were destroyed on the ground.

Before recording the dropping of the two atomic bombs and the end of hostilities, it is necessary to go back in time. For many months scientists had been working with feverish haste and in complete secrecy to produce an atomic explosion. The advances in nuclear physics had made the production of a bomb possible. Germany was working on the same project and had a considerable lead. British scientists decided that it was feasible to overcome the problems of production within a reasonable time if sufficient manpower and expenditure could be devoted to it. The United States alone had that facility. Over 120,000 people working in thirty-seven different localities were employed on the project at a cost of over $2 billion (that figure being based on the money value at that time). The obstacles were immense, but by then the full implications of the effect of the weapon were becoming apparent. The hatred engendered among the nations at war, and those enslaved, was such that the first country among the belligerents to possess the weapon would use it since, in the climate of the time, warnings of its possible use would have had no effect. The first bomb was detonated experimentally on 16 July in the New Mexico desert of America. With the bomb a reality, the urgent need to persuade Russia to enter the war against Japan receded. If a full-scale invasion of Japan had been mounted, the presence of Russian troops in Manchuria and the use of Russian bases for Allied aircraft could have had a marked effect on the outcome. As it was, Russia entered the war just in time to take her place at the peace talks.

On 6 August 1945 at 09.11, three B-29 aircraft appeared over Hiroshima, the eighth largest city in Japan. That day the first atomic bomb was dropped from 31,600 feet, and over 80,000 people died instantly, with many thousands dying later. The second bomb, on Nagasaki,

The kamikaze assault on the Allied fleets, while in no way altering the eventual outcome of the war in the Pacific, yet resulted in great loss of life and damage to every class of ship. These young pilots deliberately dived their aircraft to crash into a ship where their bomb load and burning petrol caused great havoc. Here USS Bunker Hill *is under attack, and was very severely damaged.*

265

Carrier aircraft kept up their incessant attacks on dockyards and all kinds of shipping round the coasts of Japan. Here the cruiser Aoba, a veteran of the whole war, is hit and settles on the sea bed off Yokohama.

was dropped two days later and Japan was informed that other cities would share the same fate. The Emperor intervened at a meeting of the Supreme Council on 9 August expressing his desire that Japan accept the terms laid down

at the Potsdam Conference — unconditional surrender with the proviso that the ultimate form of government in Japan should be established by the freely expressed will of the Japanese people. This was agreed and finally,

after all the misery and horror that was the war in the Pacific, hostilities ceased. Admiral Nimitz held the view that the Japanese would have sued for peace, even without the atomic bomb, because Japan, 'a maritime nation, dependent on food and materials from overseas, was stripped of her sea power', and would starve. There can be no question that had the American submarine campaign escalated over the following nine months in the way it had increased in potency over the previous period, it would have resulted in the complete collapse of Japan's mercantile marine. Had the B-29 bombers and the aircraft from the Allied fleets at sea continued to bomb Japan with the ferocity of the fire raids of the spring of 1945, then casualties would have been far more appalling. Taken together it has been argued that the war could have been brought to an end without the atom bomb. Two items will surely be a matter for deep thought. Firstly the two atomic bombs killed fewer people than did the B-29 fire raids on the major cities of Japan in two weeks, and those raids were only a foretaste of what, it seemed, was inevitably to come. Secondly the United States was now capable of detonating the bomb.

It is unreal for those who did not have the responsibility for the conduct of the war in which the survival of Britain, Europe, America and the whole of the Free World was at stake to blame those who had that power, for developing a weapon whose potency could only be guessed at. Had Germany possessed the acoustic torpedo in 1941 Britain could well have been starved into submission, and who is to say that it should not have been used to destroy Britain's ability to wage war?

The atom bombs of 6 and 8 August 1945, horrible as they were, spared Japan and the Allies infinitely greater casualties. Certainly there were overtures for peace at the time, but it is almost certain that the invasion of the Japanese mainland, planned for two months hence would have taken place. How many more hundreds of thousands of Japanese and American servicemen and countless hundreds of thousands of Japanese civilians would have had to be killed before the tight police state which then controlled Japan was finally broken, and the people themselves demanded an end to that demonic war?

More than forty years have gone by. The new Japan has emerged as a strong democratic power in the Free World and where enemies once fought they now trade in peace. Who can deny that the vibrant and fast growing people of Singapore and Malaysia, of Taiwan and Korea, and above all the emergence of a strong China, are of far greater benefit to mankind than those states that existed in the days before the dreadful war began.

This book which has sought to tell the story of the war at sea is dedicated to those who were spared the horror and who, hopefully, will never know it.

The Pacific Ocean

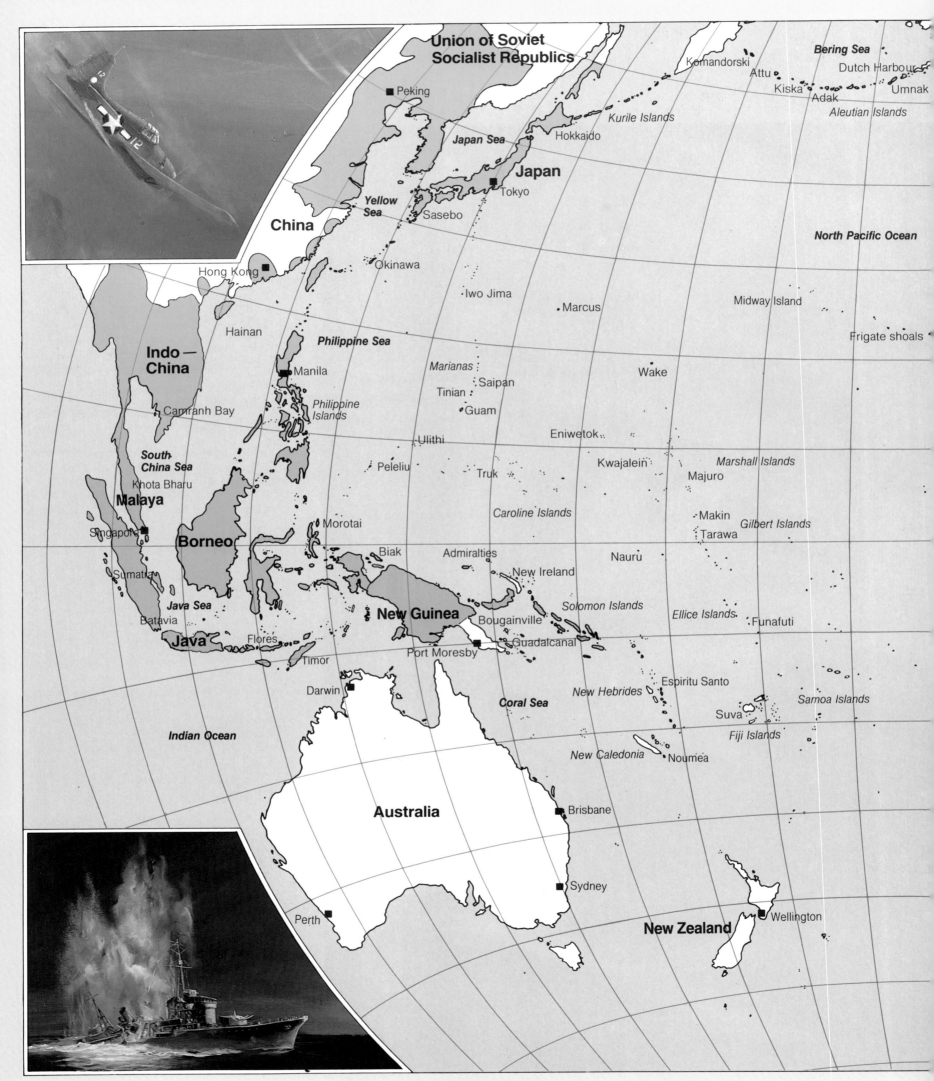

Union of Soviet Socialist Republics

Peking

Japan Sea

Hokkaido

Japan

Tokyo

Sasebo

China

Yellow Sea

Hong Kong

Okinawa

Iwo Jima

Marcus

Hainan

Indo— China

Philippine Sea

Manila

Camranh Bay

Philippine Islands

South China Sea

Khota Bharu

Malaya

Singapore

Borneo

Sumatra

Java Sea

Batavia

Java

Flores

Timor

Morotai

Biak

Darwin

Indian Ocean

New Guinea

Port Moresby

Coral Sea

Australia

Perth

Sydney

Brisbane

New Zealand

Wellington

Komandorski

Attu

Kiska

Adak

Bering Sea

Dutch Harbour

Umnak

Aleutian Islands

Kurile Islands

North Pacific Ocean

Midway Island

Frigate shoals

Marianas

Saipan

Tinian

Guam

Wake

Ulithi

Eniwetok

Peleliu

Truk

Kwajalein

Marshall Islands

Majuro

Caroline Islands

Makin

Tarawa

Gilbert Islands

Admiralties

New Ireland

Nauru

Solomon Islands

Bougainville

Guadalcanal

Ellice Islands

Funafuti

New Hebrides

Espiritu Santo

Samoa Islands

Suva

Fiji Islands

New Caledonia

Noumea

Map of the Pacific Ocean showing the principal locations of places referred to in the text. The blue area shows the extent of Japanese occupation to July 1942.

268

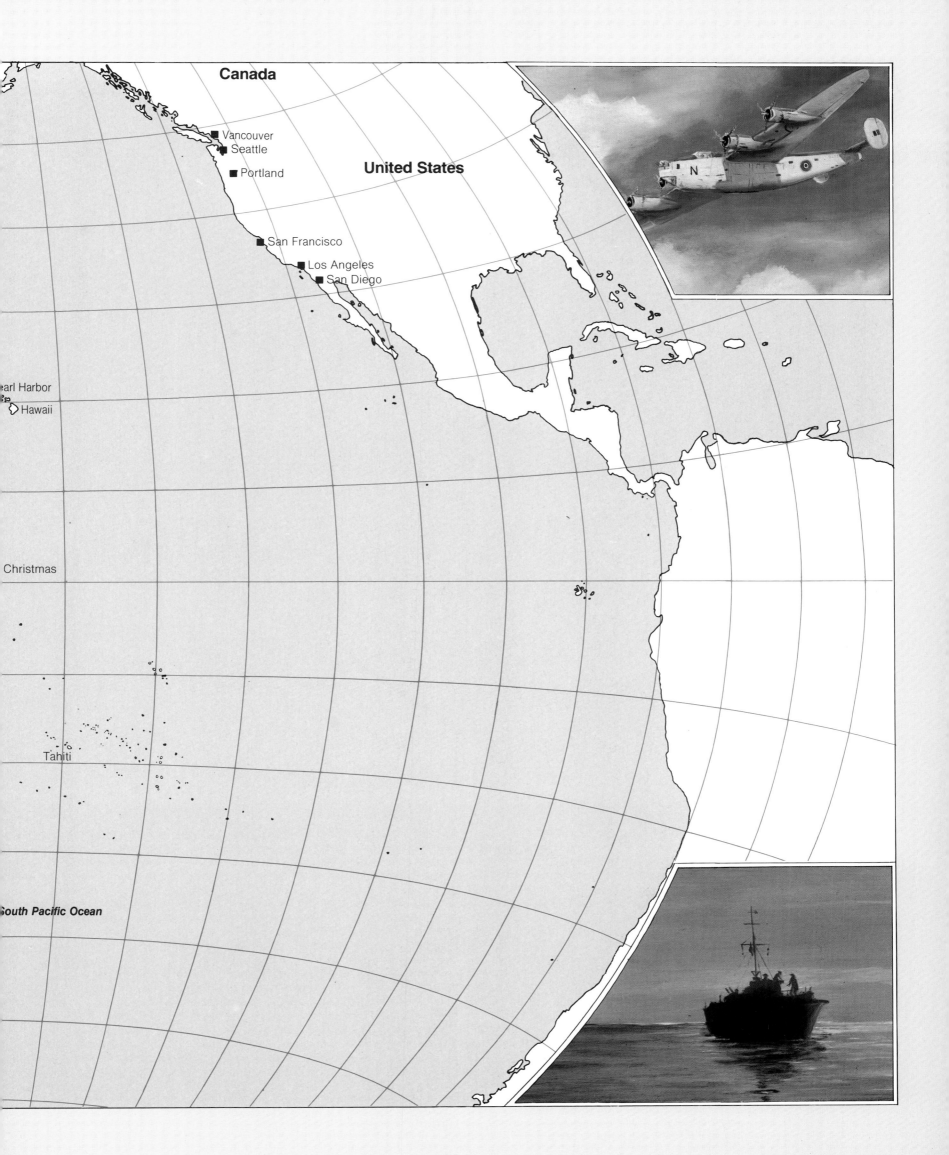

Canada

Vancouver
Seattle
Portland

United States

San Francisco
Los Angeles
San Diego

Pearl Harbor
Hawaii

Christmas

Tahiti

South Pacific Ocean

Index

M — this letter following a
page number indicates a map

Bibliography

Air raid Pearl Harbor
Naval Institute Press, USA 1981

Alden J.D.
The Fleet Submarines in the US Navy
Arms and Armour Press 1979
Allied Landing Craft of World War II
Arms and Armour Press 1985

Bagnasco
Submarines of World War 2
Arms and Armour Press 1977

Baldwin
The Crucial Years 1939 – 1941
Harper & Rowe Publishers, New York 1976

Belote J. and W.
Titans of the Seas
Harper & Rowe Publishers, New York 1975

Blair C.
Silent Victory
Lippincott (J.B.) Co., Philadelphia 1975

Breyer S.
Battleships of the world
Conway Maritime Press 1980

Brooke J.
Alarm Starboard
Patrick Stephens Ltd 1982

Brown D.
Carrier Fighters
Macdonald and Janes 1975

Brown
Carrier Operations in World War II – Vol 2
Ian Allen Ltd

Bucheim
U-Boat
William Collins Sons & Co Ltd 1974

U-Boat Kreig
R. Piper, Zurich 1976

Bulkley
At Close Quarters
Dept of the Navy, USA 1962

Bunker J.G.
Liberty Ships
Naval Institute Press, USA 1972

Busch F.O.
Prinz Eugen
Robert Hall 1960

Calhoun
Typhoon
Naval Institute Press, USA 1981

Cardin M.
Ragged Rugged Warriers
Severn House Publishers Ltd 1980

Zero Fighter
Purnell Books 1969

Coggins J.
The Campaign for Guadalcanal
Doubleday & Company, Inc, New York 1972

Collier B.
Japanese Aircraft of World War II
Sidgwick & Jackson Ltd 1971

Compton Hall
The Underwater War
Blandford Press 1982

Conway Press
All the World's Fighting Ships 1922-46
Conway Maritime Press 1980

Camera at Sea 1939 – 1945
Conway Maritime Press 1978

Cunningham
A Sailor's Odyssey
Hutchinson Publishing Group Ltd 1951

Darbye
Pacific Aircraft Wrecks
Kookaburra Publications, Australia 1979

Dickens P.
Night Action
Peter Davies Ltd 1974

Dyer G
The Amphibians came to conquer
Dept of the Navy, USA

Elliott P.
Destroyer Escorts
Almark Publications 1974

Ellis C.
**United States Navy Warship
Camouflage 1939 – 1945**
Kristall Publications Ltd 1975

Ellis J.
The Sharp end of War
David & Charles (Publishers) Ltd 1980

Encyclopedia of Sea Warfare
Spring books 1975

Feldt E.
The Coast Watchers
Bantam 1979

Francillon R.
Japanese Aircraft of the Pacific War
Putnam & Company, USA 1970

**The Royal Australian Air Force and the Royal
New Zealand Air Force in the Pacific**
Arco Publishing Inc, New York, USA 1970

Frank B.
Okinawa
Purnell Books 1969

Friedman
US Destroyers
Arms and Armour Press 1982

Fuchida M. and Okumiya M.
Midway
Hutchinson Publishing Group Ltd 1957

Green W.
Famous Bombers of the Second World War
Macdonald and Janes

Famous Fighters of the Second World War
Macdonald and Janes 1975

Green W. and Swanborough G.
US Navy and Marine Corps Fighters
Arco Publishing Inc New York, 1977

Gretton P.
Crisis Convoy
Peter Davies Ltd 1974

Griffiths S.B.
The Battle for Guadalcanal
Nautical and Aviation Publishing Co of America 1963

Hara
Japanese Destroyer Captain
Ballantyne Books, New York 1961

Hodges and Friedman
Destroyer Weapons of World War II
Conway Maritime Press 1979

Hough R.
The Hunting of Force Z
William Collins Sons & Co Ltd 1963

Hoyt
Storm over the Gilberts
Van Nostrand Reinhold Co Inc, New York 1978

HQ US Marine Corps
**History of US Marine Corps Operations in World
War 2 – 4 Vols**
Dept of the Navy, USA 1965-1971

Humble
Aircraft carriers
Michael Joseph Limited 1982

Humble R
Japanese High Seas Fleet
Pan Books Ltd 1974

Jablonski
Air War
USA Doubleday & Company, Inc, New York 1971

Jentschura H., Jung D., Michel P.
Warships of the Imperial Japanese Navy 1869-1945
Arms and Armour Press 1977

Johnson
United States PT Boats
Blandford Press 1980

Jones G
Under Three Flags
William Kimber & Co Ltd 1973

Jones J.
Graphic Art of World War II
Leo Cooper 1975

Jones K.
Destroyer Squadron 26
Chilton, USA 1959

Jones R.V.
Most Secret War
Hamish Hamilton Ltd 1978

Keegan
The Face of Battle
Jonathan Cape Ltd 1976

Kemp P.
Escape of the Scharnhörst and Gneisenau
Ian Allen Ltd 1975

Knott R.
Black Cat Raiders of World War II
Nautical and Aviation Publishing Co.
Annapolis USA 1981

Lenton H.T.
American Fleet & Escort Destroyers
Macdonald & Company (Publishers) Ltd 1971
British Cruisers
Macdonald & Company (Publishers) Ltd 1973
British Fleet and Escort Destroyers
Macdonald & Company (Publishers) Ltd 1972
British Submarines
Macdonald & Company (Publishers) Ltd 1972
German Submarines Vol 1 and 2
Macdonald & Company (Publishers) Ltd 1965
German Surface Warships
Macdonald & Company (Publishers) Ltd 1966
German Warships of the Second World War
Macdonald and Janes

Lewin R.
American Magic
Farrar Straus & Giroux, Inc, New York 1982
Ultra Goes to War
Hutchinson Publishing Group Ltd 1978

Lord W.
Day of Infamy
Bantam Books New York 1958

Lund P. and Ludlam H.
Night of the U-boats
W. Foulsham & Co Ltd 1973

The War of the Landing Craft
W. Foulsham & Co Ltd 1976

Machintyre D.
Battle of the Atlantic
Batsford (B.T.) Ltd 1961

Leyte Gulf
Purnell Books 1969

Mason D.
U-boat
Purnell Books 1968

Mayo L.
Bloody Buna
Purnell Books

Middlebrook M.
Convoy
Allen Lane 1976

Middlebrook M. and Mahoney P.
Battleship
Allen Lane 1977

Miller N.
Naval Air War
Conway Maritime Press 1980

Millot B.
Battle of the Coral Sea
Ian Allen Ltd 1974

Morison S.E.
**History of United States Naval Operations
in World War II – 15 vols**
Little Brown and Company, Boston

Two Ocean War.
Little Brown and Company, Boston 1963

Moriya
No Requiem
Hokuseido Press 1968

Muskin J.R.
The Story of the US Marine Corps
Paddington Press Ltd, New York 1979

O'Leary M
United States Naval Fighters of World War II
Blandford Press 1980

Owen F.
The Fall of Singapore
Michael Joseph Limited 1960

Pack S.C.
Crete
Ian Allen Ltd 1973

Pack W.C.
Battle of Matapan
Batsford (B.T.) Ltd 1961

Padfield P.
Dönitz
Victor Gollancz Ltd 1984

Phillips L.
The Greatest Raid of All
William Heinemann Ltd 1958

Potter
Nimitz
Naval Institute Press, USA 1976

Prange G
Miracle at Midway
McGraw-Hill Book Co, New York 1982

Preston A.
Aircraft Carriers
Hamlyn Publishing Group Ltd 1979
Cruisers
Arms and Armour Press 1980
Destroyers
Hamlyn Publishing Group Ltd 1977
V and W Class Destroyers
Macdonald & Company (Publishers) Ltd 1971

Reilly J.
US Navy Destroyers World War II
Blandford Press

Roberts J.
Aircraft Carrier Intrepid
Conway Maritime Press 1982

Robertson T.
The Golden Horseshoe
Evans Brothers Ltd 1955

Rohwer and Hummelshen
Chronology of the War at Sea – 2 vols
Ian Allen Ltd 1972

Roscoe T.
**United States Destroyer Operations
in World War II**
Naval Institute Press, USA 1953
**United States Submarine Operations
in World War II**
Naval Institue Press, USA 1949

Roskill S.W.
The War at Sea – 4 Vols
HMSO

Sakai
Samurai
Bantam 1978

Schofield
Taranto
Ian Allen Ltd 1973

The Rescue Ships
Blackwood 1968

The Russian Convoys
Batsford (B.T.) Ltd 1964

Scott P.
Battle of the Narrow Seas
Country Life 1945

Shepherd C.
German Aircraft of World War II
Sidgwick & Jackson Ltd 1975

Showell
U-boats under the Swastika
Ian Allen Ltd 1973

Siefring T.
United States Marines
Hamlyn Publishing Group Ltd 1971

US Airforce in World War Two
Hamlyn Publishing Group Ltd 1971

Silverstone
US Navy Warships
Ian Allen Ltd 1965

Simmons W.
Joe Foss, Flying Marine
Zeiger Publishing, Washington D.C. 1943

Sledge E.
With the Old Breed
Presidio USA, 1981

Smith P.
Arctic Victory
William Kimber & Co Ltd 1975
Midway
New English Library Ltd 1976
Pedestal
William Kimber & Co Ltd 1970
Task Force 57
William Kimber & Co Ltd 1969

Spector R.
Eagle against the sun
Free Press USA 1985

Steichen E.
US Navy War Photographs
Crown Publishers Inc, New York 1956

Taylor J.H. and W.R.
Encyclopedia of Aircraft
Weidenfeld and Nicolson Ltd 1978

Terzibaschitsch
Aircraft Carriers of the US Navy
Conway Maritime Press 1980

Thomas D.
Battle of the Java Sea
André Deutsch Ltd 1968

Thorpe D.W.
Japanese Naval Airforce Camouflage
Arco Publishing Inc, New York 1977

Tillman A.
Hellcat
Naval Institute Press, USA 1979

Tillman B.
Avenger at war
Ian Allen Ltd 1979
Corsair
Naval Institute Press, USA 1979
The Dauntless Dive Bomber of World War II
Naval Institute Press, USA 1976

Time Life Books
The Road to Tokyo 1979
The Second Front 1978
Island fighting 1978
Battle of the Atlantic 1977

Tuleja T.V.
Climax at Midway
J.M. Dent & Sons Ltd 1960

Turner
The Royal Air Force
Hamlyn Publishing Group Ltd 1981

Watts A.J.
Japanese Warships
Ian Allen Ltd 1966

Westwood J.N.
The Fighting Ships of World War II
Sidgwick & Jackson Ltd 1975

Willmott H.P.
Zero A 6M
Arms and Armour Press 1980

Winton J.
Air Power at Sea
Sidgwick & Jackson Ltd 1976

Sink the Haguro
Seelen Service 1978

War in the Pacific
Sidgwick & Jackson Ltd 1978

Young P.
D.Day
Bison 1981

Y'Blood
Red Sun Setting
Naval Institute Press, USA 1981